THE INTERACTION OF BORROWING AND WORD FORMATION

THE INTERACTION OF BORROWING AND WORD FORMATION

Edited by Pius ten Hacken
and Renáta Panocová

EDINBURGH
University Press

Edinburgh University Press is one of the leading university presses in the UK. We publish academic books and journals in our selected subject areas across the humanities and social sciences, combining cutting-edge scholarship with high editorial and production values to produce academic works of lasting importance. For more information visit our website: edinburghuniversitypress.com

Edinburgh University Press Ltd
The Tun – Holyrood Road, 12(2f) Jackson's Entry, Edinburgh EH8 8PJ

Typeset in Ehrhardt MT
by Servis Filmsetting Ltd, Stockport, Cheshire, and
printed and bound in Great Britain

A CIP record for this book is available from the British Library

ISBN 978 1 4744 4820 8 (hardback)
ISBN 978 1 4744 4821 5 (webready PDF)
ISBN 978 1 4744 4822 2 (epub)

Contents

List of Figures and Tables

Figures

Tables

Contributors

Marco Angster University of Zadar, Department of Linguistics.

Maria Bloch-Trojnar John Paul II Catholic University of Lublin, Department of Celtic Studies.

Silvia Cacchiani University of Modena and Reggio Emilia, Department of Studies on Language and Culture.

Angeliki Efthymiou Democritus University of Thrace, Department of Primary Education.

Livio Gaeta University of Torino, Department of Humanities.

Pius ten Hacken Leopold-Franzens-Universität Innsbruck, Department of Translation Studies.

Camiel Hamans Adam Mickiewicz University Poznań and University of Amsterdam.

Brian D. Joseph The Ohio State University, Department of Linguistics and Department of Slavic Languages and Cultures.

Vasiliki Makri University of Patras, Department of Philology (Division of Linguistics).

Renáta Panocová Pavol Jozef Šafárik University in Košice, Faculty of Arts, Department of British and American Studies.

Angela Ralli University of Patras, Department of Philology (Division of Linguistics).

Michał Rzepiela Polish Academy of Sciences, Kraków, Institute of the Polish Language.

Magda Ševčíková Charles University, Prague, Faculty of Mathematics and Physics, Institute of Formal and Applied Linguistics.

Bonifacas Stundžia Vilnius University, Department of Baltic Studies.

Alina Villalva University of Lisbon, Faculty of Letters, Department of General and Romance Linguistics.

Preface

The interaction between borrowing and word formation is a topic that has fascinated us for a long time. Given the variety of situations in which different linguistic and cultural factors determine this interaction, it is hardly possible for two people to give a proper overview of the topic. It is therefore with great pleasure that we present in this volume twelve contributions by different scholars, each with their own specialisation. These contributions are framed by an introduction setting out some general issues and a conclusion formulating some generalisations. Of course, we cannot pretend that this amounts to an exhaustive treatment, but the collection of case studies of European languages gives some new insights and highlights some previously not widely known contexts of interaction. In this way, we hope to make a useful contribution to the research on our topic.

A collection such as this is of course only possible with the active contribution of the authors of the various chapters. We would like to thank them for writing their chapter and for their prompt responses to our comments and suggestions. We would also like to thank two Lauras. Laura Williamson of Edinburgh University Press encouraged us to edit this volume and gave us advice and deadlines that helped us to produce it within a reasonable time. Laura Rebosio was a very meticulous and accurate editorial assistant, who contributed significantly to the present form of the volume.

Pius ten Hacken and Renáta Panocová

List of ISO-639 Language Codes

Throughout the volume, ISO-639 language codes are used. Where possible, we have used two-letter codes. For some historical or regional varieties, three-letter codes were necessary. This list contains all codes used in the volume.

AR	Arabic
BE	Belarusian
CA	Catalan
CS	Czech
DE	German
EL	Standard Modern Greek
EN	English
ES	Spanish
FR	French
GL	Galician
GMH	German, Middle High (c. 1050–1500)
GOH	Old High German
GOT	Gothic
GRC	Ancient Greek
GSW	Swiss German
IT	Italian
LA	Latin
LT	Lithuanian
PL	Polish
PT	Portuguese

Introduction

I

Word Formation, Borrowing and their Interaction

Pius ten Hacken and Renáta Panocová

The interaction between word formation and borrowing is not a topic that has been studied widely. A likely reason for this is that word formation and borrowing have been studied from different theoretical perspectives. Whereas word formation is usually considered a domain of morphology, borrowing is a phenomenon that has been studied in lexicography, where it has connections with etymology, language policy and contact linguistics. Therefore, we will first present these two perspectives in sections 1 and 2, before considering the possible types of interaction in section 3. This provides a background for the case studies collected in this volume. A common aspect of all case studies is the work with data. Section 4 addresses some general issues that arise in the collection and interpretation of data. Finally, section 5 introduces the chapters against this background.

1. The morphological perspective

Morphology is the part of the theory of language which is concerned with the internal structure and the formation of words. How exactly the study of words is conceived of depends on the theory adopted. Morphology is usually divided into three main domains: inflection, derivation, and compounding. It is distinguished from syntax, which is concerned with the combination of words into sentences. Which of these divisions is theoretically relevant is a question that is answered differently in different theories. A good example of these decisions is the choice between two primary divisions of the morphological domain, as illustrated in Figure 1.1.

In model A of Figure 1.1, word formation does not appear as a theoretical domain. This is the model adopted, for instance, by Selkirk (1982). In word-based approaches, e.g. Aronoff (1976) and Anderson (1992), model B is adopted. Here the idea is that word formation is a rule component in the lexicon and that lexemes are the input to word formation rules. However, Aronoff (1976) only discusses derivation, and for Anderson (1992) compounding is somewhat of an embarrassment in the sense that the resulting words have an internal structure.

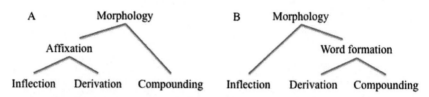

Figure 1.1 Two divisions of the domain of morphology

In the Slavic linguistic tradition based on the structuralist and functionalist theoretical framework of the Prague School of Linguistics, word formation is basically understood as a part of lexicology tightly linked with the morphological and lexical levels of language (Dokulil 1994: 127). Although this connection is straightforward, word formation is understood as having a specific position, distinct from syntax. From this perspective, Dokulil's approach is more compatible with model B in Figure 1.1.

In the generative tradition, and more generally in American structuralism, the focus of attention in morphology has always been the question of how the form of a word can be accounted for. Hockett (1954) proposed the division into Item and Arrangement (IA) and Item and Process (IP). The difference is reflected most obviously in the status of affixes. In IA, affixes are bound morphemes, so that affixation is the combination of morphemes. In IP, an affix is the phonological side effect of the application of a morphological rule to a base. Properties which in IA are assigned to the affix are in IP attributed to the corresponding process. For compounding, IA does not have to make any special provisions. In IP, we can assume, for instance, that compounds are the result of a process with more than one input element. Conversely, IP has a more straightforward solution to cases where a process changes the input in different ways than by adding an affix, e.g. *song* from *sing*. Here IA must attribute the vowel change in some way to a morpheme. In principle, IA and IP are both compatible with either model in Figure 1.1.

When the focus is on how a word form or lexeme is formed and how it is structured, borrowing is not interesting. Even if the borrowing is a complex word in the original language, it does not have structure in the language in which it is adopted. An example is the English word *kindergarten*. OED (2000 [2016]: *kindergarten*)[1] dates it to 1851. In German, *kindergarten* is a compound with the components *Kind* ('child') and *Garten* ('garden'). Depending on the morphological theory, *-er-* is a separate element (in the German terminology, a *Fugenelement*) or a part of the first component (as argued by ten Hacken 1994). In English, however, *kindergarten* is not a complex word, because the components are not elements of the English lexicon. From the perspective of morphological structure, English *kindergarten* is of the same type as *school*, i.e. it belongs to the part of the lexicon on which morphology has nothing to say.

The lack of a place for borrowing can be confirmed by a look at some current mainstream theories of morphology. Distributed Morphology, as proposed by Halle and Marantz (1993), aims to extend the domain of syntactic rules to the internal structure of words. Unless there are two or more morphemes, no rules can be applied to them. Also, in Lieber's (2004) lexical semantic approach to morphology, we first need more than one basic element in order to open the possibility of co-indexation. Booij's (2010)

Construction Morphology uses Jackendoff's (2002) approach to conceptual structure which analyses the meaning also of morphologically simple words. However, there is no rule that can be used for borrowing, so that it cannot be covered by a construction.

In sum, in a morphological perspective, word formation is covered by rules. On the basis of rules, there is little to say about borrowing. Therefore, a purely morphological perspective does not encourage the study of the interaction of word formation and borrowing.

2. The lexicographic perspective

An area where borrowing is a central issue is in lexicography. In fact, Durkin's (2016) handbook of lexicography has no separate chapter devoted to borrowings, but the index includes references to *borrowing* in twelve (of thirty-seven) chapters. The fact that borrowing is not treated as a separate topic may be due to the focus on English in many chapters. Diamond's (2016) chapter on criteria for the inclusion of entries, for instance, has a general title but in the first sentence restricts the scope to OED (2000–2019). In the lexicography of most other languages, one of the most prominent questions about the inclusion of entries in a dictionary is the proper treatment of Anglicisms. For Italian, Zoppetti (2017) is an example of a passionate plea against the use of Anglicisms and their inclusion in dictionaries.

The issue of whether to include a word as an entry or not is of course also relevant in the case of word formation. Here the question is, under which conditions a newly formed word should be entered in the dictionary. Diamond (2016: 544) discusses the case of *advisorial*. Criteria for inclusion may vary from one dictionary to another, especially in their relative weight. However, evidence of use of the word in a corpus is generally an important positive factor. By contrast, the predictability of meaning and form may be a negative factor. Atkins and Rundell (2008: 237) give *homelessness* as a good candidate for a run-on entry, i.e. a related word given without any definition at the end of a regular entry, in this case *homeless*. They mention word formation, in particular in its role as a guide to understanding the meaning, as an important factor in deciding whether a run-on entry should be used.

Another area, apart from the decision about the inclusion in dictionaries, where the phenomenon of borrowing plays a role is etymology. In etymology, the historical development of words is documented. Ten Hacken (2018) proposes an interpretation of etymological information as an account of the motivation speakers have for the use of a particular form to refer to a particular meaning. As such, *motivation* stands in opposition to the *arbitraire du signe* as stipulated by Saussure (1916). Durkin's (2009) overview of etymology devotes two entire chapters to borrowing (about one sixth of the page length). Etymology is inherently diachronic in its outlook. As such, it uses a different perspective to morphology, where the synchronic state of a rule system is the focus of attention. It is important to note this, because word formation also is one of the mechanisms that is involved in etymology. The third mechanism Durkin (2009) mentions is the change of forms and meanings of existing words.

The fact that borrowing and word formation are both among the mechanisms of etymology may suggest that at least in this field one can expect studies of their interaction. To some extent, this expectation is borne out. OED (2000 [1902]: *library*, n.[1]) gives the etymology of *library* as a borrowing from French, with a more general Romance background, where it is in turn the result of word formation. Conversely, OED (2000 [1902]: *librettist*) gives the etymology of *librettist* as a word formation based on *libretto*, which is in turn a borrowing from Italian. A crucial difference between the way word formation is invoked in etymology and in morphology, however, is the role of rules. Whereas in morphology word formation is treated as rule based, etymology is only interested in individual outputs of such rules. This means that only very limited aspects of interaction can be addressed.

Therefore, in the compilation of dictionaries, word formation and borrowing play an important role in the decision of which entries to include in a dictionary and in etymology. In both areas, the role of word formation is reduced to its application to individual cases. The interaction of the rules of word formation with borrowing is not an issue of major interest in lexicography.

3. Types of interaction

Having established that neither the morphological nor the lexicographic perspective provide an ideal background for studying the interaction of word formation and borrowing, it is now worth considering what types of interaction we can expect to find. In the case of word formation, we have both a rule system and individual applications. We can focus on the suffixation rule for *-less* or on individual words such as *treeless*. For borrowing, there is no rule system. We only have individual applications and factors that influence them. There is no rule correlating with the borrowing of, for instance, *pizza*, but at most circumstances that favour its borrowing. The interaction of borrowing and word formation can in principle take two forms. In one, they are in competition to provide the name for a concept. In the other, they influence each other's result in a way that could be called *collaboration*.

Both word formation and borrowing take place in a context where new concepts are named. In this context, *concept* is used to designate the meaning of a content word and *new* means 'not previously stored'. As argued in ten Hacken and Panocová (2011), the selection of a concept and the choice of a name are actions that can only be performed by individual speakers, but they are perceived as the activity of the speech community these speakers belong to. The role of the speech community is above all that different speakers realise how other speakers name concepts. This exchange leads to a pressure to unify the names. If 'everyone else' is perceived as using X, the pressure also to adopt X is strong. However, if different expressions are in use, one can align with one of the groups within the community.

When a new concept needs to be named, there are typically three options. One is to use an existing word, extending its meaning. This is the least prominent option in the sense that no new word is coined. An example is the use of *captain* for an officer on a plane. The second option is word formation. In word formation a new word is created, but its rule-based nature makes it possible to interpret the result. In fact, in a case such as *treeless*, it is arguably easier to retrieve the meaning of the word than for sense extensions such as *captain* in an aviation context. Both of these naming strategies are available in a purely monolingual environment. Borrowing, as in the case of *pizza*, requires a degree of access to another language. The speaker who comes up with the borrowing must know at least this particular word in the other language. In practice, both the number of speakers and the knowledge of the language of origin tend to be larger than this. Borrowing is linked to cultural contact and intercultural communication.

In principle, these three mechanisms are in competition. The requirement of language contact may seem a constraint on the use of borrowing, but there are at least three aspects that put it at an advantage. First, contexts of language contact are particularly rich in new concepts. Moreover, a culture in which new concepts arise is likely to have a certain prestige. Finally, the borrowed name is immediately available. A name arising from sense extension or word formation has to be thought up and then compete with the borrowed name that already exists.

Turning now to collaboration, it is first of all necessary to qualify some of the associations of this term. Words and linguistic processes do not act. As elaborated in ten Hacken and Panocová (2011), it is only speakers who can do that. Moreover, the process of naming new concepts and building up linguistic knowledge is largely if not entirely unconscious. Even if coming up with a new name may sometimes be a conscious action, the considerations underlying the new name are at most partially explicit. When we speak of *collaboration* between word formation and borrowing, what we mean is that both play a role in the ultimate result. This result can take the form of a new word formation rule or a new word.

Borrowing is always a matter of individual words. Moreover, as mentioned in the discussion of *kindergarten* in section 1, if the borrowed word is the result of a word formation rule in the original language, the word formation origin is lost in the receiving language. English *kindergarten* is a simplex word, although its correlate in German is a compound. Word formation rules are not borrowed. The only way they can arise in the receiving language is by re-analysis. Mühleisen (2010) describes an example of such a phenomenon in English, the suffix *-ee*. In a first phase, French words ending in *-ee* were borrowed. In a second phase, the correlation between the form and meaning of these related borrowings was noticed. The ending *-ee* was linked to a meaning which could be applied to the meaning of the base to which *-ee* was attached. In the third phase, this correlation was turned into a word formation rule. At this stage, the use of *-ee* was no longer dependent on the existence of a French word. In this way, word formation rules can emerge under the influence of another language, but this emergence is not the same as borrowing.

Another type of collaboration between word formation and borrowing occurs when the selection and application of word formation rules are influenced by the existence of a word in another language. Some relevant examples from computing in German are given in (1).

(1) a. Rechner   ('computer')   DE
     b. abstürzen   ('crash')   DE

In (1a), the German word is an agent noun derived from the verb *rechnen* ('calculate, work out'). The internal structure is based on the structure of the English word, although *compute* is more adequately translated as 'berechnen'. In (1b), we find a case where the image is taken over from one language to another. English *crash* was used for aeroplanes or the stock exchange before it came into use for computers. German *abstürzen* is the verb used in these contexts as an equivalent. Thus, in (1a) a word formation rule and in (1b) a sense extension in German are parallel to an earlier English example. The case in (1a) is usually called a calque. The phenomenon in (1b) is very similar, but it does not involve a word formation rule.

4. Collection and interpretation of data

The observation of borrowing and word formation is more complex than one might think. Data do not come labelled as one or the other. One problem is that data are generally static, whereas the phenomena constitute a change. Both borrowing and word formation are the interpretation of the relation between two situations, one the system before and the other the system after the inclusion of a new word. A second problem concerns the nature of the system. As ten Hacken (2007: 274–281) explains, named languages such as English, Dutch or Slovak are not empirical entities. They are abstractions based on the competence and/or performance of individual speakers. In order to see the consequences of this, let us consider the English pair in (2).

(2)   a.   organise   EN
       b.   organisation   EN

It seems obvious that (2b) is the result of word formation, in this case derivation with the suffix *-ation*. For (2a), the analysis is less obvious. Although *-ise* is a suffix in *neutralise* and *itemise*, the base in (2a) would be *organ*. As the meaning of *organ* (whether in the musical or in the biological sense) does not play a role in (2a), there is no reason to assume that it is the result of *-ise* suffixation. Instead, we can turn to the French translations in (3).

(3)   a.   organiser   FR
       b.   organisation   FR

For the pair in (3), it is also plausible that (3b) is derived from (3a) by suffixation. Given the well-known historical influence of French on English, it seems quite straightforward to analyse (2a) as the result of borrowing based on French (3a). The question is, now, whether (2b) is not rather a borrowing from French (3b) than a word formation based on (2a). If (2b) is a borrowing, we should not discard the possibility that (2a) is a back formation, i.e. that the verb is formed on the basis of the noun that looks like a derivative. This means that for the pair in (2), we have at least three possible analyses, as listed in (4).

(4)   a.   *organise* borrowed from FR, *organisation* by suffixation
       b.   *organise* borrowed from FR, *organisation* borrowed from FR
       c.   *organisation* borrowed from FR, *organise* by back formation

One way to decide about such options is to maximise the scope of one's theory. This is not uncommon in morphology, where in a case such as (4), only (4a) is considered at all. In some cases, even setting up bound stems is preferred to any recourse to borrowing (cf. ten Hacken 2015: 198). Here, this would result in analysing *organise* as derived from a reading of *organ* that does not appear in any other context.

If we want to base a decision on data, we can use corpora, intuitions and dictionaries. In corpora, we find words in context, but without any analysis. Even the interpretation of the expression is not in the corpus but stems from the reader's knowledge of language. One piece of information we get from corpora is the date of attestation. This is particularly relevant in historical corpora. Also, the context of use may give useful information. New words which have not been fully accepted yet are often introduced in explanatory contexts or accompanied with hedges. At the same time, records are necessarily incomplete, because not all uses of words are such that they can be retrieved for inclusion in a corpus.

The use of intuition as a source of data is controversial. While it can be argued that intuitions provide crucial information for grammatical phenomena, the structure of one's linguistic knowledge is not directly available for conscious inspection. Therefore, using intuitions about the three options in (4) is problematic.

The use of dictionaries is of a somewhat different type. As shown by ten Hacken (2009, 2012), dictionaries cannot be pure descriptions of the vocabulary of a language, although they are often invoked as authorities. A dictionary gives information about words. This information is usually based on corpora and has been compiled by lexicographers. Therefore, the information in a dictionary can be taken as a lexicographic interpretation of the available data. For (2a), OED (2019 [2004]: *organise*, v.) states that it is '[o]f multiple origins', a borrowing partly from French and partly from Latin. Also, for (2b), OED (2019 [2004]: *organisation*, n.) gives such an analysis. The suffix is only mentioned in the Latin part of the etymology. One aspect in which dictionaries can be particularly helpful is in the recording of dates of first attestation. OED gives '?*a*1425' for both words in (2). In both cases, the source of the first attestation is a translation of a French text. For French, Robert (1986) gives 1390 for the noun in (3b) and 'V. 1380' for the verb in (3a). Of course, dictionaries may represent different attitudes to the options in (4). Thus, Robert (1986) states that (3b) is derived from (3a) and (3a) from *organe*, without any reference to Latin correlates.

It is not obvious that we must choose one of the options in (4) to the exclusion of the others. Two or more may be accurate to different degrees. Such a situation can be interpreted in different ways. First, languages are abstractions from speakers. Individual speakers may have a different organisation of their mental lexicon without ever noticing these differences. For the use of the words in (2), we do not have to know their origin. On this basis, one might set up a classification of speakers according to the different options. However, these options need not be articulated. A speaker of English may start using *organisation* and store it in their mental lexicon for a combination of reasons. They may link it to the verb *organise* and a word formation rule, to the French word, or simply as a word they pick up from what others say. It is not possible to quantify the contribution of the different factors, because only the result can be observed.

Therefore, the study of the interaction of borrowing and word formation raises a number of methodological and theoretical challenges. It is important, however, to note that these challenges also emerge for the study of borrowing and of word formation in isolation. The focus on their interaction is actually an avenue to potential new insights, as we hope this volume will show.

5. Overview of the volume

The chapters in this volume are case studies of the interaction of borrowing and word formation. They illustrate situations of language contact and the response to naming needs in the competition and collaboration of these two major naming strategies. They are organised in three parts.

Part I contains five chapters focusing on compounding. Chapter 2, by Brian D. Joseph, addresses the special position of compounding in language contact and language change. Compounding is deceptively simple in its form but quite complex in its interpretation. In contact situations, this means that non-native speakers can use compounds with relative ease and shift the burden of interpretation onto the hearers. For this reason, compounding plays a much more significant role in language change than one might expect on the basis of the interpretation difficulties it causes. Two examples are discussed, one the use of Greek compounds in scientific English, the other the use of English compounds in Russian.

In the next chapter, Renáta Panocová and Pius ten Hacken discuss neoclassical compounds. In assessing the status of neoclassical compounding, they take into account the generative insight that language is ultimately based in the individual speaker's competence and the European structuralist insight that new words are a response to naming needs. The central question in this chapter is whether a language has a system of neoclassical compounding. Comparing English and Russian, Panocová and ten Hacken argue that only for English is there evidence for a substantial set of speakers who have such as system. In Russian, neoclassical compounds are generally borrowings.

Chapter 4, by Alina Villalva, is devoted to compounding in Portuguese. She explains that in Portuguese, compounding was originally not prominent in word formation. However, as a Romance language, Portuguese has a large vocabulary inherited from Latin. In the Renaissance, new Latinate words were added, some of them compounds. From the seventeenth century also neoclassical roots started appearing. Villalva argues that the influx of neoclassical compounds has not only resulted in a reinvigoration of compounding in the neoclassical domain, but also strengthened its place in native word formation, as can be shown by the appearance of new compounds that were not borrowed.

Staying within the process of compounding, in Chapter 5 Bonifacas Stundžia explores the influence of German compounding patterns on Lithuanian word formation on the basis of an eighteenth-century manuscript bilingual German-Lithuanian dictionary. German compounds are quite often rendered by Lithuanian compounds in the dictionary, but only if they consist of two stems, which corresponds to the Lithuanian word formation system. He argues that two competing patterns can be distinguished, one where the calque is only integrated into the inflectional system and one where it is also integrated in the word formation system.

Silvia Cacchiani focuses on compounding as a significant proportion of the borrowings from English that have appeared in Italian in the past decades. In Italian, N+N compounds are rare, but to the extent that they exist they are left-headed. English N+N compounds are right-headed. As a consequence, there is a pressure to adapt borrowed compounds from English. The adaptation may lead to left-headed compounds, clippings preserving only the English head or non-head, or a replacement by a more typical Italian construction. However, not all compounds are adapted. Some retain their English order of components. Cacchiani argues that despite the confusing array of alternatives, both left-headed and right-headed compounds have become more frequent in Italian.

In Part II, we turn away from compounding in language contact to focus on affixation in language contact. In the first chapter of this part, Maria Bloch-Trojnar explores the Polish suffix *-alny* which produces deverbal adjectives whose meaning can be paraphrased as 'capable of being V-ed'. It corresponds to English *-able/-ible*. The base of the Polish suffix is an imperfective, transitive verb. Traditionally, the base is also said to be [–native], but whether this is synchronically still necessary is a matter of debate. Bloch-Trojnar argues that quite a number of more recent formations can rather be analysed as morphological calques based on English. This suggests a change in the conditions governing the use of the Polish word formation rule under the influence of another language.

Chapter 8, by Camiel Hamans, discusses clippings from the perspective of the borderline between affixation and borrowing. Clipping is a traditional word formation process in Dutch, German and English. In Dutch and English, the stem is monosyllabic, but in German, disyllabic clippings ending in an unstressed vowel occur. German and English also have clippings followed by the hypocoristic suffix *-i* or *-y*. More recently, Dutch has developed clippings with the suffix *-o*. This suffix can also be attached to full forms. Hamans argues that this pattern has been borrowed from American English, where it originated from Italo-English immigrant vernacular. In German, competition from *-i* reduces its productivity.

In the next chapter on affixation and borrowing, Magda Ševčíková considers the Czech suffixes *-ismus* and *-ita* corresponding to the English *-ism* and *-ity* and to the German *-ismus* and *–ität*. She studies them on the basis of a large corpus of contemporary Czech. Words with the suffixes *-ismus* and *-ita* refer to qualities, and objects have a certain quality. Because the suffixes tend to attach to foreign bases only, the result can be analysed as a borrowing or a derivation. On the basis of corpus analysis, arguments are collected for determining which of these two analyses is better in individual cases.

The last chapter on affixation is by Angeliki Efthymiou. She explores the prefixes *iper-*, *anti-* and *para-* which derive ultimately from Ancient Greek prepositions but are used in Modern Greek as a result of a complex interplay between borrowing and word formation. The influence of calquing on the word formation processes involved and the way borrowing affects the meaning of the Modern Greek prefixes is investigated on the basis of data from two major Modern Greek dictionaries.

The three chapters that make up Part III are studies of naming in minority languages. In Chapter 11, Livio Gaeta and Marco Angster concentrate on Titsch and Töitschu, two Alemannic dialects spoken in two Aosta Valley villages. All speakers are at least bilingual, and language contact with Italian and French standard languages as well as Piedmontese and Francoprovençal regional languages has been intensive. In addition, the dialects show influence from standard German and Swiss German. On the basis of a large collection of lexical material, the relative weight of each of these influences and of native patterns in word formation, calques and borrowing is evaluated.

Angela Ralli and Vasiliki Makri investigate the borderline between word formation and borrowing in a sizeable population of Greek immigrants in the Canadian provinces of Québec and Ontario. In their variety of Greek, many English words are borrowed. The typological difference between Greek and English implies that in the integration of these words into Canadian Greek, a number of decisions have to be made to adapt them to the gender and declension system of the recipient language. On the basis of previous work and the collection of oral sources carried out in the framework of a dedicated research project, the factors determining these decisions are investigated.

The last chapter on naming in minority languages is by Michał Rzepiela. In medieval Poland, Latin was the language of the legal courts. In order to accommodate many concepts for which no Latin words were available, Polish words were borrowed into Latin. In the nominative singular, it is often difficult to determine whether a noun is Polish or Latin. Borrowing also led to the establishment of new word formation patterns in Latin. This is investigated on the basis of a dictionary and a corpus of Medieval Latin in Poland.

The concluding chapter approaches the question of how borrowing and word formation influence each other along different dimensions. Based on the case studies in Parts I, II and III, we propose some generalisations about the interaction of the two naming mechanisms.

Note

1. In references to the *Oxford English Dictionary*, the year in square brackets indicates the latest full revision of the entry.

References

Anderson, Stephen R. (1992), *A-Morphous Morphology*, Cambridge: Cambridge University Press.

Aronoff, Mark H. (1976), *Word Formation in Generative Grammar*, Cambridge, MA: MIT Press.

Atkins, B. T. Sue and M. Rundell (2008), *The Oxford Guide to Practical Lexicography*, Oxford: Oxford University Press.

Booij, Geert (2010), *Construction Morphology*, Oxford: Oxford University Press.

Diamond, Graeme (2016), 'Making Decisions about Inclusion and Exclusion', in P. Durkin (ed.), *The Oxford Handbook of Lexicography*, Oxford: Oxford University Press, pp. 532–545.

Dokulil, Miloš (1994), 'The Prague School's Theoretical and Methodological Contribution to "Word Formation" (Derivology)', in P. A. Luelsdorff (ed.), *The Prague School of Structural and Functional Linguistics: A Short Introduction*, Amsterdam and Philadelphia: John Benjamins, pp. 123–161.

Durkin, Philip (2009), *The Oxford Guide to Etymology*, Oxford: Oxford University Press.

Durkin, Philip (ed.) (2016), *The Oxford Handbook of Lexicography*, Oxford: Oxford University Press.

ten Hacken, Pius (1994), *Defining Morphology: A Principled Approach to Determining the Boundaries of Compounding, Derivation, and Inflection*, Hildesheim: Olms.

ten Hacken, Pius (2007), *Chomskyan Linguistics and its Competitors*, London: Equinox.

ten Hacken, Pius (2009), 'What is a Dictionary? A View from Chomskyan Linguistics', *International Journal of Lexicography*, 22: 399–421.

ten Hacken, Pius (2012), 'In What Sense is the OED the Definitive Record of the English Language?', in R. V. Fjeld and J. M. Torjusen (eds), *Proceedings of the XV EURALEX International Congress* (7–11 August 2012), Oslo: Department of Linguistics, pp. 834–845.

ten Hacken, Pius (2015), 'Review of L. Bauer, R. Lieber and I. Plag (2013), *The Oxford Reference Guide to English Morphology*, Oxford: Oxford University Press', *English Language and Linguistics*, 19: 188–201.

ten Hacken, Pius (2018), 'On the Interpretation of Etymologies in Dictionaries', in J. Čibej, V. Gorjanc, I. Kosem and S. Krek (eds), *Proceedings of the XVIII EURALEX International Congress, Lexicography in Global Contexts* (17–21 July 2018), Ljubljana: Ljubljana University Press, Faculty of Arts, pp. 763–773.

ten Hacken, Pius and R. Panocová (2011), 'Individual and Social Aspects of Word Formation', *Kwartalnik Neofilologiczny*, 58: 283–300.

Halle, Morris and A. Marantz (1993), 'Distributed Morphology and the Pieces of Inflection', in K. Hale and S. J. Keyser (eds), *The View from Building 20: Essays in Linguistics in Honor of Sylvain Bromberger*, Cambridge, MA: MIT Press, pp. 111–176.

Hockett, Charles F. (1954), 'Two Models of Grammatical Description', *Word*, 10: 210–231.

Jackendoff, Ray (2002), *Foundations of Language: Brain, Meaning, Grammar, Evolution*, Oxford: Oxford University Press.

Lieber, Rochelle (2004), *Morphology and Lexical Semantics*, Cambridge: Cambridge University Press.

Mühleisen, Susanne (2010), *Heterogeneity in Word-Formation Patterns: A Corpus-based Analysis of Suffixation with -ee and its Productivity in English*, Amsterdam: John Benjamins.

OED (2000–2019), *Oxford English Dictionary*, edited by J. Simpson, Oxford: Oxford University Press, 3rd edn, www.oed.com (29 June 2019).

Robert, Paul (ed.) (1986), *Dictionnaire alphabétique et analogique de la langue française*, Paris: Le Robert, 2nd edn (Alain Rey).

Saussure, Ferdinand de (1916), *Cours de linguistique générale*, edited by C. Bally and A. Sechehaye, Édition critique préparée par Tullio de Mauro, Paris: Payot (1981).

Selkirk, Elisabeth O. (1982), *The Syntax of Words*, Cambridge, MA: MIT Press.
Zoppetti, Antonio (2017), *Diciamolo in italiano: Gli abusi dell'inglese nel lessico dell'Italia e incolla*, Milano: Hoepli.

Part I Compounding

2

Compounding and Contact

Brian D. Joseph

This chapter examines the behaviour of compounds in language contact situations. Preliminaries about compounds and language contact are presented in section 1, focusing largely on questions of simplification versus complexification in language contact and of nativisation of borrowed elements as opposed to adoption without adaptation. This is followed by case studies involving Greek influence on English (section 2), Western European languages, especially English, on Russian (section 3), Western European languages, especially French, on Greek (section 4) and French influence on English (section 5). Key lessons to take away from these case studies are first that in the borrowing of compounds and compounding structures, languages seem not to engage in adaptation to native language patterns, and second that once a new structure enters a language via borrowing it takes on a life of its own, so to speak, and can take on forms that are quite different from their form in the source language.

1. Preliminaries on compounds and on contact

Vital to any serious discussion of word formation is a consideration of compounding, the process (or processes)[1] by which complex words are created out of elements that are already words or word-like along various parameters. Compounding presents an interesting analytic conundrum for linguistic theory in general, in that it is a conceptually simple operation that is nonetheless quite complex at various levels of analysis. That is, while compounding often seems to involve nothing more than simply the juxtaposition of two (or more) elements, together with the possibility of some concomitant phonological or morphophonological adjustments, it also interacts with aspects of both argument structure and lexical semantics. Moreover, given the fact that it essentially stands at the nexus of syntax, in that it involves phrasal representations, and morphology, in that it involves word-level representations, compounding raises questions as to the analytic status of the composite form as a whole as well as the status of the parts that make up the composite.

These various issues fall within the realm of theoretical problems raised by language-internal considerations. But there are important questions as well that can be asked about compounding within any framework of language contact and contact-induced change.

A good reason for considering compounding in situations of language contact is that compounding presents some elements of particular interest to language contact studies. Contact-induced change is often thought to involve simplification,[2] and thus a search on the part of speakers with some command of more than one language system,[3] i.e. bilinguals,[4] for congruent elements between the languages they control to some extent. However, there is also a view that takes contact to be a source of complexity in a language system (Nichols 1992: 193). Moreover, an influential approach to contact-induced change, specifically the position advocated in Thomason and Kaufman (1988), holds that, essentially, 'anything goes' in language contact situations and that there are no linguistic constraints on change motivated through forces external to a given language system, rather only constraints based on the social circumstances of the contact situation. Under this view, which is endorsed here, one would be led to think that compounding in situations of contact between languages could be a good testing ground for the question of simplification versus complexification in language contact outcomes. Given the multiplicity of what compounding involves and what it can do system-internally, one might expect it to be rather exempt in cases of language contact, under an assumption that speakers confronting a second language might 'take the easy way out' and look to simplify by ignoring compounding rather than to complexify. But given that the surface operation in compounding is rather simple, typically involving what appears to be just juxtaposition, enforced adjacency as it were, it might actually be seen as a handy tool for speakers to avail themselves of when using material from another language or who are faced with dealing with expressing themselves in a second language.

It is well known that in cases of borrowing, speakers of the recipient language often assimilate or adapt a foreign element of the donor language to their native language patterns and structure. Thus, words borrowed from Spanish into English with an initial voiceless stop, e.g. *taco*, are pronounced by English speakers with an English-style aspirated stop rather than the Spanish-style unaspirated stop (thus [tʰako] as opposed to [tako]). Also, to offer an example from morphosyntax, Turkish postpositions, such as *karşı* 'opposite', have generally been borrowed into other languages in the Balkans as prepositions. Such is the case in the Greek of Ottoman-era Adrianoupolis, for instance, with this particular lexeme.[5] But at the same time, when for whatever reason there is no assimilation or adaptation of the external element to the structure of the borrowing language, a degree of complexity enters the grammar. For instance, English speakers, such as myself, who pronounce the name of the famous German composer Johann Sebastian Bach with a German-style [x],[6] have introduced complexity into the phonemic system of English, first by adding an altogether new element to the phonemic inventory, and second by marking the element with severe lexical restrictions as to its occurrence. And, to turn once more to Ottoman-era Adrianoupolis Greek, the Turkish postposition *gibi* 'like' was borrowed into that language as a postposition, thus introducing a new structure into the language and thereby a degree of complexity as well to the syntax of adpositions.

How compounds fare in situations of borrowing can therefore be quite revealing with regard to matters of judging how languages complexify, or not, as the case may be. The basic conundrum here is that we might expect compounds to show assimilation/ adaptation to the borrowing language's structure, but in fact in many instances we find just the opposite. That is, often, compounding involving both foreign elements and foreign patterns provides a ready device that speakers incorporate into their usage even if at the expense of having to deal with certain anomalies these elements might cause within their native language.

Accordingly, in this chapter, in keeping with the general theme of studying borrowing and word formation, what can happen with regard to compounding under conditions of contact between speakers of different languages is examined via the presentation of various case studies. The case studies to be discussed here involve different pairs of languages, and for two of the languages involved, Greek and English, it is possible to see them both in the role of the recipient, i.e. borrowing, language and in the role of the donor language. Admittedly all of the language pairs are Indo-European in terms of their genealogical affiliation, but they are illustrative of compounding under conditions of language contact nonetheless.

Besides what these case studies show about the particular languages involved, an important lesson to be learned from them is that once elements are borrowed into a recipient language, they take on a life of their own, creating new patterns and new forms that can be quite different from what can be seen in the donor language.

2. Greek and Latin borrowings in English technical vocabulary

The first case study involves the absorption into English learnèd vocabulary of elements ultimately of Greek origin, or in some instances Latin origin, and their effect on the word formation system. The elements in question form the basis for a wide array of technical terminology having to do with medicine, science and technology more generally, but they are of interest here because they show that the borrowings bring to English a structural possibility that is not fully available with native Germanic or Anglo-Saxon elements. In a certain sense, then, the borrowings create a degree of complexity by adding to the range of structures that are available to users of English, though an attractive alternative view would say that they add to the expressive capabilities of speakers.

To illustrate this, I start with the observation that English, at least insofar as native elements are concerned, does not generally allow for so-called 'copulative' compounds (*dvandvas* in the influential terminology of the native Sanskrit grammarians of ancient times), i.e. compounds in which one item is tied to another in a composite meaning 'X and Y' but without an overt linking word like *and*. This is especially so with regard to the possibility of adding a derivational suffix to the potential compound. That is, in English it is not possible to construct words like **ear-nose-r* for 'one involved with the ear and the nose' with the agentive *-(e)r* suffix,[7] nor **red-white-ish* for 'somewhat red and white', with the approximative suffix *-ish*, in which a suffix is added onto a *dvandva* compound representing a pair of words with no overt conjunction linking the members of that compound. The *dvandva* compounding option admittedly is available in a limited way, i.e. just as the first member of a compound, as in *soda-wine mixture*, meaning 'a mixture of soda *and* wine',[8] but it is not generally possible to have such a copulative compound as input to suffixation. However, when elements that have been borrowed into English from Greek are involved, a *dvandva* compound with a suffix is possible.

For instance, in *otorhinolaryngologist*, the first three elements form a *dvandva* compound. When *oto-* for 'ear', *rhino-* for 'nose' and *laryng-* for 'throat', all representing borrowings from Ancient Greek (GRC) elements, ὠτο- (*ōto-*, oblique stem of οὖς *ous* 'ear'), ῥινο- (*rhino-*, oblique stem of ῥις *rhis* 'nose'), and λάρυγγο- (*laryngo-*, oblique stem of λάρυγξ *larynks* 'upper part of windpipe'), are simply strung together, they give a copulative sense of 'ear, nose *and* throat' even though there is no overt word for 'and'. They occur here with the complex suffix *-ologist*, also Greek in origin, referring to one who studies something. Thus, the compound means 'one who studies (i.e. is a specialist in) the ear, the nose and the throat'.[9]

The same is true with chemical names, where *dvandva*s and Greek-derived elements abound.[10] A chemical that is named entirely with Greek elements just added together is *bromochloroiodomethane*, the name for a methane molecule to which atoms of the elements bromine, chlorine and iodine are attached. The overall form is thus a determinative (*tatpuruṣa*) compound, headed by *methane*, with a composite first member *bromochloroiodo-*, where each part of the first member refers to a particular element, the free form for which in each case has the suffix *-ine*. This first member is additive in its meaning, thus a *dvandva*, but occurs without an overt word for 'and'. Here the Greek elements in the compound are the stems for βρῶμο-(ς) *brōmo-(s)* 'stench', χλωρό-(ς) *khlōro-(s)* 'light green' and ἰώδ-(ης) *iōd-(ēs)* 'bluish-green', respectively, and represent the elements derived from these stems with the Latin-derived suffix *-ine*.[11]

It must be admitted that compound words like *otorhinolaryngologist* or *bromochloroiodomethane* occur just in highly restricted sectors of the English lexicon and are hardly common garden-variety everyday household words. But they are forms that are known to and used by at least some speakers of English, and they thus qualify as a real part of the English language in a macro sense, even if jargonistic in their nature.

These words and the combining elements that they consist of exhibit a degree of productivity. One relevant fact in that regard is that they are expandable: *otorhinolaryngologist* is itself an expansion of *otolaryngologist*, literally 'a specialist in ear and throat' but conventionally, given the interconnection of the relevant body parts, a doctor who specialises in disorders of the ear, throat and nose, so that *otorhinolaryngologist* offers a more explicit enumeration of specialties. Also, *bromochloroiodomethane* can be expanded with another chemical element to *bromochlorofluoroiodomethane*, the further addition being *fluoro-* for the element *fluorine*, a Latin-derived name (*fluor* 'a flowing', cf. *fluere* 'to flow').

Moreover, new words can be formed with these elements. For instance, starting with the English medical term *encephalon* 'brain' (in anatomical usage), which is a loanword taken from GRC ἐγκέφαλος *enkephalos* '(that which is) within the head', it is possible to form the composite *encephalograph* 'brain image' with the morpheme *graph* from GRC γράφειν *graphein* 'to write'.[12] From *encephalograph*, or possibly directly from *encephalon*, the derived noun *encephalography* 'brain imaging' is created with the noun formative -*y*, from GRC -ια -*ia*, giving -*graphy* (cf. GRC γραφία *graphia* 'drawing'), and from that, *electroencephalography* 'electronic encephalography' can be formed, with *electro-* from GRC ἤλεκτρον *ēlektron* 'amber', and from that, *electro-encephalographology* 'study of electronic encephalographs' can be created (with -*logy* from GRC -λογία -*logia* (ultimately from λόγος *logos* 'word')), and so also *electro-encephalographologist* 'specialist who studies electroencephalographs' (with -*ist* from GRC -ιστης -*istēs*). Of these, by way of suggesting the productivity to these recursive processes, the last two do not occur in OED (2000–2019), the most comprehensive listing of English words.

English of course can string together elements as a compound in *brain imaging*, but to go further with non-Greek elements what is needed is either an adjective, as in *electronic brain imaging*, or more expansive non-compound syntax, as in the phrasal form *study of electronic encephalographs*, or a complex noun phrase with a relative clause, as in *specialist who studies electroencephalographs*.

It is noteworthy too that in these forms English has absorbed not only the Greek ability to string elements together copulatively, but also the Greek pattern in compounds of using a 'linking vowel' -*o*- to connect the stems in question. Thus in Greek, even though the stem for 'ear' is *ōt*- (ὠτ-) and the stem for 'nose' is *rhin*- (ῥιν), in compounds, they are joined to other stems with an -*o*-, as in GRC ὠτολαβίς *ōtolabis* 'instrument for laying hold of the ears' (lit. 'ear-taker') or ῥινολαβίς *rhinolabis* 'instrument for laying hold of the nose' (lit. 'nose-taker'). And that linking vowel -o- recurs in the Greek-derived compounds in English as well.

The various elements presented here, therefore, represent borrowings from Greek that have brought a new structural possibility into a restricted domain of English vocabulary. Thus, by one measure, these combining forms present a complexity in providing a structure not otherwise generally available in English. On the other hand, however, one could assess the contribution of these borrowed elements in a somewhat more positive light; that is, in a certain way, they expand the expressive range of English by providing a novel possibility, that of productive *dvandva* expansions, not previously available to Modern English. And within their particular jargonistic domains, these compounding patterns provide a productive means of technical nomenclature, and thus nicely fill a functional niche.

3. Analytic compounds in Russian

In the case of the Greek elements in English, the new patterns that entered the borrowing language were not particularly disruptive to the existing structure in the recipient language; they were additive in what might be viewed as a positive way. I move now to an instance of a foreign compound pattern entering a language in which the new patterns are not nativised, not adapted to existing structural possibilities, and in this way would seem to introduce a certain disruption into the recipient language system. Interestingly, though, it can be argued that the disruption is only apparent, and that the non-nativisation is rather an indication of a structural change in the language.

In particular, in a study of innovative instances of non-agreement within noun phrases in contemporary Russian, Patton (1999) discusses instances in which various compound types involving non-native elements are at odds with traditional well-entrenched structures in the language. The most revealing instances for the present purposes are cases in which the left-hand member modifies the right-hand head (thus a *tatpuruṣa* compound type) and serves an adjectival function, but, tellingly, does not inflect for case or gender in the way that a modifier in the Russian noun phrase usually does. While some of these non-agreeing elements can be categorised as indeclinable adjectives, e.g. экзотик *ekzotik* 'exotic' or беж *bež* 'beige', others involve nominal elements. An early one noted by Voroncova (1964) that shows a non-agreeing first element 'condensed' from a fuller declinable adjective is проф-билет *prof-bilet* 'union card', interestingly without the typical *-o-* joining vowel (etymologically connected with the linking vowel *-o-* in Greek discussed in section 2) as seen in compounds like рыб-о-продукты *ryb-o-produkty* 'fish products'. The Noun-Noun type mostly entered the language from foreign sources throughout the twentieth century but with a marked increase in the post-Soviet era due to greater contact with the West and with Western business and cultural practices, and thus Western languages.[13] The primary Western influences in recent years have come from America and thus, in terms of outside linguistic influence on Russian, from American English, though several of the innovative compounds Patton cites are from German.

Patton (1999: 21) notes that there generally are 'synthetic and analytic variations of a single phrase, e.g. клип-антракт *klip-antrakt* "music video intermission" v. антракт клипов *antrakt klipov* [with genitive plural *klipov*] or сервис-центр *servis-centr* "service center" v. сервисный центр *servisnyj centr* [with declinable adjective *servisnyj*]'. Nonetheless, his surveys showed that 'collocations containing indeclinable or nominal adjectives are often preferred by native speakers of Russian'.

Interestingly, Patton's findings indeed point towards a general preference by Russian speakers surveyed for the analytic, non-agreeing structures, even though, as he argues, the compounds go against existing morphosyntactic and syntactic patterning in Russian in three ways (1999: 22–23): lack of case agreement, an 'overwhelming tendency for recently acquired indeclinable adjectives to be preposed (versus the tendency of earlier borrowings to assume postposition', and 'the use of a single word form in both adjectival [= modifying] and nominal functions . . . a striking departure from typical Russian morphosyntax'. Thus, these borrowings, including forms such as футбол-клуб *futbol-klub* 'football club', with the Noun-Noun compound replacing an NP with agreeing Adjective-Noun structure, футбольный клуб *futbolnyj klub*, or офис-директор *ofis-direktor* 'office director' replacing an NP with Noun-Genitive structure, директор офиса *direktor ofisa*, and so on, represent innovations in Russian due to language contact. Among the compounding elements 'commonly found in the popular press and in speech' (Patton 1999: 21) are, from English, бизнес *biznes* (from *business*), дизайн *dizajn* (from *design*), офис *ofis* (from *office*), джаз *džaz* (from *jazz*), менеджмент *menedžment* (from *management*), секс *seks* (from *sex*) and рок *rok* (from *rock* (music)), though he ultimately lists several hundred items. Moreover, in many instances, the compounds do not reflect a foreign source directly, but show novelty, and thus some degree of productivity, within Russian; клип-антракт *klip-antrakt* 'music video intermission' and тренд-журнал *trend-žurnal* 'high fashion magazine' are examples of such novel compounds.

Importantly, however, although there are reasons for seeing the move towards Noun-Noun compounds as counter to the general structure of Russian, as noted above, Patton ultimately argues that these developments overall 'are indicative of a marked shift toward analytism' (1999: 23). Moreover, he suggests that there has been movement towards analyticism in Russian prior to the proliferation of such compounds, as argued by Comrie et al. (1996), so that the compounds with their analytic structure are not so much disrupting the general structure of Russian as perhaps just feeding an undercurrent of analyticism present in the language, thus exacerbating an already-existing tendency, though one that is admittedly innovative as compared with the Russian of, say, two centuries ago. In this view, Russian would be borrowing Noun-Noun compounds readily because it was ready to accept and develop further the structures they represent. The fact, then, that these compounds have entered Russian without nativisation would thus not be so much a matter of adding complexity to the language as enhancing what was already there, adding to the frequency of analytic structures.[14]

4. Noun-Noun compounds in Greek

As a follow-up to the Noun-Noun compounds of the previous case study, I turn now to a case where Greek, more specifically Modern Greek, plays the role not of donor, as in the first case study (where Ancient Greek is at issue), but rather as recipient, with Western European languages, especially French and English, serving as the donors. The compound type in question here is Noun-Noun compounds with the meaning 'an X which is also Y' or 'an X which is like Y'. In this case, the structure in question involves the juxtaposition of complete words, as opposed to the prevailing Greek pattern of compounding with stems. That is, as described by Mackridge (1985: 328–330) and Joseph and Philippaki-Warburton (1987: 227–228), instead of compounds with stems joined by a linking vowel, -o-, such as τσικλόφουσκα *tsikló-fuska* 'bubble-gum' (τσίκλα *tsíkla* 'gum' + φούσκα *fúska* 'bubble', joined with -o-), Modern Greek, inspired by Western European, especially French, models in the twentieth century, shows Word-Word compounds, with the juxtaposition of whole words, without the joining -o-.

The earliest examples include παιδί-θαύμα *peðí-θávma* 'child-prodigy', literally 'child-wonder', thus presumably based on German *Wunderkind*, but with the order of elements as in the English, according to Charalambakis (2014: s.v.); λέξη-κλειδί *léksi-kliðí* 'key-word', literally 'word-key', showing the order in the French model *mot clé*; and απάτη-μαμούθ *apáti-mamúθ* 'mammoth fraud', literally 'fraud-mammoth', with the order of the French *imposture mammouth*. Each member noun in these forms has its own accent, unlike the more widespread τσικλόφουσκα *tsiklófuska* type of compound where the accent of each member is effaced and the composite form has a single accent, which (as in τσικλόφουσκα *tsiklófuska*) can be different from that in each of the component parts. Moreover, although there is some variability in this regard, each member of this innovative compound type generally shows its own inflection for the appropriate case; thus, the genitive singular of 'child prodigy' is παιδιού-θαύματος *peðjú-θávmatos*, the nominative-accusative plural is παιδιά-θαύματα *peðjá-θávmata*, and the genitive plural is παιδιών-θαυμάτων *peðjón-θavmáton*. Such double inflection is quite unlike what is found in general with composite forms in Greek; τσικλόφουσκα *tsiklófuska* 'bubble-gum', for instance, has a genitive singular τσικλόφουσκας *tsiklófuskas* 'of bubble-gum', not *τσικλάσφουσκας *tsiklásfuskas*, with inflected τσικλα- *tsikla-*, or *τσικλούφουσκα *tsiklúfuska*, with a putative stem with the linking vowel -o- inflected. There are also examples in which only one member, the leftmost one, is inflected, as in (1).

(1) a. της   δεσποινίδος-θαύμα
         tis   ðespiníðos-θávma
         the.GEN.F   miss.GEN wonder.NOM
         'of the girl–wonder'
     b. του   παιδιού-θαύμα
         tu   peðjú-θávma
         the.GEN.N   child.GEN wonder.NOM
         'of the child prodigy'

Mackridge (1985: 329), for instance, cites (1a), and Joseph and Philippaki-Warburton (1987: 228) mark (1b) as acceptable, with only the first member of each in the genitive case.[15] In fact, instances of this compound occur where the two elements show a case mismatch, as in (2), from Mackridge (1985: 329).

(2) των   χωρών   μέλη
     ton   xorón   méli
     the.GEN.PL   nation.GEN.PL member.NOM.PL
     'of the member nations'

Mackridge notes that a doubly inflected compound, των χωρών μελών *ton xorón melón*, with two genitive plural forms, occurs alongside (2). As noted, the double inflection in a compound is unusual within Greek, but so too is the singly inflected type of (1a) and (2), in that the occurrence of the inflection on the left-hand member is at odds with where inflection occurs in other compounds, as τσικλόφουσκας *tsikló-fuskas* 'of bubble gum' indicates.

The entry into Greek of these Noun-Noun compounds, therefore, has led to anomalous morphosyntactic patterns in the language along various dimensions: a novel compound type with a novel accentuation pattern and novel inflectional properties. In this regard, the reaction of some native grammarians is interesting: as Mackridge (1985: 329) reports, 'such formations are condemned by Triandaphyllidis (1941: 177–178) as being alien to the spirit of the Greek language'. Alien or not, they were adopted into the language and have thrived. In fact, Mackridge (1985: 328) sees in the decades of the 1960s and 1970s 'a huge increase in the use of loose compounds' and in his estimation (1985: 329), this type has had a period of being in vogue and has come to constitute a productive pattern: 'More recent formations . . . are found frequently, particularly in journalism but also in everyday speech . . . [these] compounds may however be coined *ad hoc*, using practically any pair of nouns.'

Even with the phonological independence of each member, these inflected forms can be considered compounds for several reasons.[16] Nothing can intervene between the two pieces, there is no independent syntactic means of generating such Noun-Noun sequences in Greek, and there is no usual mechanism by which the inflectional mismatching could be generated. In instances in which a noun is in apposition with another noun, for instance, or where titles are involved, the two nouns must agree in case, as in the different case forms for 'President Stasinopulos' in (3).

(3) a. ο   πρόεδρος   Στασινόπουλος / *ο πρόεδρος Στασινόπουλο
       ο   proeðros   Stasinopulos / *o proeðros Stasinopulo
       the.NOM president.NOM Stasinopulos.NOM   NOM   ACC
   b. τον   πρόεδρο   Στασινόπουλο / *τον πρόεδρο Στασινόπουλος
       ton   proeðro   Stasinopulo   / *ton proeðro Stasinopulos
       the.ACC president.ACC Stasinopulos.ACC   ACC   NOM
   c. του   προέδρου   Στασινοπούλου / *του πρόεδρο Στασινοπούλου
       tu   proeðru   Stasinopulu   / *tu proeðro Stasinopulu
       the.GEN president.GEN Stasinopulos.GEN   ACC   GEN

It is worth noting further that unlike in Russian, in Greek there is no evidence of a trend towards analyticity. There are some uninflected and uninflectable nouns and modifiers, e.g. γιωτ *jot* 'yacht' and μπλε *ble* 'blue', but they are mostly loanwords, and very few if any are native.[17] Also, there are periphrases for genitive cases, mostly with the preposition από *apó* 'from', especially instead of the genitive plural, a form which is missing from the paradigms of many nouns (cf. Sims 2015). However, it is hard to see a trend towards uninflectability as something going on within Greek. Thus, Greek differs from Russian in this regard in that it does not appear to be ready to give up inflection, so that the presence of these Noun-Noun compounds does not seem to be an indication of any incipient (further) structural revamping of the language.[18]

These Noun-Noun compounds therefore have introduced some innovations into the grammar of Greek and yet they have found a ready home. It can be speculated that the fact that the formation of these Noun-Noun constructs is just a matter of simple juxtaposition in the source language(s) is what helped to make them an attractive addition to the language from the outside.

5. English Verb-Noun Compounds from French[19]

The preceding case studies have, quite fortuitously, involved mostly nouns used in the formation of compounds. As a final case study, I examine the development of a compound type in English with a verbal base, even though the ultimate meaning of the compound is generally nominal in nature. The source language in this case is French, and the compound itself can be exemplified by the present-day word *pick-pocket*, meaning 'someone who picks the pocket of, i.e. steals from, someone else; a thief'. This type consists of an uninflected verbal base as the first (left-hand) member and a noun serving as the object of that verb as the second (right-hand) member. The meaning is exocentric (a *bahuvrīhi* in the Sanskrit system), so that the compound as a whole generally refers to the agent of the verbal action indicated by the first member.

There are several reasons for ascribing the occurrence of this Verb-Noun compound type in English to French influence. Drawing on the discussion in Marchand (1960: 37–39),[20] it can be noted first of all that there are no such compounds to be found in Old English; compounds with verbal elements are all *tatpuruṣa*s (determinative) with the verbal element as the second (right-hand) member, e.g. *reord-berend* 'speech-bearer' (which is used figuratively to denote 'human').[21] Moreover, this Verb-Noun type begins to appear in Middle English, with the first attestations coming in the early fourteenth century, around the time that the most intense contact influence from French began to manifest itself and affect English. The earliest cited form, to judge from Marchand's presentation and the OED, appears to be *traylebastoun* (attested 1305) 'one of a class of violent evil-doers in the reign of Edward I; a particular kind of brigand or hired ruffian', from French *traille*, imperative of *trailer* 'drag', and the Old French *baston* 'stick, cudgel, club', thus literally 'a carrycudgel', i.e. 'one who trails or carries a club or cudgel'.[22] More generally, as the analysis of *traylebastoun* shows, the basis in French is a pattern with an imperative verb as the left-hand member and a noun object as the right-hand member.

Since its entrance into English, this compound type, while never overly numerous, nonetheless has remained a clear pattern that has been readily available to speakers. Marchand (1960: 37) lists a dozen early examples from the fourteenth and fifteenth centuries, and then observes that 'there has been an uninterrupted flow of coinings ever since'. Moreover, there seem to be some small clusters of these compounds with the same first element, suggesting sub-patterns that emerged in periods of a limited productivity for this type. Marchand, for instance, offers several items with first member *lick-* from the late fourteenth to the early seventeenth centuries (*lickpot* (1387), *lickdish* (1440), *lickladle* (1571), *lickplatter* (1571), *lickbox* (1611), *lickspit* (1629) and *lickspittle* (1629)), none of which has any currency today.

In fact, of the seventy-four Verb-Noun compounds that Marchand (1960: 37–38) mentions, leaving aside the seemingly stable special groups of bird names such as *wagtail* or plant names such as *catchfly*, just a little over a quarter of them (twenty-one in all) are recognisable today.[23] There are other such compounds in use today that are not mentioned by Marchand, such as *grabass* 'disruptive behaviour, horseplay', or *lackluster* 'lacking in brightness', but there are also some earlier now-obsolete ones that he does not list, such as *breakvow* 'a breaker of vows'. The unparsability and obsolete character of many that Marchand lists, e.g. *pickthank* 'toady', *turnbroach* 'boy whose office was to turn the spit' or *scaldrag* 'dyer', suggest that although Verb-Noun compounds are a legitimate type still, any general productivity for them is mostly a thing of the past.

Nonetheless, it is possible for any existing pattern in a language to serve as a model for the launching of new forms. In this regard, Baldwin (1970) is an interesting study. She discusses compounds in the works of the American humorist James Thurber, and notes that Thurber himself created numerous compounds. Among Thurber's neologistic compounds are some twenty or so instances of Verb-Noun compounds, all of which are fairly transparent as to their meanings (explained here otherwise):

blessgravy, *crumplehope*, *crunchberry*, *dampenglee*, *douselight*, *grabcheck*, *grablass*, *hidebottle*, *hugmoppet*, *kissgranny* (perhaps not so transparent, 'a man who seeks the company of older women'), *praisegravy*, *scornmuffin*, *shattermyth*, *shuncabbage*, *shushlaugh* ('one who quiets someone who is laughing'), *snatchkiss*, *sneakslug* ('a person who sneaks a slug of alcohol'), *starefrock*, *tossgravel* and *twisttongue*.

The Verb-Noun compound, while a completely novel type when it entered English from French, nonetheless seems to have found a welcome in its new language. The fact that it was at odds with existing patterns in English did not prevent it from being borrowed in the first place, suggesting that the simplicity of its mechanics, involving nothing more than juxtaposition, overrode the novelty, and thus the complication, that this pattern represented. Moreover, it seems to have successfully resisted nativisation for some seven centuries and has even shown pockets of productivity throughout its history within English.

6. Conclusion

From these several case studies, some generalisations can be developed. First, the issue of simplification versus complexification in language contact is anything but a simple one and in fact is rather complex in its own right. In particular, it is certainly not the case that languages reject in contact situations elements that are alien to their system and thus can take in foreign elements that add to the structural possibilities available to speakers. Second, it may well be, in fact, that the surface simplicity of compounds involving nothing more than juxtaposition of two (or more) elements is what makes such compound patterns easily borrowed and easily absorbed into the recipient language system, even if they would seemingly be at odds with the structure of the borrowing language. All of the case studies examined here suggest that to be a valid generalisation. Finally, based on the characteristics that these compound patterns show in the borrowing languages, it would seem to be the case, not surprisingly but tellingly nonetheless, that once a borrowed element enters a language, it takes on a life of its own and goes its own way, exhibiting properties that outstrip what was possible in the donor language. Thus, they can develop inflectional behaviour that is different from that in the donor language, they can develop degrees of productivity that go above and beyond that found in the donor language, and they can be the locus of innovation in their own right within their new environment. In this way, although compounds are synchronically special in certain ways, lying at the interface of morphology and syntax, they really are no different from other borrowed material, especially unambiguously morphological elements such as affixes; the adjective-forming suffix *-able*, for instance, while of Latinate origin, and originally restricted in Latin to occurring just with verbs, once it was borrowed into English, began to be able to combine with non-Latinate verbal bases, forming such items as *readable* or *drinkable*, based on Germanic roots, and with non-verbal bases, forming such items as *objectionable*. In contact situations, synchronically significant donor-language differences between elements can thus have less importance for the borrowing language than they do in the source language.

Notes

1. I take no position on whether the creation of, say, endocentric compounds (*tatpuruṣa*s in the influential system of the ancient Indian grammarians) differs, in terms of grammatical mechanism employed, from, say, exocentric compounds (*bahuvrīhi*s for the Indian grammarians). For the purposes of the discussion here, this matter is irrelevant.

2. Some sources for this view include Vogt (1948), Coteanu (1957), Givón (1979), Jeffers and Lehiste (1979), Mühlhäusler (1980), Whinnom (1980), Trudgill (2004) and McWhorter (2005). Thomason (2008) is an invaluable summary of the issues pertaining to simplification and complexification in language contact.

3. The discussion here focuses on contact between speakers of distinct languages, though in principle different dialects of the same language could be involved. Thus, my use of the phrasing 'language contact' should be taken to include dialect contact, even though my case studies all involve separate languages.

4. I take a broad view of what constitutes bilingualism and consider speakers with even a minimal ability in another language to be counted among the class of 'bilinguals'; see Friedman and Joseph (forthcoming: chapter 3) for discussion. Clearly, though, different degrees of ability with another language could yield different results vis-à-vis compounding.

5. See Ronzevalle (1911) on this variety of Greek and, more recently, Joseph (2019). Adrianoupolis is modern-day Edirne, now in Turkey and predominantly Turkish-speaking, but in Ottoman times it had a large Greek-speaking population.

6. See Hock and Joseph (2009: 243, 267) for some thoughts on this pronunciation.

7. Nor, alternatively, with the Greek-derived agentive suffix -*ist*: *ear-nose-ist.

8. I am deliberately overlooking *dvandva* compounds such as *farmer poet*, meaning 'a person who is a farmer and a poet' as they are not copulative in nature, and do not conjoin two distinct entities; rather, they designate two qualities of the same individual.

9. It is interesting, but beyond the scope of this study, that the acronym (or initialism, in this case) *ENT* formed from this phrase *ear, nose and throat (specialist)* has the copulative sense without any inclusion or overt representation of *and*.

10. I thank Adam Clark-Joseph of the University of Illinois for help with the matter of chemical nomenclature; see also Joseph (2017).

11. This suffix entered English from French. Note that even the head noun here, *methane*, is based on Greek, being a shortening of *methylene*, from Greek μέθυ *methu* 'wine' and ὕλη *hulē* 'wood, matter', with an adjustment of the vowel of the suffix to give -*ane* (invented to be part of a series of chemical suffixes).

12. I leave as an open question here whether the word *graph* is involved in this derivation or rather a separate but possibly related morpheme -*graph* is.

13. There is certainly more to morpholexical expansion than just outside influence. Voroncova (1964) draws attention to the effects of the 1917 revolution, for instance. As Patton (1999: 29) describes her position, she 'notes that the 1917 revolution gave rise to a process whereby compounds were introduced into the

language at a striking rate', a trend which she ascribes to 'intense social, economic and technical development at that time'.

14. For more recent views on Noun-Noun compounds in Russian, see Kapatsinski and Vakareliyska (2013). Vakareliyska (forthcoming) examines the entry of Noun-Noun compounds into other Slavic languages, especially Bulgarian, on which see also Vakareliyska and Kapatsinski (2014).

15. In fact, in that work, the doubly inflected παιδιού-θαύματος *peðjú-θávmatos* is marked as being of only marginal acceptability.

16. Mackridge (1985: 328) and Joseph and Philippaki-Warburton (1987: 227) refer to these as 'loose compounds'.

17. Some dialects have a feminine noun η γης *i jis* 'the earth' as indeclinable (genitive της γης *tis jis*, accusative τη γης *ti jis*), continuing an Ancient Greek feminine declinable noun ἡ γῆ *hē gē* (with, e.g. accusative τὴν γῆν *tēn gēn*); see Thumb (1912: §85).

18. I say 'further' because Greek did take part in a general shift towards analyticism in the medieval period due to contact with neighbouring languages (its 'involvement' in the so-called *Balkan Sprachbund*, and that shift has left its mark on the structure of Greek, with new periphrastic verbal tenses, analytic marking of adjectival degree, and so on; see Friedman and Joseph (forthcoming) for discussion).

19. I would like to thank Laurie Bauer, Bethany Christiansen, Jonathan Davis-Secord, Drew Jones and Leslie Lockett for useful leads and information regarding the history of this compound type in English.

20. See also Uhrström (1918), a work that unfortunately was not available to me.

21. I thank Jonathan Davis-Secord for supplying me with this example; I have introduced the hyphens to make the parsing clear.

22. These definitions and the etymological information are adapted from OED (2019: *trailbaston*, last accessed 3 April 2019).

23. I am basing this judgement on my own sensibilities as a well-educated native speaker as to present-day usage. The compounds I judge as still in use are *pickpocket*, *pinchpenny*, *turnkey*, *scarecrow*, *cutthroat*, *telltale*, *donothing* (as a modifier, as in *donothing Congress*), *killjoy*, *spoilsport*, *knownothing*, *spendthrift*, *daredevil*, *turnpike*, *breakfast*, *turnstile*, *stopgap*, *turnbuckle*, *breakwater*, *dreadnought*, *turntable* and *breakneck* (as a modifier, as in *breakneck speed*). It seems to me that some of these are not readily parsable to contemporary speakers (especially *turnpike*, *turnstile*, *turnbuckle* and *dreadnought*).

References

Baldwin, Alice (1970), 'James Thurber's Compounds', *Language and Style. An International Journal*, III: 3, 185–197.

Charalambakis, Christoforos (2014), *Χρηστικό Λεξικό της Νεοελληνικής Γλώσσας* [Practical Dictionary of Modern Greek], Athens: Academy of Athens.

Comrie, Bernard, G. Stone and M. Polinsky (1996), *The Russian Language in the 20th Century*, Oxford: Clarendon Press.

Coteanu, Jon (1957), *A propos des langues mixtes (sur l'istro-roumain)*, Bucharest: Mélanges linguistiques.

Friedman, Victor A. and B. D. Joseph (forthcoming), *The Balkan Languages*, Cambridge: Cambridge University Press.

Givón, Talmy (1979), 'Prolegomena to any Sane Creology', in I. F. Hancock (ed.), *Readings in Creole Studies*, Ghent: Story-Scientia, pp. 3–35.

Hock, Hans Henrich and B. D. Joseph (2009), *Language Change, Language History, and Language Relationship. An Introduction to Historical Linguistics*, Berlin: De Gruyter, 2nd edn.

Jeffers, Robert J. and I. Lehiste (1979), *Principles and Methods for Historical Linguistics*, Cambridge, MA: MIT Press.

Joseph, Brian D. (2017), 'The "Indirect" Influence of the Greek Language' (Part II of a multi-part series on the influence of Greek on the English language), *Greek Ethos*, 22: 9.

Joseph, Brian D. (2019), 'The Greek of Ottoman-era Adrianoupolis', in A. Ralli (ed.), *The Morphology of Asia Minor Greek. Selected Topics*, Leiden: Brill, pp. 315–333.

Joseph, Brian D. and I. Philippaki-Warburton (1987), *Modern Greek*, London: Croom Helm.

Kapatsinski, Vsevolod and C. M. Vakareliyska (2013), '[N[N]] Compounds in Russian: A Growing Family of Constructions', *Constructions and Frames*, 5: 1, 73–91.

Mackridge, Peter (1985), *The Modern Greek Language. A Descriptive Analysis of Standard Modern Greek*, Oxford: Oxford University Press.

McWhorter, John H. (2005), *Defining Creole*, Oxford: Oxford University Press.

Marchand, Hans (1960), *The Categories and Types of Present-Day English Word Formation. A Synchronic-Diachronic Approach*, Wiesbaden: Otto Harrassowitz.

Mühlhäusler, Peter (1980), 'Structural Expansion and the Process of Creolization', in A. Valdman and A. Highfield (eds), *Theoretical Orientations in Creole Studies*, New York: Academic Press, pp. 19–55.

Nichols, Johanna (1992), *Linguistic Diversity in Space and Time*, Chicago: University of Chicago Press.

OED (2000–2019), *Oxford English Dictionary*, edited by J. Simpson, Oxford: Oxford University Press, 3rd edn, www.oed.com (29 June 2019).

Patton, David (1999), *Analytism in Modern Russian: A Study of the Spread of Non-Agreement in Noun Phrases*, PhD dissertation, The Ohio State University.

Ronzevalle, P. Louis (1911), 'Les emprunts turcs dans le grec vulgaire de Roumélie et spécialement d'Andrinople', *Journal Asiatique. Receuil de mémoires et de notices relatifs aux études orientales publié par la Société Asiatique*, 18: 1, 69–106, 257–336, 405–462.

Sims, Andrea D. (2015), *Inflectional Defectiveness*, Cambridge: Cambridge University Press.

Thomason, Sarah G. (2008), 'Does Language Contact Simplify Grammars?', invited lecture at *Deutsche Gesellschaft für Sprachwissenschaft*, Bamberg, http://www-personal.umich.edu/~thomason/temp/simple2.pdf (29 June 2019).

Thomason, Sarah G. and T. Kaufman (1988), *Language Contact, Creolization, and Genetic Linguistics*, Berkeley: University of California Press.

Thumb, Albert [1895] (1912), *Handbook of the Modern Greek Vernacular: Grammar, Texts, Glossary*, translated from the 2nd edn (1910) by S. Angus, Edinburgh: T. & T. Clark.

Triandaphyllidis, Manolis (1941), Νεοελληνική γραμματική της δημοτικής [Modern Greek Grammar (of dhimotiki)], Athens: Organismos Ekdoseos Sxolikon Vivlion.

Trudgill, Peter (2004), 'Linguistic and Social Typology: The Austronesian Migrations and Phoneme Inventories', *Linguistic Typology*, 8: 305–320.

Uhrström, Wilhelm P. (1918), *Pickpocket, Turnkey, Wraprascal and Similar Formations in English*, Stockholm: M. Bergvall.

Vakareliyska, Cynthia M. (forthcoming), *Action Heroes: A Survey of Recent English Loanblend Open Compounds Across the South Slavic Languages* (Kenneth E. Naylor Memorial Lecture Series, 10), Oxford, MS: Balkanistica.

Vakareliyska, Cynthia M. and V. Kapatsinski (2014), 'An Anglo-Americanism in Slavic Morphosyntax: Productive [N[N]] Constructions (with Focus on Bulgarian)', *Folia Linguistica*, 48: 1, 277–312.

Vogt, Hans (1948), 'Reply to the Question, "Dans quelles conditions et dans quelles limites s'exercer sur le système morphologique d'une langue l'action du système morphologique d'une autre langue?"', in M. Lejeune (ed.), *Actes du VIe Congrès Internationale de Linguistes*, Paris: Klincksieck, pp. 31–40.

Voroncova, V. L. (1964), 'Processy razvitija morfologičeskix elementov, stojaščix na grani morfemy i slova' [Processes of the Development of Morphological Elements Standing on the Edge of Morpheme and Word], in *Razvitie Gramatiki i Leksiki sovremennogo russkogo jazyka* [Development of Grammar and Lexicon of the Contemporary Russian Language], Moscow: Nauka.

Whinnom, Keith (1980), 'Creolization in Linguistic Change', in A. Valdman and A. Highfield (eds), *Theoretical Orientations in Creole Studies*, New York: Academic Press, pp. 203–210.

3

Neoclassical Compounds between Borrowing and Word Formation

Renáta Panocová and Pius ten Hacken

Neoclassical compounds are words like *microscope*. They are complex in the sense that they consist of more than one basic component, but these components are taken from the classical languages, Latin and Greek. In the case of *microscope*, the Ancient Greek μικρός ('small, little') and σκοπέω ('examine') provide the components. Given the meaning of *microscope*, it is obvious that the word was not borrowed as an Ancient Greek compound, but combined from the components in modern languages. OED (2019 [2001]: *microscope (n.)*) gives its origin as a borrowing from Italian in the seventeenth century.[1] In this chapter, we address a number of issues regarding the interaction of borrowing and word formation as reflected in neoclassical compounds and argue for a model of historical development of neoclassical word formation. In section 1, we consider the nature of languages as they interact in borrowing and develop in word formation. Section 2 turns to the issue of naming as the main trigger for both borrowing and word formation. Against this background, we outline the model we propose in section 3. Section 4 explores the consequences of this model and gives evidence supporting it. Section 5 is a brief conclusion.

1. Language and languages

One of the immediate problems confronted in early studies of language was determining what exactly was the object of study. Saussure (1916) discusses this question systematically and arrives at the conclusion that the unit of study should be the *langue*, i.e. the language system used by a speech community. He calls this 'un objet de nature concrète' (1916: 32), i.e. an empirical object. In this view, individual languages such as English, Dutch and Slovak are the objects of study. This idea is still popular in (certain currents of) lexicography. A problem is that it is often difficult to ascertain what expressions belong to the language. This is particularly relevant in studies such as the one we present here, where the question is whether specific neoclassical compounds and the underlying system for creating them are part of a language or not.

An alternative view, which emerged as a reaction to the problems of determining what is actually part of a language, has its origin in Bloomfield (1933) and is presented in a radical, systematic way by Harris (1951). According to Harris, '[i]nvestigation in descriptive linguistics consists of recording utterances in a single dialect and analyzing the recorded material' (1951: 12). Harris shifts attention from the *langue*, in this quotation called *dialect*, to the utterances collected in a corpus. The idea that utterances (and their written counterpart) should be the object of study is still (or again) widespread in corpus linguistics and in corpus-based lexicography.

There are at least three problems in using corpora as the basis for linguistic study. First, a corpus may contain errors. Spoken language is full of unfinished sentences, sentence fragments that do not fit together, etc. Written language contains typos. We can of course accept the errors as part of the system, but then a language like English will be very different from the way we perceive it. We can also hope that errors, in particular in written language, are rare. However, a second problem is that many legitimate phenomena in language are extremely rare in corpora. It is well known that it is difficult to study idioms such as *pull someone's leg* on the basis of corpora, because of their low frequency. However, the same applies to many complex words. In particular, neoclassical compounds tend to be rare because they are often restricted to specialised language. Thus, *acrodynia* has no occurrences in COCA (28 June 2019). A third problem is that soundwaves and texts as such do not contain meaning. In order to interpret them, one has to know the language. Here *the language* cannot be taken to be 'the corpus', because that would lose the meaning of *interpretation* in circularity. Whereas an expression used in communication has a meaning, this meaning is lost in the corpus, because it only exists in the speaker's and hearer's minds. All three of these problems are relevant to neoclassical compounds. Many of these are rare, so they may be missing from a corpus and it is difficult to determine their correct form on the basis of frequency. The actual correspondence of their components to Ancient Greek or Latin words can only be verified if we have access to the meaning.

Chomsky (1965: 4) proposed a different solution to the problem of identifying the object of linguistic study by distinguishing what he calls *competence* and *performance*. Performance is the realisation of language as text or soundwaves. It corresponds to Harris's (1951) corpus. Competence is the individual speaker's grammatical and lexical knowledge that enables them to produce and understand utterances and texts. It does not correspond to Saussure's (1916) notion of *langue*, which 'n'est complète dans aucun, elle n'existe parfaitement que dans la masse' (1916: 30), i.e. it is not complete in any particular speaker, but only exists in the speech community. The difference between *competence* and *langue* highlights a problem that was first discussed by Chomsky (1980).

The discussion of the legitimacy of competence-based linguistics focused first of all on the problem of the verification of data. Whereas nobody questions that a corpus contains empirical data, grammaticality judgements as used by Chomsky were criticised as non-empirical. The behaviourist approach taken by Harris (1951) and Hockett (1954) excludes the use of such data, and Hill (1961) gives examples of problems with their verification. At the same time, it is obvious that language use requires underlying knowledge of the language. This knowledge is empirical in the sense that it exists independently of observation and is realised physically in the brain. However, the brain is individual. No two individuals share the same competence, because they would have to share the same brain. As Chomsky (1961) explains, Hill's (1961) criticism is entirely misdirected. The issue is not how to verify data, but how to explain them. There is no point in collecting an average of judgements in a population, because the language system only exists empirically in individual speakers.

As opposed to competence and performance, languages as spoken by speech communities are not empirical objects. As Uriagereka put it, 'English doesn't really exist' (1998: 27). Counter to Saussure's (1916: 32) claim, there is no concrete object corresponding to English. There is no linguistic answer to the question whether, for instance, Scots is really a dialect of English or a separate language, because there is no linguistic method for verifying either option. There is also no linguistic answer to the question of whether something is a word of English. Its inclusion in a dictionary is the result of a decision by a lexicographer. Whereas this decision is informed by observations, it cannot be determined by them. The lexicographer decides whether a word is correct and frequent enough to be included in the dictionary.

This is not to say that what constitutes English is arbitrary. However, the notion of English as a language arises only in metalinguistic observation, not in the regular use of language in communication. It is essentially the result of classifying speakers. Once we have classified speakers, we can use their competence and their performance as a basis for determining what is English. The performance can be collected and used in the form of a corpus, with competence to solve the problems of corpora as described above. However, it is not possible to determine the precise boundaries of the speech community and the precise boundaries of English. As long as we recognise that English is not an empirical concept and use *English* in a sense in which it is not necessary to refer to such boundaries, we can use the concept without running into conceptual difficulties.

2. Naming and word formation

When we consider the form and meaning of *microscope*, it is worth considering the contrast in Figure 3.1 and Figure 3.2. As mentioned, the word *microscope* is composed of two elements of Ancient Greek origin, μικρός ('small, little') and σκοπέω ('examine'). On the basis of this information, the instruments in Figure 3.1 and Figure 3.2 could both be called *microscope*. However, the name is only used for the one in Figure 3.1, never for the one in Figure 3.2. This applies to all European languages we know of. For the instrument in Figure 3.2 the name in most languages (though not in English) is derived from French *loupe* ('magnifying glass'). Thus, Slovak has *lupa* and Dutch *loep*. For French, Robert (1986: *loupe²*) gives it as the fifth meaning of a word attested from 1328 in the sense of irregularities in metal, in wood and on the skin. Collins-Robert (1987: *loupe*) gives 'magnifying glass' as the first translation, 'wen' and 'burr' for the other readings.

The non-use of *microscope* for the instrument in Figure 3.2 is often called *initial specialisation*. The idea is that when the word was first coined, it immediately specialised

Figure 3.1 Leitz microscope (1879). Photo: Timo Mappes (WikiMedia)

Figure 3.2 Magnifying glass. Photo: Tomomarusan (WikiMedia)

its meaning compared to the meaning expected on the basis of its components. This perspective is typical of generative grammar with its emphasis on generating the correct forms before they are interpreted. When we take an onomasiological perspective, the starting point is not the 'literal meaning' of *microscope* but the concept illustrated in Figure 3.1. An appropriate name is chosen for this concept. That there is another concept, illustrated in Figure 3.2, which might also have been named in this way does not come into consideration at this point at all.

The reasoning is not restricted to neoclassical compounds such as *microscope*. The same perspective can be used for the names chosen for the concept illustrated in Figure 3.2. In Slovak and Dutch, the French word *loupe* was borrowed. The fact that this word also has other meanings in French is unimportant. In French, the use of *loupe* for Figure 3.2 is an example of sense extension. In English, *magnifying glass* is a V+N compound. In Dutch, a less frequent synonym for *loep* is *vergrootglas*.[2] This is a V+N compound like the English name, with *glas* ('glass') as a head. The verb *vergroten* ('magnify') is a deadjectival prefixation of *groot* ('big'). Interestingly, *loupe* is used in English for a much smaller instrument, typically used by jewellers and watchmakers. This is a concept for which most other languages we know do not have a separate word. OED (2019 [1976]: *loupe*) gives a first attestation date of 1909.

Let us now turn to the reader's (or hearer's) perspective and compare the three Dutch words of *microscoop*, *loep* and *vergrootglas*. As far as these words are in the reader's mental lexicon, they are simply retrieved. Especially for children, however, it is quite common to come across an unknown word. The first observation is in fact that the word is not in the lexicon, from which the hypothesis can be derived that it designates a new concept. In the case of *loep*, there is not much except for the context of use that can give an indication about the meaning. It is unlikely that a reader coming across *loep* for the first time will know the French word *loupe*. For *vergrootglas*, the hypothesis about the meaning can be much more specific because of the morphological structure. The question is, then, how *microscoop* fits in this picture. To what extent does the internal structure provide information to the reader in processing this word? Should it rather be considered similar to a borrowing such as *loep* or does the structure support processing as in the case of *vergrootglas*?

A further question to be addressed concerns the role of the speech community. In ten Hacken and Panocová (2011), we discussed the relation between speech community and word formation and concluded that even though the speech community is not a given entity with clear boundaries, the social interaction within a speech community influences the individual naming acts. Each speaker knowing the word *microscope* must at some time have added it to their mental lexicon. For most speakers, this will have been done on the basis of the perception that this word exists in other speakers' mental lexicons. The actual choice of a name usually depends on a small number of speakers to whom a special authority is attributed. Depending on the concept to be named, this authority can be derived from specialised knowledge or a position as a role model (e.g. teachers, novelists, television personalities).

The question of neoclassical compounding we want to address here can thus be formulated as whether in different languages there is a system of neoclassical word formation that is realised in a sufficiently large group of speakers so that we can say that a neoclassical compound is perceived as rule based in the speech community.

3. A historical model of neoclassical compounding

The influence of Latin and Greek on English was prominent especially after 1500 when the total number of loanwords from Latin increased significantly in terms of absolute numbers (Durkin 2014: 348). In Early Modern English (c. 1500–1750),

Latin loanwords occurred in particular technical and scientific registers rather than in general vocabulary (Durkin 2014: 348). For instance, it was relatively frequent that the (borrowed) adjective-forming suffixes *-al* and *-ous* were attached to borrowed adjectives which did not have an equivalent ending in the donor language, *academical* (1549) < Latin *acadēmicus*, beside later *academic* (1579) from the same source, or *illustrious* (?1566) < Latin *illustris* (Durkin 2014: 10). Another tendency especially at that period was that some words from other languages were

> directly incorporated into complex new words in English; this is particularly a feature of how words and word elements ultimately of Latin or Greek origin were drawn upon in the terminology of the modern sciences, as in *oleiferous* 'yielding or bearing oil' (1804) < Latin *oleum* 'oil' + the (ultimately borrowed) combining form *-iferous*. (Durkin 2014: 10)

On the other hand, formations such as *aerobiosis, biomorphism, cryogen, nematocide, ophthalmopathy, plasmocyte* were first attested in the nineteenth century, but they do not seem to be loanwords or adaptations from another language (Durkin 2014: 346). New coinages of combining formatives originally from Greek or Latin continue to be formed up to present. The *Oxford English Dictionary* (OED) regularly publishes a list of new entries. The list of new entries from March 2019 includes *biofortification* 'the process by which the nutrient levels of food crops are increased through selective breeding, genetic modification, or the use of enriched fertilizers' and *biofortified* 'designating a food crop having increased nutrient levels due to selective breeding, genetic modification, or the use of enriched fertilizers', both attested after 2000.

Taking a historical perspective as a point of departure in accounting for neoclassical word formation in English, we can distinguish two different stages of borrowing presented in the model in Figure 3.3.

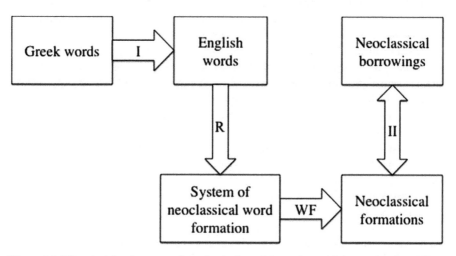

Figure 3.3 Historical development of neoclassical word formation, with borrowing (I and II), re-analysis (R) and word formation (WF)

The distinction between the two stages of borrowing in Figure 3.3 can be associated with changes in the linguistic system. The first stage can be characterised by borrowing of words from Ancient Greek or Latin into English. At this point it is not particularly important to differentiate between borrowings from Greek such as *metamorphosis* or other borrowings such as *spaghetti* from Italian or *kindergarten* from German. All these borrowed words are considered non-complex or unanalysable in English. The difference only arises in the next step.

In the case of words borrowed from Greek or Latin, a re-analysis took place. Components such as *morph(o)-* in *metamorphosis* were not only recognised as independently meaningful components but also made available for use in the formation of new words such as *isomorphism* attested in 1828 (OED 2019 [1900]), *morphology* attested also in 1828 (OED 2019 [2002]) or *hydromorphic* attested in 1938 (OED 2019 [1899]: *hydro-, comb. form*). This also means that re-analysis led to a system of neoclassical word formation. According to Durkin (2014: 347) by the middle of the seventeenth century some formatives, e.g. *auto-, poly-, -logy* or *-vorous*, begin to appear in multiple formations that are not obviously based on foreign-language models such as *granivorous* 'that feeds on grain' attested in 1646 (OED 2019 [1900]), or *piscivorous* 'fish-eating' attested in 1661 (OED 2019 [2006]). From the nineteenth century onwards, similar neoclassical formations in English tend to be extremely frequent (Durkin 2014: 374). Some examples with first attestation dates as given by OED (2019) are *autolanding*, 1959; *polycotton*, 1973; *futurology*, 1946; *algivorous*, 1856. A wildcard search on headwords yields more than twenty entries ending in *-vorous* with a first attestation from 1700 in OED (2019).

A special point about neoclassical word formation is stage II borrowing as represented in Figure 3.3. It is important to point out that the arrow goes in both directions. This indicates that neoclassical formations from English can be borrowed in other language(s) and neoclassical formations in other languages can be borrowed in English. This is true especially for many recent scientific terms, e.g *laparoscopy* 'a surgical procedure in which a fibre-optic instrument is inserted through the abdominal wall to view the organs in the abdomen or permit small-scale surgery', *nutrigenomics* 'a scientific study of the interaction of nutrition and genes', or *biofortification* mentioned above. Typically such scientific terms are almost immediately taken over by researchers in a number of other languages, usually with very little orthographic and morphological adaptation, e.g. a Slovak counterpart is *biofortifikácia*, Italian has *biofortificazione*, Spanish *biofortificación* and German *Biofortifikation*.

It is often impossible to determine the source language where a neoclassical scientific term was formed. For instance, according to the OED (2019 [1976]) the formation *laparoscopy* was actually borrowed from German to English. From the perspective of an English speaker, this information is less important and it does not affect the place of *laparoscopy* in their mental lexicon. As pointed out by Panocová (2015) it is also synchronically irrelevant because the central question is about the nature of neoclassical word formation as a system or subsystem in a speaker's mental lexicon rather than on how individual neoclassical formations developed. What is crucial is that these items which are borrowed at stage II are immediately recognised as morphologically complex not only in English but also in other languages with a system of neoclassical word formation.

4. Some consequences of the model

The status of named languages such as English, Dutch or Russian, was discussed in section 1. We argued that named languages as spoken by speech communities are not empirical objects. A direct consequence of this claim is that when evaluating the model of historical development of neoclassical word formation in Figure 3.3, we do not deal with English or another named language, but rather with individual speakers of English or another named language. This is exemplified in (1).

(1) **acrodynia** [after French acrodynie (A. Chardon 1830, in *Rev. méd. française et étrangère* 3 51)] Medicine (now hist.) a disorder characterized by swelling and pain or paraesthesia of the hands and feet, with gastrointestinal and various other symptoms, probably resulting from mercury poisoning but originally also attributed to ergotism or arsenic poisoning; (in later use) spec. = pink disease n. [. . .] (OED 2019 [2011]: *acro-, comb. form*)

The example in (1) is a lexicographic definition of a medical condition. It is used to refer to a syndrome most likely caused by mercury poisoning in children. Stedman (1997) gives two synonymous names, the phrase *pink disease* and the eponym *Swift's disease*. According to the OED entry in (1) the word in this sense originates from French and it was first used in English in a medical journal in the nineteenth century and is composed of two formatives, *acro-* used in forming terms with the meaning 'relating to peripheral parts, esp. the extremities of the body' and *-dynia* meaning 'pain' resulting in the meaning 'pain in peripheral parts of body'. Stedman (1997) lists this sense of (1) as the first one. It is probable that medical specialists speaking English have the structure of (1) in their mental lexicons and they understand its meaning without any difficulties. The same elements occur in a number of other medical terms such as *acrocyanosis* 'a condition marked by bluish or purple colouring of the hands and feet', *acromegaly* 'abnormal growth of the hands, feet, and face', *acrophobia* 'morbid fear of heights', *cephalodynia* 'headache' or *gastrodynia* 'pain in the stomach, stomachache'. At the same time, it is synchronically less relevant that the neoclassical formative *acro-* can be analysed as a borrowing from Latin *acro-* and Greek ἀκρο-. These formatives can be labelled as borrowing I in the historical model in Figure 3.3. According to OED (2019 [2011]: *acro-, comb. form*) classical Latin *acro-* and its etymon Ancient Greek ἀκρο- were used in, for instance, *acropolis* (from ἀκρόπολις) and *acronic* (from ἀκρόνυχος). Apparently, at some point these formations were re-analysed and their structure was perceived as complex. The element *acro-* was then used in naming a medical condition *acrodynia*, probably first in French. The exchange between English and French corresponds to borrowing II in Figure 3.3.

The Russian equivalent of the medical term is *акродиния* 'acrodynia'. Its meaning and structure will be obvious also to doctors or other medical specialists speaking Russian. This means that the main contrast between English and Russian medical specialists is not in their knowledge of the concept. The Russian speaker is likely to have the structure of the word in their competence because they were trained in medical terminology. However, their knowledge of meaning for the individual components is only of etymological value. This information helps them understand the motivation of this word. It is probable that to the Russian specialist the components of this word will not be available for the formation of new words. In English, by contrast, the element *acro-* appears in the scientific term *acrocentric*, first attested in 1945. It is also used in Russian, but it is likely that it was borrowed there.

In order to understand the situation of the Russian medical specialist, we can compare it to the situation in the English examples presented in (2).

(2) a. fire brigade 'an organized body of people trained and employed to extinguish fires' (OED 2019 [2015])
     b. kindergarten 'A school or establishment for the care and education of children of preschool age, a nursery school' (OED 2019 [2016])

For a non-specialist English speaker, the compound in (2a) has a complex structure and a meaning of an organised body of trained firefighters. For (2b), which was borrowed from German in the mid-nineteenth century and literally means 'children garden', from *kinder* 'children' and *garten* 'garden', it is not so straightforward that the word is complex. Some English speakers may perceive it as unanalysable in English. If they have some knowledge of German, they may recognise the individual components. Similar to the situation for the Russian medical expert mentioned above, the understanding of the complexity of the German structure of (2b) has the value of understanding the motivation of the meaning in the language of origin. This has consequences for the model of neoclassical word formation in Figure 3.3. For neoclassical word formation in Russian, we propose the model in Figure 3.4.

In contrast to the historical development of neoclassical word formation for English in Figure 3.3, we propose that for Russian no re-analysis took place. This means that there is no linguistic system of neoclassical word formation and there are no new rule-based formations from this system. All neoclassical formations in Russian are borrowings, either from ancient languages or from modern languages. Unlike for English, these formations are not re-analysed after borrowing. To our knowledge, there is no record of a neoclassical scientific term formed and used first in Russian and subsequently borrowed by other languages, especially the main languages of science.

On the other hand, Zemskaja (2002: 157) observes an increasing productivity of so-called *hybrid formations* in Russian, combining neoclassical elements with

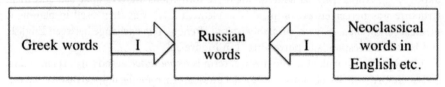

Figure 3.4 The model of neoclassical borrowing in Russian

native elements such as антигерой 'anti-hero', псевдонаука 'pseudo-science' or суперзвезда 'superstar'. Waszakowa (1994, 2000), Kleszczowa (2000), Ohnheiser (2000) and others report that a similar tendency occurs in other Slavic languages. However, the status of similar hybrid formations remains unclear as it is almost impossible to determine unambiguously whether they result from a word formation process or are half-calques (Panocová 2015: 88).

5. Evidence for the difference between English and Russian

As mentioned above, neoclassical word formation in English represents a system whereas in Russian it is not systematic in an identical way. Demonstrating the absence of a system is challenging, and we present three types of evidence for our argumentation line.

5.1 Synonymous neoclassical formations in Russian

The first piece of evidence is based on the observation that some neoclassical formatives do not seem to be used consistently as shown in (3).

(3) a. acarophobia   акарофобия, скабиофобия
            akarofobija, skabiofobija
       b. macromastia   макромастия, гигантомастия, мегаломастия
            makromastija, gigantomastija, megalomastija
       c. paramenia   парамения, дисменорея
            paramenija, dismenoreja

The examples of English neoclassical medical terms in (3) all have more than one neoclassical equivalent in Russian. When we compare synonymy cross-referencing by specialised terminological dictionaries, Stedman (1997) for English and by two English-Russian medical dictionaries for Russian (ERMD 1998; ARMS 2010), we can see the differences. For instance, for (3a), meaning 'morbid fear of small parasites', neither Stedman (1997) nor OED (2019) includes a form corresponding to скабиофобия 'scabiophobia'. By contrast, it is listed by both English-Russian medical dictionaries. This observation may suggest that in fact скабиофобия may have entered Russian from a different source language, probably from French. In fact, Quevauvilliers and Fingerhut (2001) include *scabiophobie*.[3]

The meaning of the neoclassical term in (3b) is '(the condition of having) abnormally large breasts'. The Russian medical dictionaries list three equivalents макромастия makromastija, гигантомастия gigantomastija and мегаломастия megalomastija. This contrast with the situation in Stedman (1997) and OED (2019). First of all, *gigantomastia* is given, but *macromastia* is not cross-referenced to it. In addition, Stedman (1997) and the OED (2019) do not cover the term *megalomastia* at all.

Similarly in (3c), which means 'any disorder or irregularity of menstruation', the two Russian equivalents may be used interchangeably. For English, Stedman (1997) does not indicate the terms *paramenia* and *dysmenorrhea* as synonyms. Stedman (1997) suggests *menorrhalgia* as a possible synonym of *dysmenorrhea*. In order to test our hypothesis that the donor language for the Russian medical terms in (3) is different from English, we verified the use of (3c) in French. Two French dictionaries do not include the term *paramenia*, only *dysménorrhée* 'dysmenorrhea'. Quevauvilliers and Fingerhut (2001) give English translations, but they do not indicate that English is the language of origin. The general monolingual dictionary of Robert (1986) lists *dysménorrhée* with the first attestation date of 1795. Therefore the occurrence of дисменорея 'dysmenorrhea' in (3c) suggests that in this case French is the language of origin.

The examples in (3) demonstrate that in Russian and English there are cases with more neoclassical equivalents, but these may not always be synonyms in both languages. One of the possible interpretations is that the use of pairs or triples of neoclassical synonymous terms in Russian where the synonyms are less frequent or not used at all in English may actually indicate that these were borrowed to Russian from a different donor language, very often from French. This supports our argument that in Russian there is no neoclassical word formation system that would increase consistency of neoclassical formations.

5.2 Missing Russian equivalents of English neoclassical formations

A second type of evidence for the different status of neoclassical formations in English and in Russian is that many neoclassical compounds in English have no neoclassical correspondent term in Russian. Examples are given in (4).

(4) a. chiropodalgia   боль в дистальных отделах конечностей
                            boľ v distaľnych otdelach konečnostej
                            pain in distal parts of extremities
     b. polystichia   ресницы в два и более рядов
                            resnicy v dva i boleje rjadov
                            eyelashes in two or more rows
     c. xiphoiditis   воспаление мечевидного отрастка грудины
                            vospalenie mečevidnogo otrastka grudiny
                            inflammation of the ensiform of the sternum

The English examples in (4) are neoclassical medical terms. Their Russian counterparts are explained by descriptive phrases taken from the English-Russian medical dictionary (ARMS 2010). The dictionaries do not include any Russian neoclassical equivalents. The Russian descriptive phrases in (4) explain the meaning on the basis of the meaning of the English neoclassical medical terms. The meaning of (4a) is 'pain in the hands and feet' and this can be easily deduced on the basis of the meaning of its constituents *chiro-* 'hand', *pod-* 'foot, foot-shaped', *-algia* 'pain, painful condition'. The descriptive phrase in Russian starts with боль boľ 'pain' and then it specifies which body parts are affected.

The neoclassical medical term in (4b) means 'arrangement of the eyelashes in two or more rows'. It consists of two neoclassical formatives *poly-* 'many, multiplicity' and *-stichia* originally from Greek *stichos* 'row'. Interestingly, eyelashes are not represented by any of the constituents, but these are the only things on the surface of the body that are organised in rows. The Russian description gives the information that eyelashes appear in two or more rows.

The final example in (4c) has a meaning 'inflammation of the xiphoid process of the sternum'. The internal structure has two components *xiphoid* 'sword-shaped, applied especially to the xiphoid process, ensiform' and *-itis* 'inflammation'. This meaning is directly mapped onto the Russian description. For a more detailed account of Russian neoclassical medical terms see Panocová (2015).

The examples in (4) show that in some cases Russian medical terminology was resilient to direct borrowing of neoclassical formations used in English and other languages. Instead, Russian prefers a descriptive phrase. It may be assumed that if there were a system in Russian, such terms would be taken over much more easily or almost automatically.

5.3 Dictionary coverage of neoclassical formatives and formations

The third type of evidence for the different status of neoclassical formations is based on a survey of English and Russian dictionaries which revealed that neoclassical formatives in Russian dictionaries tend to be covered to a much smaller extent as opposed to English dictionaries (ten Hacken and Panocová 2014; Panocová and ten Hacken 2016). In the collection of data we focused on neoclassical formatives used in initial position. A crucial methodological decision was to produce a list of neoclassical formatives to be investigated in English and Russian dictionaries. To avoid a biased selection we chose neoclassical formatives from the Catalan dictionary of word formation by Bruguera i Talleda (2006). Catalan is a Romance language and therefore closer to Latin than Germanic and Slavic languages. This also means that the existence of an old system of neoclassical word formation in Catalan is more probable. A list of nearly 700 initial neoclassical formatives of Greek origin was produced. It served as a basis for the search in two English dictionaries, COED (2011) and CED (2000), and two Russian dictionaries, Ušakov (1946–1947) and Efremova (2000). We classified the treatment of neoclassical formatives in the four classes given in (5).

(5) a. Class I: no mention of a neoclassical formative
     b. Class II: one formation with a corresponding neoclassical formative
     c. Class III: more than one formation with a corresponding neoclassical formative
     d. Class IV: entry for the neoclassical formative

The classes in (5) are relevant in terms of the expectations of a dictionary user. From this perspective, especially the difference between (5b) and (5c) is important. It may be assumed that a dictionary user expects that a neoclassical constituent is a separate item if there is more than one formation. The treatment of the classes of neoclassical formations in (5) in English and Russian dictionaries is given in Figure 3.5. The data in Figure 3.5 indicate several interesting findings. A comparison of the two languages clearly demonstrates that the greatest differences between English and Russian are in Class I and Class IV in (5). Approximately twice as many neoclassical formatives are

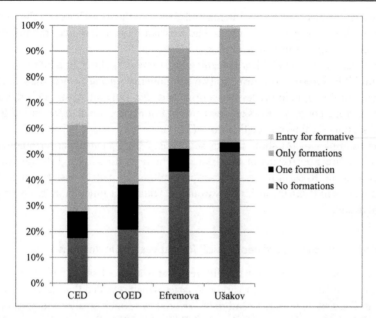

Figure 3.5 Coverage of neoclassical formatives in two English and two Russian monolingual dictionaries

not listed in Russian dictionaries. Conversely, the class with a dictionary entry of its own is significantly larger in English than in Russian, where especially the dictionary by Ušakov lists very few neoclassical formatives.

The differences between English and Russian for Class III are less striking, although in general a larger proportion of formatives is covered only by giving full neoclassical formations in Russian dictionaries. However, the number of formations is generally lower than in English. This is understandable if Russian dictionary users would not look up this information or not interpret it correctly, because they do not have a system of neoclassical word formation.

There are some differences between the two dictionaries in English. CED (2000) includes a much larger number of neoclassical formatives in Class IV and simultaneously neoclassical formations in Class II and Class III. However, COED (2011) provides a dictionary user with more detailed etymological descriptions. Similar distinctions can be observed between the two Russian dictionaries. Interestingly, considering that the dictionary by Efremova was released more than half a century later, the difference between neoclassical formations covered is very small. Although Efremova's dictionary has a higher number of separate entries for neoclassical formatives, the difference between the two dictionaries is less than 10 per cent.

The interpretation of the dictionary data in Figure 3.5 depends partly on the lexicographic policy adopted in the respective dictionaries. Following ten Hacken (2009) we assume that dictionaries cannot be considered full descriptions of the vocabulary of a language but rather are tools available to search for answers to vocabulary-related linguistic questions. From this perspective, the distinction between English and Russian dictionaries in the total numbers of the entries for neoclassical formatives seems rational. Speakers of English recognise neoclassical formatives as elements of their language because of the existence of neoclassical word formation as a system where these elements are available. For speakers of Russian, however, such information is less important due to the fact that neoclassical word formation does not constitute a system. It makes more sense to cover neoclassical formations and add etymological information for a better understanding of motivation.

6. Conclusion

We propose a model of neoclassical word formation for languages like English in which two historical stages are distinguished. In the first stage, borrowing takes words directly from classical languages. Between the first and the second stage, re-analysis takes place. After re-analysis, new neoclassical formations can have three possible origins. First, they can be borrowings from classical languages, as before. Second, they can be formed in English. Third, they can be borrowed from other modern languages that have a system of neoclassical word formation.

The crucial step in this process is the re-analysis. It is at this point that speakers stop being dependent on actual occurrences in classical languages for the extension of the set of neoclassical word formation. This re-analysis took place in a number of modern languages around the same time. This is why it is often difficult to pinpoint the actual origin of a neoclassical formation. As an internationalism, it will be adopted by several languages and analysed as a result of the mechanism for neoclassical word formation.

It is an interesting question in which languages a system of neoclassical word formation is found. Here we gave an example of the kind of evidence that can be adduced to argue for the existence or non-existence of such a system. In section 5 we showed that there is a strong case for the contention that there is a system of neoclassical word formation in English, but not in Russian. By applying the same reasoning to other languages, it should be possible to determine the cross-linguistic scope of the mechanism.

It is important to see the limitations that the general considerations in section 1 impose on such conclusions. Languages such as English and Russian are not empirical objects, so it is impossible in principle to demonstrate that they have certain properties. The evidence we presented in section 5 pertains to individual speakers. The existence of a mechanism of neoclassical word formation in English is of the same type as the existence of the word *microscope* in English. When a sufficient proportion of speakers we classify as 'speakers of English' have this word in their mental lexicon, we say that *microscope* is a word of English. This proportion is not necessarily a majority of all speakers. First of all, it is not possible to determine the number of speakers in any precise way. Second, not all speakers have an equal weight for each word. For a specialised word such as *acrodynia*, only the community of specialised speakers is taken into account. Of course, also this community does not have clearly determined boundaries.

The difference between English and Russian we argued for in section 5 is that English belongs to the set of languages in which new neoclassical formations can be formed, whereas Russian does not. Not all speakers of English will be able to coin such new formations, but a sufficient number of them have the mechanism so that a neoclassical formation can start its spread in English, even if it does not exist in any other language yet. As for Russian, not enough speakers have this mechanism for a new neoclassical formation to originate in a speech community of speakers of Russian.

Acknowledgements

This work was supported by the Slovak Research and Development Agency under the Contract No APVV-16-0035.

Notes

1. For references to the OED, we indicate the entry after the colon and the year of the last full revision of this entry in square brackets.
2. CHN (2013) gives 3,335 occurrences of *loep*, 771 of *vergrootglas*. However, there is an idiom *onder de loep nemen* (lit. 'under the magnifying-glass take', i.e. scrutinise), which accounts for most occurrences. CHN (2013) gives a frequency of 3,074 for *onder de loep* as against 107 for *onder het vergrootglas*.
3. Interestingly, Quevauvilliers and Fingerhut (2001: *scabiophobie*) give the origin as English, which is probably not correct.

References

ARMS (2010), *Anglo-russkij medicinskij slovar* [English-Russian Medical Dictionary], edited by I. J. Markovina and E. G. Ulumbekov, Moskva: GEOTAR-Media.
Bloomfield, Leonard (1933), *Language*, London: Allen & Unwin.
Bruguera i Talleda, Jordi (2006), *Diccionari de la formació de mots*, Barcelona: Enciclopèdia Catalana.
CED (2000), *Collins Dictionary of the English Language*, Glasgow: Collins, 5th edn.
CHN (2013), *Corpus Hedendaags Nederlands*, Leiden: Instituut voor Nederlandse Lexicografie, https://portal.clarin.inl.nl/search/page/search
Chomsky, Noam (1961), 'Some Methodological Remarks on Generative Grammar', *Word*, 17: 219–239.
Chomsky, Noam (1965), *Aspects of the Theory of Syntax*, Cambridge, MA: MIT Press.
Chomsky, Noam (1980), *Rules and Representations*, New York: Columbia University Press.
COCA (2008–2019), *The Corpus of Contemporary American English*, edited by M. Davies, http://corpus.byu.edu/coca/ (29 June 2019).
COED (2011), *Concise Oxford English Dictionary*, edited by A. Stevenson and M. Waite, Oxford: Oxford University Press, 12th edn.
Collins-Robert (1987), *Collins-Robert French-English English-French Dictionary*, edited by S. Atkins and A. Duval, London: Collins and Paris: Robert, 2nd edn.
Durkin, Philip (2014), *Borrowed Words: A History of Loanwords in English*, Oxford: Oxford University Press.

Efremova, Tatjana F. (2000), *Novyj slovar russkogo jazyka* [New Dictionary of the Russian Language], Moscow: Russkij Jezik, http://www.efremova.info (29 June 2019).

ERMD (1998), *English –Russian Medical Dictionary*, Moskva: Russkij Jazyk.

ten Hacken, Pius (2009), 'What is a Dictionary? A View from Chomskyan Linguistics', *International Journal of Lexicography*, 22: 399–421.

ten Hacken, Pius and R. Panocová (2011), 'Individual and Social Aspects of Word Formation', *Kwartalnik Neofilologiczny*, 58: 283–300.

ten Hacken, Pius and R. Panocová (2014), 'Neoclassical Formatives in Dictionaries', *Proceedings of the XVI EURALEX International Congress, The User in Focus*: (15–19 July 2014), Bolzano/Bozen: EURAC Research, pp. 1059–1072.

Harris, Zellig S. (1951), *Methods in Structural Linguistics*, Chicago: University of Chicago Press (reprinted as *Structural Linguistics*, 1960).

Hill, Archibald A. (1961), 'Grammaticality', *Word*, 17: 1–10.

Hockett, Charles F. (1954), 'Two Models of Grammatical Description', *Word*, 10: 210–231.

Kleszczowa, Krystyna (2000), 'Rola pozyczek w przekstalcaniu polskiego systemu slowotwórczego' [The Role of Loanwords in the Development of the Polish System of Word Formation], in K. Kleszczowa and L. Selimski (eds), *Slowotwórstwo a inne sposoby nominacju: materiały z 4 konferencji Komisji Słowotwórstwa przy Międzynarodowym Komitecie Slawistów*, (27–29 September 2000), Katowice, pp. 203–208.

OED (2000–2019), *Oxford English Dictionary*, edited by J. Simpson, Oxford: Oxford University Press, 3rd edn, www.oed.com (29 June 2019).

Ohnheiser, Ingeborg (2000), 'Ešče raz ob oposredstvovannoj motivacii' [Once More about Indirect Motivation], in K. Kleszczowa and L. Selimski (eds), *Slowotwórstwo a inne sposoby nominacju: materiały z 4 konferencji Komisji Słowotwórstwa przy Międzynarodowym Komitecie Slawistów*, (27–29 September 2000), Katowice, pp. 158–163.

Panocová, Renáta (2015), *Categories of Word Formation and Borrowing: An Onomasiological Account of Neoclassical Formations*, Newcastle upon Tyne: Cambridge Scholars Publishing.

Panocová, Renáta and P. ten Hacken (2016), 'Neoclassical Word Formation in English and Russian: A Contrastive Analysis', in L. Körtvélyessy, P. Štekauer and S. Valera (eds), *Word Formation across Languages*, Newcastle upon Tyne: Cambridge Scholars Publishing, pp. 265–280.

Quevauvilliers, Jacques and A. Fingerhut (eds) (2001), *Dictionnaire médical*, Paris: Masson, 3rd edn.

Robert, Paul (ed.) (1986), *Dictionnaire alphabétique et analogique de la langue française*, Paris: Le Robert, 2nd edn (Alain Rey).

Saussure, Ferdinand de (1916), *Cours de linguistique générale*, edited by C. Bally and A. Sechehaye, Édition critique préparée par Tullio de Mauro, Paris: Payot (1981).

Stedman (1997), *Stedman's Concise Medical Dictionary for the Health Professions*, edited by J. H. Dirckx, Baltimore: Williams & Wilkins.

Uriagereka, Juan (1998), *Rhyme and Reason: An Introduction to Minimalist Syntax*, Cambridge, MA: MIT Press.

Ušakov, Dmitrij N. (1946–1947), *Tolkovyj slovar russkogo jazyka* [Monolingual Dictionary of the Russian Language], online edition http://www.dict.t-mm.ru/ushakov (29 June 2019).

Waszakowa, Krystyna (1994), 'Tendencje rozwojowe w słowotwórstwie polszczyzny końca XX wieku' [Trends in the Development of Word Formation in Polish at the End of the 20th Century], in S. Gajda and Z. Adamiszyn (eds), *Przemiany współczesnej polszczyzny*, Opole: Instytut Filologii Polskiej, pp. 53–60.

Waszakowa, Krystyna (2000), 'Rozkładalność i kompozycjonalność struktur słowotwórczych: na przykładzie neologizmów w polszczyźnie końca XX w.' [Analysis and Compositionality of Word Formation Structures: On the Example of Neologisms in Late 20th Century Polish], in K. Kleszczowa and L. Selimski (eds), *Słowotwórstwo a inne sposoby nominacju: materiały z 4 konferencji Komisji Słowotwórstwa przy Międzynarodowym Komitecie Slawistów*, (27–29 September 2000), Katowice, pp. 63–69.

Zemskaja, Elena Andrejevna (2002), 'Specifika semantiki i kombinatoriki proizvodstva slov-gibridov' [Specific Features of Semantics and Combinatorics of the Formation of Hybrid Words], in S. Mengel (ed.), *Slavische Wortbildung: Semantik und Kombinatorik*, Münster, London and Hamburg: LIT, pp. 157–169.

4

Borrowed Compounds, Borrowed Compounding – Portuguese Data

Alina Villalva

Morphological compounding[1] is a quite recent word formation resource in Portuguese and its appearance is quite surprising since no other word formation innovation took place for more than seven centuries. This novelty was most probably triggered by an indirect situation of language contact, which yielded a particular kind of borrowing, both lexical (neoclassical roots) and structural (neoclassical compounding).

In section 1, I will briefly present a historical characterisation of the Portuguese lexicon and Portuguese borrowings, in order to locate the appearance of neoclassical compounds and neoclassical compounding in the language diachrony. In section 2, I will relate this borrowing in Portuguese to similar cases in other European languages, stressing that the same process was available, at the same time, for a large number of European languages, which facilitated a cross-linguistic spreading of these words. In section 3, I will present a description of Portuguese neoclassical compounds and the new morphological compounding process and I will conclude in section 4 that these particular loans require a reappraisal of the concept of lexical borrowing.

I. Brief survey of the history of the Portuguese lexicon and Portuguese borrowings

The Portuguese lexicon has a Latin matrix, complemented by a fuzzy set of traces from substrata languages (namely Basque, e.g. *esquerdo* 'left', and Phoenician, e.g. *ama* 'child-minder') and a poorly documented contingent of vocabulary from Germanic (e.g. *lofa* 'palm' > *luva* 'glove') and Arabic (e.g. *as-sukkar* > *açúcar* 'sugar') superstrata. Its evolution in relation to political milestones and linguistic developments is summarised in Figure 4.1.

Though we can locate the founding dates of the Portuguese kingdom between the ninth and the twelfth centuries – and though it is also possible to document that the language spoken, by that time, in the Northwestern Iberian Peninsula was no longer Latin – Portuguese as a language was not acknowledged before the thirteenth century. So, in this early period, we can find two separate language shift processes: first, from native

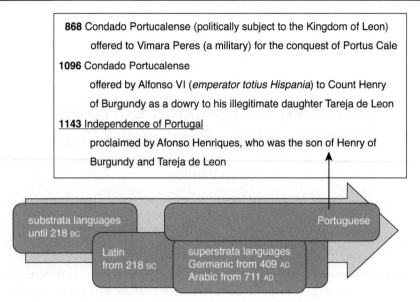

Figure 4.1 Evolution of the Portuguese lexicon

languages into Iberian Latin, and, second, from Iberian Latin into Galician-Portuguese. According to Thomason and Kaufman (1988: 37–38), we should find evidence of interference from substrata language 'as the result of imperfect learning of a target language by a group of speakers of a native language', but that is not exactly the case.

1.1 Substrata traces

In fact, we do not know much about the Iberian substrata languages, which are fully undocumented. All we have are words which have been ascribed a given origin (Mediterranean for *camurça* 'suede, chamois'; Proto-Basque for *esquerdo* 'left'; or Iberian for *chaparro* 'cork oak'), hypothetically, mostly by comparison with other (Romance) languages (cf. Castro 1991). Romanisation was an overwhelming process. Civilisational superiority combined with the lack of political unity may help to explain why this language shift (from many languages into just one) occurred so seemingly smoothly – we may even wonder why some lexical traces from the indigenous pre-Roman languages persevered. Consequently, very little interference, in the sense of Thomason and Kaufman (1988: 37–38), took place at this early stage.

1.2 The Latin lexical matrix

The process of Northwestern Iberian Vulgar Latin becoming Galician-Portuguese took more than a thousand years. The set of words of Latin origin which date back to this long period underwent a number of phonetic changes that can be used as a hint for dating them. Consider, for instance, the Latin noun *macula*, meaning 'spot, mark, stain', which is at the origin of four different words in Portuguese, as indicated in (1).

Table 4.1 Frequency of *malha*, *mancha*, *mágoa*, *mácula* (Davies and Ferreira, 2006–2019)

	13th c.	14th c.	15th c.	16th c.	17th c.	18th c.	19th c.	20th c.
malha	1	2	16	38	50	13	49	200
mancha			5	31	40	27	279	789
mágoa			2	95	41	41	592	259
mácula							49	41

(1) a. macula ('spot, mark, stain')   LA
      b. malha ('spot on the skin of animals')   PT
      c. mancha ('spot, mark, stain')   PT
      d. mágoa ('sorrow')   PT
      e. mácula ('stain, blemish')   PT

The words in (1b–d) present different phonetic solutions[2] that are related to different semantic outputs – they are old words, especially if we contrast them to (1e), which is a much more recent incorporation, as the figures regarding the diachronic distribution in Table 4.1 clearly indicate: *malha* has been attested since the thirteenth century, *mancha* and *mágoa* showed up in the fifteenth century, and *mácula* has no attestations prior to the nineteenth century.

Mácula is a phonetic replica of the Latin word. The phonetic proximity to the etymon indicates that the word is a recent borrowing, a Latinism. This is an important distinction in the Portuguese lexicon: some words of Latin origin are old words in Portuguese, so old that they became vernacular words, others are recent words in the Portuguese lexicon. The distinction is relevant for the word formation system, as we shall soon see.

Most of the early Latin heritage words are simplex words, either because they were simplex words in Latin, cf. (2a–f), or because they were lexicalised in the transition to Portuguese, losing the connection to their morphological basis, that may have also entered the language, cf. (2g–j), or not, cf. (2k–l).

(2) a. clamare   LA   >   chamar   PT   ('to call')
      b. dolore   LA   >   dor   PT   ('pain')
      c. filium   LA   >   filho   PT   ('son')
      d. lacte   LA   >   leite   PT   ('milk')
      e. luna   LA   >   lua   PT   ('moon')
      f. placer   LA   >   prazer   PT   ('pleasure')
      g. facere   LA   ('to do')   > fazer   PT   ('to do')
      h. factio   LA   ('a doing')   > feição   PT   ('form')
      i. confundere   LA   ('to mingle, to mix')   > confundir   PT   ('to mix up')
      j. confu-s-ion   LA   ('a mix, a blend')   > confusão   PT   ('confusion')
      k. auris   LA   ('ear')
      l. auricula   LA   ('external ear')   > orelha   PT   ('ear')

Derivatives have also been brought into Old Portuguese from Latin. Some of them have induced an adaptation of the Latin morphological pattern. For instance, in Latin, the suffix *-ion* attached to the supine root cf. (3). Since the paradigm of the Portuguese verb system does not include a supine, the suffix *-ion* had to take another host, which came to be the verb stem. Consequently, the suffix in (3b) has incorporated the final consonant of the supine root, which has subsequently undergone a softening due to the vicinity of the palatal vowel. In other words, the border between the base and the suffix moved to the left.

(3) a. accusare   LA   >   acusa–r   PT   ('to accuse')
     b. accusa-t [ion LA   >   acusa [ção   PT   ('accusation')

A similar process affected many other cases, especially in the domain of deverbal derivation, as in (4).

(4) a. fugit–ivus   LA   ('fugitive')   >   fugi–dio   PT   ('that escapes')
     b. escorregar   PT   ('to slip')   >   escorrega–dio   PT   ('slippery')

Furthermore, like in other Romance languages, the noun *mente* that occurred in a semi-frozen adverbial phrase was grammaticalised and became a (quite peculiar) suffix that selects fully inflected adjectives (feminine if the adjectives are variable), as shown in the 13th century example (5).

(5) directa mente   LA   ('lit. direct mind')   >   dereytamente   PT   ('rightfully')

The examples (3–5) look like clear cases of interference, though not necessarily raised by an imperfect learning of the target language, but to its making.

Curiously, Latin compounds, or prefixed words, were treated quite differently. Generally speaking, they were all lexicalised (see the example in (6)). Therefore, no compounding pattern was available in Old Portuguese.

(6) LA *bene*] [*dictio*- 'praising' > *benção* 'blessing'

So, in its initial state, Portuguese word formation received no other strong influence than from Latin, and it clearly favoured affixation to the point of a total neglect of compounding.

1.3 Superstrata loanwords

Superstrata languages came with the Germanic rule that arrived after the fall of the Roman Empire, and, four centuries later, with the Muslim conquest of most of the Iberian Peninsula. Germanic rule was not hostile to the Latin model that had shaped Iberia, so Latin was preserved as the dominant language. Only a few loanwords (see the examples in (7)) kept the memory of the Gothic heritage.

(7) a. gasalja GOT ('companion') > agasalhar PT ('to muffle')
    b. spitus GOT ('spit') > espeto PT ('spit')
    c. gans GOT ('goose') > ganso PT ('goose')
    d. lofa GOT ('palm') > luva PT ('glove')
    e. rauba GOT ('spoils') > roupa PT ('clothing')

So, in this case, no interference took place. These words are very early borrowings into the local variety of Vulgar Latin.

The same may be said about Arabic, though the presence of this language had a more long-lasting effect. Latin was still retained as the dominant language, but Arabic left a durable lexical imprint in the large set of borrowed words, most of which are still in use. Arabic borrowings which were introduced during a period of direct language contact (eighth–ninth centuries AD) brought the definite article from the source language, reinterpreted as a kind of prefix. The examples in (8) represent direct Arabic loans.

(8) a. al–qatifa AR > alcatifa PT ('carpet')
    b. ar–ruzz AR > arroz PT ('rice')
    c. as–sukkar AR > açúcar PT ('sugar')
    d. at–tunn AR > atum PT ('tuna')
    e. ad–dayha AR > aldeia PT ('village')

The same borrowing process can be found in Castilian, unlike most other languages (see the examples in (9)).

(9) a. arroz açúcar atum PT
    b. arroz azúcar atún ES
    c. arroz azucre atún GL
    d. arròs sucre tonyina CA
    e. riz sucre thon FR
    f. riso zucchero tonno IT
    g. rice sugar tuna EN
    h. Reis Zucker Thunfisch DE

Interestingly, TLFi presents some French equivalent words (i.e. *riz* and *sucre*) as borrowings from Italian,[3] while others (cf. *thon*) are assigned to a Latin etymon,[4] but they are all documented much later than the Portuguese equivalents.

Moreover, if we consult the entry *zucchero* in an Italian etymological dictionary (such as Pianigiani 1907, 1926),[5] we will find the connection between Arabic and Italian in Sicily, which implies that, most probably, the spreading of these words came from this origin and time (Sicily, thirteenth–fourteenth centuries).

The contrast between Arabic borrowings in Iberian languages and elsewhere also helps to understand a set of Arabic borrowings in Portuguese that lack the definite article (e.g. *âmbar*, *sofá*). This is due to the fact that they are indirect loans or later borrowings, as in (10).

(10)	a.	hanbar	AR	>	[1256]	âmbar	('amber')	PT	
	b.	wa xá,lláh	AR	>	[1495]	oxalá	('hopefully')	PT	
	c.	xaráb	AR	>	[13th c.]	xarope	('syrup')	PT	
	d.	miskin	AR	>	mezquino	ES	>	mesquinho	('petty')	PT
	e.	haxxíxín	AR	>	assassino	IT	>	assassin	('assassin')	PT
	f.	suffa	AR	>	sofa	FR	>	sofa	('sofa')	PT

The words of Arabic origin in (10a–c) are very early borrowings into the local variety of Vulgar Latin, and (10d–f) are indirect borrowings into Portuguese. Both substrata and superstrata languages offered the Northwestern Iberian Vulgar Latin/Romance a considerable amount of words. There is no reason to believe that the process was more than strictly lexical, not even when the incorporation of the Arabic determiner played a role, since it was not recognised as such in Portuguese and the constraint was no longer active a few centuries later. Therefore, substrata and superstrata languages left no traces in the Portuguese word formation system.

1.4 Borrowings from non-European languages

From Old Portuguese to the Enlightenment nothing has really changed in the domain of word formation. The Portuguese lexicon has received borrowings from a wide variety of languages (see the examples of borrowings from African languages in (11), Amerindian languages in (12) and Asiatic languages in (13)).

(11)	a.	banana	('banana')
	b.	carimbo	('stamp')
	c.	cubata	('African hut')

(12)	a.	canoa	('canoe')
	b.	tomate	('tomato')
	c.	amendoim	('peanut')

(13)	a.	leque	('fan')
	b.	bengala	('cane')
	c.	chá	('tea')

Words such as (11–13) entered the language, slowly and steadily, at all stages of its history, especially those that were brought from maritime expansion, but they have never interfered with the general nature of Portuguese morphology.

1.5 The borrowing typology

Table 4.2 presents Thomason and Kaufman's (1988: 77) typology for borrowings. Germanic and early Arabic borrowings do not fit easily into the typology: language contact between Vulgar Latin and these languages was quite intense, which suggests category 4, but, since no structural borrowing took place, they must fall under category 1. Category 1 fits all other words of whatever origin that were introduced by

Table 4.2 Typology for borrowings (adapted from Thomason and Kaufman (1988: 77))

1.	Casual contact: lexical borrowing only	Lexicon: content words (non-basic vocabulary borrowed for cultural and functional reasons)	Germanic borrowings? Early Arabic borrowings? Later Arabic borrowings Borrowings from European languages Borrowings from non-European languages
		Structure: −	
2.	Slightly more intense contact: slight structural borrowing	Lexicon: function words (conjunctions and adverbial particles) Structure: minor phonological, syntactic and lexical semantic features (that cause little or no typological disruption)	
3.	More intense contact: slightly more structural borrowing	Lexicon: function words (prepositions and adpositions; derivational affixes added to native vocabulary; personal and demonstrative pronouns, numerals, etc.) Structure: phonemicisation of previously allophonic alternations; aspects of moving from SOV to SVO, e.g. borrowed postpositions in a prepositional language (or vice versa).	
4.	Strong cultural pressure: moderate structural borrowing	Lexicon: − Structure: major structural features that cause relatively little typological change (e.g. extensive word order changes, borrowed inflectional affixes and categories, etc.).	Germanic borrowings? Early Arabic borrowings?
5.	Very strong cultural pressure: heavy structural borrowing	Lexicon: − Structure: major structural features that cause significant typological disruption (e.g. changes in word structure rules, etc.).	

subsequent waves of lexical borrowings, but it does not suit the first two, that came under a quite intense contact that triggered no structural borrowing. Maybe the intensity of language contact needs to be calibrated by other factors, such as the prestige of each language.

None of these categories seems to apply to the so-called Latinisms either. Though they originate in the same language as most of the early Portuguese lexicon, as we have seen with *mácula*, Latinisms have very specific (phonetic, prosodic and semantic) properties. No real language contact took place in this case, so this is a challenge to Thomason and Kaufman's (1988: 77) typology. A minus 1 category, specific for literary language contact, as in Table 4.3, could prove to be quite useful in this case.

Table 4.3 Supplement to Thomason and Kaufman's (1988) borrowing typology in Table 4.2

-1.	Literary contact	Lexicon: content words (non-basic vocabulary) borrowed	Latinisms
		for cultural and functional reasons	
		No structural borrowing	

Table 4.4 Frequency of *experiência, herdamento, herança* (Davies and Ferreira, 2006–2019)

	13th c.	14th c.	15th c.	16th c.	17th c.	18th c.	19th c.	20th c.
experiência				139	254	118	543	2302
herdamento	113	140	37	10				
herança	3	22	71	129	124	29	308	579

Renaissance writers, such as Garcia de Resende (1470–1536) or Luís de Camões (1524–1579/1580), pioneered the reshaping of the Portuguese lexicon and the introduction of this particular kind of lexical borrowings (cf. Silva 1931; Carvalho 1984), often under the influence of Castilian words created by an identical intervention (cf. Castro 2011). Words like *experiência*, in (14a), illustrate a direct loan from Latin that took place in the sixteenth century (see Table 4.4); *herdamento* and *herança*, which are both semantically related to the verb *herdar* ('to inherit') show that a vernacular word (i.e. *herdamento*) could rival a latinate derivative (cf. *herança*), eventually under the influence of Castilian, and lose the dispute, as the diachronic distribution in Table 4.4 clearly demonstrates.

(14) a. experientia LA   ('experiment')   > experiência PT   ('experiment')
     b. haerere   LA > haerentia   LA > herencia   ES > herança PT
        ('heritage')
     c. hereditare LA > herdar   PT > herdamento PT   ('heritage')

This literary initiative complied with a political programme that was designed for the affirmation of Portugal as a nation. In their opinion, the claim that the vernacular language was as worthy of consideration as Latin was sustained by the demonstration that Portuguese was very similar to Latin (at least in the lexical aspect).

The general framework of neoclassicism favoured the relatinisation of Portuguese even more. Classical Latin could then be used to introduce new words, although not always straightforwardly. Raphael Bluteau (1638–1734) was a clergyman of French origin who lived in London and Italy, and finally came to Portugal, where he became the author of the first reference dictionary for Portuguese. It is a masterpiece compiled to provide words for the usage of educated people. In his *Vocabulário*, published between 1712 and 1728, we can find entries such as *connivencia*, which he describes as 'a Latin word that I have not found in Portuguese authors yet. But, since it may be useful to mean consent, I decided to mention it here' (my translation (AV)).[6] In fact, the word is hard to find in Latin authors as well, at least in classical authors, as the entry in Lewis and Short (1879) demonstrates:

cōnīventĭa, ae, f. coniveo, II. B.,
I. connivance (post-class. and rare)

The meaning that the word acquired in Portuguese is not exactly, as Bluteau originally intended, 'consent', but 'consent to a wrongdoing', which may be seen as a metaphorical extension of the meaning of the Latin base verb: *coniveo* 'to shut the eyes'. But the relevance of this example comes from the fact that it documents the process of relatinisation and the positive state of mind of the target language promoters of the process.

2. Latinisms in Portuguese and other languages

Though early Latinisms were full words, the morphological devices available in Portuguese allowed their segmentation – from a structural point of view, these words were not that different from vernacular words. So, modern scholar contact with Latin (including a Latinised Ancient Greek) allowed Portuguese (like many other modern languages) to create and share a parallel lexicon, meant to be used for word formation, particularly in academic/literary/technical environments. Thus, roots and suffixes that roughly correspond to Latin and Ancient Greek roots and affixes, processed by language-specific adaptation requirements, form this neoclassical lexicon and morphosemantic needs.

In Portuguese, neoclassical roots behave quite differently from vernacular roots. In fact, they display a quite systematic complementary distribution:

- vernacular roots, such as *peix-* (cf. (15a)), are used in simple words (cf. (15b)), in vernacular derivatives (cf. (15c)) and morpho-syntactic compounds (cf. (15d)). If we compare these words cross-linguistically, we will conclude that they are predominantly language-specific, even though they may share a common origin cf. (15b–d);
- neoclassical roots, like the Latinate *pisc-* (cf. (15e)) and the Hellenistic *icti-* (cf. 15h)) never occur in simple words; they just occur with neoclassical suffixes (cf. (15f) and (15i)) and within neoclassical compounds (cf. (15g) and (15j)). These words are frequently shared, with minor differences, by other languages.

(15) a. peix-
     b. peixe   Eng. fish   Fr. Poisson
     c. peixeiro   Eng. fishmonger   Fr. Poissonnier
     d. peixe-espada   Eng. swordfish   Fr. Espadon
     e. pisc-
     f. piscina   Eng. swimming pool   Fr. Piscine
     g. piscicultura   Eng. fish farming   Fr. Pisciculture
     h. icti-

i. ictiose   Eng. ichthyosis   Fr. Ichthyoses
j. ictiofobia   Eng. ichthyophobia   Fr. ichtyophobie

The introduction of these neoclassical roots (and affixes) may hardly be seen as a normal case of borrowing – it is rather the output of a translation exercise, in the context of a source language that has no native speakers. Their lexica can be adopted by other languages, as an extra lexical resource that can be used for special purposes, such as scientific and technological naming requirements.

After the borrowing of Classical Latin words and their analysis into constituents, the road to using them in word formation was wide open. Since affixation is involved in quite familiar word formation processes in Romance languages, neoclassical derivation merely implied the enlargement of the affix set. New affixes, such as *-ose*, *-ite* or *-ismo* attached to neoclassical roots that translate the vernacular words (cf. (16a–c)), but they have quickly acquired the capacity to select vernacular bases (cf. (16d–f)).

(16) a. -ose   ictiose ('ichthyosis')   cf. icti-   vs. peixe ('fish')
     b. -ite   rinite ('rhinitis')   cf. rin-   vs. nariz ('nose')
     c. -ismo   nepotismo ('nepotism')   cf. nepot- vs. sobrinho ('nephew')
     d. avari(a)   ('damage')   cf. avariose ('syphilis')
     e. amendoim   ('peanut')   cf. amendoinite ('overdose of peanuts')
     f. Salazar   (PM from 1932–1968)   cf. salazarismo ('Salazar's regime')

In time, neoclassical affixes became normal affixes and no noticeable changes in the word formation system took place.

The borrowing of neoclassical compounds had other consequences in Portuguese. The adjunction of a root to another root was well known since Vulgar Latin, by means of prefixation. As shown in Table 4.5, the set of prefixes that is contemporarily

Table 4.5 Portuguese prefixes of Greek and Latin origin

	prepositional origin		adjectival origin	
Greek origin	[anti] balas	('anti-bullet')	[auto] ajuda	('self help')
	[hiper] mercado	('hypermarket')	[mega] sucesso	('mega-success')
	[hipo] glicemia	('hypoglycaemia')	[poli] cultura	('poly-culture')
			[pseudo] ciência	('pseudo-science')
Latin origin	[co] autor	('co-author')	[mini] saia	('miniskirt')
	[contra] argumento	('counter-argument')	[multi] colorido	('multi-coloured')
	[ex] polícia	('former policeman')	[pluri] disciplinar	('multidisciplinary')
	[infra] som	('infrasound')	[recém] casado	('newly-married')
	[inter] ligação	('interconnection')	[semi] automatic	('semiautomatic')
	[pós] exílio	('post-exile')		
	[pré] acordo	('pre-agreement')		
	[pró] americano	('pro-American')		
	[sub] mundo	('sub-world')		
	[super] herói	('super-hero')		
	[ultra] resistente	('ultra-resistent')		

available includes the diachronic output of Latin and Ancient Greek prepositions and adjectives.

These prefixes are modifiers of the head to their right, as illustrated in (17).

(17) a. des$_{modifier}$ – contente   ('unhappy')
     b. sem$_{modifier}$ – abrigo   ('homeless')
     c. bem$_{modifier}$ – vindo   ('welcome')
     d. neo$_{modifier}$ – realism   ('neo-realism')
     e. vice$_{modifier}$ – reitor   ('vice-rector')

Neoclassical compounds added noun roots to this list. From a structural and functional point of view they are not that diverse, but this was an absolute novelty in the domain of Portuguese word formation.

3. Neoclassical compounding

In a way, borrowed roots in borrowed compounds triggered the borrowing of a new word formation process that became particularly useful to find names for all sorts of substances, ideas or new findings. Bluteau (1712–1728), again, provides a very nice example of the invention of a neoclassical compound to replace a word that he considered inadequate. The making of *pirilampo* ('firefly'), literally ('fire torch'), shows that the source language could also be Ancient Greek, probably brought to their knowledge via Latin translations of classical Ancient Greek texts, and it demonstrates that the compound word structure had by now become familiar.

> PIRILAMPO. Nas Conferencias Academicas, que se fizeraõ no anno de 1696, na livrarya do Conde da Ericeira, foy proposto, se ao insecto luzente, vulgarmente chamado *Cagalume*, se daria em papeis, ou discursos serios, outro nome mais decoroso, como v.g. Pirilampo à imitação de Plinio Histor. Que chama a este insecto *Lampyris*, nome composto de *Lampas*, que em Grego val o mesmo que *Tocha*, & *Pyr*, que quer dizer fogo. A alguns pareceo este nome *Pirilampo* affectado, outros foraõ de parecer, que se admitisse em obras Epicas; por ser *Cagalume* incompativel com o nobre, & magestoso estylo. Sebastiaõ Pacheco Varella no seu livro intitulado Num. Vocal, pag. 373, fallando neste bichinho, diz, (Quem depois de ver o dia claro, fará estimação do desprezado *Insecto luzente*, só porque de noite pareceo Astro brilhante? *Vid.* Cagalume.[7]

This new source of lexical enrichment is not bound to Portuguese, nor to any other language; it is a process shared by all languages that used neoclassical roots for scientific writings. Hence, the transfer of these words from language to language became usual and frequent – spreading the knowledge entailed by the words.

The afflux of neoclassical compounds coming from other languages has probably helped to consolidate its conformity to Portuguese. Consider two examples. The word *psicologia* ('psychology') is first attested in Portuguese in 1839,[8] but it was not coined in Portuguese, nor was it coined at this time – it is certainly a loan. Krstic (1964) discusses the original coinage and use of a Latin version of the word in these terms:

In technical and encyclopaedic literature one can find somewhat different information about when the word "psychology" was formed and who was the first to use it. In the main psychological and philosophical dictionaries, textbooks, and leading world encyclopaedias there are for the most part three different opinions of the origin of this term which, as the word denoting scientific or philosophic dealing with the phenomena of psychic (subjective, conscious) life, has now come into very wide use.

And he goes on:

All the three names connected with the formation of the term "psychology" are the names of the people of German origin from the 16th century [. . .] However, in a document known for years there is a detail which has unfortunately remained unnoticed until now and which fully entitles us to a complete revision of the established opinion on the first appearance of the word "psychology" in the scientific language of Europe. At least 66 years before [the German 16th-century philosopher] Göckel [. . .] the term "psychology" was used by our great humanist, the poet of "Judita", Marko Marulic (1450–1524) in one of his Latin treatises not as yet found but whose title "Psichiologia de ratione animae humanae" is preserved in a list of Marulic's works given by the poet's fellow-citizen, contemporary, and friend Bozicevic-Natalis in his "Life of Marko Marulic from Split". (Krstic 1964: 7)

Indeed, each neoclassical term tells a story, which is not always easy to reach and often related to epistemological issues, but, in this case, if Krstic (1964) is right, we may locate the appearance of the Latinate word *psichiologia* in Central Europe, at the beginning of the sixteenth century. Its arrival in the Portuguese lexicon was delayed by three centuries and certainly by a number of different languages, but it ultimately arrived.

Another testimony is provided by the word *antroponímia*. According to Portuguese etymologists (such as Leite de Vasconcelos 1931: 3; Machado 1977), a Portuguese anthropologist coined this word in 1887 to refer to the 'study of the names of human beings'. He could have used some vernacular expression, but the replacement of *pessoa* ('person') by *antrop-* and *nome* ('name') by *onom-* was certainly meant to bring some *gravitas* to this recent discipline. Then, according to the TLFi, the French word *anthroponimie* was borrowed from the Portuguese word *antroponímia*.

We may have found the thread of events that led to the introduction of neoclassical compounding as an available word formation resource in Portuguese. None of these compounds may be seen as borrowings from Latin or Ancient Greek, they are borrowings from neighbouring languages or original coinages. It is the process of neoclassical compounding that may be seen as a structural borrowing, which brings us back to Thomason and Kaufman's (1988: 77) typology. Once again, we find no suitable category for this kind of neoclassical borrowing. Changes in word structure rules fall under category 5, which implies very strong cultural pressure, but this is not the case here. Hence, we may now suggest filling the 'structure' part of the above-suggested -1 category. In Table 4.6, the information from Tables 4.2 and 4.3 is combined and revised.

Table 4.6 Revised borrowing typology after Thomason and Kaufman's (1988) typology

-1.	Literary contact	Lexicon: content words (non-basic vocabulary) borrowed for cultural and functional reasons	Latinisms
		Structure: new word formation patterns	neoclassical compounding
1.	Casual contact: lexical borrowing only	Lexicon: content words (non-basic vocabulary borrowed for cultural and functional reasons)	Germanic borrowings? Early Arabic borrowings? Later Arabic borrowings Borrowings from European languages Borrowings from non-European languages
		Structure: −	
2.	Slightly more intense contact: slight structural borrowing	Lexicon: function words (conjunctions and adverbial particles) Structure: minor phonological, syntactic and lexical semantic features (that cause little or no typological disruption)	
3.	More intense contact: slightly more structural borrowing	Lexicon: function words (prepositions and adpositions; derivational affixes added to native vocabulary; personal and demonstrative pronouns, numerals, etc.) Structure: phonemicisation of previously allophonic alternations; aspects of moving from SOV to SVO, e.g. borrowed postpositions in a prepositional language (or vice versa)	
4.	Strong cultural pressure: moderate structural borrowing	Lexicon: − Structure: major structural features that cause relatively little typological change (e.g. extensive word order changes, borrowed inflectional affixes and categories, etc.).	Germanic borrowings? Early Arabic borrowings?
5.	Very strong cultural pressure: heavy structural borrowing	Lexicon: − Structure: major structural features that cause significant typological disruption (e.g. changes in word structure rules, etc.)	

The success of the neoclassical compounding pattern led to its expansion into a more general morphological compounding pattern that is now able to recruit vernacular roots as well, either in one (cf. (18a)) or both structural positions (cf. (18b–d)).

(18) a. sambódromo   ('sambadrome')
     b. lusodescendência   ('Portuguese descent')
     c. sul-americano   ('south American')
     d. toxicodependente   ('drug addict')

Morphological compounding is also responsible for the formation of a kind of semantic doublet of previously existing words, illustrated in (19). It provides a terminological version for a general language word previously available.

(19) a. mata-ratos   ('rat poison') vs. raticida   ('rat poison')
     b. matador   ('killer')   vs. homicida   ('homicide')
     c. dentista   ('dentist')   vs. odontologista ('odontologist')
     d. dor de cabeça ('headache')   vs. cefalgia   ('headache')

It is also interesting to note that a series of new roots can be obtained by truncation
of some of these compounds. The resulting clips correspond to shorter equivalents of
their compound base, although they look like neoclassical roots (see the examples in
(20)).

(20) automóvel ('car')   autoestrada ('highway')
      auto- ('self')   ≠   auto- ('car')
      ecologia ('ecology')   eco-turismo ('ecotourism')
      eco- ('environment') ≠   eco- ('ecological')
      geografia ('geography')   geolocalização ('geolocation')
      geo- ('earth')   ≠   geo- ('geographic')

Now, the properties of morphological compounding are quite subtle, as I have
described elsewhere (cf. Villalva 1994, 2000; Villalva and Gonçalves 2016: 180–182).
First, we need to acknowledge two different structures: an adjunction head final structure, as in (21a), and a coordination exocentric structure, as in (21b). The distinction
is, of course, semantic, but some formal contrasts are also detectable.

(21) a. [[toxic]$_{modifier}$ o [dependent]$_{head}$]$_{compound\ root}$ e   ('drug addict')
     b. [[historic]$_{coordinated\ string}$ o [politic]$_{head}$]$_{coordinated\ string}$ o ('historical and political')

Both compound structures share the same configurational design: all morphological compounds are compound roots formed by roots typically mediated by a linking
vowel; in adjunction structures, the left-hand root is a modifier and the right-hand
root is the head, as in (21a); in coordination structures, both roots are coordinated
strings, as in (21b).

In these representations, I have intentionally left the linking vowel, which is a very
interesting constituent, unanchored. The isolation of the linking vowel is generally
ignored in neoclassical root lists, but their autonomy is easily demonstrated if we
compare the form they take when they occupy the left-hand position, as in (22a) and
(22c) with their form when they take the right-hand position, as in (22b) and (22d).

(22) a. **cardi**-o-vascular   ('cardiovascular')
   b. taqui-**cardi**-a   ('tachycardia')
   c. **tóxic**-o-depend-ent-e   ('drug addict')
   d. neur-o-**tóxic**-a / o   ('neurotoxic')

Thus, the linking vowel is an independent constituent. Its main role, as a boundary marker between roots, is phonetic. The European Portuguese vowel system is formed by eight vowels in stressed position (i.e. [i e ɛ ɐ a u o ɔ]) and four vowels in unstressed positions (i.e. [i ɨ ɐ u]). The reduction is obtained by raising and centralisation, as *festival* and *violino* in (23) illustrate.

(23) a. f[ɛ]st-a   ('party')   f[i]stival   ('festival')
   b. vi[ɔ]l-a   ('guitar')   vi[u]lin-o   ('violine')

But there are cases that block the unstressed vowel raising process. One of these cases is the linking vowel [ɔ], in morphological compounds. In compositional structures, the vowel height is kept, even though it is unstressed (see the examples in (24)).

(24) a. toxic   [ɔ]   dependent   e
   b. historic   [ɔ]   polític   o

A raised linking vowel indicates that the compound has been lexicalised, as in (25a–b). In fact, the presence of a low rounded linking vowel marks recent (compositional) words, as in (25c). This may be why clipped roots are always followed by a low rounded linking vowel, as in (25d–i).

(25) a. fil[u]sof-i-a   ('philosophy')
   b. histori[u]graf-i-a   ('historiography')
   c. vide[ɔ]confer-ênc-i-a   ('videoconference')
   d. ec[ɔ]turism-o   ('ecotourism')   cf. ec[u]logia   'ecology'
   e. ec[ɔ]system-a   ('eco-system')
   f. ec[ɔ]eficiênci-a   ('eco-efficiency')
   g. ge[ɔ]local-iz-a-ção   ('geolocation')   cf. ge[u]grafia   'geography'
   h. ge[ɔ]estratég-ic-o   ('geo-strategic')
   i. ge[ɔ]politic-o   ('geo-political')

Furthermore, the linking vowel appears to be sensitive to some etymological information. The roots listed in (26a–l) form a set of Latinate forms that select the linking vowel [i]. Unattested words such as those in (26m–p) show that the choice of the linking vowel sets the line between admissible and inadmissible compounds.

(26) a. cid   ('kill')   e.g. fung[i]cid-a   ('fungicide')
   b. cultur   ('produce')   e.g. hort[i]cultur-a   ('fruit farming')
   c. dic   ('say')   e.g. fat[i]dic-o   ('fateful')
   d. fer   ('have')   e.g. aqu[i]fer-o   ('aquifer')

e. fic   ('give')   e.g. honor [i] fic-o   ('honorary')
f. fug   ('repel')   e.g. centr [i] fug-o   ('centrifugal')
g. form   ('shape')   e.g. cruc [i] form-e   ('cross-shaped')
h. loqu   ('speak')   e.g. ventr [i] loqu-o   ('ventriloquist')
i. par   ('generate')   e.g. ov [i] par-o   ('egg-layer')
j. ped   ('foot')   e.g. palm [i] ped-e   ('palmiped')
k. son   ('sound')   e.g. un [i] son-o   ('unison')
l. vor   ('eat')   e.g. crud [i] vor-o   ('raw food eater')
m. banan [i] vor-o   ('banana eater')   cf. *banan [ɔ] vor-o
n. banan [ɔ] fag-o   ('banana eater')   cf. *banan [i] fag-o
o. estudant [i] cid-a   ('student murderer')   cf. *estudant [ɔ] cid-a
p. estudant [ɔ] craci-a   ('student rule')   cf. *estudant [i] craci-a

In sum, the phonetic nature of the linking vowel is sensitive to an idiosyncratic feature of the head root.

4. Concluding remarks

The existence of morphological compounding patterns in Portuguese is quite recent and its appearance is quite surprising since no other word formation innovation had occurred for more than seven centuries of language evolution. Apparently, this innovation was triggered by a particular situation of language contact, which yielded a peculiar kind of borrowing, both lexical (neoclassical roots) and structural (neoclassical compounding). The introduction of this 'innovative' word formation resource may have found a smooth path into the Portuguese language through the similarity with prefixation, but the key to success was probably the fact that the same kind of language contact took place, at the same time, between Classical Latin and many European languages, but crucially (for Portuguese) French (mostly during the 1700s and 1800s) and English, more recently. Since Portuguese borrowed many neoclassical compounds formed in French or English, the sudden abundance of data may have increased the pressure that favoured the settlement of root compounding in Portuguese.

In sum, neoclassical loans have reached much higher than expected. They have formed a parallel lexicon in contemporary Portuguese and they have induced the birth of a new word formation process in this language. Apart from its language-specific relevance, the case is also quite interesting for a general theory of borrowing and borrowing typologies (e.g. Thomason and Kaufman 1988), since it involves a pair of languages (Ancient Greek and Portuguese) that were never in direct contact and even belong to different Indo-European genetic branches, but also because the borrowing occurs between languages that belong to different synchronies.

Notes

1. According to Villalva (1994, 2000: 353–389), morphological compounds are compound roots, formed exclusively by roots that are generally mediated by a linking vowel (see also Villalva and Gonçalves (2016: 180–182)).

2. *macula* > *malha*: [kul] > [kl] > [ʎ]

   macula > *mancha*: [kul] > [kl] > [ʃ]

   macula > *mágoa*: [k] > [g] + [ula] > [wa].

3. *riz* – Empr. à l'ital. riso 'riz', att. dep. le XIVe s. (d'apr. DEI) mais prob. plus anc. (cf. Marco Polo, supra, et lat. médiév. risus av. 1241[. . .].

   sucre – Empr. à l'ital. zucchero 'sucre', att. dep. le XIIIe s. (dér. zuccherato 'sucré', [. . .] zucchero au XIVe s., [. . .], lui-même empr. à l'ar. sukkar qui, de même que le gr., lat. saccharum, est d'orig. indienne (skr.); ce sont en effet les Arabes qui ont introduit la culture de la canne à sucre en Andalousie et en Sicile.

4. *thon* – Du lat. thunnus, thynnus, de même sens, gr. 'id.', peut-être par l'intermédiaire du prov. ton 'id.' (att. seulement dep. le XVe s. ds LEVY Prov.).

5. '**zúcchero**, ant. **zúccaro** [. . .] *dall'arab.*|AS|SOKKAR [. . .] avendo gli Arabi coltivato lo zucchero in Sicilia e nella Spagna [. . .]'.

6. '**Connivencia**. He palavra Latina, da qual até agora naõ acho exemplo em Authores Portuguezes. Mas como poderá ser necessario o uso della para sinonymo de consentimento [. . .] me pareceo bem fazer aqui mençaõ della.'

7. '**Firefly**. During the Academic Conferences held in 1696 at the library of the Earl of Ericeira, someone suggested that the lightning insect commonly called *Cagalume* should get a more decorous name, better fit to be used in serious speeches, like Pirilampo [. . .] this name is compounded by *Lampas*, that in Greek means "torch" and *Pyr*, that means "fire".[. . .].' (My translation (AV))

8. Silvestre Pinheiro Ferreira is the author of *Noções Elementares de Filosofia Geral e Aplicada às Ciências Morais e Políticas (Ontologia, Psicologia, e Ideologia)*, a book published in Paris, in 1839. This may be the first or one of the first occurrences of the word in Portuguese.

References

Carvalho, José Gonçalo Herculano de (1984), 'Contribuição de *Os Lusíadas* para a renovação da língua portuguesa', *Estudos Linguísticos*, III: 77–125.

Castro, Ivo (1991), *Curso de História da Língua Portuguesa* (with R. Marquilhas and J. L. Acosta), Lisboa: Universidade Aberta.

Castro, Ivo (2011), 'A língua de Camões', in V. Aguiar e Silva (ed.), *Dicionário de Luís de Camões*, Lisboa: Caminho, pp. 461b–469a.

Davies, Mark and M. Ferreira (2006–2019), *Corpus do Português: 45 Million Words, 1300s–1900s*, http://www.corpusdoportugues.org/hist-gen/ (Historical/Genres) (16 August 2018).

Krstic, Kruno (1964), 'Marko Marulic. The Author of the Term "Psychology"', *Acta Instituti Psychologici*, 36: 7–13, https://psychclassics.yorku.ca/Krstic/marulic.htm (16 August 2018).

Leite de Vasconcelos, José (1931), *Opúsculos. III. Onomatologia*, Coimbra: Imprensa da Universidade, http://cvc.instituto-camoes.pt/conhecer/biblioteca-digital-camoes/explorar-por-autor.html?aut=183 (16 August 2018).

Lewis, C. T. and C. Short (eds) (1879), *A Latin Dictionary. Founded on Andrews' Edition of Freund's Latin Dictionary*, Oxford: Clarendon Press, http://www.perseus.tufts. edu/hopper/text?doc=Perseus:text:1999.04.0059 (29 June 2019).

Machado, José Pedro (1977), *Dicionário Etimológico da Língua Portuguesa*, Lisboa: Livros Horizonte.

Pianigiani, Ottorino (1907, 1926), *Vocabolario Etimologico della Lingua Italiana*, Roma: Dante Alighieri, Firenze: Ariani, http://www.etimo.it/?pag=hom (20 December 2018).

Silva, Carlos. E. C. (1931), *Ensaio sobre os latinismos dos Lusíadas*, Coimbra: Imprensa da Universidade, http://archive.org/details/CORREADASILVAENSAIOSOBR EOSLATINISMOSDOSLUSIADAS] (16 August 2018).

Thomason, Sarah. G. and T. Kaufman (1988), *Language Contact, Creolization, and Genetic Linguistics*, Berkeley, LA and Oxford: University of California Press.

TLFi (n.d.), *Le Trésor de la Langue Française informatisé*, ATILF-CNRS and Université de Lorraine, http://www.atilf.fr/tlfi (16 August 2018).

Villalva, Alina (1994, 2000), *Estruturas Morfológicas. Unidades e Hierarquias nas Palavras do Português*, Lisboa: Fundação Calouste Gulbenkian, Fundação para a Ciência e Tecnologia.

Villalva, Alina and Carlos A. Gonçalves (2016), 'The Phonology and Morphology of Word Formation', in L. Wetzels, S. Menuzzi and J. Costa (eds), *Handbook of Portuguese Linguistics*, Oxford: Wiley-Blackwell, 167–187.

5

Compound Calques in an Eighteenth-Century German-Lithuanian Dictionary

Bonifacas Stundžia

Compound calques are a widespread type of structural borrowing that was created by an item-by-item translation of the source compound (cf. the definition of *calque* in general, Haspelmath 2009: 39). In this chapter, I distinguish between absolute compound calques, i.e. item-by-item copies of donor language compounds, including both the pattern of a compound and the semantics of its members, and non-absolute (or creative) compound calques that have differences in the semantics of one member, in the pattern of the compound, or in both.

This chapter has been divided into five sections. Section 1 introduces the data, research methods and aim, while section 2 discusses the sociolinguistic and cultural situation in East Prussia in the eighteenth century. Section 3 presents nominal compounding in the eighteenth-century German-Lithuanian dictionary by Jacob Brodowski, including the overall characteristics of Lithuanian compounds and their German equivalents. Section 4, which is central to this chapter, presents research on Lithuanian determinative, possessive and verbal governing compound calques in the said dictionary. The chapter ends with the conclusions (section 5).

1. The data, research methods and aim

The material for this chapter is taken from an eighteenth-century manuscript, the *German-Lithuanian Dictionary* by Jacob Brodowski (1011 pp., ~1744, hereafter referred to as *B*); the documentary edition containing a facsimile, transcript and word register was published in 2009 (see Drotvinas 2009). The compiler of the dictionary, Jacob Brodowski (LT Jokūbas Brodovskis, ~1692–1744), studied at Königsberg University. From 1713 until his death, he was a teacher at a church school in the parish of Trempai (DE Trempen, currently Novostrojevo, Kaliningrad district, Russia) in the eastern part of the Duchy of Prussia, which used to be called Lithuania Minor as opposed to Lithuania Major, a territory of the United Polish-Lithuanian Commonwealth inhabited by Lithuanians (for more see Zinkevičius 1996: 272; Drotvinas 2009: I, XXI–XXIII). It is unclear whether Brodowski's native language was Lithuanian, Polish or even

German (he could have descended from an ethnically mixed family), nevertheless his Lithuanian and German were proficient (for more see Plaušinaitytė 2010: 43–46). It is worth noting that for more than thirty years Brodowski collected Lithuanian words, expressions, proverbs and riddles from ordinary people living in Trempai and the neighbouring parishes. The data of spoken Lithuanian (and German), which he referred to as *Vocabula Domestica*, comprise a significant layer of *B* and in most cases can be distinguished from the written language data taken mostly from the 1735 translation of the Bible with references known as *Vocabula Biblica Veteris et Novi Testamenti*. Therefore, as regards the Lithuanian language, *B* is not a bilingual dictionary based on a compilation of earlier dictionaries but rather a rich database of words and expressions used both in the Lithuanian community and writings in the Duchy of Prussia in the eighteenth century. In the majority of cases, the Lithuanian words and expressions, as a rule augmented with synonyms, are given as equivalents of German words and expressions which are taken from both German-Latin, German-Lithuanian dictionaries, spoken language and from concordances of the German Bible (for more see Plaušinaitytė 2010: 161–245). There are also Lithuanian words, expressions, proverbs and riddles without German equivalents or translation.

The present research is based mostly on the description of structural patterns of nominal compounds used in cognate languages that are in contact with each other and possess a similar morphological structure, including that of nominal compounds. The main differences between the two languages are as follows:

- a) in German, compounding is about several times more frequent than in Lithuanian;
- b) the structural patterns Ncase+N (dependent determinative compounds the first member of which comprise a case form of a noun, mostly gen.sg. or pl.) and N/A+V+Suffix (synthetic compounds) are characteristic only of German;
- c) only two-stem compounds are characteristic of Lithuanian.

The aim of the chapter is to address and answer the following questions:

- What types of compound calques (for the term see Haugen 1953: 393–394; Haspelmath 2009: 38–40; Wohlgemuth 2009: 129) were characteristic of the eighteenth-century Lithuanian used in the Duchy of Prussia?
- Does the process of borrowing (copying, loan translation) show any signs of integrating compound calques into the word formation system of Lithuanian?
- How strong was the Germanic influence on Lithuanian compounding? Did Lithuanian compounding become closer to German compounding?

2. The sociolinguistic and cultural situation in East Prussia in the eighteenth century

The Duchy of Prussia was a multinational and multilingual state with Germans belonging to the higher class, hence German functioned as the dominant and prestige language here. Lithuanians were the largest non-German ethnic group and, together with other local Baltic ethnic groups, belonged to the lower class of inhabitants of the Duchy. A unique Lithuanian ethnic group was spread mostly in the villages of the eastern part of the Prussian state, in Lithuania Minor. In many parishes of East Prussia, Lithuanians were in the majority and were mostly monolingual (the number of bilingual and even multilingual Lithuanians began to increase from the eighteenth century onwards). Even after the terrible plague at the beginning of the eighteenth century and the subsequent colonisation of Lithuania Minor by German-speaking people, the northern regions of East Prussia 'were still predominantly Lithuanian [. . .] The Germanization of Lithuanians during the entire period was quite weak' (Zinkevičius 1996: 270).

Prussian Lithuanians 'played a very important role in the history of Lithuanian culture [. . .] Up to the very end of the 18th century. Lithuanian culture was more intensively spread here than anywhere else' (Zinkevičius 1996: 228). They had Lithuanian schools, periodicals, a standard written language, the norms of which were codified in the *Grammatica Litvanica* by Daniel Klein in 1653, and the Lithuanian Language Seminar for teachers and priests founded at Königsberg University in 1718. The eighteenth century saw the translation of the Bible (prepared collectively and published in 1735), the world-famous poem 'Seasons of the Year' by Kristijonas Donelaitis (1714–1780), as well as active linguistic debates about the quality of written Lithuanian which, because of many borrowed words and phrases, was hardly understandable to ordinary people. Puristic attitudes were widespread among educated people who published Lithuanian grammars, dictionaries and texts in the seventeenth and particularly eighteenth centuries. These people included both Germans and Lithuanians but all of them were bilingual or multilingual.

Having been influenced by these debates, it seems that Jacob Brodowski decided to collect Lithuanian words and expressions from ordinary people for his dictionary. There were several manuscript German-Lithuanian dictionaries, as well as a small Lithuanian-German and German-Lithuanian dictionary by Friedrich W. Haack (1730) before *B* in East Prussia, while the first Polish-Latin-Lithuanian dictionary was published by Konstantinas Sirvydas (~1620) in Lithuania Major (there is no information suggesting that Brodowski was aware of it). Due to the fact that the author of *B* collected a large amount of spoken language data, the results of the present analysis at least partly reveal the status of compounding and compound calques in the eighteenth-century variety of Lithuanian used in the Duchy of Prussia, as well as the Germanic influence on Lithuanian compounding.

3. Nominal compounding in *B*

In this chapter, I distinguish between the following categories of compounds:

1. determinative compounds covering the subcategories of dependent and attributive compounds,
2. possessive compounds,

3. verbal governing compounds, and
4. copulative compounds.

For more on this classification, which is commonly used by Indo-Europeanists, see Olsen (1999: 657–759, and 2002). The last category is extremely rare and is not included in the present research.

3.1 The overall characteristic of Lithuanian compounds in B

According to productivity, the main categories of B's Lithuanian compounds distribute as follows:[1]

1. determinative compounds (~55 per cent, 239/433), e.g. *kirv-kot-is* (< *kirv-is* 'axe' + *kot-as* 'handle' + IP *-is*) 'axe handle',
2. possessive compounds (~25 per cent, 106/433), e.g. *plik-galv-is* masc., *plik-galv-ė* fem. (< *plik-a* 'bald' + *galv-a* 'head' + IPs *-is, -ė*) 'bald-head', and
3. verbal governing compounds (~20 per cent, 86/433), e.g. *sviest-muš-is* 'butter churn' (< *sviest-as* 'butter' + *muš-ti* 'beat' + IP *-is*) lit. 'butter-beat'.

Similar ratios between the main classes of nominal compounds are characteristic of Baltic languages in general (concerning Old Lithuanian, see Drotvinas 1967: 171, concerning Old Latvian, see Bukelskytė-Čepelė 2017: 47–50). The majority of determinative compounds belong to the subcategory of the dependent determinatives and have an N+N structure which can be viewed as prototypical, e.g. *kirv-kot-is* given above. The majority of the subcategory of attributive determinative compounds fall into the structures A+N or V+N, e.g. *skers-vag-a* 'cross-furrow' (< *skers-a* 'cross' + *vag-a* 'furrow' + IP *-a*). Most of the possessive compounds have the structures A+N or Num+N (e.g. *plik-galv-is, -ė*, see above), and all except one verbal governing compounds fall into the structure N+V, e.g. *sviest-muš-is* (cf. above).

With regard to the formal characteristics of the compound patterns discussed, it is worth noting that all Lithuanian compounds in B have a two-stem structure (as a rule, there is no interfix between the stems) and many of them are assigned to the generalised inflectional paradigms masc.nom.sg. *-is* (unstressed) or *-ys* (stressed), fem.nom. sg. *-ė*, and therefore are fully integrated into the word formation system (for more see section 4.5). The second verbal member of verbal governing compounds coincides with the past or present tense stem as is shown by the 3rd person which is identical in singular and plural (the verbal member can also be based on infinitive stem). Similar characteristics are typical of compounds of modern Lithuanian as well (see Stundžia 2016: 3090–3092).

As far as the origin of the members of Lithuanian compounds is concerned, the pattern with two native members prevail, but there are distinct differences among the main categories of compounds. The most indigenous are possessive and verbal governing compounds, having ~9 per cent and ~13 per cent of borrowed members respectively, while attributive determinative compounds have ~17 per cent of borrowed members, and most non-native are dependent determinative compounds with ~33 per cent of borrowed members. Among dependent determinative compounds, half of the attested cases have at least one borrowed member. The highest percentage of borrowed members in the group of dependent determinative N+N compounds could be at least partly explained by the fact that nouns 'cover the most differentiated domain for labelling concepts, objects, and roles' and thus are the most borrowable class of vocabulary (Matras 2009: 168).

Based on the etymological analysis of vocabulary by Hock (2015) and Smoczyński (2018), the majority of matter borrowings include members of compounds which are Slavisms, mostly old ones (~74 per cent), also used in the dialects of Lithuania Major, e.g. *aliej-us* <Allejus>[2] 'oil' (from BE *oléj* 'id.'), *vyn-as* <Wÿnas> 'wine' (from PL *mino* or BE *vinó*). There are old Germanisms as well, e.g. *šarv-as* <Szarwas> 'armour' (from GMH *sarwes* 'id.'), nevertheless most Germanisms are new ones, including borrowings from Prussian German, e.g. *likt-is* <Liktis> 'candle' (from DE *Licht* 'id.'), *pypk-is* <Pÿpkis> 'pipe' (from Prussian German *pīpke*) (~22 per cent).

3.2 Lithuanian compounds and their German equivalents in *B*

In most cases *B*'s Lithuanian compounds are rendered by compounds in German of an identical or a different pattern. The choice of the pattern mostly depends on the category of the compound. With regard to the dependent determinative compounds (part of them as well as compounds of other categories comprise calques), cf. examples (1–4).[3]

(1) a. kirv-kot-is (< kirv-is + kot-as + IP -is) <Kirwkotis> LT
     b. Axt-en-helm (< Axt + IF -en + Helm) <Axtenhelm> DE
         'axe-handle' (N+[IF]+N) both LT and DE, i.e. handle of an axe. B180.

(2) a. lauk-aguon-ai, pl. (< lauk-as + aguon-ai, pl. of aguon-as + IP -ai)
         <Laukagůnai> LT
     b. Feld-mohn (< Feld + Mohn) <Feld Mohn> DE
         'field-poppy' (N+N) both LT and DE. B273.

(3) a. kalk-kakal-ys (< kalk-is + kakal-ys + IP -ys) <Kalkkakalÿs> LT
     b. Kalk-ofen (< Kalk + Ofen) <Kalck Offen> DE
         'lime-stove' (N+N) both LT and DE. B767.

(4) a. karal-žaisl-is (< karal-ius + žaisl-as + IP -is) <Karal-Zaislis> LT
     b. König-s-spiel (< König-s, gen.sg. + Spiel) <Königs Spiel> DE
         'king-game' (N+N) LT vs. 'king's game' ($N_{gen.sg.}$+N) DE, i.e. chess. B811.

The examples (1–4) illustrate the prototypical N+N structure of dependent determinative compounds which are based on two nominal members having an identical meaning in both languages. As regards the formal relation between the members of compounds, German formations in (1b) and (4b) differ from their Lithuanian equivalents in the following: the members of (1b) are connected with the interfix

which occurs rarely in the compounds of Lithuania Minor, while the first member of
(4b) does not represent a nominal stem but rather a genitive singular form (*König*-s
'king's') which is not peculiar for Lithuanian compounding. The characteristic
feature of Lithuanian compounding in (1a) and (4a) is the generalised IP *-is/-ys*
(masc.) (for more see section 4.5). LT *lauk-aguon-ai* (2a) and *kalk-kakal-ys* (3a) have
IPs *-ai* (pl.) and *-ys* inherited from *aguon-ai* and *kakal-ys* which stand in the position
of the second members of compounds. As to the origin of the members of Lithuanian
examples, the compound (1a) is based on the native nouns *kirvis* 'axe' and *kotas*
'handle', while the one in (3a) is based on the Germanisms *kalkis* 'lime' and *kakalys*
(DE *kachel*) 'stove'. One member of the compounds (2a) and (4a) is borrowed from
German (*aguonas* 'poppy') or Slavic (*karalius* 'king'), while the other one is native
(*laukas* 'field', *žaislas* 'game').

The German compound equivalents of Lithuanian attributive determinative compounds fall mostly into A+N (5b), V+N (6b) and N+N (7b) structures.

(5) a. skers-vag-a (< skers-a + vag-a + IP -a) <Skérs Wagga> LT
     b. Quer-furche (< Quer + Furche) <Quer Furche> DE
         'cross-furrow' (A+N) both LT and DE. B508.

(6) a. skir-kel-is (< skir-ti INF + kel-ias + IP -is) <Skirkelis> LT
     b. Scheid-weg (< scheid-en + Weg) <Scheidweg> DE
         'divide-road'(V+N) both LT and DE, i.e. crossroad. B41.

(7) a. gyv-plauk-ai, pl. (< gyv-i, pl.masc. of gyv-as + plauk-ai, pl. of plauk-as + IP -ai,
         pl.) <Gÿwplaukai> LT
     b. Milch-haar (< Milch + Haar) <Milch Haar> DE
         'live-hair' (A+N) LT vs. 'milk-hair' (N+N) DE, i.e. soft hair. B913.

The examples (5–6) show A/V+N structure of attributive determinative compounds
which contain two members that carry the same meaning in both languages, while
the example (7a) illustrates an attributive Lithuanian compound with an A+N structure which is rendered by a dependent determinative N+N compound in German
(7b). In (6a) the Lithuanian compound has the generalised IP *-is*. All members of the
Lithuanian compounds in (5–7) are native words, i.e. *skersas*, masc., -a, fem. 'cross',
vaga 'furrow' (5a), *skirti* 'divide', *kelias* 'road' (6a), *gyvas*, masc., -a, fem. '(a)live',
plaukas 'hair' (7a).

Most Lithuanian possessive compounds have German compound equivalents, as a
rule belonging to the A/Num+N structure, see examples (8–9).

(8) a. plik-galv-is (< plik-a + galv-a + IP -is), both noun and adjective <Plikgalwis> LT
     b. Kahl-kopf (< kahl + Kopf), noun <Kahl Kopff> DE
         'bald-head'/'bald-headed' (A+N) LT vs. 'bald-head' DE. B766.

(9) a. devyn-ak-iai, pl. (< devyn-ios + ak-ys, pl. of ak-is + IP -iai, pl.), noun
         <Dewynakiei> LT
     b. Neun-auge (< Neun + Auge), noun <Neunauge> DE
         'nine-eye' (Num+N) both LT and DE, i.e. nine-eyed (lamprey). B474.

The examples in (8–9) illustrate a prevailing A/Num+N structure of Lithuanian possessive compound nouns and adjectives, while in German the same structure is typical only for nouns. Concerning adjectives, German has a peculiar structure A+N+SF, which is to be viewed through the frames of derivation (for more see Neef 2015: 582–584), e.g. DE *kahl-köpf-icht* <Kahl Köpfficht> B812 (mod. *Kahl-köpf-ig*) 'bald-headed' (< *Kahl-kopf*). The Lithuanian compounds (8a, 9a) have generalised IP masc. *-is*, pl. *-iai* (for more see section 4.5) and their members are the native words *plikas*, masc., *-a*, fem. 'bald', *galva* 'head', *devyni*, masc., *-ios*, fem. 'nine' and *akis* 'eye'.

Lithuanian verbal governing compounds are also rendered mostly by German compounds manifesting different patterns, see examples (10–12).

(10) a. seil-ė-tek-is (< seil-ės, pl. + IF -ė- + tek-a PRS3 of tek-ė-ti + IP -is) <Seiletekis> LT

  b. Geifer-fluss (< Geifer + Fluss < fließ-en) <Geiffer Fluß> DE 'saliva-stream' (N+V) both LT and DE, i.e. salivation. B542.

(11) a. šien-pjov-ys (< šien-as + pjov-ė PST3 of pjau-ti + IP -ys) <Szenpjowis> LT

  b. Heu-hau-er (< Heu + Hau-er < hau-en) <Heu Hauer> DE 'hay-mowe' (N+V) LT vs. 'hay-mow-er' (N+V+SF) DE, i.e. haymaker. B694.

(12) a. sviest-muš-is (< swiest-as + muš-ti INF + IP -is) <Swiestmuszis> LT

  b. Butter-fass (< Butter + Fass) <Butter Faß> DE 'butter-beat' (N+V) LT vs. 'butter-dish' (N+N) DE, i.e. butter churn. B305.

The examples (10a–12a) show that Lithuanian verbal governing compounds manifest the N+V structure and, as a rule, the generalised IP masc. *-is/-ys* (feminine forms are rare in *B*), e.g. *sviest-muš-is* (N+V+IP *-is*) 'butter churn' (12a), *šien-pjov-ys* (N+V+IP *-ys*) 'haymaker' (11a). The second verbal member of this category of compounds represents the stem of present tense (10a), past tense (11a) or infinitive (12a) form, while the nominalised forms of the type [†]*tekis*, [†]*pjovys* and [†]*mušis* do not exist.[4] The members of the Lithuanian compounds in (10–12) are native words. Interfixes such as *-ė-* in (10a) were rare in Lithuanian compounds in East Prussia.

German compound equivalents of Lithuanian verbal governing compounds are represented by:

a) the N+V pattern with V functioning as a nominalised verbal form, e.g. *Geifer-fluss* lit. 'saliva-stream' (10b),

b) synthetic compounds having the pattern N+deverbal noun formed with the suffix *-er* (N+V+SF; see Neef 2015: 584f., Barz 2016: 2391ff.), e.g. *Heu-hau-er* lit. 'hay-mow-er' (11b), and

c) dependent determinative N+N compounds, e.g. *Butter-fass* 'butter churn' (12b).

Part of *B*'s Lithuanian compounds, irrespective of their category, are rendered in German by simplicia, derivatives, as well as by word combinations, see examples (13–15).

(13) a. šon-kaul-is (< šon-as + kaul-as + IP -is) <Szonkaulis> LT
     b. Rippe <Ribbe> DE
         'side-bone', i.e. rib. B1016.

(14) a. šun-malk-is (< šuo [stem šun-] + malk-as + IP -is) <Szunmalkis> LT
     b. Säuf-er (< sauf-en) <Sauffer> DE
         'dog-mouthful' LT vs. 'swill-er' DE, i.e. drunkard. B1042.

(15) a. žiem-mit-is, masc., žiem-mit-ė, fem. (< žiem-a + mit-o PST3 of mis-ti + IPs -is,
         -ė) <Ziemitis, Ziemitte> LT
     b. jährig Pferd, jährige Kuh <jährig Pferdt, jährige Kuh> DE
         'winter-feed' LT, i.e. animal feed during winter vs. 'yearling horse, cow' DE.
         B972, 826.

The examples (13–15) illustrate Lithuanian compounds with native members and represent all the categories discussed above, i.e. determinative (13a), possessive (14a) and verbal governing (15a) compounds with generalised IPs and zero interfixes. These Lithuanian compounds are rendered by non-compound equivalents in German. In (13), an N+N dependent determinative compound in Lithuanian corresponds to a simplex noun in German. In (14), an N+N possessive compound in Lithuanian has a German suffixed -er derivative as a counterpart. The Lithuanian compound noun (15a) is characterised by both masculine and feminine forms. It is an N+V verbal governing compound, where German has a word combination.

4. Lithuanian compound calques in B

There is almost no mention of previous research on calques and borrowings in B. A short overview of the origin of Lithuanian vocabulary can be found in the introductory chapter to the documentary edition of B (Drotvinas 2009: I, XXXIV–XXXVII). Drotvinas pays attention to lexical borrowings as well as hybrids. He has also briefly described Lithuanian calques based on German compounds in the German-Lithuanian dictionaries of the seventeenth century. He distinguishes between regular and non-regular calques. The first type covers those Lithuanian compounds that are absolute equivalents of German compounds, cf. LT karšt-lig-ė <Karßtligge> 'fever' (< karšt-is 'fever' + lig-a 'illness' + IP -ė) and DE Hitz-krankheit <Hitzkranckheit> (< Hitze 'fever' + Krankheit 'illness') lit. 'fever-illness'. The second type of calques includes Lithuanian nominal word combinations based on German compounds, cf. LT Dievo [gen.sg.] baimė <Diewo baime> 'fear of god', lit. 'God's fear', and DE Gott-es-furcht (< Gott-es gen.sg. 'God's' + Furcht 'fear') (Drotvinas 1989: 76–78). The term semi-calque is used to denote those cases when the semantics of one member of a compound calque differs from the semantics of the compound member in a donor language, cf. LT žiurk-žolės, pl. <Żurk-Żoles> 'rat-poison' (< žiurk-ė 'rat' + žol-ės, nom.pl. of žol-ė 'herbs; grass' + IP -ės, pl.) lit. 'rat-herbs' and DE Ratte-n-pulver <Ratze-n-pulver> (< Ratte-n, gen.pl. of Ratte 'rat' + Pulver 'powder') lit. 'rat-powder' (1989: 78–79).

4.1 The identification and overall characteristic of compound calques

In my analysis, I identified compound calques on the basis of linguistic and extra-linguistic criteria. The linguistic criteria are as follows:

- The use of a suspected calque in written sources only
- The existence of non-compound synonyms of a suspected compound calque
- The category of a suspected compound calque
- The part of speech of a suspected compound calque
- The semantics of a suspected compound calque

The extra-linguistic criterion includes various innovations in people's material and spiritual life, because in many cases the process of calquing and borrowing in general is culturally and socially motivated (Haspelmath 2009: 35–37, 46–50; Matras 2009: 168–172).

It stands to reason that the criteria given above are interdependent. The more criteria that can be applied, the higher probability for a compound in hand to be analysed as a calque. For example, if a compound is known from written sources only and is a noun representing an N+N pattern with a cultural meaning, it is a strong candidate to the class of calques. The next step is finding a source in a donor language. On the basis of comparison of a recipient language compounds and their equivalents in a donor language, different types of calques can be distinguished. Absolute compound calques are illustrated in (16) and (17).

(16) a. psalm-giesm-ė (< psalm-as + giesm-ė + IP -ė) <Psalm=Giesme> LT
     b. Psalm-lied (< Psalm + Lied) < Psalm Lied > DE
         'psalm-song' (N+N) both LT and DE, i.e. a psalm. B987.

(17) a. klyst-kel-ias/ -is (< klyst-a PRS3 of klys-ti + kel-ias + IPs -ias/ -is) <Klystkelas/ Klýstkelis> LT
     b. Irr-weg (< irr-en + Weg) <Irr Weg> DE
         'to mistake-road' (V+N) both LT and DE, i.e. mistaken path. B256, 41.

Absolute compound calques is the name I use for what Haugen (1953: 393–394) and Haspelmath (2009: 39) call *loan translations* or *calques*. They show a stem to stem copy of a compound in the donor language and also copy the semantics of the members and the pattern of the compound. The examples (16–17) illustrate names for cultural concepts.[5] In both languages, (16) has a prototypical N+N pattern and (17) a V+N pattern. The nominal members of the Lithuanian compound calques can both be native, as *giesmė* ('sacred song') in (16a) and *kelias* ('road') in (17a) and borrowed, as *psalmas* ('psalm'), a Slavism, in (16a) nouns, while the verbs are only native, cf. *klyst-a* PRS3 of *klys-ti* 'to mistake' (17a).

Another type is non-absolute compound calques, of which (18–20) are examples.

(18) a. zyl-klėtk-a (< zyl-ė + klėtk-a + IP -a) <Zylkletka> LT
     b. Meise-kasten (< Meise + Kasten) <Meise Kasten> DE
         'tit-cage' (N+N) LT vs. 'tit-box' (N+N) DE, i.e. a cage/ box for a tit. B906.

(19) a. pyv-neš-is (< pyv-as + neš-ti INF + IP -is) <Piwneszis> LT
     b. Bier-träg-er (< Bier + Träg-er < trag-en + SF -er) <Bier Träger> DE
         'beer-carry' (N+V) LT vs. 'beer-carri-er' (N+V+SF) DE, i.e. beer carrier.
         B987.

(20) a. vyn-spaud-a (< vyn-as + spaud-ė PRS3 of spaus-ti + IP -a) <Wyn Spauda> LT
     b. Wein-kelter (< Wein + Kelter) <Wein=Kelter> DE
         'grape-to press' (N+V) LT vs. 'grape-press' (N+N) DE, i.e. a press for grapes.
         B777.

In *non-absolute* or *creative compound calques*, complex words (compounds or derivatives) or combinations of words in the donor language give rise to partial copies in the borrowing language. For Lithuanian creative compound calques based on German compounds I distinguish three main types of compound calques according to the type of differences from the compounds in the donor language:

• in the semantics of one member of a compound;
• in the pattern of a compound (except for cases with/without interfix);
• in the pattern of a compound and semantics of one member of it.

Example (18a) illustrates a non-absolute N+N dependent determinative cultural compound calque *zyl-klėtk-a* 'a cage for a tit' (cf. DE *Meise-kasten* 'a box for a tit') with a semantic difference compared to the second member of a compound, i.e. the DE *Kasten* 'box' is rendered by the LT Slavism *klėtka* 'cage' and not by the Slavism *dėžė* 'box'. Example (19a) shows a non-absolute verbal governing compound calque with the difference in the pattern of compound, i.e. a German synthetic N+V+SF compound *Bier-träg-er* 'beer carrier' is rendered by the N+V[+IP] compound *pyv-neš-ys*, the pattern of which is widespread in Lithuanian (the exact morpheme to morpheme copy would be †*pyv-neš-ėj-as*, i.e. N+V+SF[+IP]). It is clear from example (20a) that the Lithuanian N+V[+IP] verbal governing compound *vyn-spaud-a* 'grape-press' was creatively modelled on the basis of a German dependent determinative N+N compound *Wein-kelter* with a difference in the pattern of the compound and the semantics of its second member, i.e. the noun DE *Kelter* 'press' was rendered by the verb LT *spausti* 'to press' with the subsequent change in the pattern of compound. An absolute copy of this German compound would be †*vyn-pres-as* or †*vyn-pres-is* (< *vyn-as* 'grape' + *pres-as* 'press' + IPs *-as/-is*). The first member of the Lithuanian compound (18a) is the native noun *zylė* 'tit' with the Slavic loanwords *pyvas* 'beer' and *vynas* 'grape; vine' in (19a–20a).

Calques are copious among Lithuanian compounds in *B*, while material-borrowings are rare.[6] The amount of calques depends directly on the category and pattern of compounds. Calques are most copious in the group of determinative compounds, in particular in the case of prototypical N+N formations that represent, as a rule, the dominant pattern of cultural borrowings. Calques in other categories of compounds, many of which are language specific, are comparatively rare and mostly rendered by means of the productive A+N (possessive compounds) and V+N (verbal governing compounds) patterns. Further detailed analysis of Lithuanian calques in *B* will be based on the main categories of compounds reviewed above (see section 3).

4.2 Determinative compound calques

The category of determinative compounds is most subject to the process of calquing. The majority of calques in hand are absolute copies of German dependent compounds represented by the prototypical N+N pattern. The members of compound calques can be both native and borrowed nouns. The most widespread are patterns with one loanword used twice more frequently in the position of the first member (21a, 22a) than in the position of the second member (23a) of a compound.

(21) a. budel-bern-is (< budel-is + bern-as + IP -is) <Buddelbernis> LT
     b. Büttel-knecht (< Büttel + Knecht) <Büttel Knecht> DE
         'butcher-labourer' (N+N) both LT and DE, i.e. butcher's assistant. B305.

(22) a. kros-but-is (< kros-as + but-as + IP -is) <Krosbuttis> LT
     b. Färbe-haus (< Farbe + Haus) <Färbe Hauß> DE
         'dye-house' (N+N) both LT and DE. B451.

(23) a. kaln-altor-ius (< kaln-as + altor-ius + IP -ius) <Kaln=altorus> LT
     b. Berg-altar (< Berg + Altar) <Berg Altar> DE
         'mountain-altar' (N+N) LT and DE, i.e. altar on a mountain. B191.

The examples in (21–23) as well as in (2), (4) and (16) illustrate dependent determinative absolute compound calques having the N+N structure and both the first (21, 22, 4, 16) and the second (23, 2) borrowed members. The first members of the Lithuanian calques (21a), (22a), (4a) and (16a) are represented by the Germanism *budelis* 'butcher' and the Slavisms *krosas* 'dye', *karalius* 'king' and *psalmas* 'psalm', while the second members are represented by native nouns *bernas* 'labourer', *butas* 'house', *žaislas* 'game' and *giesmė* 'sacred song'.

The first member of the Lithuanian calques *kaln-altor-ius* (23a) and *lauk-aguon-ai* (2a) is represented by native nouns *kalnas* 'mountain' and *laukas* 'field', while the second members are loanwords, i.e. a Slavism *altorius* 'altar' (24a) and a Germanism *aguonai* pl. 'poppy' (2a). On the integration of compound calques into the word formations system of Lithuanian see section 4.5.

Dependent determinative compound calques can also have both borrowed members, see examples (24a–25a).

(24) a. alyv-kodž-ius (< alyv-a + kodž-ius + IP -ius) <Alÿw Kodzius> LT
     b. Öl-krug (< Öl + Krug) <Oel Krug> DE
         'oil-jug' (N+N) both LT and DE. B958.

(25) a. rot-pon-as/-is (< rot-a + pon-as + IPs -as/-is) <Rot=Ponas/ Rót=Ponis> LT
     b. Rat-herr (< Rat + Herr) <Rath Herr> DE
         'council-gentleman' (N+N) both LT and DE, i.e. a member of council. B996.

Both members of the Lithuanian dependent determinative cultural compound calques (24a) and (25a) as well as *kalk-kakal-ys* 'lime-stove' in (3a) are borrowed nouns, i.e. the Slavisms *alyva* 'oil', *kodžius* 'jug' (24a) and *ponas* (25a) and the Germanisms *rota* 'council' (25a), *kalkis* 'lime' and *kakalys* 'stove' (3a).

About half of the Lithuanian dependent determinative compounds contain both native members, and more than half of these formations can be attributed to the calques, see examples (26a–28a).

(26) a. kepen-žol-ės, pl. (< kepen-os, pl. + žol-ės, pl. + IP -ės, pl.) <Képen' Zóles> LT
b. Leber-kraut (< Leber + Kraut) <Leber Kraut> DE
'liver-grass' (N+N) both LT and DE, i.e. violet, liverwort. B855.

(27) a. šiaur-vėj-is (< šiaur-ė + vėj-as + IP -is) <Szaur=Wejis> LT
b. Nord-wind (< Nord + Wind) <Nord Wind> DE
'north-wind' (N+N) both LT and DE, i.e. northern wind. B951.

(28) a. vair-virv-ė (< vair-as + virv-ė + IP -ė) <Wair=wirwe> LT
b. Ruder-band (< Ruder + Band) <Ruder Band> DE
'oar-rope' (N+N) both LT and DE, i.e. the rope for a boat. B1025.

The examples (26a–28a) illustrate absolute dependent determinative N+N compound calques possessing both native members, i.e. *kepenos* 'liver' and *žolės*, pl. 'grass' (26a), *šiaurė* 'north' and *vėjas* 'wind' (27a), *vairas* 'oar' and *virvė* 'rope' (28a). In the case of (27a), there is a frequently-used Lithuanian paradigmatic derivative, *šiaur-ys*, with the same meaning.

Besides the predominant absolute dependent determinative compound calques, there are also cases of non-absolute calques that have differences both in the semantics (29a–30a) and structure (31a–32a) of the compounds.

(29) a. riešut-lazd-a (< riešut-as + lazd-a + IP -a) <Reszut'Lazda> LT
b. Nuss-baum (< Nuss+ Baum) <Nuß Baum> DE
'nut-stick' (N+N) LT vs. 'nut-tree' (N+N) DE, i.e. walnut. B953

(30) a. vyn-med-is (< vyn-as + med-is + IP -is) <Wÿnmedis> LT
b. Wein-stock (< Wein + Stock) <Wein Stock> DE
'vine-tree' (N+N) LT vs. 'vine-stick' (N+N) DE, i.e. grape. B265, 682.

(31) a. kar-kamar-a (< kar-as + kamar-a + IP -a) <Kar-Kamára> LT
b. Krieg-s-kammer (< Krieg-s, gen.sg. + Kammer) <Kriegs Cammer> DE
'war-cabinet' (N+N) LT vs. 'war's-cabinet' (N$_{gen.sg.}$+N) DE, i.e. a state institution in East Prussia. B823.

(32) a. šun-žvaigžd-ė (< šuo [stem šun-] + žvaigžd-ė + IP -ė) <Szun'Zwaigzde> LT
b. Hund-s-stern (< Hund-s, gen.sg. + Stern) <Hunds Stern> DE
'dog-star' (N+N) LT vs. 'dog's-star' DE (N$_{gen.sg.}$+N), i.e. dog-star (Syrius). B732.

The Lithuanian dependent determinative compounds (29a, 30a) are an illustration of cultural calques *riešut-lazd-a* (cf. DE *Nuss-baum*) 'walnut' and *vyn-med-is* (cf. DE *Wein-stock*) 'grape' which show difference in semantics of one of the members of a compound, i.e. of the second member in this case, cf. LT *lazda* 'stick' and DE *Baum* 'tree' (29), LT *medis* 'tree' and DE *Stock* 'stick' (30). The first member LT *riešutas* 'nut' is a native noun (29a), while *vynas* 'vine' is a Slavism (30a).

The examples (31b, 32b) illustrate German dependent determinative $N_{gen.sg.}$ + N compounds, the so-called case compounds *Krieg-s-kammer* and *Hund-s-stern*, which are rendered by Lithuanian N+N, i.e. stem+stem, compounds *kar-kamar-a* and *šun-žvaigžd-ė* during the process of calquing. As a matter of fact, in this case a pattern peculiar to German compounding is rendered by a prototypical N+N pattern in Lithuanian. The members of calques comprise both native nouns (*karas* 'war', *šuo* 'dog', *žvaigždė* 'star') and borrowings (a Slavism *kamara* 'cabinet').

The Lithuanian attributive determinative compound calques based on German attributive compounds are not copious, see examples (33a–34a).

(33) a. skers-stuk-is (< skers-as + stuk-is + IP -is) <Skerstukis> LT

b. Quer-stück (< Quer + Stück) <Quer Stück> DE
   'cross-strip' (A+N) both LT and DE, i.e. cross-strip (of land). B991.

(34) a. papild-apier-a (< papild-o PRS3 of papild-y-ti + apier-a + IP -a)
   <Papild=Apiera> LT

b. Füll-opfer (< füll-en + Opfer) <Füllopffer> DE
   'supplement-sacrifice' (V+N) both LT and DE, i.e. extra sacrifice. B507.

The examples (33, 34) illustrate absolute attributive determinative compound calques, cf. LT *skers-stuk-is* and DE *Quer-stück* (A+N) 'cross-strip (of land)'[7] (33), LT *papild-apier-a* and DE *Füll-opfer* (V+N) lit. 'supplement-sacrifice' (34). The second members of Lithuanian compounds are loanwords from German (*stukis* 'strip, piece', 33a) and Slavic (*apiera* 'sacrifice', 34a). As regards the first members of these Lithuanian compounds, they originate from the native adjective *skersas*, masc. 'cross' (33a) and the present tense form of the verb *papildyti* 'add, supplement' (a prefixed *pa-* derivative) (34a).

4.3 Possessive compound calques

The equivalents of Lithuanian possessive compounds are in most cases also compounds in German, but only about a quarter of them can be viewed as a source of calques in Lithuanian. Lithuanian possessive compound calques are both absolute and non-absolute. As the examples of Lithuanian absolute possessive compound calques (9a) in section 3.2 and (35a) below demonstrate.

(35) a. gruč-pilv-is (< gruč-ė + pilv-as + IP -is) <Grucz=Pilwis> LT

b. Grütze-bauch (< Grütze + Bauch) <Grütze Bauch> DE
   'porridge-belly' (N+N) both LT and DE, i.e. having a belly full of porridge. B610.

The possessive compounds above have Num+N (9) and N+N (35) patterns in both languages. Both members of the Lithuanian compound (9a) and the second member of the formation (35a) are native words, while the first member of the compound (35a) is a Slavic loanword.

Non-absolute Lithuanian possessive compound calques differ from donor language compounds mostly in the structure of a compound, see example (36a).

(36) a. liūt-galv-is (< liūt-as + galv-a + IP -is) <Lutgalwis> LT
     b. Löwe-n-kopf (< Löwe-n, gen.sg. + Kopf) <Löwen Kopff> DE
        'lion-head' (N+N) LT vs. 'lion's-head' ($N_{gen.sg.}$+N) DE. B884.

The examples in (36) illustrate the process of calquing in which the German possessive compound is rendered into Lithuanian as a possessive compound, except for the specific Germanic feature, of the gen.sg. form of the first member. The first member of the Lithuanian calque is a Slavism *liūtas* 'lion', while the second one is a native noun *galva* 'head'.

4.4 Verbal governing compound calques

Half of the equivalents of Lithuanian verbal governing compounds are also compounds in German, but only about a quarter of them can be viewed as a source of calques in Lithuanian (the same ratio is characteristic of possessive compounds, see section 4.3). There are only non-absolute Lithuanian verbal governing N+V compound calques, which are coined following the example of both German N+V+SF synthetic (37b, 19b) or N+N dependent determinative compounds (38b). The choice of a donor language compound pattern depends mostly on the semantics of the compound. The verbal governing compound calques having the meaning of agent are, as a rule, patterned after the example of German synthetic N+V+SF compounds.

(37) a. kalk-deg-is (< kalk-is + deg-ti + IP -is) <Kalkdegis> LT
     b. Kalk-brenn-er (< Kalk + Brenn-er < brenn-en + SF -er) <Kalck Brenner> DE
        'lime-burn' (N+V) LT vs. 'lime-burn-er' (N+V+SF) DE, i.e. one who burns lime. B767.

The Lithuanian verbal governing compound calques (37a) and (19a) in section 4.1 have an agent meaning and an N+V[+IP] structure, while the compounds of the donor language (37b) and (19b) belong to the synthetic type N+V+SF-*er*. The second members of the Lithuanian compounds at hand are the native verbs *degti* 'burn' and *nešti* 'carry', while the first members are borrowings, i.e. a Germanism *kalkis* 'lime' (38a) and a Slavism *pyvas* 'beer' (19a) (native nouns are also possible in this case).

The Lithuanian verbal governing compound calques having the meaning of instrument are, as a rule, patterned after the example of German dependent determinative compounds (the difference in semantics of the second member in this case is inevitable), cf. (10) and (20). The Lithuanian verbal governing compound calques (10a) and (20a) have an instrument meaning and an N+V structure, while the compounds of the donor language belong to the prototypical N+N type. The second members of Lithuanian compounds (37a), (10a) and (20a) are the native verbs *degti* 'burn' (37a), *mušti* 'beat' (10a) and *spausti* 'press' (20a), while the first members can be native nouns, e.g. *sviestas* in (10a), or borrowed, e.g. *vynas* in (20a), a Slavism, and *kalkis* in (37a), a Germanism.

Coming to the end of the analysis of Lithuanian compound calques in *B*, one feature of the process of calquing should be mentioned, viz. very rare cases when calques are patterned on German compounds that have a three-stem structure, see example (38a).

> (38) a. šun-laišk-ai/-iai, pl. (< šuo [stem šun-] + laišk-ai, pl. + IPs -ai/ -iai, pl.) <Szunlaiszkai/ Szunlaiszkei>LT
>
> b. Hund-s-zunge-n-kraut (< Hund-s, gen.sg. + Zunge-n, gen.pl. + Kraut) <Hunds Zungen Kraut> DE
> 'dog-leaves' (N+N) LT vs. 'dog's-tongue's-grass' ($N_{gen.sg.}$ +$N_{gen.pl.}$ +N) DE, i.e. hound's tongue. B732, 273.

The example (38a) illustrates a Lithuanian possessive compound calque coined after a German dependent determinative compound with three stems. As a matter of fact, the process of calquing results in a two-stem formation characteristic of Lithuanian compounding, i.e. a grass the leaves of which have a connection to dog (38).

All in all, throughout the analysis of Lithuanian compound calques in *B*, it was discovered that the patterns that were not characteristic of Lithuanian compounding were not involved in the process of calquing. For example, one can find only a few item-to-item compound calques modelled on German-specific synthetic compounds, see example (39a).

> (39) a. lent-žaid-ik-as (< lent-a + žaid-ik-as < žaid-ė PST3 from žais-ti + SF -ik- + IP -as) <Lentzaidikkas> LT
>
> b. Brett-spiel-er (< Brett + Spiel-er < spiel-en + SF -er) <Brett Spieler> DE
> 'board-play-er' (N+V+SF) both LT and DE, i.e. chess-player or draughts-player. B290.

The example (39) illustrates a very rare Lithuanian absolute compound calque which patterns morpheme to morpheme German synthetic compound. A creative calque with the same meaning could be †*lent-žaid-ys* (N+V[+IP -*ys*]).

4.5 The integration of compound calques into the word formation system of Lithuanian

The majority of compounds of modern Lithuanian are integrated into the word formation system by means of generalised inflectional paradigms -*is*/-*ys* (masc.) and -*ė* (fem.) (for more see Urbutis 1965: 447f., 453f., 460, 467; Stundžia 2016: 3091). This generalisation seems to be characteristic of compounding also in *B*; nevertheless, as regards compound calques, part of them have the generalised inflectional paradigms and others are only adapted with IPs -*a*, -*(i)as* (pl. -*(i)ai*) and -*(i)us* taken from the second nominal member. The latter cases are more typical of determinative compound calques which have borrowed second members, particularly representing loanwords that are not old, cf. *(kar-)kamara* 'war-cabinet' and *kamar-a* (31a), a Slavism, *(papild-)apier-a* 'supplement sacrifice' and *apier-a* (34a), a Slavism, *(lauk-)aguon-ai* 'field-puppy' and *aguon-ai* (2a), a Germanism, *(alyv-)kodž-ius* 'oil-jug' and *kodž-ius* (24a), a Slavism, *(kaln-)altor-ius* 'mountain-altar' and *altor-ius* (23a), a Slavism. In the light of this finding, one can hypothesise that dependent determinative compound calques having a second borrowed nominal member are more weakly integrated into the word formation system of Lithuanian, and that a certain interrelation between matter and pattern borrowing exists.

I have also found rare cases of variation of inflectional paradigms of compound calques and compounds in general in *B*. Examples we have seen above include (17), (25) and (38). Another example *is kiaul-uog-a* sg. (IP -a)/ *kiaul-uog-ės* pl. (IP -*ė*, pl. -*ės*) lit. 'pig-berry' (cf. *uog-a*, pl. *uog-os* 'berry'), B201, 272. The competition of the two variants of the N+N pattern, i.e. the one which is only morphologically adapted and the other which is characterised by generalised inflectional paradigms, shows the ongoing development towards integration of the compound calques into the word formation system of eighteenth-century Lithuanian. It is worth noting that in the Lithuanian-German dictionary by Kurschat (1883), which came more than 100 years later than *B*, almost all compound calques have the generalised inflectional paradigms.

5. Conclusions

The main results of the present research can be summarised as follows:

- Only two-stem absolute and non-absolute compound calques are character-istic of eighteenth-century Lithuanian as shown by the data of the dictionary by Brodowski (the two-stem structure is an essential feature of composition in Lithuanian).
- Compounding patterns characteristic of German were not introduced into Lithuanian apart from single cases.
- The most copious examples of both absolute and non-absolute compound calques have been revealed in the category of determinative compounds; in particular, in those belonging to the prototypical N+N formations, which as a rule represent cultural borrowings. Possessive and verbal governing compound calques occur relatively rarely, and most of them are non-absolute copies of German compounds.
- The semantics of members of compound calques are rendered both with borrowed and native nouns. Patterns that have borrowed member(s) prevail, and that is an argument for the interrelation between material and structural borrowing.
- The coexistence of two types of compound calques can be identified from the point of view of their integration into the word formation system of Lithuanian:

    a)   calques which are fully integrated into the word formation system by generalising inflectional paradigms *-is/-ys* (masc.) and *-ė* (fem.), which are characteristic of Lithuanian nominal compounding;

    b)   calques which take the inflectional paradigms *-a, -(i)as* or *-(i)us* from the second nominal member of a compound and are therefore only morphologically adapted and not integrated into the word formation system.

- Infrequent cases of competition between the two types of calques show an ongoing development towards the integration of compound calques into the word formation system of eighteenth-century Lithuanian.

The findings listed above show that the overall Germanic influence on Lithuanian compounding in the eighteenth century was not strong. It seems that it was limited mostly to the increase of compound calques based on common patterns, in particular on the prototypical N+N pattern. The patterns exclusively characteristic of German compounding were rendered by patterns that were typical of Lithuanian compounding in the process of calquing. Therefore, Lithuanian compounding did not get closer to German compounding. The outcomes of the Lithuanian and German language contact summarised here can be partially explained by puristic attitudes that were spread among educated Lithuanians and Lithuanian-oriented Germans or Poles in East Prussia.

What are the general lessons that can be learned from this case study? It seems that the productivity of calquing depends on the type of formations, the intensity of language contact, as well as on the attitudes of educated people and the prestige of the donor language. One could expect the use of foreign structural patterns of formations when the influence of a prestige donor language is strong and there are no puristic attitudes, while when the influence is not strong and/or puristic attitudes are involved, the structural patterns that are common for a donor and a recipient language or typical of the latter will be used in the process of calquing.

Abbreviations used for explaining examples

A	adjective
gen.	genitive
IF	interfix (linking element)
INF	infinitive
IP	inflectional paradigm (inflection class marker)
N	noun
Num	numeral
pl.	plural (always nominative)
PRS	present
PST	past
sg.	singular
SF	suffix
V	verb

Acknowledgements

I would like to thank Hannah Lucy Shipman (Vilnius University) for editing my English in this chapter. Needless to say, all potential errors are mine.

Notes

1. A list of abbreviations for grammatical markers used in this chapter is given at the end of the chapter.
2. For the Lithuanian examples both the modern and original spelling have been provided (for the latter spelling, angle brackets are used).
3. The numbered examples are given with morpheme breaks in modern spelling and original orthography in angle brackets as follows:

   a. Compound (< 1st member + [IF] + 2nd member + IP) <original spelling> LT
   b. Compound (< 1st member + [IF] + 2nd member + [SF]) <original spelling> DE

   The order is glosses, patterns, translation and source. The number at the end indicates the position in the dictionary.
4. Words that are not attested in any Lithuanian text are marked †.
5. The original and widespread Lithuanian compound that has the same meaning is *šun-kel-is*, lit. 'dog-path' (< *šuo*, stem [šun-] + *kel-ias* + IP *-is*).
6. There are about thirty morphonologically adapted lexical borrowings based on German compounds, the majority of which represent specific terms used in the life and structure of German society, e.g. LT *Pucmeseris* <Pucmesseris> (< DE *Putz Meßer*) 'shaving knife' B956, LT *širmokeris* <Szirmokeris> (< DE *Geschir Macher*) 'dish-maker' B562.
7. The original Lithuanian word carrying the identical meaning is a paradigmatic derivative *padal-ė* <padale> B991 (< *padal-y-ti* 'to divide').

References

Barz, Irmhild (2016), 'German', in P. O. Müller, I. Ohnheiser, S. Olsen and F. Rainer (eds), *Word-Formation. An International Handbook of the Languages of Europe*, Berlin: De Gruyter, vol. 4, pp. 2387–2410.

Bukelskytė-Čepelė, Kristina (2017), *Nominal Compounds in Old Latvian Texts in the 16th and 17th Centuries*, PhD dissertation, Stockholm: Stockholm University.

Drotvinas, Vincentas (1967), *XVI–XVIII a. lietuviškų raštų sudurtiniai daiktavardžiai* [16th–18th-Century Patterns of Lithuanian Compound Nouns], PhD dissertation (manuscript), Vilnius: Vilnius University.

Drotvinas, Vincentas (1989), 'Leksikos vertiniai XVII a. vokiečių-lietuvių kalbų žodynuose' [Lexical Calques in 17th-Century German-Lithuanian Dictionaries], *Baltistica*, 25: 1, 75–82.

Drotvinas, Vincentas (ed.) (2009), *Jokūbas Brodovskis. Lexicon Germanico-Lithvanicum et Lithvanico-Germanicum* [Manuscript Dictionary of the 18th Century;

Documentary Edition Containing a Facsimile, Transcript and Word Register], Vilnius: Lietuvių kalbos institutas, vols 1–3.

Haspelmath, Martin (2009), 'Lexical Borrowing: Concepts and Issues', in M. Haspelmath and U. Tadmor (eds), *Loanwords in the World's Languages: A Comparative Handbook*, Berlin: De Gruyter, pp. 35–54.

Haugen, Einar (1953), *The Norwegian Language in America*, Philadelphia: University of Pennsylvania Press.

Hock, Wolfgang (ed.) (2015), *Altlitauisches etymologisches Wörterbuch*, Hamburg: Baar, vols 1–3.

Kurschat, Friedrich (1883), *Wörterbuch der littauischen Sprache. 2. Theil: Littauisch-Deutsches Wörterbuch*, Halle: Verlag der Buchhandlung des Waisenhauses.

Matras, Yaron (2009), *Language Contact*, Cambridge: Cambridge University Press.

Neef, Martin (2015), 'Synthetic Compounds in German', in P. O. Müller, I. Ohnheiser, S. Olsen and F. Rainer (eds), *Word-Formation. An International Handbook of the Languages of Europe*, Berlin: De Gruyter, vol. 1, pp. 582–593.

Olsen, Birgit A. (1999), *The Noun in Biblical Armenian: Origin and Word-Formation: With Special Emphasis on the Indo-European Heritage*, Berlin: De Gruyter.

Olsen, Birgit A. (2002), 'Thoughts on Indo-European Compounds – Inspired by a Look at Armenian', *Transactions of the Philological Society*, 100: 1, 233–257.

Plaušinaitytė, Lina (2010), *Jokūbo Brodovskio žodyno leksikografinis metodas* [The Lexicographic Method of Jacob Brodowski's Dictionary], unpublished PhD dissertation, Vilnius: Vilnius University.

Smoczyński, Wojciech (2018), *Lithuanian Etymological Dictionary*, Berlin: Peter Lang.

Stundžia, Bonifacas (2016), 'Lithuanian', in P. O. Müller, I. Ohnheiser, S. Olsen and F. Rainer (eds), *Word-Formation. An International Handbook of the Languages of Europe*, Berlin: De Gruyter, vol. 5, pp. 3089–3106.

Urbutis, Vincas (1965), 'Sudurtiniai daiktavardžiai' [Compound Nouns], in K. Ulvydas (ed.), *Lietuvių kalbos gramatika*, Vilnius: Mintis, vol. 1, pp. 437–473.

Wohlgemuth, Jan (2009), *A Typology of Verbal Borrowings*, Berlin and New York: De Gruyter.

Zinkevičius, Zigmas (1996), *The History of the Lithuanian Language*, Vilnius: Mokslo ir enciklopedijų leidykla.

6

(Pseudo-)Anglicisms as Nominal Compounds in Italian

Silvia Cacchiani

The occurrence of Anglicisms and pseudo-Anglicisms in Italian has steadily increased over the last few decades. The phenomenon is often referred to as the Anglicisation of the Italian language and appears to be moving Italian towards a new standard. The present study reports on a qualitative investigation into foreign patterns of word formation in contact-induced language change. My research question, therefore, is one about the convergence of word formation patterns across English and Italian (section 1): while English shows a strong preference for the right-hand head rule, Italian generally adheres to left-headedness in nominal compounding (section 2). Taking a broadly functional-cognitive perspective on the outcomes of contact with English right-headed word formation, the analysis discusses Italian classifying and identifying compounds primarily mediated through the press or coined for use as proper names (N_{PR}) and trademarks (section 3). As will be seen, reductions to simplexes (section 4), loan translations, calques and Anglicisms (section 5), as well as second-generation neoclassical compounds, right-headed hybrid analogues and constructs with cognate bases that are formed in Italian (section 6) only ever have a reinforcing effect on word formation patterns that are already available to Italian, favouring their spread from learned to non-learned word formation.

1. (Pseudo-)Anglicisms in Italian

Over the last decades, a growing number of lexical borrowings from English have entered Italian. Whereas until the mid-twentieth century the core vocabulary of Italian numbered very few early Anglicisms (1a), borrowings since the 1950s (1b) and recent Anglicisms (1c) now count among the highly – or most – frequent words in the Italian core vocabulary (NVdB 2016).

(1) a. baby (1877), bar (1892), sport (1829)
     b. design (1954), gay (1959), pop (1964), show (1954)
     c. email (1991), internet (1997), post (1996), web (1996)[1]

Together with the incremental increase in pseudo-Anglicisms (i.e. forms that depart from the English source form but 'sound English' to non-native Italian users, e.g. IT *autogrill*, N 'motorway service area', 1963 < IT *Autogrill®*, N_{PR}), they are a sign of high Anglicisation (McArthur 2002) and appear to be moving Italian towards a new standard (Bombi 2017).[2]

Additionally, while derivations formed by an Italian affix plus foreign word are standard practice (2a), (sets of) complex words are formed with borrowings that are in general use or are generally understood by the average Italian speaker (2b).

(2) a. lowcostismo (2005) 'low cost -ism', i.e. low-cost mantra
     b. aereo killer (1989)' killer plane'
         afa-killer (1994) 'killer heat'
         caldo-killer (1994) 'killer hot weather'
         gambero killer 'killer crayfish', i.e. red Louisiana crayfish
         squalo killer 'killer shark'
         zanzara killer 'killer mosquito'

Unlike native adjectives and nouns, IT *killer* (1936) – an Anglicism and a highly frequent lexeme in the Italian core vocabulary – is uninflected. The examples in (2b) specify the relation 'N1 is a killer' in the pattern 'N + *killer*', which reverses English constituent order.

Coining new words may go all the way to extra-grammatical compounding (Dressler 2000; Ronneberger-Sibold 2010, 2012; Mattiello 2012; Cacchiani 2015), as in (3).

(3) a. IT Renxit (2016) < (Matteo) Renzi, N_{PR} + exit (1978)[3]
     b. IT tenager (2015) 'tween' < ten (1967) + teenager (1951) [SC][4]

In (3a), Renxit illustrates the case of pseudo-Anglicisms formed via analogy on individual Anglicisms or sets of Anglicisms. The blend of personal name plus noun extends the set of analogical borrowings that include *Grexit* < *Greece* + *exit* (2012), *Brexit* < *Britain* + *exit* (2016) and, possibly, *Czexit*, *Frexit*, *Spexit* and *Swexit*, with limited currency in Italian. In (3b), recourse is made to paronymy (see also (5a) below), which involves phonemic substitution and phonological similarity to established neighbours (Konieczna 2012; Cacchiani 2016, 2017; Mattiello 2017): the speaker analyses *teenager* as a composite structure and forms the blend *tenager*, with alignment of SW1 and SW2 at the left edge and phonemic substitution of a SW2 segment (/i/ for /ɛ/) in pretonic syllable (Cacchiani 2016).

Overall, speakers of Italian as a recipient language have become agents of borrowing (Winford 2010). Loanwords have oftentimes entered Italian as necessary loans, i.e. with the corresponding innovation (Öhmann 1961) (4).

(4) a. www (1992) / web (1993) / World Wide Web
     b. internet (1997)
     c. blog (2000)

In the exceptional case of (4), thanks to technological diffusion and the democratisation of means to access the current online environment, *web* in (4a), though not *www* and *World Wide Web*, as well as (4b–c) have acquired the special status of most frequent lexemes in the core vocabulary of Italian (NVdB 2016), along with very few other Anglicisms (e.g. *bar*, 1892, *film*, 1889, *ok/okay*, 1931, *quiz*, 1949, *test*, 1895).

A second reason behind borrowing is prestige. As a matter of fact, the widespread perception of English as the socially dominant and most prestigious contact language has favoured recourse to (pseudo-)Anglicisms and luxury loans in Italian media discourse and the press, politics, marketing campaigns and the language of advertising in general (cf. among others Iacobini 2015; Bombi 2017). As described in Öhmann (1961), luxury loans exist in parallel to near-equivalents in the recipient language (5).

(5) a. IT Halloweek, N_{PR} (2016) < Halloween, N_{PR} (1995) + week[5]
     b. IT revisione di spesa; IT spending review (2012) < EN spending review

Luxury loans are used for a number of stylistic and pragmatic effects. For instance, (5a), *Halloweek* 'Halloween week' [IT settimana di Halloween] illustrates how business and marketing exploit English as a valuable linguistic commodity (Cameron 2012) for foreign branding. In the case of (5b) the luxury loan *spending review* is used in Italian politics for other reasons, including intentional disguise (Galinsky 1967).

2. Headedness in Italian nominal constructs

It has long been noted that the unmarked order in SVO languages like Italian is for modifiers to follow the head (Greenberg 1963) and for left-headed compounding in general. For instance, in (6a) the Italian left-headed compounds *navetta spaziale, nave spaziale, navicella spaziale*, with a relational adjective (*spaziale*) as second constituent, render right-headed English equivalents (*space shuttle* and *spaceship*, with a relational noun as first constituent). However, right-headed neoclassical compounds with identical meaning are also available to Italian (6b).

(6) a. IT navetta spaziale (1974) 'space shuttle' < EN space shuttle
         IT nave spaziale, navicella spaziale (1974) 'spaceship' < EN spaceship
     b. IT cosmonave (1961) 'cosmo-COMB.FORM ship', i.e. spaceship
         IT astronave (1961) 'astro-COMB.FORM ship', i.e. spaceship

But 'nominal compounds with their head to the right are [generally understood to be] either survivals from Latin or loan words from other languages' (Scalise 1992: 198), as in (7). The former (Hatcher 1951; Scalise 1992; Bisetto 2004; Iacobini 2004) comprise lexicalised forms (7a) and remains from earlier stages in the development of the language (7b).

(7) a. IT terremoto (1294) 'earth movement', i.e. earthquake < LA terrae mŏtu(m)
         'earth-GEN movement'

     b. IT lungomare (1942) 'along sea', i.e. beach front;
        IT mezzanotte (1313–1319) 'midnight'

Importantly, *lungomare* forms the bottom level of a marginal pattern, the Prep-Noun schema for exocentric nouns. Other specifications are given in (8), where the Italian translations alternate and compete with the Anglicisms in product names.

(8) a. IT dopobarba 'aftershave' (1956), aftershave (1959) < EN aftershave
     b. IT doposole 'aftersun' (1970), aftersun < EN aftersun

Here, English matter came to reinforce a parallel Italian pattern. As to attributive compounds such as lexicalised *mezzanotte* 'midnight' (7b), research on foreign word formation in Italian (Iacobini 2015; Bombi 2017) suggests that English contributes extensively to enhancing the pattern via a number of non-adapted specified $[A-N]_N$ compounds, with a direct modification relation between constituents and inversion of the unmarked Noun-Adj order that is characteristic of Italian (9a). This is also the unmarked order in (9b), *(il) caso Mattei* (vis-à-vis *the Obama case*, with reverse order), with a commemorative relation (Warren 1978; Ortner and Müller-Bolhagen 1991; Schlücker 2016; section 3) established between a juxtaposed noun (*caso* 'case') and a family name (*Mattei*).

(9) a. IT personal computer (1977)
       IT fast food (1982)
       IT new economy (1988)
     b. IT il caso Mattei 'the Mattei- N_{PR} case'

On the other hand, neoclassical compounding is still productive – i.e. not only available but also profitable to different degrees (Corbin 1987; Bauer 2001; see Panocová 2015 for a discussion) – in contemporary Italian (NPN 2008). If language contact involves an increase in convergence of patterns (Bolonyai 1998; Myers-Scotton 2006), then it is safe to assume extensions of neoclassical compounding via the inclusion of base forms (Arndt-Lappe 2015) borrowed from English and second-generation elements, i.e. formatives that have achieved word status, for example IT *foto/foto-* (Iacobini 2004; Radimský 2015; section 6.1). It goes without saying, however, that I am by no means making a case for contact as the sole source of revitalisation. Another key factor is the form-compressing nominal style (Koptjevskaja-Tamm 2013) that characterises press headlines (Bisetto 2004: label jargon), administrative and scientific texts, as well as brand naming for marketing purposes. Among others, this appears to be at play in *Halloweek* or *Renxit* (5) as well as in (10).

(10) a. IT calcioscommesse (1985) 'football bets', i.e. match-fixing scandal
      b. IT parco divertimenti 'amusement-PL park', i.e. fun fare, children's recreation
         area' < IT parco dei divertimenti 'park of amusements'
      c. IT Mauro foto, N_{PR} 'Mauro- N_{PR} photo', i.e. Mauro's photography shop
        IT Foto Mauro, N_{PR} 'photo Mauro- N_{PR}', i.e. Mauro's photography shop

In (10a) we see an external head, (10b) is right-headed, and in (10c) there are two examples of naming mirror constructs.

3. Data selection and theoretical underpinnings

For purposes of this chapter, I share with Booij's (2010) *Construction Morphology* the basic ideas of constructional schemas and of a hierarchical lexicon. I understand constructs as empirically attested tokens of constructions, or constructional schemas with different degrees of abstractness. Constructs unify properties at the phonological, syntactic and semantico-pragmatic levels, thus forming the bottom level of a specific pattern or schema. Since it is not easy to determine whether a construct would count as a compound or a phrase (cf. Lieber and Štekauer 2009), I do not try to draw a line between the two but rather follow Radimský (2015; drawing on Booij 2010) in using *construct* as a cover term for both categories.

At this stage of research, the analysis is strictly qualitative and primarily descriptive, based on a pool of 400 nouns and 400-plus names. Though I have occasionally relied on my own experience and on the acceptability judgements of ten Italian informants with tertiary education [SC], most units were gathered from the relevant literature, dictionaries and databases (last accessed 12 September 2018).

For nouns, I compiled a preliminary catalogue of existing reductions from Anglicisms, and (sets of) analogues (complex forms) and base forms (in the sense of Arndt-Lappe 2015) shared in the analogues drawing on the literature on new words and foreign word formation in Italian (Vogel 1990; Adamo and Della Valle 2006; Lombardi Vallauri 2008; Radimský 2013; Iacobini 2015; Bombi 2017). The list was further expanded and all items were cross-checked against the etymological and morphological information provided in the entries of the following dictionaries and databases: dictionaries of Anglicisms (Görlach 2001) and pseudo-Anglicisms (Furiassi 2006); dictionaries, databases of neologisms and word lovers' blogs of new words (NPN (2008) – *Neologismi. Parole nuove dai giornali*; ONLI (n.d.) – *Osservatorio neologico della lingua italiana*; the NT (n.d.) blog – *Neologismi Treccani Online*); encyclopaedic dictionaries of Italian, including *Vocabolario Treccani* (Treccani 2018), *Grande Dizionario Italiano dell'Uso 2007* (GRADIT 2007), *Il Nuovo De Mauro* (NDM 2001–2018), *Dizionario Sabatini Coletti 2007* (DISC 2008), *loZingarelli2017* (Zingarelli 2016), *il Devoto-Oli. Vocabolario della lingua italiana 2017* (Devoto Oli 2016).

For naming constructs, I searched the online database of the *Ufficio italiano brevetti e marchi* (UIBM n.d.) ('Italian Registration Office for Patents and Trademarks', the Italian counterpart of the UK Intellectual Property Office) for patents, brand names, product names, trademarks formed with the bases already identified for nominal constructs. For additional examples, I relied on the regularly updated word list of the NT blog (*Neologismi Treccani Online*), the Italian word lover's guide to new words from the quality press.

Where available, information about etymology, sense(s) and date of first attestation of English and Italian regular words, borrowings and English-Italian hybrids under consideration was gathered via a cross-check of these data sources, the *Oxford English Dictionary* online (OED) and the *Merriam-Webster* dictionary online

(Merriam-Webster). Information about frequency and currency of use of complex (pseudo-)Anglicisms and particular base forms was retrieved from individual entries in De Mauro's *GRADIT* (GRADIT 2007) and from the word list of the *Nuovo vocabolario di base della lingua italiana* (NVdB 2016).[6]

Working along the lines of Iacobini (2015), the analysis proceeds from reductions of English complex words to simplexes in Italian (section 4), through adapted translations, calques and English borrowings (section 5) to second-generation neoclassical combining forms, lookalikes, Anglicisms, semantic equivalents and cognates in right-headed constructs (section 6).

I will address pattern borrowing and similarity across patterns in terms of proportional analogies of the type a:b = c:x. That is, the relation between 'a' and 'b' serves as a model or analogue for the formation of 'x' on the basis of some perceived similarity between the elements of the equation (Arndt-Lappe 2015). In its turn, similarity can be graded in the two fuzzy categories of local analogy and schemas. Local analogy is at play when the language user analyses the composite structure of the analogue – here, also adapted borrowings – and substitutes one component. Ideally, analogy is strictly 'local' – based on one particular analogue or analogue base – involves a high degree of similarity and might bring about a limited pattern (Arndt-Lappe 2015). However, it is not always possible to trace the new word to one analogue. Sets of analogues may give rise to a relevant pattern and bring about a gradual shift from local analogy to schemas, or more general representations with different degrees of abstractness. Analogy-based and schema-based accounts, Booij's (2010: 91) argument goes on, can coexist when the base word is still easily and immediately recognisable among a number of complex words and reinforces the entrenchment of the symbolic schema to which it is still linked.

The semantics of the linking rule in the composite structure is only addressed in section 6, when discussing second-generation neoclassical compounding, English-Italian lookalikes and English base forms. The main emphasis here lies on the following elements: *acqua/aqua* and *foto*; *terapia, dipendenza* and *pensiero*; *boy, centre, city, day, point* and *story*. For the purposes of this chapter, I shall broadly refer to Jackendoff's (2009, 2010, 2016) work on argument and modifier schemata. The argument schema introduces the configuration 'an N_2 of/by N_1'. Additionally, in the modifier schema N_1 and N_2 can be related in that arguments of a function F, as expressed by the paraphrase 'an N_2 such that F is true of N_1 and N_2'. A generative system accounts for the (promiscuous) semantic structure of nominal compounds based on the possible interaction of multiple variables. Hence, (often reversible) basic functions may combine to account for semantic structures with action modalities like 'occupation' (for a particular proper function PF), 'habitual activity' and 'ability', include co-composition of material from the meaning of the noun with F, or involve metonymic extension or metaphor coercion. Recursion of all variables is possible. However, because a thorough linguistic analysis of the semantics of the rule R is beyond the scope of this research, I will do away with theoretical modelling into detailed morphosyntactic and conceptual-semantic structures, set aside the formalisation of generative schemata and only proceed equipped with a list of relations and paraphrases that I do not state formally. For my purposes, the lists of basic functions and corresponding paraphrases

from Jackendoff (2009, 2010, 2016) seem to be a reasonable simplification for the characterisation of semantic relations in complex Italian (pseudo-)Anglicisms and English-
Italian cognates. Recall, however, that I draw a (non-discrete) line between appellative
nouns, which are prototypically classificatory and non-referential, and proper names,
which are prototypically identifying and used for unique individuals (cf. Anderson
2007; van Langendonck 2007). As in this context CLASSIFY comes across as too
general for identifying compounds as names, I suggest an additional function: reversible *COMMEMORATE (X, Y)* 'N2 is named after $N_{PR}1$', 'N1 is named after N2' (as
per Warren 1978; Ortner and Müller-Bolhagen 1991; Schlücker 2016).

4. Reductions to simplexes

Reductions of English complex words to the first constituent are an obvious indication
of the SVO order and a reference for the left-headedness in Italian. Examples from
Vogel (1990) are the pseudo-Anglicisms in (11a). Note that Vogel (1990) also includes
IT *night* and *plaid* in her list, though Italian dictionaries also give *nightclub*, and OED
also gives *plaid* in the same sense (11b).

(11) a. IT smoking 'tux suit' (1891) < EN smoking jacket
         IT scotch < EN scotch tape
     b. IT plaid < EN plaid blanket/plaid
         IT night/nightclub (1958) < EN nightclub
     c. IT la play, N < IT Playstation, N_{PR} / playstation, N (1995) < EN Playstation®,
         N_{PR}

As can be seen, the target forms retain the modifier, which specifies the subcategory
of the head. For nouns, a well-known case of reduction to the left in informal settings
is (11c).

In like manner, a Google search shows that complex names of bands in Italian allow
reduction to the left-most constituent (12a). This is in line with Italian's preference for
left-headedness. While the meaning of the borrowed construct is retained, reduction
to the initial constituent might suggest little implicit or explicit awareness of different
morphological structures or of the semantics of the compounding rule. Importantly,
however, competing patterns of reductions are at work with other names (12b). This
appears to be in line with the overall preference for the second constituent in reductions of English band names in Italian (12c).

(12) a. IT gli Alma, N_{PR} 'the Soul' < IT gli Almamegretta, N_{PR} 'the soul migrated-PSPL',
         i.e. the Migrated soul, a band
     b. IT i Modena, N_{PR} 'the Modena'
         IT i City Ramblers, N_{PR} 'the City Ramblers'
         IT i City, N_{PR} 'the City'
         IT i Ramblers, N_{PR} 'the Ramblers'
         < IT i Modena City Ramblers 'the Modena City Ramblers' < EN the Dublin City
         Ramblers

    c. IT gli Stones, N_{PR} 'the Stones'
        IT i Rolling, N_{PR} 'the Rolling'
        < IT i Rolling Stones, N_{PR} 'the Rolling Stones'
    d. IT i Pink, N_{PR} 'the Pink'
        IT i Floyd, N_{PR} 'the Floyd'
        < IT i Pink Floyd, N_{PR} 'the Pink Floyd'[7]

(12b) shows that *i Modena City Ramblers*, which in fact names an Italian band on the model analogue *the Dublin City Ramblers*, can undergo reduction to *i Modena, i City Ramblers, i City, i Ramblers*. Moving on to English band names (*Rolling Stones* and *Pink Floyd*), reductions to the left and right constituent of *i Rolling Stones* and *i Pink Floyd* are possible in Italian (12c–d). However, data from a Google search suggest that reductions to the right far outnumber reductions to the left: *gli Stones* (9,720 hits) vs. *i Rolling* (800 hits); *i Floyd* (3,520 hits) vs. *i Pink* (1,730 hits).

Reductions to the final element are common with appellative pseudo-Anglicisms (13a), including luxury loans in specialised domains such as *spread* (13b), which still alternates with the Italian left-headed counterpart, *spread BTP-BUND*, in its most recent sense.

    (13) a. IT lifting (1946) < EN face lifting
            IT spinning (1993) < EN aqua spinning
        b. IT differenziale 'spread'; IT spread (1990) < EN credit spread/bid offer spread
            IT spread, spread BTP-BUND < EN BTP/BUND spread

Altogether, it seems safe to claim that reduction of foreign matter to the first constituent is a fact in Italian, but isolated cases of reduction to the right constituent might follow contact with English borrowings.

5. Adapted translations, calques and Anglicisms

English words can enter Italian as loan translations, calques or Anglicisms. Loan translations which reshuffle constituent order run into the thousands. Because native left-headed compounds replace right-headed English constructs, the latter cannot have a reinforcing effect on right-headedness in Italian compounding. As an instance of the opposite case, coexistence of left-headed Italian constructs and right-headed English equivalents (14) is assumed to have a positive effect on implicit metalinguistic awareness of mirror structures in speakers of the recipient language and thus boost the analysability of the English borrowing vis-à-vis Italian. Note, however, that Italian constructs and Anglicisms may alternate to different extents, with an Anglicism eventually taking over. Consider the examples in (14).

    (14) a. IT quartiere della moda 'district of fashion', i.e. fashion district
            IT fashion district (2010) < EN fashion district
        b. IT fine settimana 'weekend'
            IT weekend (1905) < EN weekend

    c. IT Coppa dei Campioni (d'Europa), N_{PR} 'Cup of the champions of Europe', i.e.
        Champions League
        IT Champions League, N_{PR} < EN (UEFA) Champions League

In Standard Italian, *quartiere della moda* 'disctrict of fashion' (14a) does not alter-nate with *fashion district*, a recent luxury loan in the fashion industry. As to (14b), right-headed *weekend* is part of the core vocabulary of Italian (NVdB 2016); instead, GRADIT labels IT *fine settimana*, left-headed, as used and understood by the average Italian speaker. (14c) is yet another case: IT *Coppa dei Campioni* and the Anglicism *Champions League* are still in competition in current Italian, in spite of the official name shift to *Champions League* in 1992/1993.[8]

In principle, borrowings that have been effortlessly accepted into Italian along with their referent can provide repeated encounters with modifier-head constructs (15).

    (15) IT file sharing (2001) < EN file sharing
           IT credit crunch (2003) < EN credit crunch
           IT crowdsourcing (2006) < EN crowdsourcing
           IT energy drink (2006) < EN energy drink
           IT fashion blogger (2007) < EN fashion blogger
           IT wedding planner (2007) < EN wedding planner

Yet, this is more likely true when regular English complex structures with highly fre-quent or easily understood base forms are used as models for coining new words, as in the pseudo-Anglicisms and hybrid specifications in (16a–b).

    (16) a. IT Pony Pizza Pisa, N_{PR} (2001) 'pony pizza (restaurant in) Pisa'
             IT Roma Pony Pizza, N_{PR} 'pony pizza (restaurant in) Rome' < IT pony pizza
             (2001) 'pony express rider that delivers pizzas', i.e. restaurant that delivers to you
             < IT pony express (1986) 'pony express rider', i.e. delivery boy for a postal service
             < EN Pony Express rider (1860–1861)/Pony Express® (1893)
        b. IT Batmobile < EN Batmobile
             IT Batcaverna (2011) < EN Batcave
             IT Bat-villa 'Bat-villa' (2011) < IT Bat-casa < EN Bat-home

Importantly, in IT *pony pizza* (16a), the name of a postal service (*Pony Express®*) is extended metonymically (van Langendonck 2007) from name to appellative noun in order to describe delivery boys that work there. In turn, *pony express* serves as the analogue base for the noun *pony pizza* (2001), 'delivery boy for pizza restaurants', and the name *Pony Pizza*, which identifies a pizza restaurant that delivers takeaway food. The construct may enter recursive modification in information-compressing (Koptjevskaja-Tamm 2013) naming units like *Pony Pizza Pisa* 'Pony Pizza shop in Pisa' and the mirroring structure *Roma Pony Pizza* 'Pony Pizza shop in Rome', which specify location.

    Turning to the set of *Bat*-nouns in (16b), though some speakers might see the *Batmobile* as formed by analogy on IT *Papamobile* 'Pope's car', *Batmobile* 'Batman's car' is adapted from EN *Batmobile* /ˈbætmə‚biːl/ to IT /batˈmɔbile/. *Batcaverna* translates EN *Batcave* in Batman's comics and in the Batman movies. More recently, it was used in the press along with *Bat-casa* and *Bat-villa* (2011), formed via analogy on *Bat-casa*.[9]

6. Second-generation neoclassical combining forms and lookalikes

As is well known, most Italian right-headed compounds are based on initial neoclassical combining forms. One contribution of English to Italian is the introduction of so-called second-generation combining forms, or lookalikes of neoclassical combining forms that have achieved word-like status with non-learned meaning (Radimský 2006, 2013; Iacobini 2015). In this context, the following items are generally mentioned in the relevant literature: IT *acqua/acqua-/aqua-*, *cine/cine-*, *foto/foto-*, *moto/moto-*, *tele/tele-* and *video/video-*, together with *baby* as a premodifier in Anglicisms and hybrid compounds. In section 6.1 *acqua/acqua-/aqua-*, *idro-* and *foto/foto-* are considered in more detail. The remaining sections look into constructs formed with IT *terapia* and *dipendenza* (section 6.2), and the Anglicisms *boy*, *centre*, *day*, *point* and *story* (section 6.3).

6.1 Initial combining forms

For our purposes, it is essential to note that it is not always easy nor possible to reconstruct the direction of borrowing of neoclassical compounds that did not originate in Latin or Greek. The ability to link the word to a specific publication or person, however, can help reconstruct the language of origin of the word formation (ten Hacken and Panocová 2014; Panocová 2015).

acqua/acqua-/aqua-, idro-

IT *acqua*, *acqua-* and *aqua-* (borrowed from Latin via English) are lookalikes and orthographic neighbours. The neoclassical forms EN *hydro-* and IT *idro-* (from GRC ὕδωρ [hýdōr] 'water') combine with learned words in hard sciences – for instance, to name pathologies, minerals and elements (OED: *hydro-*; GRADIT: *idro-*), as in (17a). Additionally, EN *hydro-* and IT *idro-* are used in the aeronautics and navigation industries for vehicles that can move in or on water, as in (17b).

(17) a. EN hydrocephalus (1671) < LA < GRC ὑδροκέφαλον < ὑδρο- 'water' κεφαλή
        'head'
        IT idrocefalo (1698) < GRC ὑδροκέφαλον
        EN hydrogen (1791); IT idrogeno (1795) < FR hydrogène
        EN hydromagnesite; IT idromagnesite < DE Hydromagnesit (1835)[10]
     b. EN hydroplane (1901); IT idrovolante (1907) < FR hydravion (1900)[11]

Another combining form used in chemistry and pharmacy in words for liquids, solutions and, in Italian, essences is EN *aqua-* / IT *aqua*, from LA *aqua* 'water'

(OED: *aqua-*; GRADIT: *aqua*). GRADIT further adds that *aqua* is now an obsolete variant of *acqua* 'water' in Italian. Hence the dictionary equivalents EN *aqua regia* and IT *acqua regia*, coined in Latin in the Middle Ages for nitro-muriatic acid (18a). Recently, however, EN *aqua-* has been attested in classifying and identifying constructs that mostly denote aquatic entertainment and equipment for aquatic sports and activities (OED: *aqua-*). One early example is EN *Aqua-Lung*, a trademark originally registered in France for the first scuba apparatus and widely known in Italian, at least among divers. IT *acqua-* and *aqua-* have thus come to render EN *aqua-* (18b) and EN *water* (18c) plus an English constituent in locative compounds ('N_2/Comb. form is in N_1') that classify types of aquatic entertainment, routines in water and aquafit equipment.[12] Note that in the fitness industry IT *idrobike* (18c), based on the trademark *Hydrobike*, alternates with IT *acquabike* and *aquabike* in rendering EN *aquabike* and *waterbike*.

> (18) a. EN aqua regia 'water royal'; EN aqua regis 'water king–GEN' (1224); IT acqua regia 'water royal', i.e. royal water or nitro–muriatic acid < LA aqua regia 'water royal'
>
> b. IT aquabike, acquabike (1998), idrobike (1999) < EN aquabike, water bike, IT Hydrobike, N_{PR} < EN motor bike
> IT aquacycling (2012) < EN aqua cycling
>
> c. IT aquagym, acquagym (1998) < EN water gym/water gymnastics
> IT acquascooter (1989) < EN waterscooter, AcquaScooter, N_{PR} < EN motor scooter

Turning to naming units in Italian, the examples in (19) illustrate the case of pseudo-Anglicisms.

> (19) a. IT Acquapark, N_{PR} 'water park'
> b. IT Acquafan, N_{PR} 'fun in water' < acquapark + fun/fan i.e. aqua fun waterpark (for fans of water entertainment)

Acquafan (park) (19b) plays on the homophony of the borrowings and orthographic neighbours *fan* and *fun*, both pronounced /fan/ in Italian, to explicitate the function of *Acquapark* 'water park' ('N_2 is in/is made of N_1') (19b) as follows: 'N_2 whose proper function is to enable someone to have fun in N_1'.

foto/foto-

IT *foto/foto-* has multiple meanings and uses. As a neoclassical combining form derived from GRC *photo-* 'light', *foto-/-foto* means 'light, related to light', it forms terms like IT *fotoallergia* (1956) and EN *photoallergy* (1936), IT *fotoconducibilità*, which renders EN *photoconductivity* (20).

> (20) IT fotoallergia (1956); EN photoallergy (1936)
> IT fotoconducibilità (1956) < EN photoconductivity (1873)[13]

Another sense of IT *foto-* is 'photography, photographic, that uses photography'. IT *foto* /ˈfɔto/ matches the minimal prosodic unit for Italian nouns. It was first attested in 1931 as IT *fotó*, a simplex adapted from FR *photo* /foˈto/ (1839), in its turn a shortening of FR *photographie*. OED describes *photo*, N/A (1860) as a shortening formed within English from EN *photography*, in its turn 'formed within English, by compounding, probably after French *photographie*' (OED: *photo, photography*), but IT *fotografia* (1840) is said to be modelled on FR *photographie* or EN *photography*, both first attested in 1839 (GRADIT: *fotografia*). That is, the direction of borrowing is not clear.

With *fotografia, foto* (uninflected) counts among the most frequent words in the Italian core vocabulary (NVdB 2016). It is regularly found in classifying and naming constructs (21).

(21) a. IT fotolitografia 'photo-COMB.FORM litography' (1865) < FR photolitographie; fotocopia 'photo-COMB.FORM copy' (1917) < FR photocopie
IT fotomontaggio (1933) 'photomontage' <FR photomontage
IT fotocamera 'photo-COMB.FORM camera', i.e. camera (1965) < IT foto- + DE Kamera
IT fototessera (1966), foto tessera 'photo-COMB.FORM card', i.e. passport photo
IT fotoamatore (1965) 'photo-COMB.FORM lover', i.e. amateur photographer
IT ritocco fotografico 'photographic editing', i.e. photo editing, fotoritocco 'photo-COMB.FORM editing' (1994) < EN photo editing, photo retouching

b. IT il Fotoamatore, N_{PR} 'the photo lover', i.e. the shop called Amateur photographer < IT fotoamatore
IT Foto gallery, N_{PR} < EN Photo Gallery
IT Foto Atelier 'photo atelier', i.e. photographer's studio/shop
IT Foto Studio, N_{PR} 'photo studio', i.e. photographer's studio/shop
IT Foto discount, N_{PR}
IT Foto Roma, N_{PR} 'photo (in) Rome- N_{PR}' vis-à-vis IT Livorno Foto '(in) Livorno- N_{PR} photo'
IT Foto Mauro, N_{PR} 'Photo-N (by) Mauro- N_{PR}'; IT Foto Sposini, N_{PR} 'Photo-N (by) Sposini-NPR' vis-à-vis IT Walter foto, N_{PR} '(by) Walter- N_{PR} photo-N'

(21a) suggests that the bound form *foto-* 'involving or using photography' is used in early translations of French source words (e.g. IT *fotocopia* 'photocopy'). Examples from the 1960s are compounds with foreign simplexes (e.g. IT *fotocamera* 'camera' < *foto-* + DE *Kamera*) or Italian bases, e.g. IT *fotoamatore* 'amateur photographer', or IT *fototessera* and its variant with the free form *foto tessera* 'passport photo'. The English influence is more clearly apparent with IT *fotoritocco*, which competes with IT *ritocco fotografico*, a phrase with relational adjective, in rendering English *photo editing*. Arguably, the meaning of the relational adjective *fotografico* 'photographic' is identical to that of the corresponding noun (ten Hacken 2019) and of *foto* in particular.

Moving across the noun-name divide (21b), IT *il Fotoamatore*, N_{PR} ('the photo lover's shop', is coined via conversion from the noun *fotoamatore*. Hyphenated and solid compounds, however, are not an option when the naming construct does not have a complex nominal counterpart in Italian. For instance, the pseudo-Anglicism *Foto gallery*, possibly adapted from Microsoft's *Windows Photo Gallery*, names a retail shop and is the identifying counterpart of IT *galleria fotografica* ('photographic gallery'). Other examples are IT *Foto Atelier* and IT *Foto Studio* – with the noun phrases IT *studio fotografico* 'photographic shop' and *atelier fotografico* 'photographic shop' as their classifying counterparts – or the hybrid *Foto discount* 'cheap photographic shop', with an argument schema.

When it comes to naming units in mirror constructs like IT *Foto Roma* vis-à-vis *Livorno Foto*, the basic commemorative and locative functions compose and are reversible ('N is named after N_{PR} and N is in N_{PR}'). Commemorative relation and proper function ('sell') can be said to co-compose in *Foto Mauro* and *Foto Sposini* and the mirror construct *Walter foto*. These mirror constructs, however, might be misleading. Certainly, the standard commemorative schema available to Italian for naming places juxtaposes noun and name (Lombardi Vallauri 2008: composti intitolativi 'commemorative compounds'), as in IT *Via Cavallotti* 'Street-N Cavallotti- N_{PR}' vs. EN *Queensberry Place*; but with recently registered names that specify the product being sold the data shows a strong preference for juxtaposing name and noun, as in IT *Riccardo Corredi* 'Riccardo's trousseau shop', IT *Roberta Pelle* 'Roberta's leather shop', IT *Parlanti Auto* 'Parlanti the car dealer', IT *Ghelardini Ferramenta* 'Ghilardini's hardware shop', IT *Nosari Biliardi* 'Nosari's billiard shop'.

To recapitulate, French can be used to account for early uses of *foto-* 'of or relating to photography, concerning or using photography' as a bound form and for the adoption of IT *foto* as a simplex noun. Additionally, it seem safe to claim that English word formation patterns have most definitely influenced Italian word formation (as in IT *fotoritocco* from EN *photo editing*). Third, the contrast between the bound form *foto-* and its homonym *foto* in recent Italian constructs could be attributed at least in part to the contrast between classifying and identifying uses.

6.2 Compounds with cognate heads as second constituents

Form compression (Bisetto 2004; Koptjevskaja-Tamm 2013) appears to be an important trigger of right-headed analogical sets of pseudo-Anglicisms and full specifications of foreign patterns with regular English-Italian cognates. Following Koptjevskaja-Tamm (2013: 280) I understand form compression as the provision of 'concise and efficient labels for entities that would otherwise need more cumbersome or at least longer descriptions'.

The option is demonstrated by constructs with IT *terapia* 'therapy' and *dipendenza* 'dependence, addiction' as second constituents in patterns with nouns as first constituents and arguments.[14]

terapia

IT *terapia* is used as a second constituent and the head of neoclassical compounds in specialised discourse (22a), but the schema appears to have been recently extended to allow non-learned nouns in first position, in solid and hyphenated compounds (22b–c).

(22) a. IT elioterapia (1899); EN heliotherapy (1890)
IT idroterapia (1852); EN hydrotherapy (1876) < FR hydrothérapie
b. IT aromaterapia (1981) < EN aromatherapy (1949) < FR aromathérapie
IT luce-terapia, terapia della luce 'therapy of/through (artificial) light' < EN light therapy
IT terapia dell'acqua 'therapy of/through water < EN water therapy
IT profumoterapia 'perfume therapy', EN essence therapy
c. IT Lunaterapia 'moon therapy'
IT cioccolato-terapia 'chocolate therapy'
IT coccole-terapia 'cuddle therapy'
IT Riccardo-terapia 'Riccardo- N_{PR} therapy' [SC][15]

The shift from neoclassical combining form to noun modifier is attested in both Italian and English, as in the case of compounds like EN *light therapy* and IT *luce-terapia*, in medicine (22b), IT *aromaterapia*, adapted from EN *aromatherapy*, and *profumoterapia*, for EN *essence therapy*, in complementary and alternative medicine. It is not difficult to find examples that seem to vouch for the influence of English: interestingly, NPs might alternate with the compound (e.g. IT *luce-terapia* and *terapia della luce* 'therapy through light') or contribute to blocking a compound (e.g. IT *terapia dell'acqua* 'therapy through water' for EN *water therapy*). Yet, sets of analogues are formed easily in Italian, as illustrated in (22c). Like IT *aromaterapia* or *profumoterapia*, classificatory nouns and names with *terapia* in final position describe all sorts of treatments in or outside complementary medicine, where 'N_1 enables N_2' and 'N_2 by N_1': in IT *Lunaterapia*, a name, the first constituent specifies the instrument or agent, where *luna* emerges as identical to or as enabling *terapia*; this is a special treatment offered by Italian holistic health clinics. Further instantiations and extensions are oftentimes occasional formations that describe enticing treats, e.g. IT *cioccolato-terapia* 'chocolate-based therapy', IT *coccola-terapia* 'cuddle therapy' and IT *Riccardo-terapia* 'therapy by/with Riccardo'.

dipendenza

Compounds with *dipendenza* 'dependency, addiction' as a second constituent are formed in medicine, media language and in informal settings to denote addictions and dependencies (23).

(23) a. IT tossicodipendenza 'substance dependence' (1978)
IT teledipendenza 'TV addiction'(< tele(visione) 'television' + dipendenza 'dependence') < IT tossicodipendenza
IT videodipendenza 'TV addiction' (1983) < IT tossicodipendenza 'substance addiction'
IT polidipendenza 'poli-COMB.FORM addiction', i.e. multiple addictions (1998)
IT internet-dipendenza, cyberdipendenza, netdipendenza (1996) 'cyberaddiction' < EN cyberaddiction
IT alcool-dipendenza 'alcohol addiction' < EN alcohol addiction
IT gioco-dipendenza 'gambling addiction' (2012)
IT ludopatia 'ludo-COMB.FORM + -pathy-COMB.FORM', i.e. gambling disorder

    b. IT clerodipendenza 'church dependence', i.e. dependence on the church
       IT mamma-dipendenza 'dependence on mums', i.e. excessive dependence on one's
       mum' [SC]
       IT Riccardo-dipendenza 'dependence on Riccardo- N_{PR}' [SC]

A reinforcement effect from English onto Italian can be readily accounted for by assuming the increasing global recourse to English as a lingua franca in the hard and soft sciences. The results here are adapted modifier-head constructs and right-headed word formations within Italian. Competition with semantically equivalent NPs is not unusual, as is the case with IT *tossicodipendenza* 'substance dependence' vis-à-vis *dipendenza da sostanze stupefacenti* 'addiction to drugs' or IT *alcool-dipendenza* 'alcohol addiction' vis-à-vis *dipendenza da alcool* 'addiction to alcohol'. The shift from learned neoclassical compound (e.g. IT *polidipendenza* 'multiple addictions') to non-learned word formation can be observed with IT *teledipendenza* and IT *videodipendenza* 'TV dependence', formed by analogy with IT *tossicodipendenza* 'substance dependence'. Another case in point are the neoclassical compounds IT *ludopatia* and, though extremely rare, EN *ludopathy* vis-à-vis IT *gioco-dipendenza* and EN *gambling addiction*, all referring to problem gambling.

    The distinction between (23a) on the one hand and (23b) on the other depends on (non-)institutionalisation. IT *clericodipendenza* was playfully coined in the press to describe the dependency of Italian politicians on the Catholic Church; other playful nonce-formations are IT *mamma-dipendenza* 'dependence on one's mum', for IT *mammismo* 'excessive attachment to one's mother' and IT *Riccardo-dipendenza* 'dependence on Riccardo', with a given name as modifier.

6.3 Foreign heads in right-headed constructs

Forming names and nouns after right-headed borrowings that are often part of our daily lives suggests the ability of Italian speakers to analyse and extend borrowed patterns based on low-level non-native schemas. The compounds that I will briefly address in this section are nouns and names formed with a second constituent that was borrowed from English and is now part of Standard Italian: *boy, day, point* and *story*.

boy

One right-headed pattern that has formed of late has *boy* as the second constituent. *Boy* was originally borrowed from English in 1892 to label a young valet, junior servant or shop assistant; it is now used with reference to 'a male child or youth' (GRADIT: *boy*). It is also found in loanwords like *cowboy* and *golden boy* (24a). For our purposes, what is interesting are the classifying examples in (24b), which specify the low-level pattern or schema [Name of Italian political leader-*boy*]$_N$.

    (24) a. IT cowboy (1918) < EN cowboy
          IT golden boy < EN golden boy

    b. IT papaboy (1999) 'Pope boy', i.e. young supporter of the Pope
       IT Berlusconi boy (1993), i.e. young supporter of Berlusconi
       IT Ciampi boy (1994), i.e. young supporter of Ciampi
       IT RAIboys 'RAI boys', i.e. RAI employees

In (24b), *Berlusconi boy* serves as the model analogue for sets of right-headed analogues with names of Italian politicians as first constituents. *Ciampi boy* and many more formations instantiate the same low-level pattern or schema, where *boy* is a young supporter of the politician identified by the name ('N_2 has the proper function to support/celebrate Name$_1$'). *Papaboy* also belongs here in that the Pope is the Bishop of Rome and a highly influential head of state. One extension of the pattern is *RAIboys*, used in context to denote 'dedicated employees that did their very best to support RAI (Italian broadcasting service) behind the scenes of the Festival di Sanremo (the Italian pop music festival) and thus turn it into a successful event'.

centre, point

Sets of analogues with *centre* and *point* (25) as second constituents appear to be either Anglicisms or pseudo-Anglicisms.

  (25) a. IT infopoint (1992) < EN infopoint
          IT internet point (1992) < EN internet cafe
      b. IT Beauty point, N_{PR}; Fitness point, N_{PR}; Wellness point, N_{PR}
      c. IT beauty centre (1990) < EN beauty centre, beauty salon
          IT fitness centre < EN fitness centre
          IT wellness centre < EN wellness centre

In (25a), IT *infopoint* (1992), for 'N_2 whose proper function is to sell/give N_1', is an Anglicism; instead, *internet point* (1992) is a pseudo-Anglicism formed in Italian to render EN *internet cafe*. Also, while *point* is found in complex identifying names in Italian, *centre* appears to be used in loans from English nouns that retain their classifying function in Italian, e.g. *Fitness point* vis-à-vis *fitness centre*, *Wellness point* vis-à-vis *wellness centre* (alternating with IT *centro benessere*), and *Beauty point* vis-à-vis *beauty center* (1990), in its turn alternating with IT *centro estetico, centro estetica, estetista*.[16]

day

IT *day* (before 1980; Devoto Oli 2016: *day*) is a slightly different case. Institutionalised Anglicisms such as IT *President Day* and *Columbus Day* (26a), with a commemorative function, serve as model analogues to form *Papa Day* 'Pope's day' and extensions in sets of analogues with names of Italian politicians, e.g. *Veltroni Day* 'Veltroni's day' (26b), or nouns and nominalisations (26c).

  (26) a. IT President Day < EN President Day
          IT Columbus Day < EN Columbus Day

    b. IT Papa Day 'Pope('s) Day', i.e. events to celebrate/commemorate the Pope

       IT Veltroni Day 'Veltroni('s)- N_{PR} day', i.e. events to celebrate/commemorate Veltroni

    c. IT referendum day

       IT restitution day < IT election day < EN election day

       IT commemoration day < EN commemoration day

       IT clic-day

       IT Vaffa-Day, V-day (2007) 'go-away day' < EN D-Day (1944)

In the context of names for unique individuals (26a–b), it is easy to infer a 'celebrate' interpretation. The default activity is explicitated when nouns and nominalisations with eventive/resultative readings replace names for unique individuals and nouns for roles of public and political figures, as in (33c). Hence, IT *referendum day* and *restitution day*, modelled on Anglicisms like *election day* or *commemoration day* ('N_2 is N_1', 'N_2 whose proper function is to participate in N_1') or IT *clic–day* and the analogue *Vaffa-Day*. *Vaffa Day* 'go-away day', or a day devoted to telling politicians to pack, describes a rally organised and held by Beppe Grillo, former Italian comedian and founder of the anti-establishment Five Star Movement, to militate against the then government. Somewhat ironically, the event was shortened to *V-day*. This turned a very offensive compound into a paronym and a close orthographic neighbour of *D-Day*, naming the set of the Allies' landing operations to invade Europe in June 1944.

    In all cases, *day* loses its standard meaning and describes an organised public event that takes place at a particular date and comes with a specific function (in short, a social artefact).

story

We can assume a low-level pattern or schema [Name of Italian political leader-*story*]$_N$ for *Berlusconi story* 'Berlusconi's sorry saga'. *Story* was borrowed into Italian in 1960 (GRADIT: *story*). A number of Anglicisms have *story* as a head, e.g. *love story* (1971), *spy story* (1983), *detective story*, *ghost story* ('N_2 has the proper function to inform about N_1') (27a). The hybrids in (27b), formed in Italian, specify the same schema.

    (27) a. IT love story (1971) < EN love story

         IT spy story (1983) < EN spy story

         IT detective story < EN detective story

         IT ghost story < EN ghost story

      b. IT tangenti story 'bribery story', i.e. bribery scandal

         IT mafia story

         IT la Berlusconi story (1993) 'the Berlusconi story' < the Obama story

In (27b), *mafia story* extends the schema via a metonymic shift (in the sense of Benczes 2006) from effect (*mafia*) to cause (the mafia organisation, syndicate), thus working towards reinforcing the negative connotations for 'despicable or scandalous event' that associate with *tangenti story* and are also an aspect of one sense of IT *storia* 'scandalous love affair'. Constructs such as IT *la Berlusconi story* 'the Berlusconi story', where the politician's name, *Berlusconi*, is used metonymically to stand for the politician's actions, retain these negative connotations (hence '[report on] Berlusconi's sorry saga, Berlusconi's dystopian epic', also sarcastically called *Berlusconeide* < *Berlusconi* + *Eneide* 'Eneid'). This is quite a long way from the positive associations arising from possible analogue models such as EN *the Obama story*.

7. Conclusions

My goal has been to analyse foreign word formation in Italian. Particularly, qualitative data analysis was meant to set the scene for future research on the influence of English word formation patterns as part of the re-standardisation of the language (Bombi 2017).

The chapter demonstrates the general adherence of Italian to the left-hand head rule in case of reductions from English compounds to Italian simplexes (IT *smoking* < EN *smoking suit*): the meaning of the borrowed construct is retained, and reduction to the initial constituent might suggest little implicit or explicit awareness of different morphological structures or of the semantics of the compounding rule. However, the data also suggest a reinforcing effect that foreign word formation might have on right-headed patterns in Italian. For instance, reductions from names of foreign bands show that Italian is open to competition between opposite variants (IT *i Pink* 'the Pink', *i Floyd* 'the Floyd' < IT *i Pink Floyd* 'the Pink Floyd'). If rare, reductions to the second constituent in pseudo-Anglicisms from English compounds are also possible (IT *lifting* < IT *face lifting*).

English words can enter Italian as loan translations, calques or Anglicisms. Loan translations that reshuffle constituent order run into the thousands. Because native left-headed compounds replace right-headed English constructs, the latter cannot have a reinforcing effect on right-headedness in Italian compounding. Anglicisms that have been readily accepted into Italian along with their referent can provide repeated encounters with modifier-head constructs and thus increase awareness of non-native structures. Yet, coexistence of left-headed native constructs and right-headed English equivalents (*fine settimana* and its more frequent alternate, *weekend*) is expected to have a stronger effect on implicit metalinguistic awareness of mirror structures in speakers of the recipient language. In fact, implicit metalinguistic awareness may develop or be enhanced in the recipient language through comparison of competing English loans and Italian equivalents, e.g. IT *revisione di spesa* and the equivalent *spending review*, English source form and adaptations, as well as exclusive recourse to English borrowings for new referents (*crowd sourcing*). Cross-linguistic cognates in right-headed patterns (IT *terapia*, EN *therapy*, IT *dipendenza*, EN *dependence*) can further boost the process and work towards convergence (Weinreich 1953). IT *terapia* and IT *dipendenza* are used as a second constituent and the head of neoclassical compounds in specialised discourse, but the schemas appears to have been recently extended to allow non-learned nouns in first position, in solid and hyphenated compounds (IT *elioterapia*, EN *heliotherapy*; IT *aromaterapia* < EN *aromatherapy*; IT *coccole-terapia* 'cuddle therapy').

What this means for foreign compounding in Italian is not that new patterns are expected but rather that English right-headed borrowings can have a support effect and favour right-headed compounding in marginal word formation processes or in right-headed neoclassical compounding. In line with recent literature on new words and foreign word formation in Italian (Iacobini 2015), we have seen that neoclassical compounding has indeed been revitalised in contact with borrowings.

For instance, EN *aqua-* (as in *Aqua-Lung* or *aquagym*) has revitalised the use of IT *aqua-* and *acqua* 'water' in non-learned classifying and naming solid compounds formed in Italian (*aquagym, aquagym, Acquafan* vis-à-vis IT/EN *aqua regia* and nouns of solutions and essences). As for IT *foto/foto-*, French can be used to account for early uses of *foto-* 'of or relating to photography, concerning or using photography' as a bound form and for the adoption of IT *fotografia* and its shortening *foto* as a simplex noun. English word formation patterns, however, appear to influence Italian word formations and the shift from NPs with relational adjective to compound (IT *ritocco fotografico* 'photographic editing', IT *fotoritocco* < EN *photo editing*). The contrast between the bound form *foto-* and its homonym *foto* in recent Italian constructs appears to depend, at least in part, on the contrast between classifying and identifying uses (IT *fototessera* 'passport photo'; IT *Foto Mauro, Mauro Foto*).

Moving away from second-generation neoclassical combining forms, sets of hybrid analogues exhibit Anglicisms that are part of common language. For example, in the native left-headed pattern: *killer* (*aereo killer* 'killer plane'); and in the foreign right-headed pattern: *boy* (*Berlusconi boy*), *centre* and *point* (loans such as IT *wellness centre*, for IT *centro benessere*, vis-à-vis IT *Beauty point* 'Beauty salon, Beauty centre'), *day* (*Veltroni Day*), *story* (*Berlusconi story*).

Notes

1. Unless otherwise specified (e.g. using [SC] for examples discussed with my informants or footnotes with details for additional sources), corpus data were retrieved from the primary references and secondary literature discussed in section 3. Where available, the date of first attestation provided for the nominal constructs under scrutiny is the earliest date gathered through cross-verification from the dictionaries and databases that I used as main source for collecting nouns and names.
2. Other terms adopted in Italian linguistics are *italiese* (Dardano 1986), *itangliano* (McArthur 2002; Beccaria 2006) and *italo-inglese* (Stammerjohann 2003).
3. *Renxit* (3a) ironically denotes the withdrawal of support for Matteo Renzi, Italy's Prime Minister in 2016, rather than the withdrawal of individual countries from the EU, as in *Grexit* or *Brexit*.
4. The occasionalism *tenager* (3b) was uttered by an eight-year-old girl playing with a schoolmate (Cacchiani 2016).
5. *Halloweek* (5a) was coined by Ferrero running a Halloween marketing campaign for Kinder chocolate in 2016.
6. Throughout the chapter, I render De Mauro's (GRADIT (2007), NVdB (2016)) usage labels as follows: FO, or 'fondamentale', used in 90 per cent of the texts

under scrutiny in De Mauro (GRADIT (2007), NVdB (2016)): most frequent core vocabulary; AU, or 'di alto uso', found in 6 per cent of the texts: highly frequent core vocabulary; AD 'di alta disponibilità', not used but well known to the average speaker: highly available core vocabulary; CO or 'comune': generally known and understood by speakers with primary and/or secondary education.

7. The data discussed in (12) comes from manual selection of the hits returned by an advanced Google search for the expressions '"gli Alma" -megretta' and '"i Megretta"', '"i Modena" -City Ramblers', '"i City" -Modena -Ramblers' and '"i Ramblers" -Modena City', '"i Rolling" -Stones', '"gli Stones"', '"i Pink" -Floyd' and '"i Floyd"' (data retrieved on 1 August 2017).

8. Contrary to *Coppa dei Campioni* and *Champions League* in (14c), IT *Coppa UEFA* has rendered *UEFA European Championship* and *UEFA Cup* in the years 1971–2009. In the 2009–2010 season the competition was renamed *(UEFA) Europa League* and commonly referred to as *UEFA Euro* (as in *UEFA Euro 2012, UEFA Euro 2016, UEFA Euro 2020*), while new regulations came into force. Therefore, *Coppa UEFA* and *(UEFA) Europa League* are not in competition but designate different concepts.

9. *Bat-casa*, *Bat-villa* and *Batcaverna* (16b) are used for the young Moratti's luxurious house and basement in Milan, very much like Bruce Wayne's villa and basement.

10. *Hydromagnesite* (17a) is the oldest *hydro*-mineral recorded in the IMA Database of Mineral Properties (n.d.). Because research on hydromagnesite was first published in German, EN *hydromagnesite* and IT *idromagnesite* can be understood as translating DE *Hydromagnesit*.

11. As regards *hydravion* 'hydroplane' (17b), I depart from the date of first attestation provided by TLFi (n.d.: *hydravion*). Though the word was 'in the air' (ten Hacken and Panocová 2014; Panocová 2015), I take EN *hydroplane* and IT *idroplano* to translate FR *hydravion*. Additionally, based on the object only (and not on evidence of the word being used), I give 1900 as its first date of attestation, so as to account for early prototypes, which were designed and built in France in the last decades of the nineteenth century. The French engineer Henri Fabre succeeded in undertaking the first flight ever by hydroplane in 1910 (Encyclopédie Larousse: *Fabre*).

12. Another set of analogues that instantiate a location function comprises *snowshoeing* (1994) and winter sports that take place in *snowparks* (2001). For example, IT *snowboard/snowboarding* (1989), *snowbike/snowbiking* (1998), *snowtubing* (2001).

13. The scientist W. Smith first reported the results of his experiments on photoconductivity (20) in *Nature*'s 1873 February issue (Stöckmann 1973). This suggests that the term was first formed in English and later adopted in Italian and other languages.

14. I deliberately exclude from the analysis modifier-head constructs that do not have English model analogues. This is the case of form compressions from possessive NPs that were initially coined in the press to cater for the combined need to be concise and attract the reader's attention, e.g. IT *Berlusconi-pensiero* (1989) 'Berlusconi('s)- N_{PR} view' ('N_2 of Name$_1$'), for *il pensiero di Berlusconi*, i.e. the editorial line of Berlusconi's Italian TV channels about politics, society and morality

some years before he officially joined the political fray (1994). Notice that over time constructs with *pensiero* have gained ground in informal, colloquial interactions where expressing one's views cannot have any impact on the socio-political panorama, and the name of the public character, institution or organisation has been replaced by given names, as in *Silvia pensiero* 'Silvia('s)- N$_{PR}$ view' [SC].

15. I draw from my own experience for *cioccolato-terapia* 'chocolate therapy', *coccole-terapia* 'cuddle therapy' and *Riccardo-terapia* 'Riccardo therapy' (28c). My informants judged all three examples acceptable, further adding to the list of potential treats. None of them was aware of the fact that IT *cioccolato-terapia* and IT *coccole-terapia* have equivalents in English.
16. A similar example is the name *Computer City*, formed in Italian on model analogues such as the global retailer *PC City*.

References

Adamo, Giovanni and V. Della Valle (2006), 'Tendenze nella formazione di parole nuove dalla stampa italiana contemporanea', in G. Adamo and V. Della Valle (eds), *Che fine fanno i neologismi? A cento anni dalla pubblicazione del Dizionario moderno di Alfredo Panzini*, Firenze: Leo S. Olschki, pp. 105–122.

Anderson, John M. (2007), *The Grammar of Names*, Oxford: Oxford University Press.

Arndt-Lappe, Sabine (2015), 'Word-formation and Analogy', in P. O. Müller, I. Ohnheiser, S. Olsen and F. Rainer (eds), *Word-Formation. An International Handbook of the Languages of Europe*, Berlin and New York: De Gruyter, vol. 2, pp. 822–841.

Bauer, Laurie (2001), *Morphological Productivity*, Cambridge: Cambridge University Press.

Beccaria, Gian Luigi (2006), *Per difesa e per amore. La lingua italiana oggi*, Milano: Garzanti.

Benczes, Réka (2006), *Creative Compounding in English: The Semantics of Metaphorical and Metonymical Noun-Noun Combinations*, Amsterdam and Philadelphia: John Benjamins.

Bisetto, Antonietta (2004), 'Composizione con elementi italiani', in M. Grossmann and F. Rainer (eds), *La formazione delle parole in italiano*, Tübingen: Niemeyer, pp. 33–50.

Bolonyai, Agnes (1998), 'In-between Languages: Language Shift/Maintenance in Childhood Bilingualism', *International Journal of Bilingualism*, 2: 21–43.

Bombi, Raffaella (2017), 'Anglicisms in Italian. Typologies of Language Contact Phenomena with Particular Reference to Word-formation Processes', in M. Cerruti, C. Crocco and S. Marzo (eds), *Towards a New Standard. Theoretical and Empirical Studies on the Restandardization of Italian*, Boston and Berlin: De Gruyter, pp. 269–292.

Booij, Gert (2010), *Construction Morphology*, Cambridge: Cambridge University Press.

Cacchiani, Silvia (2015), 'On Italian Lexical Blends: From Language Play to Innovation', *Neologica. Revue internationale de néologie*, 9: 169–186.

Cacchiani, Silvia (2016), 'On Italian Lexical Blends: Borrowings, Hybridity, Adaptations, and Native Word Formations', in S. Knospe, A. Onysko and M. Goth (eds), *Crossing Languages to Play with Words. Multidisciplinary Perspectives*, Berlin: De Gruyter, pp. 305–336.

Cacchiani, Silvia (2017), 'From Analogues to New Words and Constructs through Paronymy, Local Analogy and Schemas', in A. Schröder and C. Haase (eds), *Analogy, Copy, and Representation. Interdisciplinary Perspectives*, Bielefeld: Aisthesis Verlag, pp. 37–46.

Cameron, Deborah (2012), 'The Commodification of Language: English as a Global Commodity', in T. Nevailanen and E.-C. Traugott (eds), *The Oxford Handbook of the History of English*, Oxford: Oxford University Press, pp. 352–363.

Corbin, Danielle (1987), *Morphologie dérivationnelle et structuration du lexique. Vols I-II*, Tübingen: Niemeyer.

Dardano, Maurizio (1986), 'The Influence of English on Italian', in W. Wiereck and W.-D. Bald (eds), *English in Contact with Other Languages*, Budapest: Akadémiai Kiadò, pp. 231–252.

Devoto Oli (2016), *Il Devoto-Oli Digitale 2017*, edited by G. Devoto and G. C. Oli, Milano: Le Monnier. [CD-ROM]

DISC (2008), *Il Sabatini Coletti. Dizionario della lingua italiana 2007*, edited by F. Sabatini and V. Coletti, Milano: Rizzoli Larousse. [CD-ROM]

Dressler, Wolfgang U. (2000), 'Extragrammatical Versus Marginal Morphology', in U. Doleschal and A. M. Thornton (eds), *Extragrammatical and Marginal Morphology*, Munich: LINCOM, pp. 1–9.

Encyclopédie Larousse (n.d.), https://www.larousse.fr/encyclopedie (12 September 2018).

Furiassi, Cristiano (2006), *False Anglicisms in Italian*, Monza: Polimetrica International Scientific Publisher.

Galinsky, Hans [1963] (1967), 'Stylistic Aspects of Linguistic Borrowing. A Stylistic View of American Elements in Modern German', in B. Carstensen and H. Galinsky (eds), *Amerikanismen der deutschen Gegenwartssprache. Entlehnungsvorgänge und ihre stilistischen Aspekte*, Heidelberg: WINTER, pp. 35–72.

Görlach, Manfred (2001), *A Dictionary of European Anglicisms*, Cambridge: Cambridge University Press.

GRADIT (2007), *Grande Dizionario Italiano dell'Uso, Vols. I–VIII*, edited by T. De Mauro (2007), Torino: UTET, 2nd edn. [CD-ROM]

Greenberg, Joseph H. (1963), 'Some Universals of Grammar with Particular Reference to the Order of Meaningful Elements', in J. H. Greenberg (ed.), *Universals of Language*, Cambridge, MA: MIT Press, pp. 61–113.

ten Hacken, Pius (2019), 'Relational Adjectives Between Syntax and Morphology', *SKASE Journal of Translation and Interpretation*, 19: 1, 77–92.

ten Hacken, Pius and R. Panocová (2014), 'Neoclassical Formatives in Dictionaries', in A. Abel, C. Vettori and N. Ralli (eds), *Proceedings of the XVI EURALEX International Congress, The User in Focus* (15–19 July 2014), Bolzano/Bozen: EURAC Research, pp. 1059–1072.

Hatcher, Anna G. (1951), *Modern English Word-Formation and Neo-Latin: A Study of the Origins of English (French, Italian, German) Copulative Compounds*, Baltimore, MD: Johns Hopkins Press.

Iacobini, Claudio (2004), 'Composizione con elementi neoclassici', in M. Grossmann and F. Rainer (eds), *La formazione delle parole in italiano*, Tübingen: Niemeyer, pp. 69–96.

Iacobini, Claudio (2015), 'Foreign Word-formation in Italian', in P. O. Müller, I. Ohnheiser, S. Olsen and F. Rainer (eds), *Word-Formation. An International Handbook of the Languages of Europe*, Berlin and New York: De Gruyter, vol. 3, pp. 627–659.

IMA Database of mineral properties (n.d.), http://rruff.info/ima/ (1 August 2017).

Jackendoff, Ray (2009), 'Compounding in the Parallel Architecture and Conceptual Semantics', in R. Lieber and P. Štekauer (eds), *The Oxford Handbook of Compounding*, Oxford: Oxford University Press, pp. 105–129.

Jackendoff, Ray (2010), *Meaning and the Lexicon: The Parallel Architecture, 1975–2010*, Oxfrod: Oxford University Press.

Jackendoff, Ray (2016), 'English Noun-Noun Compounds in Conceptual Semantics', in P. ten Hacken (ed.), *The Semantics of Compounding*, Cambridge: Cambridge University Press, pp. 15–37.

Konieczna, Ewa (2012), 'Analogical Modelling and Paradigmatic Word Formation as Attention Seeking Devices', in A. Ralli, G. Booij, S. Scalise and A. Karasimos (eds), *On-Line Proceedings of MMM8, the 8th Mediterranean Morphology Meeting*, University of Patras, Greece, pp. 168–189, https://geertbooij.files.wordpress.com/2014/02/mmm8_proceedings.pdf (12 September 2018).

Koptjevskaja-Tamm, Maria (2013), 'A *Mozart Sonata* and the *Palme Murder*: The Structure and Uses of Proper-name Compounds in Swedish', in K. Börjas, D. Denison and A. K. Scott (eds), *Morphosyntactic Categories and the Expression of Possession*, Amsterdam and Philadelphia: John Benjamins, pp. 253–290.

Langendonck, Willy van (2007), *Theory and Typology of Proper Names*, Berlin and New York: De Gruyter.

Lieber, Rochelle and P. Štekauer (2009), 'Status and Definition of Compounding', in R. Lieber, and P. Štekauer (eds), *The Oxford Handbook of Compounding*, Oxford: Oxford University Press, pp. 3–18.

Lombardi Vallauri, Edoardo (2008), 'Composti intitolativi in italiano: un'oscillazione', in E. Cresti (ed.), *Prospettive nello studio del lessico italiano*, Firenze: Firenze University Press, vol. 2, pp. 555–562.

McArthur, Tom (2002), *Oxford Guide to World Englishes*, Oxford: Oxford University Press.

Mattiello, Elisa (2012), *Extra-Grammatical Morphology in English. Abbreviations, Blends, Reduplicatives and Related Phenomena*, Berlin and Boston: De Gruyter.

Mattiello, Elisa (2017), *Analogy in Word-formation: A Study of English Neologisms and Occasionalisms*, Berlin and Boston: De Gruyter.

Merriam-Webster (2018), *Merriam-Webster's Dictionary and Thesaurus*, Springfield, MA: Merriam-Webster, Inc., https://www.merriam-webster.com/ (12 September 2018).

Myers-Scotton, Carol (2006), *Multiple Voices: An Introduction to Bilingualism*, Oxford: Blackwell.

NDM (2001–2018), *Nuovo De Mauro*, edited by T. De Mauro, Milano: Mondadori-Pearson, http://dizionario.internazionale.it/ (12 September 2018).

NPN (2008), *Neologismi. Parole nuove dai giornali*, edited by G. Adamo and V. Della Valle, Roma: Istituto dell'Enciclopedia Italiana.

NT (n.d.), *Neologismi Treccani*, http://www.treccani.it/lingua_italiana/neologismi/searchNeologismi.jsp (12 September 2018).

NVdB (2016), *Il Nuovo vocabolario di base della lingua italiana*, edited by T. De Mauro, https://www.internazionale.it/opinione/tullio-de-mauro/2016/12/23/il-nuovo-vocabolario-di-base-della-lingua-italiana (12 September 2018).

OED (2000–2019), *Oxford English Dictionary*, edited by J. Simpson, Oxford: Oxford University Press, 3rd edn, www.oed.com (12 September 2018).

Öhmann, Emil (1961), 'Prinzipienfragen der Fremd- und Lehnwortforschung', *Mitteilungen Universitätsbund Marburg*, 3–12.

ONLI (n.d.), *Osservatorio Neologico della Lingua Italiana*, http://www.iliesi.cnr.it/ONLI/intro.shtml (12 September 2018).

Ortner, Lorelies and E. Müller-Bolhagen (1991), *Deutsche Wortbildung: Typen und Tendenzen in der Gegenwartssprache. Vierter Hauptteil: Substantivakomposita*, Berlin and New York: De Gruyter.

Panocová, Renatá (2015), *Categories of Word Formation and Borrowing*, Newcastle upon Tyne: Cambridge Scholars Publishing.

Radimský, Jan (2006), *Les composes italiens actuels*, Paris: Cellule de recherche en linguistique.

Radimský, Jan (2013), 'Position of the Head in Italian N-N Compounds: The Case of Mirror Compounds', *Linguistica Pragensia*, 23: 1, 41–52.

Radimský, Jan (2015), *Noun+Noun Compounds in Italian. A Corpus-based Study*, Prague: Jihočeská Univerzita v Českých Budějovicích.

Ronneberger-Sibold, Elke (2010), 'Word Creation. Definition – Function – Typology', in F. Rainer, W. U. Dressler, D. Kastovsky and H. C. Luschützky (eds), *Variation and Change in Morphology. Selected Papers from the 13th International Morphology Meeting* (February 2008), Amsterdam and Philadelphia: John Benjamins, pp. 201–216.

Ronneberger-Sibold, Elke (2012), 'Blending Between Grammar and Universal Cognitive Principles: Evidence from German, Farsi, and Chinese', in V. Renner, F. Maniez and P. J. L. Arnaud (eds), *Cross-Disciplinary Perspective on Lexical Blending*, Berlin and Boston: De Gruyter, pp. 115–143.

Scalise, Sergio (1992), 'Compounding in Italian', *Rivista di linguistica*, 4: 1, 175–199.

Schlücker, Barbara (2016), 'Adjective-noun Compounding in Parallel Architecture', in P. ten Hacken (ed.), *The Semantics of Compounding*, Cambridge: Cambridge University Press, pp. 178–191.

Stammerjohann, Harro (2003), 'L'italiano e le altre lingue di fronte all'anglicizzazione', in N. Maraschio and T. Poggi-Salani (eds), *Italia linguistica anno Mille. Italia linguistica anno Duemila*, Roma: Bulzoni, pp. 77–101.

Stöckmann, Fritz (1973), 'Photoconductivity – A Centennial', *phys – stat – sol (a)*, 15: 381.

TLFi (n.d.), *Le Trésor de la Langue Française informatisé*, ATILF – CNRS and Université de Lorraine, http://www.atilf.fr/tlfi (1 August 2017).

Treccani (2018), *Vocabolario Treccani*, http://www.treccani.it/vocabolario/ (12 September 2018).

UIBM (n.d.), *Ufficio italiano brevetti e marchi*, http://www.uibm.gov.it/index.php/2012-06-18-11-45-40 (12 September 2018).

Vogel, Irene (1990), 'English Compounds in Italian', in W. U. Dressler, H. C. Luschützsky, O. E. Pfeiffer and J. R. Rennison (eds), *Contemporary Morphology*, Berlin and New York: De Gruyter, pp. 99–110.

Warren, Beatrice (1978), *Semantic Patterns of Noun-Noun Compounds*, Göteborg: Acta Universitatis Gothoburgensis.

Weinreich, Uriel (1953), *Languages in Contact. Findings and Problems*, New York: Linguistic Circle of New York.

Winford, Donald (2010), 'Contact and Borrowing', in R. Hickey (ed.), *The Handbook of Language Contact*, Oxford: Wiley-Blackwell, pp. 170–177.

Zingarelli (2016), *Lo Zingarelli*, edited by M. Cannella and L. Lazzarini, Milano: Zanichelli. [CD-ROM]

Part II Affixation

7

The Role of Borrowing in the Derivation of Passive Potential Adjectives in Polish

Maria Bloch-Trojnar

This chapter deals with the role of the [±native] marking in the formation of deverbal adjectives terminating in the suffix *-alny* in Polish. The class in question corresponds to *-able/-ible* derivatives in English and conveys the concept of 'passive possibility' as expressed in the paraphrase 'capable of being V-ed' (Bauer 1983) (e.g. *manageable*). Diachronically, the English formations arose under the influence of French, in which, like in other Romance languages, the suffix is related to the Latin *-bilis*. In synchronic terms, the suffix *-able* is counted among the most productive.

By contrast, the relevant suffix in Polish is native in origin but it lags behind its English opposite number in terms of what Corbin (1987) calls *rentabilité* ('profitability'). The suffix *-alny* is synchronically active since, alongside well-entrenched lexical items such as *przewidywalny* 'predictable', *widzialny* 'visible', *uleczalny* 'curable', there are numerous neologisms and nonce-formations, such as *definiowalny* 'definable', *manipulowalny* 'manipulable', *negocjowalny* 'negotiable' (Jadacka 2001: 102).[1] It will be argued that the influx and subsequent adaptation of English verbs, coupled with the speakers' awareness that *-able* and *-alny* discharge similar roles in their respective systems of word formation, has a role to play in raising the productivity of the suffix. This is also possible because, counter to previous analyses (Laskowski 1975; Kowalik 1977; Szymanek 2010), the [±native] marking of the base is not relevant in determining the domain of the process.

This chapter is divided into two parts: a qualitative and a quantitative analysis. In section 1, earlier analyses are presented and critically evaluated and a new proposal is advanced, on which the set of eligible bases is delimited by referring to the semantico-syntactic properties of base verbs. Section 2 offers a frequency analysis supported by diachronic information, which will allow us to separate the well-entrenched lexical items from the latest arrivals, including *hapax legomena*, and trace the latest developments in the formation of passive potential adjectives (henceforth PPAs).

1. Constraints on the derivation of passive potential adjectives in Polish

As far as semantico-syntactic constraints are concerned, PPAs in Polish are based on transitive eventive verbs (e.g. *wykonalny* 'doable', *zmywalny* 'washable', *odnawialny* 'renewable'). Verbs of propositional attitude and psychological verbs do not serve as bases and so there are no *-alny* equivalents of English *lovable*, *credible* and *admirable*. On the other hand, they are possible with verbs of perceiving and sensing such as *widzialny* 'visible', *słyszalny* 'audible' and *namacalny* 'palpable'. The domain of *-alny* suffixation primarily includes transitive bases, but occasionally intransitive verbs with a selected PP are attested (e.g. *odpowiedzialny* 'responsible', *porównywalny* 'comparable'). There are also isolated cases of an intransitive verb with a locative (e.g. *mieszkać* 'live' – *mieszkalny*).[2] Some verbs allow two uses, e.g. *mierzyć* ('measure') as in (1).

> (1) a. On mierzy dwa metry.
>   'He measures two metres', i.e. He is two metres tall.
>   b. Mierzą prędkość nowego modelu.
>   'They are measuring the speed of the new model.'

In such cases only the passivisable variant can be adjectivised. The adjective *mierzalny* 'measurable' can be formed only in reference to the situation in (1b), which implies a causative change of state.

Like in English, potential adjectives can be based on roots characterised as [±native], but they show no phonological differences in the base in terms of the stress pattern, allomorphy or truncation, as observed in the case of *-able/-ible* affixation (Aronoff 1976).

The positive conditions on *-alny* attachment are as general as in the case of its English counterpart, namely that the base verb be [+transitive] (Chapin 1967; Aronoff 1976; Bauer 1983; Fabb 1984; Rainer 1993), and yet the number of actual words recorded in dictionaries is relatively small, slightly exceeding one hundred. Szymanek (2010) concludes that the category in Polish must be far more constrained and goes on to identify the phonological and morphological constraints which restrict the applicability of the process. In Bloch-Trojnar (2017), I extend Oltra-Massuet's (2013) analysis of *-ble* adjectives in English, couched in the Distributed Morphology framework (Halle and Marantz 1993), to Polish. In this analysis, potential adjectives are viewed as modalised passive participles, i.e. both a semantic and a formal link is established with the passive participle, which has hitherto gone unnoticed.[3] The outline of this analysis is presented below, following the discussion of previous proposals.

1.1 Previous accounts

The very identification of the suffix and the base are fraught with difficulty due to the fact that Polish morphology is stem based and the status of thematic elements is not immediately evident. The citation form of verbs is the infinitive, which normally terminates in *-ć*, e.g. *robi·ć* 'do', *pisa·ć* 'write'.[4] Theme-forming elements will be separated from the verbal root with a dash, i.e. *rob-i·ć* 'do', *pis-a·ć* 'write'. They precede inflectional endings and their identity plays a key role in the assignment of stems to particular conjugations. However, some of them surface in deverbal derivatives (Czaykowska-Higgins 1998) and discharge an aspectual function (Młynarczyk 2004).[5] Therefore, following Czaykowska-Higgins (1998) a formal distinction is recognised between thematic elements which contribute to the derivational stem (verbalising suffixes type 1 VS1: *-i, -ew/ej, -ow, -iw/yw*) and thematic elements which form the inflectional stem (VS2: *-a, -e, -aj*).

Earlier analyses of the category of passive potential adjectives placed great emphasis on formal constraints (Laskowski 1975; Kowalik 1977). For Laskowski (1975: 135–136) the suffix *-aln·y* can be regarded as an intermorphic extension of the basic adjective-forming suffix *-n·y*. His solution, proposed in the abstract phonology framework, involves the second degree (*·l*) stem which is homophonous with the 3rd person sg. praeterite form, e.g. (2).

(2)   *wykrywa·ć* 'to discover' > *wykrywał* 'he discovered' > *wykrywał-n·y*

This means that the derivational stem contains *-al-*, the actual derivational ending being *-n-*.

However, Szymanek (2010: 105–112) follows the traditional assumption that there exists the suffix *-aln·y* and identifies two classes of bases to which it is attached. The first class of bases to which the suffix *-aln·y* is productively attached are Secondary Imperfective (SI) transitive verbs. SIs arise by shifting a derived perfective verb into the imperfective class, a process in which the thematic suffix *-a* and *-i/-y* in the base is substituted with *-iwa/ywa* and *-a* respectively in the SI, illustrated in Table 7.1.[6]

Szymanek emphasises that it is not just any imperfective verb that can serve as the base (e.g. *rządzić* 'rule' – **rządzalny*, *leczyć* 'treat' – **leczalny*, *grać* 'play' – **gralny*, *znać* 'know' – **znalny*) and concludes that 'the category "Secondary Imperfective" is grammatically significant and available to the rules of word-formation' (Szymanek 2010: 110).

The second class of bases eligible for *-aln·y* affixation are verbs marked as imperfective, transitive and [–native]. Such verbs typically belong to the learned/scientific lexicon and bear the nativising thematic element *-ow-* (sometimes preceded by the stem extensions *-ik*, *-iz*), e.g. (3).

Table 7.1 Secondary Imperfective verbs as bases for the derivation of PPAs

Verb	PPA
pisać[IPFV] 'write' – przepisać[PFV] 'copy' przepisać[PFV] 'copy' – przepisywać[IPFV(SI)] 'copy'	przepisywalny 'copiable'
widzieć[IPFV] 'see' – przewidzieć[PFV] 'predict' przewidzieć[PFV] 'predict' – przewidywać[IPFV(SI)] 'predict'	przewidywalny 'predictable'
kryć[IPFV] 'cover' – odkryć[PFV] 'discover' odkryć[PFV] 'discover' – odkrywać[IPFV(SI)] 'discover'	odkrywalny 'discoverable'

(3) a. transformować 'transform' – transformowalny 'transformable'
     b. weryfikować 'verify'   – weryfikowalny 'verifiable'
     c. analizować 'analyse'   – analizowalny 'analysable'

In sum, Szymanek (2010: 110–111) proposes two disjoint classes of imperfective verbs serving as input to *-alny* suffixation: '(a) native verbs, which must meet the condition of belonging to the category of Secondary Imperfectives [. . .] and (b) non-native verbs, which do not observe this condition'. He also remarks that 'we take it for granted that a feature like [±native], or its analogue, is a synchronically significant lexical designation'.

Szymanek's account accurately describes the data. He selects the first-degree rather than the second-degree stem in *-ł-*, which allows him to get around problematic cases such as *palny* 'inflammable' < *palić (się)* 'burn', which are best described as relating to *pal-* rather than *palił-*. The selection of the imperfective form is made only on formal and not semantic grounds. The addition of the affix *-alny* to the present (first-degree) stem is constrained by a mixture of properties, i.e. reference is made to the syntactic transitive feature, the morphological property of the Secondary Imperfective, and the lexical property [±native]. We do not learn why non-derived imperfective native stems are not suitable whereas the adapted foreign ones are.

In what follows I will consider another option, i.e. I will establish whether there is anything to be gained from an analysis in which *-alny* adjectives are regarded as modalised passive participles. I propose yet another segmentation of the derived adjective where the *-al-* element supplies modality, whereas the *-n-* morpheme reflects the presence of passive morphology in the structure (Jabłońska 2007; Biały 2008). The theme vowel in the verbal stem of the passive participle is replaced with the modal element *-al-*, as presented in Table 7.2.

Notably, the formatives contributing to the verbal derivational stem are retained (i.e. verbalising suffixes of type 1 in Czaykowska-Higgins's (1998) analysis: *-i*, *-ew/ ej*, *-ow*, *-iw/yw*). Thematic elements whose sole function is the spell-out of conjugation class features (verbalising suffixes of type 2: *-a*, *-e*, *-aj*) do not appear in the potential adjective.

1.2 Potential adjectives as modalised passive participles

The passive participle is formed from transitive verbs with the aid of the suffixes *-n·y* and *-t·y*, and it is the participle form in *-ny* that serves as the base for the derivation

Table 7.2 Passive participles as bases for the derivation of PPAs

Verb	Passive participle	Potential adjective
odwróc-i·ć^{PFV} odwrac-a·ć$^{IPFV(SI)}$ 'reverse'	odwróc-o-n·y odwrac-a-n·y	odwrac-al-ny
przewidzi-e·ć^{PFV} przewid-yw-a·ć$^{IPFV(SI)}$ 'predict'	przwidzi-a-n·y przewid-yw-a-n·y	przewid-yw-al-ny

Table 7.3 Passive participles in -*ny* as bases for the derivation of PPAs in -*alny*

Verb	Passive participle	PPA
pi·ć^{IFPV} – wy-pi·ć^{PFV} 'drink'	pi-t·y – wy-pi-t·y	pit-n·y
ścier-a·ć^{IFPV} – zetrz-e·ć^{PFV} 'erase'	ścier-a-n·y – star-t·y	ścier-al-n·y
dotyk-a·ć^{IFPV} – dotk-ną·ć^{PFV} 'touch'	dotyk-a-n·y – dotk-nię-t·y	dotyk-al-n·y
wykr-y·ć^{PFV} – wykr-yw-a·ć^{IFPV} 'discover'	wykr-y-t·y – wykr-yw-a-n·y	wykr-yw-al-n·y

of passive potential adjectives. If the participle ends in -*ty*, as is the case with the verb *pić* 'drink', it is excluded from its domain. These regularities are illustrated in Table 7.3.

Only those passive participles which can be passivised can serve as bases for -*alny*, i.e. participles related to [Agent, Theme] verbs which take an internal argument in the accusative case. There are two other types of passive participles in Polish which are not a component of the passive voice, i.e. participles relating to mental activities such as *pomyślany* 'think-PPRT', *upragniony* 'desire-PPRT', *wymarzony* 'dream-PPRT', *wytęskniony* 'miss-PPRT', *znany* 'know-PPRT' and participles relating to intransitive verbs, e.g. *wyspany* 'sleep-PPRT', *uśmiechnięty* 'smile-PPRT', *zmarznięty* 'be cold-PPRT'. None of these can serve as the base for potential adjectivisation (*pomyślalny, *wyspalny). We can conclude that there is not only a formal but also a functional link with the passive in that only passive participles occurring in passive sentences can act as bases for potential adjectivisation.

Another interesting feature of PPAs in Polish is that it is primarily imperfective verbs that serve as bases. This statement is, by and large, true but it is in need of a slight modification. According to Oltra-Massuet (2013), the suffix -*ble* in English is inserted in a little *a* node c-commanding a ModP.[7] The modal component induces stativity and genericity and -*ble* adjectives are generic characterising predicates (Krifka et al. 1995). They are individual-level predicates which express permanent properties of individuals. As such, in Polish they are more felicitous with the imperfective aspect. According to Condoravdi (1989), in languages with a perfective-imperfective aspectual distinction, middles, and all generic sentences, are marked with the imperfective aspect. In Polish, unlike in English, the imperfective is the semantically and morphologically unmarked member in the aspectual opposition. The morphologically marked perfective refers to a single, well-delimited event occurring on a specific occasion. In semantic terms, the 'imperfective aspect is a non-aspect' (Willim 2006: 205) and imperfective sentences convey a wide array of meanings such as 'progressiveness, imperfectiveness, iterativity, habituality/genericity, ingressiveness, perfectivity and resultativity' (Willim 2006: 200) (see also Śmiech 1971: 44; Comrie 1976: 59, 113; Laskowski 1999: 160–161). In the majority of cases the imperfective member of the aspectual pair acts as the base for the derivation of PPAs. However, the perfective stem is not impossible, as illustrated by the examples in Table 7.4.

Table 7.4 Perfective passive participles as bases for the derivation of PPAs

Verb	Passive participle	PPA
wykonać^{PFV} wykonywać^{IPFV} 'perform'	wykonany wykonywany	wykonalny
leczyć^{IPFV} uleczyć^{PFV} 'cure'	leczony uleczony	uleczalny
niszczyć^{IPFV} zniszczyć^{PFV} 'destroy'	niszczony zniszczony	zniszczalny
twierdzić^{IPFV} stwierdzić^{PFV} 'claim'	twierdzony stwierdzony	stwierdzalny
rozerwać^{PFV} rozrywać^{IPFV} 'tear'	rozerwany rozrywany	rozerwalny

Table 7.5 Derivational doublets related to the imperfective and perfective passive participle

Verb	Passive participle	PPA
rozwiązać^{PFV} rozwiązywać^{IPFV} 'solve'	rozwiązany rozwiązywany	rozwiązalny rozwiązywalny
odwołać^{PFV} odwoływać^{IPFV} 'cancel'	odwołany odwoływany	odwołalny odwoływalny
stostować^{IPFV} zastosować^{PFV} 'utilise'	stosowany zastosowany	stosowalny zastosowalny
palić^{IPFV} zapalić^{PFV} 'burn, set fire to'	palony zapalony	palny zapalny

This has led me to the conclusion that it is not so much the actual morphological aspectual marking that matters, but the fact that the verbal root in question underlies an aspectual pair, i.e. it denotes a situation that can be viewed as an activity with a potential result. This intuition seems to be confirmed by the existence of occasional derivational doublets, presented in Table 7.5, which can be related to both the imperfective and perfective form of the base verb.

Furthermore, there is no need to make reference to the [±native] contrast. The borrowed verbs are imperfective and transitive, but it suffices to say that they participate in an aspectual opposition, i.e. they can be conceived of as events with a potential result. The aspectual contrast is expressed by means of prefixation and it is the

Table 7.6 PPAs derived from [–native] verbs forming aspectual pairs

Verb	Passive participle	PPA
obserwować[IPFV]	obserwowany	obserwowalny
zaobserwować[PFV]	zaobserwowany	
'observe'		
akceptować[IPFV]	akceptowany	akceptowalny
zaakceptować[PFV]	zaakceptowany	
'accept'		
modyfikować[IPFV]	modyfikowany	modyfikowalny
zmodyfikować[PFV]	zmodyfikowany	
'modify'		

Table 7.7 PPAs in -*ny* related to participles in -*(o)n·y* and -*t·y*

Verb[IPFV] ↔ Verb[PFV]	Passive participle	PPA
pal-i·ć – s-pal-i·ć 'burn'	(s)pal-o–ny	pal–ny
kos-i·ć – s-kos-i·ć 'mow'	(s)kosz-o–ny	koś–ny
dziel-i·ć – po-dziel-i·ć 'divide'	(po)dziel-o–ny	podziel–ny
rob-i·ć – z-rob-i·ć 'do'	(z)robi-o–ny	–
jeść – z-jeść 'eat'	(z)jedz-o–ny	–
pi·ć – wy-pi·ć 'drink'	(wy)pi-ty	pi-t–ny
bi·ć – z-bi·ć 'beat'	(z)bi-ty	–

unprefixed, imperfective pair member that serves as the base for the -*alny* adjective, as in Table 7.6.[8]

Borrowed verbs which are classified as *imperfectiva tantum*, i.e. verbs that inherently lack the perfective counterpart, cannot give rise to -*alny* derivatives, e.g. *stymulować* 'stimulate', *hospitalizować* 'hospitalise', *izolować* 'isolate' and *snifować* 'sniff amphetamine'.

The presence of an aspectual marker, i.e. a perfectivising prefix or an imperfectivising suffix, is an overt indicator that the verb participates in an aspectual contrast. Either type is possible but derived stems with imperfective markers are preferred because of the semantic restrictions on the derivative, or, to put it in constructionist terms, on account of genericity requirements associated with the modal operator.

The lack of potential adjectives in -*alny* relating to morphologically simplex imperfective transitive verbs which form aspectual pairs may be due to the existence of adjectives in -*ny*. The virtually unproductive suffix -*ny* is selected if the passive participle ends in -*(o)n·y* or -*t·y*, as shown in Table 7.7.

Because the formation of the potential adjective is marginally productive with the participle in -*ony*, in some cases the system falls back on the habitual stem, e.g. *jadać* 'eat habitually' – *jadalny* 'edible'. The habitual stem is available to a handful of lexically marked roots, and since it is semantically compatible with the genericity requirement imposed by the modal operator the formation of the adjective is not blocked

Table 7.8 PPAs derived from verbs forming aspectual pairs and simplex verbs lacking an aspectual counterpart excluded from the domain of PPA formation

Simplex verb^{IPFV}	Verb^{PFV} ↔ Verb^{SI}	PPA
myć 'wash'	umyć – umywać 'wash'	umywalny
myć 'wash'	zmyć – zmywać 'wash'	zmywalny
grzać 'warm'	ogrzać – ogrzewać 'warm'	ogrzewalny
lać 'pour'	wylać – wylewać 'pour out'	wylewalny
znać 'know'	poznać – poznawać 'get to know'	poznawalny

(e.g. *pijać* 'drink habitually' – *pijalny* 'drinkable' and *sypiać* 'sleep habitually' – *sypialny* 'that can be slept in' as in *wagon sypialny* 'sleeping car').

Furthermore, simplex imperfective roots will not give rise to potential adjectives if their perfective counterparts have ceased to be regarded as the truly perfective counterpart in an aspectual pair. A clear indicator of this is the formation of the Secondary Imperfective and it is the SI form that gives rise to the *-alny* adjective, as shown in Table 7.8.[9]

The formation of the SI is not blocked since it has a different meaning from the basic imperfective verb to which the prefixed verb is related. Tenuous as it may be, this difference seems to be related to iteration, durativity or intensity.[10] Simple imperfective roots give rise to a plethora of derived perfective forms (e.g. *pisać* 'write' > *dopisać* 'add, write in', *nadpisać* 'overwrite', *przypisać* 'ascribe', *zapisać* 'fill with writing', *spisać* 'draw up', etc.) (Śmiech 1986). Since the derived verbs express a variety of meanings in addition to perfectivity, the system generates their proper aspectual counterparts, which are traditionally called Secondary Imperfectives, although they are, in fact, aspectual counterparts of derived verbs. It is these imperfective forms that are selected for the formation of potential adjectives (*dopisywalny*, *nadpisywalny*, *przypisywalny*, *zapisywalny*, *spisywalny*, *przypisywalny*). Simplex imperfective forms are thus greatly outnumbered and since they express basic meanings there may be pragmatic limitations on their usage as bases.[11] After all, potential adjectives are supposed to express non-trivial properties.

1.3 Summary of the qualitative analysis

Potential adjectives are characterised by modal, passive and generic content. Only passivisable verbs, i.e. verbs which take the internal argument and involve external causation, can serve as bases. The imperfective form is selected because the imperfective is the semantically unmarked member in the aspectual opposition and it is compatible with the non-specificity required of generic characterising predicates. The base verb must be a member of an aspectual pair, i.e. it must denote a situation with a potential result. Thus, it is not enough for the verb to be imperfective, and at times perfective stems are actually taken as a base. Morphologically simplex imperfective roots will find their way to a passive potential adjectival structure provided that they denote a process with a potential result. There is no *leczalny or *znalny but there is uleczalny 'curable' and poznawalny 'cognoscible'. There is no need to make reference to the notion of 'Secondary Imperfective' and the [±native] distinction. Suffice to say that the base verb is to be associated with an internal theme argument, an implication of causation and a change of state. The best match is an aspect variable [Agent, Theme] verb. The rest follows from the constraints on the structure, i.e. the fact that -alny adjectives are modalised passive participles.

If we can show that both native and borrowed/adapted verbs contribute to enlarging the stock of -alny derivatives, this will be tangible evidence in favour of the proposed analysis.

2. Frequency analysis of -alny derivatives based on [±native] verbs from a diachronic perspective

A corpus-based measure of the number of types (type frequency), i.e. different words with a given affix, is preferable to the dictionary-based measures, since it is conducted on a representative language sample (Biber 1993) and does not involve arbitrary decisions as to whether or not to include a given lexical item in the list. The measure of the occurrence of the affix with the same base (token frequency) demonstrates which items are used more frequently and are thus more firmly established in the speakers' memory and have a stronger representation in the lexicon. Words which occur only once in a corpus (the so-called hapax legomena) point to the existence of an active morphological rule, which makes possible their decomposition into constituent parts and their semantic interpretation (Baayen 1992, 1993; Baayen and Renouf 1996; Plag et al. 1999).

In what follows I will try to establish whether the influx of verbs borrowed from English has the potential to influence the productivity of the rule. I will first look into the proportion of native and foreign bases in the domain of the rule and subsequently I will look at their token frequencies and discuss the number of hapaxes in the relevant subdomains. Finally, I will consider the rise of new derivatives in a diachronic perspective in order to formulate some predictions for the future. The hypotheses will be tested on the data obtained from the National Corpus of Polish (NKJP) (Przepiórkowski et al. 2012). The balanced version of the NKJP amounts to 300 million words and its full version contains c. 1,500 million words.[12] An extensive unbalanced pool of texts can be useful when we investigate low-frequency phenomena for which the balanced version of the corpus gives few or no occurrences. The PELCRA search engine devised for the NKJP by Pęzik (2012) makes it possible to search both versions of the corpus and retrieve all word forms of a given lexical item, which is extremely useful when studying inflectionally rich languages like Polish. It also provides information on token frequency and dates of attestation/publication. PELCRA enables collocation search, register and time distribution plots (Górski et al. 2012). Since deverbal derivatives, as such, belong to very low-frequency phenomena, we expect to find a real difference between the balanced and the full version of the NKJP, the latter being crucial to finding the hapaxes. Additionally, in order to establish the type frequency, our corpus searches are supported with the data contained in two reverse dictionaries, one edited by Grzegorczykowa and Puzynina (1973) and the other edited some thirty years later by Tokarski (2002).

2.1 Type and token frequency analysis

The reverse dictionary edited by Grzegorczykowa and Puzynina (1973), compiled on the basis of the most comprehensive dictionary of Polish edited by Doroszewski, contains c. 170 items terminating in *-alny* that can be related to verbal bases. Interestingly, almost all of them are based on native verbs with the notable exception of *obserwowalny* 'observable'. When confronted with the NKJP, the list has to be shortened by c. 40 lexical items that are not attested.[13] The list to be found in Tokarski (2002) has been amended in such a way as to exclude these items, but only five new entries have been added (i.e. *przystosowalny* 'adjustable', *rozwiązalny* 'solvable', *weryfikowalny* 'verifiable', *komunikowalny* 'communicable', *reformowalny* 'reformable'), of which only the last three can be regarded as derivatives based on non-native verbs. The relevant data have been broken down into three classes and full lists are provided in Appendices 7.2–7.4, with the numbers in parentheses indicating the token frequencies in the balanced and full version of the NKJP. *Hapax legomena* come last and are marked in bold.

In the first group there are twenty-seven items with a token frequency exceeding 100 in the balanced corpus (see Appendix 7.2) and only five of them have a frequency higher than 500.[14] Notably, these entrenched high-frequency units frequently show additional lexicalised senses inasmuch as they have a deontic flavour or are devoid of any passive interpretation whatsoever, e.g. *karalny* 'punishable', *doświadczalny* 'experimental', *opłacalny* 'profitable', *powitalny* 'welcoming' and *pochwalny* 'laudable'.

In the second group there are eighty-three items with a token frequency below 100 (see Appendix 7.3), five of which have the status of *hapax legomena* (i.e. *dosięgalny* 'reach-PPA' (1-1), *dobieralny* 'assort-PPA' (1-1), *powątpiewalny* 'doubtful' (1-1), *włączalny* 'include-PPA' (1-1), *namaszczalny* 'anoint-PPA' (1-1)).

The third group contains twenty-five items which are not attested in the balanced version and can only be found in the full version of the NKJP (see Appendix 7.4). There are six hapaxes in this group, namely *wymłacalny* 'thresh-PPA' (0-1), *skracalny* 'shorten-PPA' (0-1), *przeświecalny* 'translucent' (0-1), *wyciągalny* 'draw out-PPA' (0-1), *przesączalny* 'drainable' (0-1) and *zaświadczalny* 'testify-PPA' (0-1).

In sum, there are 135 derivatives, of which eleven have the status of hapaxes. What we can deduce is that we are dealing with a truly productive process of word formation, characterised by a low number of high-frequency items, a high number of low-frequency items and giving rise to neologisms, nonce-formations and hapaxes. The tendencies are in line with Plag's (2004: 8–9) remark that

> productive processes are [. . .] characterized by large numbers of low frequency words and small numbers of high frequency words. The many low frequency words keep the rule alive, because they force speakers to segment the derivatives and thus strengthen the existence

of the affix. Unproductive morphological categories will, in contrast, be characterized by a preponderance of words with rather high frequencies and a small number of words with low frequencies.

A detailed study of the data in the NKJP allowed us to identify another ten derivatives based on native verbal bases, two of which are hapaxes (i.e. *skalowalny* 'scalable' (23-285), *stopniowalny* 'gradable' (12-34), *ladowalny* 'loadable' (3-11), *kasowalny* 'deletable' (2-6), *różniczkowalny* 'differentiable' (1-27), *zdejmowalny* 'removable' (0-6), *wyjmowalny* 'removable' (0-3), *opodatkowalny* 'taxable' (0-2), *cytowalny* 'quotable' (0-1) and ***drukowalny*** (0-13) 'printable').

However, far more interesting is the number of derivatives based on non-native (i.e. English) verbs. They are divided into two groups depending on whether they have been attested in the balanced corpus (see Appendix 7.5) or not (see Appendix 7.6). The former contains thirty-seven items and the latter forty-eight. In the first subclass there are ten hapaxes. The second subclass contains nineteen hapaxes. They are marked in bold in the appendices.

The number of nonce-formations based on adapted foreign verbs amounts to eighty-five, of which twenty-nine are hapaxes. To sum up, the ratio of native to non-native bases in passive adjective formation is 142:88.[15] The ratio of hapaxes with native bases to hapaxes with non-native ones is 13:29. Since they are a significant source of new formations, derivatives based on non-native verbs are an important factor in maintaining the productivity of the rule. Their low token frequency stems from the fact that they are relatively recent arrivals, most of them making their appearance in the 1990s, at a time coinciding with the fall of communism, the introduction of English into the school curriculum and widespread access to the internet and computer-mediated communication.[16] This issue is addressed in more detail in the following section.

2.2 A diachronic perspective

The PELCRA concordancer can produce diagrams showing how the relative frequency of a word (measured against its number of occurrences in a given year) changes in time (Górski et al. 2012; Pęzik 2012).

According to Fischer (1998: 174) one of the indicators of institutionalisation is a decrease in frequency after a certain frequency peak value. This tendency can be illustrated for two relatively well-entrenched adjectives based on foreign bases, namely *obserwowalny* 'observable' and *akceptowalny* 'acceptable'.

Figures 7.1 and 7.2 demonstrate the time prior to the coining of the derivative followed by the peak of its frequency, subsequent drop and then continuation at a lower rate. With the PELCRA tool we can produce similar charts for all tokens terminating in *-izowalny*, *-ifikowalny* and *-owalny*.

Figure 7.3 demonstrates that *-alny* derivatives based on foreign verbs ending in *-izować* made their appearance in the early 1990s, reached their frequency peak in 2003 and now continue to be used at a lower rate.

Figure 7.4 shows that *-alny* derivatives based on foreign verbs ending in *-ifikować* appeared most recently and they do not seem to have reached their frequency peak yet.

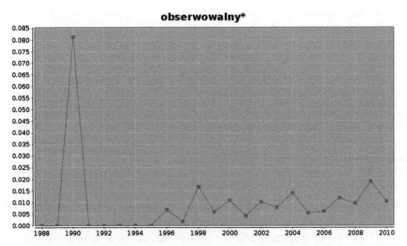

Figure 7.1 Diachronic frequency profile for query *obserwowalny* 'observable'

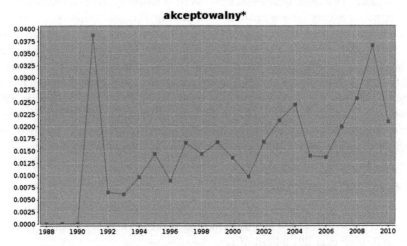

Figure 7.2 Diachronic frequency profile for query *akceptowalny* 'acceptable'

Because verbs ending in -*ować* can be related to native and foreign bases (including those ending in -*izować* and -*ifikować*), we can see in Figure 7.5 that the corresponding -*alny* derivatives have been attested since the late 1980s and the frequency peak value is more than ten times higher in comparison to peak values in Figures 7.3 and 7.4. Most importantly, we can observe that there is a rising tendency for the use of -*alny* derivatives.

Another interesting phenomenon which has transpired during the investigation of -*alny* derivatives based on native verbs is that, apart from a few well entrenched derivatives such as *mieszkalny* 'inhabitable' (Figure 7.6), they are relatively recent arrivals dating back to the 1990s, as shown in Figures 7.7 and 7.8 for *mierzalny* 'measurable' and *rozpoznawalny* 'recognisable'.

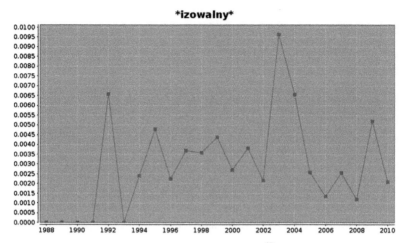

Figure 7.3 Diachronic frequency profile for query –*izowalny*[17]

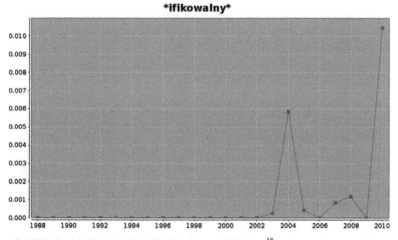

Figure 7.4 Diachronic frequency profile for query –*ifikowalny*[18]

Figures 7.7 and 7.8 demonstrate that both derivatives appeared in the early 1990s and reached their frequency peak in 2009. The fall in frequency in 2010 may indicate either that the process of their institutionalisation has started or that the items are on their way to be discarded. The fact remains that the appearance of these and similar native derivatives has coincided with the expansion of the lexicon with -*alny* derivatives based on adapted foreign verbs.

2.3 Borrowing – word formation interactions

My contention is that the productivity of the process of forming PPAs in Polish has recently been given a fillip thanks to the influx of English verbs, with the number of

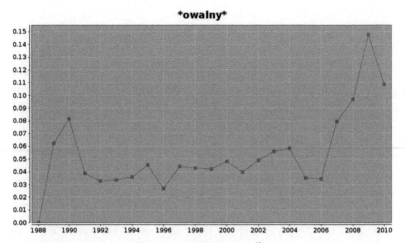

Figure 7.5 Diachronic frequency profile for query *-owalny*[19]

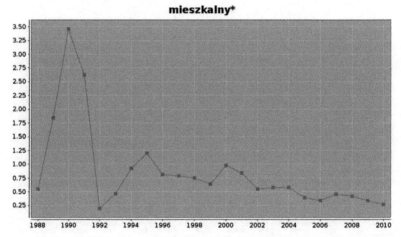

Figure 7.6 Diachronic frequency profile of a well-entrenched lexical item for query *mieszkalny* 'habitable'

foreign-based hapaxes being twice as numerous as in the case of adjectives based on native verbs. The rise of adjectives based on native verbs has also been noticeable, with the majority of new adjectives making their appearance in the 1990s, and the process shows a steady tendency for expansion, e.g. *wszczepialny* 'implantable' and *wyłączalny* 'turn off-PPA' appeared between 2000–2003. Whereas *wszczepialny* could be regarded as the native equivalent of the foreign-sounding *implantowalny* 'implantable', which also features among the hapaxes, there seems to be no English model for *wyłączalny* 'such that can be turned off'. Actually, a sizeable group of adjectives based on adapted foreign bases and listed in Appendices 7.5 and 7.6 would require such a periphrastic gloss, which means that they have no English *-able* opposite numbers.

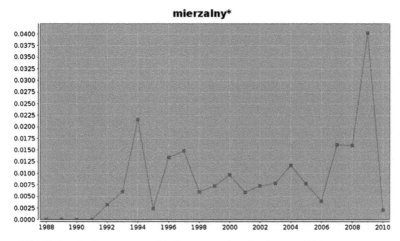

Figure 7.7 Diachronic frequency profile for query *mierzalny* 'measurable'

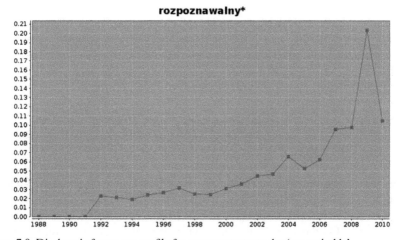

Figure 7.8 Diachronic frequency profile for query *rozpoznawalny* 'recognisable'

At the same time, it is possible to encounter cases where the *-alny* formation is a direct calque from English, since the complex form has a higher token frequency than its supposed simplex base (Seifart 2015). The adjective *biodegradowalny* 'biodegradable' is a case in point. The adjective has 142 occurrences in the full NKJP compared to five occurrences of word forms of the verb *biodegradować* 'biodegrade'. By contrast, the word forms of *akceptować* occur 17,949 times in the corpus, whereas the corresponding adjective *akceptowalny* has only 753 occurrences in the corpus. Furthermore, the token frequency of the verb *obserwować* far exceeds that of the adjective *obserwowalny* (44, 721:358), which is indicative of a derivational relationship.

Szymanek (2010) rightly observes that the PPA relating to the simplex imperfective intransitive verb *grać* 'play', i.e. **gralny*, is impossible. At the same time, in English the verb is transitive, as in *play computer games*. Most gamers in Poland have a pressing

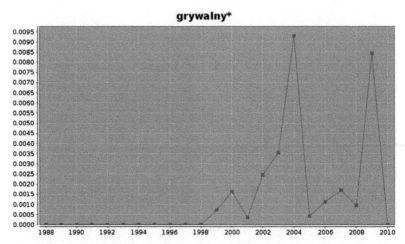

Figure 7.9 Diachronic frequency profile for query *grywalny* 'playable'

need for the Polish equivalent of *playable* and they seem to have taken care of this lexical gap, as the full version of NKJP contains ninety-seven occurrences of the adjective *grywalny* 'playable', which is related to the habitual form *grywać* 'play habitually', e.g. (4).

(4) Warhammer okazał się bardziej grywalny, ale lubię mroczność w innym wydaniu niż fantasy.
'Warhammer turned out to be more playable, but I prefer darkness in a convention other than fantasy.'

Given the growing role of the internet in the lives of the younger generation, the adjective might become part of the linguistic norm despite the fact that it does not meet the constraints on the relevant WFR (*grać* 'play' – *grywać* 'play habitually' do not form an aspectual pair). On the other hand, since the institutionalisation of a word correlates with a multi-topical distribution in a variety of texts, this word may share the fate of other nonce-formations coined to meet the needs of a limited linguistic community. As Figure 7.9 demonstrates, the adjective has recently lost its popularity, which may mark its ephemeral status.

3. Conclusion

Whereas in English the distribution of the *-able* and *-ible* allomorphs hinges on the native/Latinate origin of the verbal bases, in Polish the identification of the bases eligible for *-alny* suffixation need not make recourse to the [±native] marking of the base.

The emergence of particular lexical items may be due to borrowing, but since there is a verbal base available for each *-alny* formation and the frequency of occurrence of verbs exceeds the frequency of related adjectives and many *-alny* formations have no *-able* correlates in English, it is plausible to assume that these adjectives are products of word formation rather than borrowing. In the course of the past fifty years we have witnessed a substantial rise in the profitability of the rule from 170 derivatives attested in Grzegorczykowa and Puzynina (1973) to 230 attested in Tokarski (2002). Forty derivatives had been discarded by the turn of the millennium as evidenced in Tokarski (2002), while 100 new formations have been added since. Tokarski (2002) identified five new derivatives, while the present study discussed ninety-five new -*alny* formations, of which ten are based on native verbs and eighty-five can be related to adapted foreign verbs.

The intensified character of Polish–English linguistic contact, coupled with a greater proficiency of Poles in English after the fall of communism, the introduction of English to the school curriculum, unconstrained access to the internet and a wave of Polish emigration to the United Kingdom and Ireland, have, to varying degrees, resulted in the influx of foreign verbs which serve as input to passive potential derivation. As far as *hapax legomena* are concerned, at least for the time being, the rule produces twice as many in the foreign subdomain. However, the formation of -*alny* derivatives on borrowed/adapted stems seems to have given a new impulse to the formation of adjectives based on native bases. This is due to the fact that the rule is operative on transitive [Agent, Theme] verbs forming aspectual pairs, irrespective of whether they are [±native].

Appendix 7.1

Items from the reverse dictionary edited by Grzegorczykowa and Puzynina (1973) which are not listed in the balanced and full version of the NKJP (forty derivatives):

domacalny 'grope-PPA'
zalecalny 'recommend-PPA'
skręcalny 'twist-PPA'
nasycalny 'saturate-PPT'
oddalny 'stave off-PPA'
smagalny 'lash-PPA'
urabialny 'work-PPA'
podstawialny 'place-PPA'
zestawialny 'correlate-PPA'
dowidzialny 'see-PPT'
zaspokajalny 'satisfy-PPA'
poczekalny 'wait-PPA'
uciskalny 'press-PPA'
żegnalny 'part-PPA'
przypominalny 'remind-PPA'
zasuwalny 'draw-PPA'
odsuwalny 'push away-PPA'
zsuwalny 'draw in-PPA'
ogrzewalny 'warm-PPA'
wychowalny 'bring up-PPA'

powinszowalny 'congratulate-PPA'
polaryzowalny 'polarise-PPA'
oderwaly 'tear off-PPA'
pralny 'wash-PPA'
potrząsalny 'shake-PPA'
chwytalny 'catch-PPA'
zawalny 'fell down-PPA'
przerywalny 'interrupt-PPA'
rozwiązalny 'solve-PPA'
odsączalny 'drain-PPA'
wyćwiczalny 'drill-PPA'
spuszczalny 'release-PPA'
oczyszczalny 'purify-PPA'
rozrządzalny 'govern-PPA'
ruszalny 'move-PPA'
rozprowadzalny 'distribute-PPA'
pocieszalny 'comfort-PPA'
obciążalny 'burden-PPA'
poruszalny 'move-PPA'

Appendix 7.2

Derivatives with a token frequency higher than 100 in the balanced NKJP (twenty-seven derivatives):

mieszkalny 'habitable' (3892-23, 238)
dopuszczalny 'permissible' (1035-5282)
porównywalny 'comparable' (941-5247)
doświadczalny 'experimental' (741-4432)
pożegnalny 'farewell' (585-2713)
odnawialny 'renewable' (486-3165)
zauważalny 'noticeable' (474-2145)
rozpoznawalny 'recognisable' (473-2687)
opłacalny 'profitable' (453-2322)
przewidywalny 'predictable' (373-1797)
widzialny 'visible' (355-2815)
jadalny 'edible' (333-2019)
namacalny 'palpable' (325-1876)
słyszalny 'audible' (299-1097)

karalny 'punishable' (278-2060)
wyczuwalny 'detectable' (235-958)
przypuszczalny 'presumable' (230-2266)
powitalny 'welcoming' (214-834)
sypialny 'for sleeping' (210-717)
dostrzegalny 'noticeable' (188-816)
powtarzalny 'repeatable' (170-1089)
wymagalny 'necessary' (146-663)
osiągalny 'attainable' (142-729)
rozpuszczalny 'soluble' (120-874)
palny 'combustible' (119-746)
wymienialny 'replaceable' (114-484)
pochwalny 'laudable' (111-736)

Appendix 7.3

Derivatives with a token frequency below 100 in the balanced NKJP (with the *hapax legomena* coming last and marked in bold) (eighty-three derivatives):

mierzalny 'measurable' (80-469)
sprawdzalny 'verifiable' (76-385)
dotykalny 'tangible' (65-162)
wykonalny 'manageable' (61-296)
wypłacalny 'solvent' (62-294)
przyswajalny 'ingestible' (58-530)
rozszczepialny 'fissile' (56-216)
odwracalny 'reversible' (54-543)
wybieralny 'elective' (54-314)
dosłyszalny 'audible' (45-59)
uleczalny 'curable' (43-238)
grzebalny 'bury-PPA' (42-350)
wyobrażalny 'imaginable' (37-149)
obliczalny 'calculable' (31-140)
obserwowalny 'observable' (29-388)
wykrywalny 'detectable' (28-151)
obieralny 'elective' (27-104)
zbywalny 'transferable' (26-135)
zmywalny 'washable' (26-135)
przepuszczalny 'permeable' (25-191)

rozporządzalny 'manageable' (25-87)
poznawalny 'cognoscible' (23-288)
weryfikowalny 'verfiable' (22-510)
wyleczalny 'curable' (20-153)
wytłumaczalny 'explicable' (18-106)
reformowalny 'reformable' (15-134)
przeliczalny 'calculable' (14-451)
policzalny 'calculable' (14-154)
rozwiązywalny 'solvable' (14-105)
ubieralny 'dress-PPA' (11-18)
postrzegalny 'observable' (12-41)
ściągalny 'collectible' (10-43)
rozkładalny 'foldable' (10-29)
umarzalny 'sink (a debt)-PPA' (10-102)
wybaczalny 'forgivable' (9-48)
przebłagalny 'propitiative' (8-258)
usuwalny 'removable' (8-58)
przekładalny 'translatable' (8-36)
zanurzalny 'submersible' (7-15)
rozszerzalny 'extensible' (6-28)

zniszczalny 'destructible' (5-41)
wyróżnialny 'distinguishable' (5-22)
przenikalny 'permeable' (5-13)
wypowiadalny 'pronounceable' (5-9)
rozstrzygalny 'decide-PPA' (4-35)
ścieralny 'erase-PPA' (4-22)
rozbieralny 'dismantle-PPA' (3-39)
całkowalny 'integrable' (3-36)
przetłumaczalny 'translatable' (3-25)
odtwarzalny 'reproducible' (3-25)
wszczepialny 'implantable' (3-18)
przemijalny 'transient' (3-17)
wymierzalny 'mete out-PPA' (3-15)
komunikowalny 'communicate-PPA'
(3-14)
spłacalny 'pay off-PPA' (3-13)
przemakalny 'soak-PPA' (3-13)
sprowadzalny 'importable' (3-11)
odwoływalny 'call off-PPA' (3-11)
stosowalny 'usable' (2-27)
zastępowalny 'replaceable' (2-17)
wystarczalny 'sufficient' (2-14)

przekazywalny 'transmissible' (2-10)
wyłączalny 'turn off-APP' (2-10)
obracalny 'revolve-PPA' (2-9)
przystawalny 'adhere to-PPA' (2-8)
przesuwalny 'movable' (2-7)
ziszczalny 'materialise-PPA' (2-2)
wyrażalny 'expressible' (1-22)
odkształcalny 'buckle-PPA' (1-18)
przekraczalny 'transgressible' (1-10)
odwołalny 'revocable' (1-7)
rozłączalny 'detachable' (1-7)
obrabialny 'workable' (1-5)
spostrzegalny 'noticeable' (1-5)
nastawialny 'reposition-PPA' (1-5)
nawracalny 'convert-PPA' (1-4)
wzruszalny 'movable' (1-4)
zamienialny 'changeable' (1-2)
dosięgalny 'reach-PPA' (1-1)
dobieralny 'assort-PPA' (1-1)
powątpiewalny 'doubtful' (1-1)
włączalny 'include-PPA' (1-1)
namaszczalny 'anoint-PPA' (1-1)

Appendix 7.4

Derivatives not attested in the balanced NKJP (twenty-five derivatives):

używalny 'usable' (0-19)
stwierdzalny 'state-PPA' (0-14)
zgrzewalny 'weld-PPA' (0-7)
liczalny 'countable' (0-7)
mieszalny 'miscible' (0-7)
odłączalny 'separable' (0-6)
rozwiązalny 'solvable' (0-6)
działalny 'act-PPA' (0-5)
wysuwalny 'exsert-PPA' (0-5)
rozsuwalny 'draw back-PPA' (0-5)
oswajalny 'tameable' (0-4)
obejmowalny 'embrace-PPA' (0-3)
skrawalny 'cut-PPA' (0-3)

rozerwalny 'tear-PPA' (0-3)
spawalny 'weld-PPA' (0-3)
naruszalny 'breach-PPA' (0-3)
przeszczepialny 'transplantable' (0-2)
zginalny 'foldable' (0-2)
przystosowalny 'adjustible' (0-2)
wymłacalny 'thresh-PPA' (0-1)
skracalny 'shorten-PPA' (0-1)
przeświecalny 'translucent' (0-1)
wyciągalny 'draw out-PPA' (0-1)
przesączalny 'drainable' (0-1)
zaświadczalny 'testify-PPA' (0-1)

Appendix 7.5

Derivatives based on non-native verbs attested in the balanced NKJP (thirty-seven derivatives):

akceptowalny 'acceptable' (119-753)
programowalny 'programmable' (44-175)
konfigurowalny 'configurable' (25-73)
biodegradowalny 'biodegradable' (21-142)
identyfikowalny 'identifiable' (18-79)
definiowalny 'definable' (15-224)
modyfikowalny 'modifiable' (15-44)
bootowalny 'bootable' (10-18)
sterowalny 'steerable' (9-108)
kontrolowalny 'controllable' (8-27)
kwalifikowalny 'qualify-PPA' (5-31)
egzekwowalny 'execute-PPA' (3-19)
redukowalny 'reducible' (3-15)
edytowalny 'editable' (3-15)
negocjowalny 'negotiable' (3-11)
konstruowalny 'constructible' (2-18)
rejestrowalny 'register-PPA' (2-12)
interpretowalny 'interpretable' (2-12)
adaptowalny 'adaptable' (2-11)
falsyfikowalny 'falsifiable' (1-109)

testowalny 'testable' (1-14)
manipulowalny 'manipulable' (1-11)
kwantyfikowalny 'quantifiable' (1-7)
implantowalny 'implantable' (1-4)
dywersyfikowalny 'diversify-PPA' (1-2)
finansowalny 'finance-PPA' (1-2)
formowalny 'form-PPA' (1-2)
dokowalny 'dock-PPA' (1-1)
inwestowalny 'invest-PPA' (1-1)
iterowalny 'iterate-PPA' (1-1)
dedukowalny 'deducible' (1-1)
hydrolizowalny 'induce hydrolysis-PPA' (1-1)
segregowalny 'segregate-PPA' (1-1)
eksportowalny 'exportable' (1-1)
inwestowalny 'investable' (1-1)
administrowalny 'administer-PPA' (1-1)
komercjalizowalny 'commercialise-PPA' (1-1)

Appendix 7.6

Derivatives based on non-native verbs not attested in the balanced NKJP (forty-eight derivatives):

realizowalny 'realise-PPA' (0-32),
obiektywizowalny 'objectivise-PPA' (0-24)
googlowalny (0-23)/*guglowalny* (0-15) 'googleable'
lokalizowalny 'localisable' (0-8)
kopiowalny 'copiable' (0-7)
kwalifikowalny 'qualify-PPA' (0-6)
symulowalny 'simulate-PPA' (0-5)
montowalny 'install-PPA' (0-5)
kalibrowalny 'calibrate-PPA' (0-5)
dekodowalny 'decode-PPA' (0-5)
adresowalny 'address-PPA' (0-4)
konwertowalny 'convertible' (0-4)
werbalizowalny 'verbalise-PPA' (0-4)
diagonalizowalny 'diagonalise-PPA' (0-4)
klasyfikowalny 'classify-PPA' (0-4)
deformowalny 'deformable' (0-4)
notowalny 'rate-PPA' (0-3)

blokowalny 'block-PPA' (0-2)
dysponowalny 'administer-PPA' (0-2)
serwisowalny 'provide services-PPA' (0-2)
manewrowalny 'manoeuvre-PPA' (0-2)
operowalny 'operable' (0-2)
importowalny 'importable' (0-2)
edukowalny 'educable' (0-2)
estymowalny 'estimate-PPA' (0-2)
analizowalny 'analysable' (0-2)
absorbowalny 'absorptive' (0-2)
algorytmizowalny 'create an algorithm for-PPA' (0-2)
korygowalny 'corrigible' (0-1)
transferowalny 'transferable' (0-1)
aplikowalny 'applicable' (0-1)
nawigowalny 'navigable' (0-1)
eksploatowalny 'exploitable' (0-1)
konsumowalny 'consumable' (0-1)
ewoluowalny 'evolve-PPA' (0-1)

digitalizowalny 'digitalise-PPA' (0-1)
formalizowalny 'formalise-PPA' (0-1)
materializowalny 'materialise-PPA' (0-1)
certyfikowalny 'certifiable' (0-1)
pacyfikowalny 'pacifiable' (0-1)
ignorowalny 'ignore-PPA, negligible' (0-1)

kompresowalny 'compress-PPA' (0-1)
kserowalny 'xerox-PPA' (0-1)
eksplikowalny 'explicable' (0-1)
filtrowalny 'filter-PPA' (0-1)
eliminowalny 'eliminate-PPA' (0-1)
hakowalny 'hack-PPA' (0-1)

Notes

1. The concept of passive possibility can also be expressed by other less productive markers, such as *-ny* (e.g. *palić* 'burn' – *palny* 'combustible'), *-(el)ny* (e.g. *czytać* 'read' – *czytelny* 'legible') and *-liwy* (e.g. *tłoczyć* 'stamp (metal)' – *tłoczliwy* 'drawable') (Kallas 1999; Szymanek 2010). Since their role is marginal, they will be disregarded in this analysis.

2. PPAs can be classified as passive dispositions with an existential modal force (see Cohen 2016), i.e. they refer to the type of disposition, where the agent's power to perform an action or not does not have to be realised but can be realised (hence they are existential, not universal dispositions) and the bearer of the disposition is not an agent/causer (hence they are passive). However, this type of disposition requires the presence of a sentient agent with a will and understanding. The presence of a sentient agent with a will and understanding in the situation expressed by the base verb seems to override the transitivity requirement. It allows us to explain why Subject-Experiencer verbs such as *kochać* 'love' and *podziwiać* 'admire' are excluded from its domain, while verbs referring to powers (as opposed to states) such as *widzieć* 'be able to see' and *słyszeć* 'be able to hear' are not. If intransitive verbs are allowed, these are primarily unergative verbs whose subjects are agents (Perlmutter 1971) such as *mieszkać* 'live'. I have come across only one case with an unaccusative verb acting as the base (i.e. *przemakalny* 'permeable').

3. Interestingly, in some languages the expression of potential semantics interacts with passive morphology, as demonstrated by Oltra-Massuet (2013) for Georgian, Turkish and Hungarian. Cinque (1990) argues that *-bile* in Italian is lexically built on the past participial form. Passive morphology is detectable in potential adjectives in Latin (Leumann et al. 1963), Greek (Alexiadou 2001), Nahuatl (Sullivan 1983) and Irish (Bloch-Trojnar 2016).

4. Where explicit reference to the internal structure of the word form is relevant, the purely inflectional markers are separated with a raised dot (·), and derivational elements or elements of unclear status with a dash (Szymanek 2010: 17).

5. According to Laskowski (1975) and Szpyra (1989), the verbalising suffix (VS) is listed in the lexicon together with the root and is the marker of the category verb and of the conjugation class. However, Czaykowska-Higgins (1998) argues that the lexicon contains roots abstractly specified for the conjugation class features. The VSs are like the theme vowels/suffixes in other Indo-European languages and function merely as the phonetic spell-out of these features. These markers can be

further differentiated into VS1 suffixes, which participate in the formation of the derivational stem constituent, and VS2 suffixes, whose sole function is to form the inflectional stem, i.e. they precede tense and person/number marking, as depicted below, with optional elements in parentheses: $[_{VW} [_{DS} \text{(Prefix)} [\sqrt{\text{ROOT}}] \text{(VS1)} _{DS}]$ $\text{(VS2)} - \text{TM} - \text{(P/N)}_{VW}]$.

6. There are also other less productive suffixes *-wa* and *-ewa*, which are used to form SIs, e.g. *lać*^{IPFV} 'pour' – *wylać*^{PFV} 'pour out'– *wylewać*$^{IPFV(SI)}$ 'pour out' (Wróbel 1999: 565–568).

7. There is general agreement that the suffix *-ble* expresses modality (Vendler 1968; Lyons 1977; Bauer 1983; Di Sciullo 1997).

8. There seems to be a more general constraint on the use of prefixed perfective verbs in derivation. For example, the nominalising suffix *-(a)cja* can be added exclusively to the imperfective member of an aspectual pair, even though the nominalisations are aspect neutral and, depending on context, may denote an activity or an event (Waszakowa 1994) (e.g. *obserwacja* 'observation' – **zaobserwacja*, *akceptacja* 'acceptance'– **zakceptacja*, *modyfikacja* 'modification' – **zmodyfikacja*).

9. Empty prefixes, such as those in Table 7.6 above, do not form SIs. If it is not possible to form an SI, and the only way to express the imperfective is to go back to the original verb, we are dealing with a true aspectual pair (Svenonius 2004a: 195).

10. According to Svenonius (2004a:192–196, 2004b) the numerous prefixes can be classified into three types: lexical, aktionsartal (or superlexical) and aspectual. Lexical prefixes may give rise to unpredictable, idiomatic readings (e.g. *kupić* 'buy' – *przekupić* 'bribe', *gotować* 'cook' – *przygotować* 'prepare'). Superlexical prefixes modify the inherent temporal or modal characteristics of the base verb and convey different types of lexical aspect (*Aktionsart*), such as INCEPTIVE (*zapłakać* 'start crying'), COMPLETIVE (*dojeść* 'eat up'), PERDURATIVE (*przespać* 'sleep through'), DELIMITATIVE (*pospacerować* 'walk for a while') and many others (Antinucci and Gebert 1977; Śmiech 1986; Karolak 1996). The semantic contribution of aspectual prefixes is limited to perfectivity, hence they are regarded as 'empty'. Crucially, the prefixes on verbs in Table 7.7 do not fall in the aspectual class. Consequently, simple imperfective verbs do not form aspectual pairs and cannot act as the base for *-alny* adjectives.

11. The potential adjective relating to the root *pis-* 'write' which underlies the aspectual pair *pisać* – *napisać* is not impossible, but is confined to a highly specialised context:

    (i) Podział tekstu na czytalny i *pisalny* wprowadził Roland Barthes w latach 70-tych.

    'Distinction of-text in readable and writable introduced Roland Barthes in the years 70'

    i.e. 'Roland Barthes introduced the distinction into readable and writeable text in the 1970s'

12. The balanced corpus aims at being representative of the average speaker of Polish in terms of frequency of words, grammatical structures, collocations etc. The structure of the corpus is as follows: books 29 per cent (16 per cent literature, 5.5 per cent factual literature, 2 per cent educational literature, 5.5 per cent

guidebooks and lifestyle magazines), 50 per cent newspapers and 4 per cent other written texts (official documents, letters), 7 per cent internet sources (blogs, fora, websites) and 10 per cent spoken material (natural conversations, mass-media discourse, parliamentary proceedings). All texts are dated to after 1945.

13. A complete list of items from Grzegorczykowa and Puzynina (1973) which are not attested in the balanced and full version of the NKJP is given in Appendix 7.1. This situation indicates that we are dealing with a truly productive process and, as is usually the case, only a fraction of possible derivatives/nonce-formations successfully goes through all the stages of institutionalisation (Hohenhaus 2005).

14. According to Fischer (1998: 172) a word can be regarded as institutionalised if it occurs at least forty times in a corpus of about 25,000,000 words within at least a few years. Given the size of the balanced version of NKJP this number would have to be multiplied by twelve, and consequently, by her definition, only the first six items listed in Appendix 7.2 could be regarded as fully institutionalised. These include: *mieszkalny* 'habitable' (3892-23, 238), *dopuszczalny* 'permissible' (1035-5282), *porównywalny* 'comparable' (941-5247), *doświadczalny* 'experimental' (741-4432), *pożegnalny* 'farewellADJ' (585-2713) and *odnawialny* 'renewable' (486-3165).

15. In should be borne in mind that three of the 135 *-alny* formations listed in Tokarski (2002) are based on non-native verbs and the corpus analysis conducted in this study has yielded another ten derivatives based on native verbs. Hence the number on PPAs based on native bases equals 142, whereas the number of PPAs based on foreign bases amounts to eighty-eight.

16. A detailed account of English-Polish linguistic contact is available in, e.g. Walczak (1983), Sękowska (2007) and Mańczak-Wohlfeld (1995, 2006, 2010).

17. See http://nkjp.uni.lodz.pl/?q=ycglhejc (21 August 2017).

18. See http://nkjp.uni.lodz.pl/?q=yajd7tgh (21 August 2017).

19. See http://nkjp.uni.lodz.pl/?q=yblut4c4 (15 July 2017).

References

Alexiadou, Artemis (2001), *Functional Structure in Nominals: Nominalization and Ergativity*, Amsterdam: John Benjamins.

Antinucci, Francesco and L. Gerbert (1977), 'Semantyka aspektu czasownikowego' [The Semantics of Verbal Aspect], *Studia Gramatyczne*, 1: 7–43.

Aronoff, Mark (1976), *Word Formation in Generative Grammar*, Cambridge, MA: MIT Press.

Baayen, Harald (1992), 'Quantitative Aspects of Morphological Productivity', in G. Booij and J. van Marle (eds), *Yearbook of Morphology 1991*, Dordrecht: Kluwer Academic Publishers, pp. 109–149.

Baayen, Harald (1993), 'On Frequency, Transparency and Productivity', in G. Booij and J. van Marle (eds), *Yearbook of Morphology 1992*, Dordrecht: Kluwer Academic Publishers, pp. 181–208.

Baayen, Harald and A. Renouf (1996), 'Chronicling *The Times*: Productive Lexical Innovations in an English Newspaper', *Language*, 72: 69–96.

Bauer, Laurie (1983), *English Word Formation*, Cambridge: Cambridge University Press.

Biały, Adam (2008), 'Verbal Syntax in Nominalization and Adjectivization', *Poznań Studies in Contemporary Linguistics*, 44: 3, 284–301.

Biber, Douglas (1993), 'Representativeness in Corpus Design', *Literary and Linguistic Computing*, 8: 241–57.

Bloch-Trojnar, Maria (2016), 'Constraints on the Derivation of Potential Adjectives in Irish', in M. Bloch-Trojnar, R. Looby, M. Ó Fionnáin and A. Bednarski (eds), *New Trails and Beaten Paths in Celtic Studies*, Lublin: Wydawnictwo KUL, pp. 133–153.

Bloch-Trojnar, Maria (2017), 'A Note on the Structure of Passive Potential Adjectives in Polish', in P. Łozowski and A. Głaz (eds), *Route 66: From Deep Structures to Surface Meanings. A Festschrift for Henryk Kardela on his 66th Birthday*, Lublin: Maria Curie Skłodowska University Press, pp. 165–187.

Chapin, Paul (1967), *On the Syntax of Word-derivation in English*, Cambridge, MA: MIT Press.

Cinque, Gugliemo (1990), 'Ergative Adjectives and the Lexicalist Hypothesis', *Natural Language and Linguistic Theory*, 8: 1–39.

Cohen, Ariel (2016), 'The Square of Disposition', in F. Martin, M. Pitteroff and T. Pross (eds), *Morphological, Syntactic and Semantic Aspects of Dispositions. Working Papers of the SFB 732 Incremental Specification in Context*, University of Stuttgart, pp. 51–64, https://elib.uni-stuttgart.de/bitstream/11682/8886/5/Dispositions-Volume.pdf (28 June 2018).

Comrie, Bernard (1976), *Aspect*, Cambridge: Cambridge University Press.

Condoravdi, Cleo (1989), 'The Middle Voice: Where Semantics and Morphology Meet', in P. Branigan, J. Gaulding, M. Kubo and K. Murasugi (eds), *Student Conference in Linguistics 1989. MIT Working Papers in Linguistics* 11, Cambridge, MA: MIT Press, pp. 16–30.

Corbin, Danielle (1987), *Morphologie dérivationnelle et structuration du lexique*, Tübingen: Niemeyer.

Czaykowska-Higgins, Ewa (1998), 'Verbalizing Suffixes and the Structure of the Polish Verb', in G. Booij, and J. van Marle (eds), *Yearbook of Morphology 1997*, Dordrecht: Kluwer Academic Publishers, pp. 25–58.

Di Sciullo, Anna Maria (1997), 'Selection and Derivational Affixes', in W. U. Dressler, M. Prinzhorn and J. R. Rennison (eds), *Advances in Morphology*, Berlin and New York: De Gruyter, pp. 79–95.

Fabb, Nigel (1984), *Syntactic Affixation*, PhD dissertation, MIT.

Fischer, Roswitha (1998), *Lexical Change in Present-day English: A Corpus-based Study of Motivation, Institutionalization, and Productivity of Creative Neologisms*, Tübingen: Narr.

Górski, Rafał, B. Lewandowska-Tomaszczyk, M. Bańko, P. Pęzik, M. Łaziński and A. Przepiórkowski (2012), 'Practical Applications of the National Corpus of Polish', *Prace Filologiczne*, 13: 231–240, https://courses.helsinki.fi/sites/default/files/course-material/4443507/CEEOL-3.pdf (28 June 2018).

Grzegorczykowa, Renata and J. Puzynina (eds) (1973), *Indeks a tergo do Słownika języka polskiego pod redakcją Witolda Doroszewskiego* [Reverse Index to the Dictionary of the Polish Language Edited by Witold Doroszewski], Warszawa: Wydawnictwo Naukowe PWN.

Halle, Morris and A. Marantz (1993), 'Distributed Morphology and the Pieces of Inflection', in K. Hale and S. J. Keyser (eds), *The View from Building 20: Essays in Honour of Sylvain Bromberger*, Cambridge, MA: MIT Press, pp. 111–176.

Hohenhaus, Peter (2005), 'Lexicalization and Institutionalization', in P. Štekauer and R. Lieber (eds), *Handbook of Word Formation*, Dordrecht: Springer, pp. 353–373.

Jabłońska, Patrycja (2007), *Radical Decomposition and Argument Structure*, PhD dissertation, University of Tromsø.

Jadacka, Hanna (2001), *System słowotwórczy polszczyzny* [The Polish Word Formation System], Warszawa: Wydawnictwo Naukowe PWN.

Kallas, Krystyna (1999), 'Przymiotnik' [The Adjective], in R. Grzegorczykowa, R. Laskowski and H. Wróbel (eds), *Gramatyka współczesnego języka polskiego. Morfologia*, Warszawa: Wydawnictwo Naukowe PWN, pp. 469–523.

Karolak, Stanisław (1996), 'O semantyce aspektu (w dwudziestą rocznicę publikacji rozprawy F. Antinucciego i L. Gerbert "Semantyka aspektu czasownikowego")' [On the Semantics of Aspect (on the 20th Anniversary of the Publication of "The semantics of Verbal Aspect" by F. Antinucci and L. Gerbert)], *Biuletyn Polskiego Towarzystwa Językoznawczego*, 52: 9–56.

Kowalik, Krystyna (1977), *Budowa morfologiczna przymiotników polskich* [The Morphological Structure of Polish Adjectives], Wrocław: Ossolineum.

Krifka, Manfred, F. J. Pelletier, G. N. Carlson, A. ter Meulen, G. Chierchia and G. Link (1995), 'Genericity: An Introduction', in G. N. Carlson and F. J. Pelletier (eds), *The Generic Book*, Chicago and London: The University of Chicago Press, pp. 1–124.

Laskowski, Roman (1975), *Studia nad morfonologią współczesnego języka polskiego* [Studies on the Morphophonology of Contemporary Polish], Wrocław: Ossolineum.

Laskowski, Roman (1999), 'Kategorie morfologiczne języka polskiego – charakterystyka funkcjonalna' [The Morphological Categories of Polish – Functional Characteristics], in R. Grzegorczykowa, R. Laskowski and H. Wróbel (eds), *Gramatyka współczesnego języka polskiego. Morfologia*, Warszawa: Wydawnictwo Naukowe PWN, pp. 151–224.

Leumann, Manu, J. B. Hofmann and A. Szantyr (1963), *Lateinische Grammatik auf der Grundlage des Werkes von Friedrich Stolz und Joseph Hermann Schmalz*, München: C. H. Beck.

Lyons, John (1977), *Semantics*, Cambridge: Cambridge University Press.

Mańczak-Wohlfeld, Elżbieta (1995), *Tendencje rozwojowe współczesnych zapożyczeń angielskich w języku polskim* [Tendencies in the Development of Contemporary English Borrowings in Polish], Kraków: Universitas.

Mańczak-Wohlfeld, Elżbieta (2006), *Angielsko-polskie kontakty językowe* [English-Polish Language Contacts], Kraków: Wydawnictwo Naukowe UJ.

Mańczak-Wohlfeld, Elżbieta (2010), *Słownik zapożyczeń angielskich w polszczyźnie* [A Dictionary of English Borrowings in Polish], Warszawa: Wydawnictwo Naukowe PWN.

Młynarczyk, Anna (2004), *Aspectual Pairing in Polish*, Utrecht: LOT.

Oltra-Massuet, Isabel (2013), *Deverbal Adjectives at the Interface: A Crosslinguistic Investigation into the Morphology, Syntax and Semantics of -ble*, Berlin: De Gruyter.

Perlmutter, David (1971), *Deep and Surface Structure Constraints in Syntax*, New York: Holt, Rinehart and Winston.

Pęzik, Piotr (2012), 'Wyszukiwarka PELCRA dla danych NKJP.' [The PELCRA Search Engine for the Data of the Polish National Corpus], in A. Przepiórkowski, B. Mirosław, R. Górski and B. Lewandowska-Tomaszczyk (eds), *Narodowy Korpus Języka Polskiego*, Warszawa: Wydawnictwo Naukowe PWN, pp. 253–273.

Plag, Ingo (2004), 'Productivity', in K. Brown (ed.), *Encyclopedia of Language and Linguistics*, Amsterdam: Elsevier, 2nd edn, pp. 1–26.

Plag, Ingo, C. Dalton-Puffer and H. Baayen (1999), 'Morphological Productivity across Speech and Writing', *English Language and Linguistics*, 3: 209–228.

Przepiórkowski, Adam, M. Bańko, R. Górski and B. Lewandowska-Tomaszczyk (eds) (2012), *Narodowy Korpus Języka Polskiego* [The National Corpus of the Polish Language], Warszawa: Wydawnictwo Naukowe PWN.

Rainer, Franz (1993), *Spanische Wortbildungslehre*, Tübingen: Niemeyer.

Seifart, Frank (2015), 'Direct and Indirect Affix Borrowing', *Language*, 91: 3, 511–532.

Sękowska, Elżbieta (2007), 'Wpływ języka angielskiego na słownictwo polszczyzny ogólnej' [The Influence of English on the Vocabulary of Polish General Language], *Poradnik Językowy*, 5: 44–53.

Śmiech, Witold (1971), *Funkcje aspektów czasownikowych we współczesnym języku ogólnopolskim* [The Role of Verbal Aspect in Contemporary Polish General Language], Wrocław: Zakład Narodowy im. Ossolińskich.

Śmiech, Witold (1986), *Derywacja prefiksalna czasowników polskich* [The Derivation of Polish Verbs by Prefixation], Wrocław: Ossolineum.

Sullivan, Thelma (1983), *Compendio de la gramática náhuatl*, México: Universidad Nacional Autónoma de México.

Svenonius, Peter (2004a), 'Slavic Prefixes: Introduction', in P. Svenonius (ed.), *Nordlyd 32.2: Special Issue on Slavic Prefixes*, Tromsø: University of Tromsø, pp. 177–204, http://wwwub.uit.no/munin/nordlyd (28 June 2018).

Svenonius, Peter (2004b), 'Slavic Prefixes Inside and Outside VP', in P. Svenonius (ed.), *Nordlyd 32.2: Special Issue on Slavic Prefixes*, Tromsø: University of Tromsø, pp. 205–253, http://wwwub.uit.no/munin/nordlyd (28 June 2018).

Szpyra, Jolanta (1989), *The Phonology–Morphology Interface: Cycles, Levels and Words*, London and New York: Routledge.

Szymanek, Bogdan (2010), *A Panorama of Polish Word Formation*, Lublin: Wydawnictwo KUL.

Tokarski, Jan (ed.) (2002), *Schematyczny indeks a Tergo polskich form wyrazowych* [Schematic Reverse Index of Polish Word Forms]. Warszawa: Wydawnictwo Naukowe PWN.

Vendler, Zeno (1968), *Adjectives and Nominalizations*, The Hague: De Gruyter.

Walczak, Bogdan (1983), 'The Earliest Borrowings from English into Polish', *Studia Anglica Posnaniensia*, 16: 121–131.

Waszakowa, Krystyna (1994), *Słowotwórstwo współczesnego języka polskiego. Rzeczowniki sufiksalne obce* [Word Formation of Contemporary Polish. Nouns with Foreign Suffixes], Warszawa: Wydawnictwa Uniwersytetu Warszawskiego.

Willim, Ewa (2006), *Event, Individuation, and Countability: A Study with Special Reference to English and Polish*, Kraków: Jagiellonian University Press.

Wróbel, Henryk (1999), 'Czasownik' [The Verb], in R. Grzegorczykowa, R. Laskowski and H. Wróbel (eds), *Gramatyka współczesnego języka polskiego. Morfologia*, Warszawa: Wydawnictwo Naukowe PWN, pp. 536–583.

8

How an 'Italian' Suffix Became Productive in Germanic Languages

Camiel Hamans

This chapter discusses the complicated interplay between some examples of borrowing and subsequent word formation. It will demonstrate how speakers of Dutch and German re-analyse disyllabic forms, which have recently been borrowed from American English, and how they subsequently use the pattern applied in these clippings more widely, which results in a word formation process that resembles clipping and subsequent suffixation as it appears in American English. However, the application differs. Dutch, for example, borrowed disyllabic models such as *lesbo* and *afro* on the one hand and *kiddo* and *creepo* on the other hand. The first two lexemes can be described as monosyllabic clipped forms to which subsequent suffixation applied, while in the latter two suffixation applied to a monosyllabic base word. However, in Dutch the new word formation process also accepts disyllabic and trisyllabic base words and thus results in trisyllabic and quadrisyllabic words such as *gewono* and *positivo*.

In the first part of this chapter, traditional monosyllabic clipping in English, Dutch and German is discussed. In the second part, clipping is compared with hypocoristic formations in German and English. In the third part, the focus is on recent disyllabic forms ending in unstressed *-o*. In this section it will also be demonstrated how the *-o* pattern has been borrowed in Dutch and German. In addition, some data from Swedish will be presented to support the claim made in this chapter. The data discussed here come from the literature about clipping and from focused Google searches by the author.

1. Clipping: general

In this section, first a few remarks from the literature about clippings will be presented. Subsequently a preliminary analysis of different types of English clipping follows. Finally, examples from languages such as Dutch and German will be discussed.

1.1 Arbitrariness

Stockwell and Minkova (2001: 10) devote a short paragraph to clipping, which they call 'creation by shortening', in which the authors state:

> Shortening may take any part of a word, usually a single syllable, and throw away the rest, like *quiz* from *inquisitive, phone* from *telephone, plane* from *airplane, flu* from *influenza*. Shortening is sometimes called "clipping." The process often applies not just to an existing word, but to a whole phrase. Thus, *mob* is shortened from *mobile vulgus* "fickle rabble." *Zoo* is from *zoological gardens. Ad* and British *advert* are transparently based on *advertisement* (. . .) Many shortenings have entered the language and speakers have lost track of where they came from. How many people would recognize *gin* as in *gin and tonic* as coming from *Genève?*[1]

The examples given by Stockwell and Minkova suggest that almost every part may be thrown away: the beginning of a word, the final part(s) or even the first plus the last syllables. Marchand (1969: 441) approaches clipping from a different point of view. According to him, clipping is more a stylistic or a sociolinguistic phenomenon than a morphological process:

> What makes the difference between *mag* and *magazine, maths* and *mathematics,* is the way the long word and the short word are used in speech. They are not interchangeable in the same type of speech. *Magazine* is the standard term for what is called *mag* on the level of slang. The substitution of *Mex* for *Mexican* implies another shift in linguistic value in that it involves a change of emotional background, based on original slang character of the term. Moreover, the clipped part is not a morpheme in the linguistic system (nor is the clipped result for that matter), but an arbitrary part of the word form. It can at all times be supplied by the speaker. The process of clipping, therefore, has no grammatical status that compounding, prefixing, suffixing and zero-derivation have, and it is not relevant to the linguistic system (la langue) itself but to speech (la parole).

Aronoff (1976: 20–21) calls clipping a linguistic oddity which therefore does not deserve serious attention in morphological studies.

1.2 Types of clippings

Although most of the traditional literature suggest that clipping is highly unsystematic, Marchand (1969: 441–448) distinguishes three main types: back, fore, and middle clipping.[2] Mattiello's (2013: 75) classification roughly follows Marchand's format. Examples of these three types are (1–3).

(1) a. sax   < saxophone
     b. nip(s)   < nipple(s)
     c. tute   < tutor

(2) a. coon   < racoon
     b. droid   < android
     c. vator   < elevator

(3) a. jams   < pyjamas
     b. quiz   < inquisitive
     c. script   < prescription

In (1), we find examples of back clipping, in (2) of fore clipping and in (3) of middle clipping. It is remarkable that most of these traditional clipped forms are monosyllabic and are mostly of the form CVC.[3]

Van de Vijver (1997: 223), who discusses clipping in Dutch in an Optimality Theory (OT) framework, only accepts one type of shortening, back clipping:

> There are two constraints that will be unviolated in clippings. The first is that the left edge of the clipping and the left edge of the base match. This means that the first segment of the base is also the first segment of the clipping. This constraint is called ANCHOR-LEFT (McCarthy and Prince 1994). The second constraint is that the order of the segments in the base is carried over to the segments of the clipping. In other words, there is no intrusion of segments in the clipping, as compared to the base, nor is there any skipping of segments in the base, as compared to the clipping. This constraint is called CONTIGUITY (McCarthy and Prince 1994).

Van de Vijver's restriction to back clipping (repeated in Hinskens 2001) is less determined by his theoretical approach than might be expected. The vast majority of clipping cases in English, German, Dutch, French, Spanish, Polish, Swedish, Icelandic, Bahasa Indonesia are indeed instances of back clipping (cf. Hamans 1996, 1997a, 2004a, 2004b; Fisiak and Hamans 1997). Instances of back clipping are numerous, whereas examples of middle clipping are very rare (Mattiello 2013: 75). In addition, fore clipping is far less frequent than back clipping (Marchand 1969: 443; for a similar conclusion for German, see Balnat 2011: 44).[4] The preference for back clipping, and thus for forms in which the initial part is still present, can be explained in terms of information structure (Lambrecht 1994). The prominence of the initial part of words can be seen as an instance of the importance of initial parts in general. This preference can be seen in all languages discussed here. If the beginning of a word is retained, this means that an ANCHOR-LEFT constraint operates. All languages discussed here share this preference. Consequently, back clipping must be much more frequent than any other type in these languages (Mattiello 2013: 72). The examples produced here are all nouns, which is not by accident. There exist a few examples of clipped adjectives e.g. *fab* for *fabulous* and *preg* for *pregnant* and for verbs such as *to dis* for *to disrespect*, but the clear majority of clippings are nouns.[5]

What the examples also show is that usually there is a difference in register between the source word and the clipped form (cf. Marchand 1969: 441). Most of the resulting nouns belong to an informal or even slangy register or are part of youngsters' or student language or of a specialised jargon. However, this is not an automatic result of clipping. See for instance (4–6).[6]

(4) a. sex   < sexual activity
     b. movie   < moving picture
     c. pub   < public house

(5) a. plane   < aeroplane
     b. bus   < omnibus
     c. varsity < university

(6) a. flu   < influenza
     b. fridge   < refrigerator
     c. tec   < detective

In (4) we find examples of back clipping, in (5) of fore clipping, and in (6) of middle clipping. These examples show that clipped forms, which have been around for a longer period, may become accepted at a certain point in time and so rise in standing from an informal register to a more accepted one.

1.3 Monosyllabic clippings in Dutch and German

Since middle clipping is really rare in Dutch and German, only examples of back and fore clipping are presented here. In (7) some Dutch examples of back clipping are given and in (8) some examples of fore clippings.

(7) a. buur   < buurman ('neighbour')
     b. Jap   < Japanner ('Japanese')
     c. lab   < laboratorium ('laboratory')

(8) a. bam   < boterham ('sandwich')[7]
     b. bus   < omnibus ('bus')
     c. toffels[8] < pantoffels ('slippers')

Van der Sijs (2002) collected more Dutch clippings. Her examples confirm that traditional clipping in Dutch follows a monosyllabic CVC pattern, as the examples of older Dutch clipped forms in (9) show.

(9) a. loods   < loodsman ('pilot')   – already attested in the 17th c.
     b. mum   < minimum ('wink')   – attested since 1940
     c. pas   < paspoort ('passport')   – already attested in the 17th c.
     d. pon   < japon ('nightie')   – attested in the early 20th c.
     e. prol   < proleet ('plebeian')   – attested in the 1930s
     f. soos   < sociëteit ('club')   – already attested in the 19th c.
     g. spijs   < amandelspijs ('almond paste') – attested since 1875

In German, monosyllabic clipped forms are less common than in English or Dutch. However, there are a few examples, such as the back clippings in (10) and the fore clippings in (11).

(10) a. Bib   < Bibliothek ('library')
     b. Lok   < Lokomotive ('locomotive')
     c. Rep   < Republikaner ('republican')

(11) a. Rad   < Fahrrad ('bicycle')
     b. Bahn   < Eisenbahn ('railway')
     c. Schirm   < Regenschirm ('umbrella')

From the examples presented in (7–11) one may conclude that Dutch and German share a traditional CVC clipping pattern with English. However, in German one also finds a disyllabic pattern with a final unstressed vowel. This pattern is much more common than the CVC pattern, cf. (12–13).

(12) a. Abi   < Abitur ('finals')
     b. Krimi   < Kriminalroman ('detective novel')
     c. Uni   < Universität ('university')

(13) a. Demo   < Demonstration ('demonstration')
     b. Kino   < Kinematograph ('cinema')
     c. Tacho   < Tachograph ('tachograph')

There is no parallel disyllabic pattern in Dutch nor in English.

2. Hypocoristics

An example such as German *Uni* presented in (12) very much resembles a form such as German *Studi*, informal for *Student*, or *Ossi*, informal for *Ostdeutscher* 'person from East-Germany'.[9] A similar *-i* appears in German hypocoristics, such as *Mutti* and *Omi*, respectively 'mother'and 'grandmother'. Therefore, hypocoristics are discussed in this section, first German hypocoristics, subsequently English hypocoristics. A comparable pattern does not exist in Dutch, probably due to the highly regional and informal connotation of the diminutive suffix *-ie* (cf. Hamans 1997b, 2015).

2.1 German hypocoristics

The German examples presented so far are all rather recent, which does not mean that clipping is a young phenomenon in German. On the contrary, Balnat and Kaltz (2006: 199) produce a couple of old examples such as *Lanz* from *Lanzknecht* 'footman, soldier' and *Ländi* from *Landjäcker* 'policeman', which were attested as early as the sixteenth century.[10] The fact that there are hardly any data available for older periods of German is most likely due to the informal register to which clippings usually belong. Consequently, the standard written sources of older stages of German on which the prescriptive handbooks are based contain hardly any clipped forms. In Modern German, however, the shortening of words is a normal and frequent process (Angst 2000: 210). Balnat (2011) even claims that the productivity of clipping started to increase around

1900. From this moment on, 'it is impossible to imagine life without clipped forms' (2011: 287). As we will see below, this is in conformity with findings in other languages. However, this does not imply that clipping was an exotic and infrequent process before 1900. It is not well-attested, and just as many of the recent clippings never exceed the threshold level to become more acceptable,[11] and thus may disappear again, older clippings may have got lost and never have made their way to the recorded lexicon.

Another interesting aspect of the examples Balnat and Kaltz quote is the final -*i* in *Ländi*. As we have seen in (12) final -*i* is quite common in German clippings.[12] It is even more frequent than all other comparable vocalic endings. In (12) the vowel *i* is part of the source words, whereas in *Landjäcker* there is no vowel but a glide <*j*>. Balnat (2011: 75–76) quotes a few other early examples with final -*i*, which originate in Southern German, especially in Bavarian German: *Spezi* from *Spezialfreund* 'special friend', with *i* from its source word, and *Gspusi* from *Gespons* 'sweetheart' with added -*i*. This final *i*, which is frequently used in the formation of names in Bavarian, 'became popular *again* in the 1950s and later, especially in the formation of first names' (Balnat 2011: 76).

Hamans (2015: 28–29) discusses examples such as (14–16).

(14) a. Heini   < Heinrich
     b. Ul(l)i   < Ulrich
     c. Peti   < Peter
     d. Willi   < Wilhelm

(15) a. Schumi   < Michael Schumacher (*1969)
     b. Lewi   < Hans-Jürgen Lewandowski
     c. Gorbi   < Michael Gorbachev (*1931)
     d. Honni   < Erich Honecker (1912–1994)[13]

(16) a. Schmitti   < Jürgen Schmitt (*1949)
     b. Krammi   < Markus Kramm[14]

The main difference between the examples in (12) and (14–16) is that -*i* in (12) is part of the original word, of the root, whereas in (14–16) -*i* is added. This segment -*i* is a kind of a suffix.

What the examples in (14) show is that the addition of the hypocoristic suffix -*i* is obligatory, since forms such as Hein, Ul, Peet or Will are virtually excluded in German. Here clipping must obligatorily be followed by suffixing. This is also true for (15).[15] In Modern German, just as in Dutch and English, the trochee is the unmarked metrical pattern, and this explains why in the examples of (14) and (15) a monosyllabic clipped form is dispreferred. The examples of (16) show how dominant the trochaic character of Modern German is; that it can even change the form of a name. Because of their trochaic pattern *Schmitti* and *Krammi* appear to be preferred and thus seem to be better forms of colloquial Modern German than *Schmitt* and *Kramm*.

Hypocoristic -*i* is not restricted to names as the examples in (17) and (18) show. It also appears in familial forms of address (17) and in hypocoristic forms (18).

(17) a. Bubi   < Bube ('boy')
     b. Mutti   < Mutter ('mother')
     c. Omi   < Oma ('grandmother')
     d. Vati   < Vater ('father')

(18) a. Schocki   < Schockolade ('chocolate')
     b. Pulli   < Pullover ('pullover')
     c. Hunni   < Hundert Euro Schein ('hundred-euro banknote')
     d. Spüli   < Spülmittel ('rinse aid')

In a way, the examples in (17), being forms of address, can still be compared with the names in (14–16). However, no proper names can be recognised in the forms in (18). All these forms share a certain form of endearment and informality, which is not surprising, knowing that the -*i* suffix originally is a diminutive suffix (Würstle 1992: 54).[16]

Balnat (2011: 76) explains the productivity of -*i* formations by pointing to the immense popularity of English and especially of English names ending in -*y*/-*ie* in the 1950s in Germany, which was partly occupied by British and American troops. Köpcke (2002: 294) disagrees with this explanation since most of the new borrowed clipped forms do not have a parallel full form in English. He points, just as Greule (2006: 424–430) does, to the -*i* hypocoristic pattern, discussed before, as a starting point. However, what was even more important for the success of this new pattern is that Modern German is a predominantly trochaic language. This fact, already mentioned by Féry (1997), who even speaks about *Trochäuszwang* 'trochee coercion', greatly facilitated this process of suffixation. In addition, Köpcke (2002: 300) demonstrates how important the trochaic character of Modern German is by pointing to the stress shift in clipped forms such as *Ábi* from *Abitúr* 'graduation from high school' and *Stúdi* from *Studént*.

In these examples clipping operated first, and then was followed by obligatory suffixation as the unacceptability of **Mut*, **Om* and **Vat* demonstrates.[17] Subsequently, final -*i* became so frequent in informal language that the speakers of German gradually came to the implicit conclusion that -*i* was no longer only a marker of endearment, but it was at the same time a marker of possible clipped forms. Consequently, the suffix -*i* could be used in examples such as (19), where one finds clipped nouns followed by a suffix -*i*.

(19) a. Fundi   < Fundamentalist ('fundamentalist')
     b. Ossi   < Ostdeutscher ('East-German')
     c. Profi   < professioneller Sportler ('professional sportsman')
     d. Studi   < Student ('student')

Again, clipping and subsequent suffixation operated here. However, it is no longer the feature of endearment which is prominent here. Other semantic aspects of the diminutive suffix prevail, which is even more visible in (20), where pejorative nouns are presented that end in a suffix -*i*.

(20) a. Blödi ('boy')   < blöd ('stupid$_{ADJ}$')
     b. Gifti ('junk')   < Gift ('drugs$_{NOUN}$')
     c. Hirni ('intellectual')   < Hirn ('brain$_{NOUN}$')
     d. Schwuli ('gay$_{NOUN}$')   < schwul ('gay$_{ADJ}$')

The examples of (20) can best be compared to those of (16). In neither case does clipping operate. It is only a matter of suffixation. However, the source words to which this suffixation process applies are monosyllabic. In this respect, they correspond to the clipped bases in (14), (15), (17–19). The result is again the most preferred German phonological word, a disyllabic trochee. In addition, these examples show that when the source word has a pejorative meaning, the suffix -*i* cannot change the overall meaning. Finally, examples (14–17) and (19–20) suggest that the suffix -*i* may imply the feature [+human], whereas the final -*i* which originates from the source word, as in (12), never includes such a feature. The suffix -*i* in (20) definitely contains a feature [+human], since the resulting nouns in (20) all refer to human beings. In addition, the suffix contains a formal feature that involves a transition of word class, from adjective to noun.

What the examples discussed here show is that three factors determine clipping in German:

- The Modern German preference for the unmarked metrical word pattern, the trochee, explains why most Modern German clippings are disyllabic. Unfortunately, there are not enough data available from earlier stages of German. Therefore, it is impossible to analyse older German clippings in detail. Whether in earlier stages of German the most frequent form of clipping also resulted in disyllabic forms or possibly in monosyllabic clipped forms is impossible to say. However, the instances of early name clippings discussed by Greule (2006) are often monosyllabic, which suggests that older patterns of clippings may have had a preference for monosyllabic forms, just as Dutch and English.
- The frequency of final -*i* in clipped contexts brings the language user to the idea that this final -*i* has a special function and meaning, especially since this final -*i* resembles hypocoristic -*i* in many respects. A common segment is called a *confusivum* by Zabrocki (1962) in his theory of diacrisis.
- This confusivum subsequently becomes the most prominent marker of German clipped forms. Since part of the meaning of this marker -*i* is that it signals informality and a certain degree of endearment (or other semantic aspects of the meaning of diminutive suffixes), these aspects may get more prominence and so finally the marker -*i* can also be used without clipping the base.

Final -*i* is not the only suffix which can be added to clipped forms in German, although it is the normal pattern (Féry 1997; Wiese 2001). Very recently, final -*o* came up and displayed a similar behaviour. However, before we can discuss this most recent development, the English counterpart of German -*i* will be analysed first.

2.2 English hypocoristics ending in -ie/-y[18]

In English, one can easily find similar examples with the hypocoristic suffix *-ie* or *-y*. The difference in spelling between *-ie* and *-y* is not systematic and has no special meaning. The oldest examples, *hussy* 'housewife' and *chappy* 'chapman', are attested as early as in 1530 and 1550 respectively (Antoine 2000: xx–xxi). The occurrence of this suffix is discussed in detail by Antoine (2000: xxxi):

> "-ie/-y" is a true suffix, with a hypocoristic meaning, which was first used in Scots; it (. . .) was used very early in combination with clipping (**hussy, chappy**). This suffix is commonly used with clippings of Christian names (Andy, Cathy, Eddie, Ronnie, etc.) or of family names (Fergie, Gorby, Schwartzy, etc.). It is also used in the coining of nicknames (Fatty, Froggie, etc.) or of endearing terms (dearie, sweetie, etc.) – this is thoroughly recorded. However, the use of "-ie/-y" in combination with clippings of common nouns goes largely unnoticed or seems at least to be considered a marginal phenomenon. The *OED* notes that "Bookie for Bookmaker is a formation of a rare type; cf. nighty for nightdress".

In his corpus Antoine collected 1,482 clipped words, of which about 200 end in *-ie/-y*. The suffix can take a number of different meanings, as Antoine (2000: xxxi–xxxii) shows.

> It can serve, as in the case of proper nouns, to obtain a hypocoristic diminutive (e.g.: pressie, shortie, woodie, biccy, chewie, hottie, preemie) though such words can also be used humorously, or ironically, or even pejoratively. It is to be noted further that the suffix "-ie/-y" is added to clippings of words that already have negative overtones – the change of ending often results in an even more pejorative word; "-ie/-y" thus serve to enhance the negative trait in words that designate individuals whose social or political behaviour is frowned upon by the speaker, character traits or behaviours that are deemed to be and presented as pathological ones. The political lexicon offers instances of this, with words like commie, lefty, rightie, but other fields also do. Thus the corpus contains words that designate nationalities (Argie, Frenchie, Jerry, Russky and also limey [British CH]), sexual or other tendencies (lesbie, lessie but also alkie, dipsy, loony, prosti, yachtie)[19] and even some trades (from pressie [president CH] to wharfie [docker CH] through newsie [newspaper seller CH] and umpie [umpire CH]), in which it is very often difficult not to sense, if not a clearly pejorative nuance, at least an ironical or condescending overtone, which both the context and the stress put on the word will make even clearer. Such words make it clear that the merely hypocoristic value is far from being the only one the suffix "-ie/-y" can have.

The English suffix *-ie/-y* may be added after a clipped form, as in (21), or after a monosyllabic full word as in (22) and (23).

(21) a. telly   < television set
     b. movie(s) < moving pictures
     c. footy   < football
     d. Aussie   < Australian

  e. commy < communist
  f. nunky < (n)uncle

(22) a. hottie < hot
  b. dearie < dear
  c. cutie < cute

(23) a. yuppie < yup[20]
  b. junkie < junk
  c. hippie < hip

The difference between (22) and (23) lies in their connotation. The nouns in (22) are usually evaluated positively, whereas the ones in (23) are clearly negative. This corresponds to the way in which diminutives can be used.

 Most of these forms are highly informal, appear mainly in spoken language and date from the twentieth century. However, a now-obsolete form such as *nunky* was already attested in the eighteenth century, which shows that the process of truncation followed by suffixation with *-i* has a much longer history. Examples such as *junky* and *hippie* go back to the 1920s and 1960s respectively.[21]

 The data presented here show a process that matches the one sketched above for German clipped nouns. First comes clipping to a monosyllabic base form and subsequent suffixation; later suffixation of monosyllabic adjectives and nouns without prior clipping has become possible. However, there is one big difference between the German and the English process. There are hardly any clipped forms in English ending in an *-ie/-y* that originate from a clipped source word.

 In (21), suffixation is obligatory, just as in most of the following examples of (24) and (25). Monosyllabic clipped forms such as **tel*, **Aus*, **nunk*, etc., are excluded. However, monosyllabic clipped forms as such were not excluded.

 As in German, English hypocoristic names may be formed by truncation followed by suffixation.

(24) a. Andy < Andrew
  b. Gerry < Gerald
  c. Frankie < Franklin[22]

(25) a. Aggie < Agnes
  b. Izzy < Isabella
  c. Vicky < Victoria

It is clear that the predominantly trochaic character of English must have influenced the process, see for instance the stress shift in *Austrálian > Aússie* or *Victória > Vícky*. However, the unmarked trochaic pattern does not play a role with respect to stress shift only. The prosody also determines the overall outcome of the process: the preference for disyllabic trochaic forms prevents monosyllabic outputs, such as **tel*, **Aus*, **nunk*, **And*, **Ag*, etc. However, the preference for disyllabic trochaic forms does not go so far as to trigger the removal of all existing monosyllabic words or names from the language.

Semantically the suffix does not seem to add much to the forms. The clipped form itself has already an endearment, familiar or similar reading, which may be the reason why the suffix *-ie/-y* can be added so easily to fulfil the prosodic preference, as the examples in (26) show, where full words are clipped to monosyllabic forms, which are subsequently suffixed by hypocoristic *-ie/-y*.

(26) a. Chevrolet > Chev > Chevy
     b. Cigarette > cig   > ciggie
     c. Stephen   > Steve > Stevie

Semantically, there is not much difference between *Chev* and *Chevy* or between *cig* and *ciggie* or *Steve* and *Stevie*. Unfortunately, there are not enough data available to sketch the historic changes in detail and with certainty. What is known is that a form such as *cig* turned up in the late nineteenth century, whereas *ciggie* made its entrance only more than half a century later, around 1960. A well-known form such as *hanky* (from *handkerchief*), however, also dates back to the late nineteenth century. This brings us to the assumption that the change from clipping only to clipping followed by suffixation is not an abrupt change but a gradual process of diffusion of innovation. What is clear from the literature is that the few instances of early historical clipping that have been recorded are mainly monosyllabic (Marchand 1969: 449; Kreidler 1979).

To summarise, the English data presented here show several aspects:

- First, that clipping is an old phenomenon. Unfortunately, it is scarcely documented because it belongs to informal, spoken registers. However, scrutiny of dramatic texts and informal sources such as letters may possibly reveal more data.
- Second, that there seems to be an ongoing change in clipping preference. It starts with monosyllabic clipping first, followed by monosyllabic clipping plus *-ie/-y* suffixation and finally also simple *-ie/-y* suffixation. The upcoming preference for a trochaic pattern plays an important role in this change (cf. Hamans 2012).
- Third, that the frequency of *-ie/-y* suffixation, after clipping to monosyllabic base forms, brings the language user to the conclusion that this suffix is not only a diminutive marker with all its possible connotations, but that the suffix also signals informality, which is a characteristic feature of short, clipped forms. Subsequently the suffix can be used, as in the case of *deary*, to mark these new word forms as informal and affective, or in the case of *junkie* as informal and derogatory.

3. A new pattern

Recently a new, disyllabic pattern of clipped forms originated. It appeared in Dutch for the first time in the late 1970s and 1980s. In this section, first the Dutch development is discussed. Then the comparable pattern in English is analysed and finally the emergence of the phenomenon in German and Swedish is discussed.

3.1 Final -o in Dutch

(27) a. aso   < asociaal ('antisocial person')
     b. impo   < impotent ('impotent person')
     c. pedo   < pedofiel ('paedophile')

(28) a. alto ('alternative person')   < alternatief ('alternative')
     b. depro ('depressed person')   < depressief ('depressed')
     c. sago ('cantankerous person')   < chagrijnig ('cantankerous')

(29) a. lullo ('dumb person')   < lul ('prick')
     b. duffo ('dull person')   < duf ('dull')
     c. jazzo ('fan of old-style jazz music')   < jazz ('jazz')

In Dutch one comes across numerous examples with clipping only, as in (27). The naïve language user notices that all these forms end in -o and that they have certain semantic, stylistic and formal features in common: [+human], [+negative], [+informal] and [+preceded by a monosyllable]. Thus, s/he reinterprets this final -o as a suffix-like element with the features mentioned. The next step is that the language user introduces this suffix-like element after truncation, such as in (28). The final step is (29): -o becomes a suffix that may be added after monosyllabic nouns. The process matches German hypocoristic formation and clipping followed by -i suffixation.

The three examples presented in (27) are from the three last decades of the twentieth century. Only two earlier forms ending in -o and referring to persons have been attested. The first one is the word *indo* from *Indonesian*, which was in use for mixed Dutch-Indonesian people in the then-Dutch colony of the Dutch Indies, now Indonesia, before the Second World War. The other example is *provo*, from *provocateur*, for 'member of the *provo* movement in Amsterdam in the 1960s'. This word was consciously coined by the Dutch criminologist Buikhuisen (1965). Also, the forms in (28) and (29) appeared for the first time in the late 1970s and 1980s, together with some clear loanwords from American English youth language and slang such as *lesbo*, *macho* and *creepo*. Kuitenbrouwer (1987) published a collection of clipped forms called *afko's*, which is a clipped form of *afkortingen* 'abbreviations' (or shortenings, since the forms he collected are mostly clipped forms).[23] Many of his examples are clipped forms ending in -o, with or without subsequent suffixation and some with -o suffixation only. This collection, which was meant to present the most recent innovations in Dutch, showed how much innovation actually was borrowing from American English, how influential American English examples were and how rapidly the innovation progressed.

3.2 Final -o in English

American English and Australian English recently also developed an -o pattern.

(30) a. psycho   < psychopath
     b. homo   < homosexual
     c. dipso   < dipsomanic

(31) a. afro   < African hairstyle
     b. lesbo   < lesbian
     c. relo   < relative_N

(32) a. sicko   < sick
     b. kiddo   < kid
     c. creepo   < creep

The process of recognition, generalisation and reinterpretation of final -*o* by the naïve English language user must have been like that of the naïve speaker of Dutch. However, the process started earlier and in Australian English even earlier than in American English. In American English, the process became productive after the Second World War, whereas in Australian English this had already happened a few decades earlier.[24]

This is not the place to describe how final -*o* became popular in American and Australian English, but it is most likely that the suffix finds its origin in the language of Italian immigrants (for a detailed discussion see Hamans 2018). After all, Italian has a hypocoristic final -*o*. Although Italian final -*o* has different functions, a certain association of final -*o* with trochaic, apparently clipped forms, informal register and male referents is not unlikely in the ears of speakers of American English exposed to Italian names. Nor is a somewhat negative connotation unlikely, since the Italian community was long seen as a group of mafiosi, laundry bosses and nightclub crooners. So -*o* became iconic for informal and negative. In addition, the existence of a hypocoristic pattern with final -*y*/-*ie* may have supported the emergence and the diffusion of the new pattern. This is more likely, since the existing hypocoristic pattern was also trochaic.

3.3 Extension of the pattern

The question now remains of how this American English pattern became popular in the Netherlands. Hamans (2004a, 2004b) describes how the language of popular music and media brought the innovation to the Netherlands, a country that is famous for its hospitality towards foreign influences, also when it comes to language. In addition, the preferred Dutch word form is trochaic. Therefore, the innovation was able to adjust the process of clipping to the prototypically trochaic Dutch word form (for a detailed description see Hamans 2012).

However, the naïve speaker of Dutch also uses the new suffix in new formal environments.

(33) a. positivo ('someone with too positive an attitude')   < positief ('positive_ADJ')
     b. gewono ('dull, normal person')   < normal ('normal_ADJ')
     c. lokalo ('representative of a local political party')   < lokaal ('local_ADJ')

The semantic and stylistic features of the new suffix -*o* remain the same in the examples in (33). However, the set of words to which the suffix can be added is no longer restricted to monosyllabic ones, but also contains words of two or even three syllables.

In addition, the base words are adjectives. The suffix also causes a transposition of word class, since the resulting forms are nouns. As will be clear, this is an extension of the application of the new suffixation process and this is a Dutch 'innovation'. However, it should be noted that the last part of the examples presented in (33) show a trochaic pattern: *positívo*, *gewóno* and *lokálo*; all with main stress on the penultimate syllable.

3.4 Final -o in German

In German, examples of pure clipping resulting in [+human] clipped forms ending in -*o* are scarce, due to the frequency of the competing suffix -*i*. Steinhauer (2000: 10) describes -*o* as a younger suffix. A few [+human] examples of pure clipping with final -*o* are presented in (34).

(34) a. Homo   < Homosexueller ('gay$_{NOUN}$')
      b. Pedo   < Pädophiler ('paedophile')
      c. Psycho < Psychopath ('psychopath')

(35) a. Nudo   < Nudist ('nudist')
      b. Prolo   < Proletarier ('proletarian')
      c. Stino   < stinknormale (Person) from stink[25] ('boringly normal person')

(36) a. Normalo[26] ('normal person')   < normal ('normal$_{ADJ}$')
      b. Heino ('artist name')   < Hein(z), name of a singer[27]
      c. Kloppo ('nickname')   < Jürgen Klopp, German football coach

The process in German is hampered by the productivity of the -*i* suffix. However, forms such as *Realo* ('realist') versus *Fundi* ('fundamentalist') are quite common in Modern German and show that -*o* clipping and suffixation have gained a foothold in German. As Balnat (2011: 78) claims, this is due to recent American English influence. Fleischer (1969: 210) and Angst (2000: 223) both describe the order in which the innovation took place as follows. First came clipping, resulting in -*o* (or -*i*), later followed by clipping plus suffixation. This corresponds to the way the process is described here, and it follows from the initial recognition of a common segment, *confusivum*, as described in Zabrocki's theory. Although the German data show that the development in this language is slower than in, for instance, Dutch, because of the presence of a competing native suffix, the pattern of the development appears to be similar. In both languages, the influence of a prestigious foreign language together with a process of diacrisis – which is the recognition of a common segment, followed by assigning morphological status to this segment – leads to the systematic emergence of a new suffix and a new pattern.

However, it remains unclear why an existing hypocoristic/clipping pattern with final -*i* hampers the introduction of a competing pattern with final -*o* in German, whereas the disyllabic hypocoristic pattern with final -*y*/-*ie* is considered to be supportive for the pattern with final -*o* in English. An explanation might be that the

German -*i* pattern is more than a hypocoristic system; it is a full-fledged system of clipped forms. One may assume that such a system opposes innovations with a similar function. The American English hypocoristic -*y*/-*ie* system cannot be described as a full-fledged system of clippings, as shown. In American English the trochaic pattern of the hypocoristic pattern most likely paved the way for -*o* clipping.

3.5 Final -*o* in Swedish

The most common and most preferred pattern of clippings in Swedish is a disyllabic pattern (Nübling and Duke 2007: 234). However, this pattern does not end in an open syllable, as for instance in German, but is characterised by a suffix -*is*.

(37) a. alkis   < alkoholisk ('alcoholic')
     b. kompis   < kompagnon ('mate')
     c. skådis   < skådespelare ('actor')

(38) a. doldis ('anonymous public figure')   < dold ('hidden')
     b. kändis ('public figure')   < kand ('well-known')
     c. snackis ('snacker')   < snack ('snack')

As the examples in (38) show, the suffix is no longer restricted to previously truncated forms. Both types, those of (37) and (38), share a negative or at least emotional connotation and both belong to a colloquial style (Nübling and Duke 2007: 234–235). However, the productivity of the patterns differs considerably. Whereas truncation followed by suffixation, as in (37), is highly productive, examples with suffixation only, as in (38), are scarce.

Recently a new disyllabic pattern came up in Swedish (Parkvall 1998): disyllabic clippings with final -*o*. Examples are given in (39–41).

(39) a. alko   < alkoholist ('alcoholic')
     b. lycko   < lyckost ('extremely lucky person')
     c. psyko   < psykopat ('psychopath')

(40) a. aggro ('aggressive person')   < aggressiv ('aggressive$_{ADJ}$')
     b. hygglo ('nice person')   < hygglig ('reasonable$_{ADJ}$')
     c. pucko ('stupid person')   < puckad ('puck$_{NOUN}$')

(41) a. fetto ('fat person')   < fet ('fat$_{ADJ}$')
     b. fyllo ('drunkard')   < full ('full$_{ADJ}$')[28]
     c. slappo ('lazy bump')   < slapp ('soft$_{ADJ}$')

The process in Swedish looks exactly the same as those in English and Dutch. In (39) only truncation applies, resulting in clipped forms ending in a final segment -*o*. The data in (40) are examples of truncation and suffixation, whereas (41) shows that only suffixation also applies to monosyllabic words. So, one may explain this innovation in a similar way. It is the power of the identical part, the confusivum -*o*, that triggers the innovation. However, without the influence of a foreign language the innovation was unlikely to happen, especially since Swedish has a preferred and quite different system of clipping of its own. It is the influence of a foreign language, American English, that seduces or invites the speaker of the receiving language to start the innovation consciously or unconsciously. Since clipping in Swedish has been less well-described in the literature than in Dutch or German, there are not yet enough data to demonstrate how the change really progressed. But it should be noted that all the Swedish data presented here are from the last twenty-five to thirty years. They cover the same period as in Dutch, which makes it very likely that the innovation started under American English influence. Anyway, the Swedish culture is as open as the Dutch, and pop culture and media occupy a similar position in the lives of Swedish youth as in those of the Dutch.

4. Conclusion

The data presented and discussed in this contribution demonstrate how naïve speakers of different languages operate in the same way. They establish an identity in the form and function of a (final) segment in different words. Subsequently they reinterpret this segment as having a morphological status, a suffix in the examples discussed here. This suffix can be used in a similar way as in the language in which it originated. However, the application of the suffixation process may even expand.

A question that could not be answered is whether the naïve speakers of the receiving language borrow the suffix -*o* directly or whether they borrow word forms with final -*o* and subsequently detect the possible system behind final -*o* for themselves. Unfortunately, there are not enough accurate data available. It is unclear which words were borrowed or produced first. However, the data that are available for Dutch suggest that first a small number of foreign American English words were borrowed. What is known about the German and Swedish innovation supports this impression. If this is true, first foreign words with final -*o* were borrowed. Subsequently, the underlying pattern was found by the speakers of the receiving language. Finally, the speakers introduced the system into their own grammar. As will be clear, in this chapter this view is implicitly adopted when explaining the borrowing of the clipping process and the associated suffix.

Notes

1. This etymology is not correct: *gin* is an abbreviation of *geneva* (Klein 1971: 312), which comes from Dutch *genever* or *jenever* (Klein 1971: 308), a type of distilled drinking alcohol flavoured by juniper berries.
2. Also called *edge clipping* or *fore and back clipping*. Actually, *middle clipping* is a confusing term since it is not the middle part which is truncated but just the two edges. However, *middle clipping* is used commonly for this kind of example where the 'middle of the word is retained' (Marchand 1969: 444; Steinhauer 2015: 357). When the middle part is really deleted, one may speak of *median clipping* (Jamet

2009: 10; Mattiello 2013: 75). However, examples such as *breathalyser*, from *breath* and *analyser*, make clear that one should rather describe this type of formation in terms of blending.

3. Kreidler (1979) shows that traditional English clipped forms are monosyllabic. The examples Marchand (1969: 449) offers of older clipped forms are also predominantly CVC.

4. Diachronically the picture is different. Minkova (2018) showed that clipping in early English is restricted to fore clipping, which peaked between 1300 and 1600 and then decreased quite sharply. Back clipping was practically unattested until the end of the Middle English period, whereupon it rapidly became the dominant model.

5. Whereas in English, German and Dutch clipping is mainly restricted to nouns, this may be different in other languages. In Swedish, for instance, clipped adjectives and even verbs are much more common (Nübling 2001; Leuschner 2006; Nübling and Duke 2007).

6. The well-known clipped form *pram* is also an instance of back clipping. Of the original form *perambulator* the first vowel got reduced completely before clipping took place.

7. The form *bam* looks as if the middle segment *oterh* is deleted. Such a process, which is extremely rare, is known as *mid-clipping, median clipping* or *contraction*. Median clipping, of course, is a way to describe the resulting form *bam*, just as *proctor* from *procurator* in English (Mattiello 2013: 75). However, it is much more attractive to describe *bam* as a process of fore clipping, which should have resulted in *ham*. This form should have coincided with an existing noun *ham* 'ham'. Since clipped forms should be as transparent as possible semantically, because of their required semantic retrievability (Hamans 2008: 156–157), the clipped form *ham* is blocked. Thus, for the onset of the output another consonant of the source word must be selected. *Tam* and *ram* are existing Dutch words, so the only remaining option is *bam*. *Bam* is attested for several dialects of the province Noord-Brabant (eWND 2015–2019: *bam*). However, the diminutive *bammetje* is much more frequent. It appeared already as the title of a newspaper article in van Kleef (2005).

8. *Toffels* is of course disyllabic. There are a few more monosyllabic examples of nominal fore clipping in Dutch, such as *net* < *internet*, *bas* < *contrabas* 'double bass' and *fax* < *telefax*. However, these forms may have been taken over directly from other languages as clipped nouns. The total number of fore clippings is very small.

9. In *Uni* the final vowel is part of the original source word, whereas in *Studi* and *Ossi* the final *-i* is added.

10. Greule (2006) produces instances of clipped names which have been attested much earlier than the sixteenth century.

11. As the two corpus descriptions of Mattiello (2013, 2017) show, a great number of clipped words (and blends) disappear quickly. In order to become accepted, words must reach a certain frequency and have to exceed an unspecified threshold level (Seuren 2013).

12. So far there are no extensive corpora of clipped forms in different languages. However, a quick search through an internet corpus of German Kurzwörter 'clipped words' results in a great number of clipped words with final -*i* (http://www.mediensprache.net/de/basix/oekonomie/kurzwort/liste_kw.aspx), whereas Hamans (1997a) and Hinskens (2001) only were able to produce a very small number of Dutch examples.

13. Respectively German Formula 1 racing driver, German commercial film director, leader of the Soviet Union (1985–1991), leader of the DDR, the communist East German republic (1971–1989).

14. Respectively German artist and German poker player.

15. Monosyllabic clipped names are not excluded in German – see for instance *Hans* or *Gert/Gerd* (cf. Kürschner 2014). However trochaic disyllabic names are dominant. For standard Dutch it is different: monosyllabic clipped names are quite common and fully acceptable. However, in the informal slang of traditional Amsterdam, disyllabic names are preferred: *Hansie* instead of *Hans* and *Pietje* instead of *Piet*.

16. Diminutives belong to what is usually called *evaluative morphology*. Quite often they not only express smallness but also familiarity and a positive or negative attitude towards the referent (see for instance Schneider 2013). Diminutive suffixes are widely used to express endearment. In Polish, for instance, in which a plurality of diminutive suffixes are used to form common first names, as in for instance the suffix -*ek*: *Dariusz* > *Darek*, *Sławomir* > *Sławek* and *Tadeusz* > *Tadek*. Note that suffixation follows clipping here, just as in the examples presented above.

17. *Bub* is also found next to *Bubi* in (17a), which shows that suffixation is not always obligatory.

18. Lappe (2007) discusses English clipped forms and hypocoristics in detail. The results of her analysis are opposite to the analysis presented here. She assumes that disyllabic forms must be given priority. Monosyllabic forms are derived from disyllabic forms according to her. Hamans (2012) discusses her analysis.

19. *Yachtie* differs from the other examples presented here. A *yachtie* may be somebody who travels around the world at sea at somebody else's expense. A sexual load is not immediately evident in this meaning. However, *yacht* is also an acronym in youngsters' slang: "Young and Coming Home Tonight, which means that you scored and some fly ass coochie is going to come home with you!" (Urban Dictionary 1999–2019: *Yacht*).

20. *Yup* is an acronym: *young urban professional*. It was coined in the early 1980s.

21. *Hippie* was already attested in the 1940s, but the word only became common from the 1960s on.

22. *Frankie* may also be derived from Frank but in this case naturally no truncation takes place.

23. The form *afko* illustrates how clippings follow the normal rules of Dutch syllable structure. Whereas *o* in *afkorting* is short or lax, the corresponding vowel in *afko* is long or tensed due to open syllable lengthening, just as in *info* from *informatie* 'information' or *demo* from *demonstratie* 'demonstration'.

24. The examples Jespersen (1942: 223) produces are mostly examples of Australian English. A number of his examples are still not attested in American English.

However, as early as 1858 an example such as *dipso* is already attested in American English, just as *kiddo* in 1893, *wino* in 1915, *psycho* 1927 and *pinko* in 1936. Some years later, a wave of new formations in *-o* arrived, resulting in, among others, forms such as *fatso* (1944), *weirdo* (1955) and *sicko* (1977).

25. Related to the verb *stinken* 'smell'. The prefixoid functions as an intensifier semantically, as in *stinksauer* 'pissed off'.

26. If German hypocoristic and clipped forms are all disyllabic, then *Normalo* is an exception in which the first syllable is not parsed. However, one can imagine that *Normalo* is one of the first examples that consisted of more than two syllables, similar to the Dutch examples in (33). This last assumption is supported by the fact that German *normal* is an adjective and that, just like in (33), there is also transposition of word class here.

27. The standard form *Heini* acquired a negative meaning (Balnat 2011: 74; Elsen 2011: 70) since the name became part of compounds such as *Trödelheini* 'sorehead'. That is why the popular singer Heinz Georg Kramm (and others) called himself *Heino*, which has a positive connotation, which is also due to the association with the old Germanic name *Haim* or *Heimo*, which contains the element *Heim* 'house' and which means 'calm, well-balanced ruler (of the house)' (Gerr 2011: 123). The form *Heino* may also be influenced by Frisian boys' names such as *Dodo, Eggo, Eicko, Enno, Friko, Habbo, Hano, Hemmo*, etc.

28. The vowel change may be due to the related form *fylld* 'stuffed'.

References

Angst, Gerhard (2000), 'Gefahr durch lange und kurze Wörter', in G. Stickel (ed.), *Neues und Fremdes im Deutschen Wortschatz: Aktueller Lexikalischer Wandel*, Berlin: De Gruyter, pp. 210–238.

Antoine, Fabrice (2000), *An English-French Dictionary of Clipped Words*, Louvain-La-Neuve: Peeters.

Aronoff, Mark (1976), *Word Formation in Generative Grammar*, Cambridge, MA: MIT Press.

Balnat, Vincent (2011), *Kurzwortbildung im Gegenwartsdeutschen*, Hildesheim: Georg Olms Verlag.

Balnat, Vincent and B. Kaltz (2006), 'Zu einigen theoretischen Problemen der Kurzwortbildung', *Beiträge zur Geschichte der Sprachwissenschaft*, 16: 195–218.

Buikhuisen, Wouter (1965), *Achtergronden van nozemgedrag*, Assen: Van Gorcum & Comp.

Elsen, Hilke (2011), *Grundzüge der Morphologie des Deutschen*, Berlin: De Gruyter.

eWND (2015–2019), *elektronische Woordenbank van de Nederlandse dialecten (eWND)*, edited by N. van der Sijs, Amsterdam: Meertens Instituut, www.meertens.knaw.nl/ewnd/ (12 July 2019).

Féry, Caroline (1997), '*Uni* und *Studis*: Die besten Wörter des Deutschen', *Linguistische Berichte*, 72: 461–489.

Fisiak, Jacek and C. Hamans (1997), 'Memento for a Lefto', in A. Ahlqvist and V. Čapková (eds), *Dán do oide. Essays in memory of Conn R.Ó Cléirigh*, Dublin: Institiúd Teangeolaíochta Éireann, pp. 157–163.

Fleischer, Wolfgang (1969), *Wortbildung der Deutschen Gegenwartsprache*, Leipzig: VEB Bibliographisches Institut.

Gerr, Elke (2011), *Das Große Vornamenbuch*, Hannover: Humboldt, 12th edn.

Greule, Albrecht (2006), 'Kurzwörter in historischer Sicht', *Neuphilologische Mitteilungen*, 107: 4, 423–434.

Hamans, Camiel (1996), 'A Lingo of Abbrevs', *Lingua Posnaniensis*, 38: 69–78.

Hamans, Camiel (1997a), 'Clippings in Modern French, English, German and Dutch', in R. Hickey and S. Puppel (eds), *Language History and Linguistic Modelling: A Festschrift for Jacek Fisiak on his 60th Birthday*, Berlin: De Gruyter, pp. 1733–1741.

Hamans, Camiel (1997b), 'Im Westen nichts Neues: over de opkomst van een beschaafd morfeem', in A. Van Santen and M. Van der Wal (eds), *Taal in tijd en ruimte*, Leiden: SNL, pp. 237–245.

Hamans, Camiel (2004a), 'From *rapo* to *lullo*', in A. Duszak and U. Okolsk (eds), *Speaking from the Margin: Global English from a European Perspective*, Frankfurt am Main: Peter Lang, pp. 69–75.

Hamans, Camiel (2004b), 'The Relation between Formal and Informal Style with Respect to Language Change', in C. B. Dabelsteen and J. N. Jorgensen (eds), *Languaging and Language Practicing* (Copenhagen Studies in Bilingualism), Copenhagen: University of Copenhagen, Faculty of Humanities, vol. 36, pp. 168–195.

Hamans, Camiel (2008), 'Why Clipped Forms should be Accepted as Nouns', *Lingua Posnaniensis*, 50: 95–109.

Hamans, Camiel (2012), 'From Prof to Provo: Some Observations on Dutch Clippings', in B. Botma and R. Noske (eds), *Phonological Explorations: Empirical, Theoretical and Diachronic Issues*, Berlin: De Gruyter, pp. 25–40.

Hamans, Camiel (2015), 'De relatie tussen verkleinwoorden en verkortingen: Een vergelijking tussen drie West-Germaanse talen', *Brünner Beiträge zur Germanistik und Nordistik*, 29 (2): 21–33.

Hamans, Camiel (2018), 'Between *Abi* and *Propjes*: Some Remarks about Clipping in English, German, Dutch and Swedish', *SKASE Journal of Theoretical Linguistics* 15 (2): 24–59.

Hinskens, Frans (2001), 'Hypocoristiche vormen en reductievormen in het hedendaagse Nederlands', *Neerlandica Extra Muros*, 39: 37–49.

Jamet, Denis (2009), 'A Morphophonological Approach to Clipping in English', *Lexis*, HS 1.

Jespersen, Otto (1942), *A Modern English Grammar. Part 4: Morphology*, Copenhagen: Ejnar Munksgaard.

van Kleef, Bas (2005), 'Bammetje', *de Volkskrant* (22 November 2005), Amsterdam, https://www.volkskrant.nl/wetenschap/bammetje~b992ea8f/ (10 July 2019).

Klein, Ernest (1971), *A Comprehensive Etymological Dictionary of the English Language*, Amsterdam, Oxford and New York: Elsevier.

Köpcke, Klaus-Michael (2002), 'Die sogenannte *i*-Derivation in der deutschen

Gegenwartsprache: Ein Fall outputorientierter Wortbildung', *Zeitschrift für germanistische Linguistik*, 30: 293–309.

Kreidler, Charles W. (1979), 'Creating New Words by Shortening', *Journal of English Linguistics*, 13: 24–36.

Kuitenbrouwer, Jan (1987), *Turbotaal: Van Socio-babbel tot Yuppiespeak*, Amsterdam: Aramith.

Kürschner, Sebastian (2014), 'Familiennamen als Basis der Spitznamenbildung: Ein deutsch-schwedischer Vergleich', in F. Debus, R. Heuser and D. Nübling (eds), *Linguistik der Familiennamen*, Hildesheim: Georg Olms, pp. 441–473.

Lambrecht, Knud (1994), *Information Structure and Sentence Form. Topic, Focus and the Mental Representations of Discourse Referents*, Cambridge: Cambridge University Press.

Lappe, Sabine (2007), *English Prosodic Morphology*, Dordrecht: Springer.

Leuschner, Torsten (2006), 'Nederlands tussen Duits en . . . Zweeds. Grafonemische afkortingen (*Kurzwörter*) in taalvergelijkend perpsectief', in M. Hüning, U. Vogl, T. Van der Wouden and A.Verhagen (eds), *Nederlands tussen Duits en Engels: Handelingen van de workshop op 30 september en 1 oktober 2005 aan de Freie Universität Berlin*, Leiden: SNL, pp. 141–162.

McCarthy, John and A. Prince (1994), 'The Emergence of the Unmarked: Optimality in Prosodic Morphology', in M. Gonzalez (ed.), *Proceedings of NELS North-Eastern Linguistic Society 24*, Amherst, MA: GLSA Publications, pp. 333–379.

Marchand, Hans (1969), *The Categories and Types of Present-Day English Word-Formation*, Munich: C. H. Beck, 2nd edn.

Mattiello, Elisa (2013), *Extra-grammatical Morphology in English*, Berlin: De Gruyter.

Mattiello, Elisa (2017), *Analogy in Word-Formation*, Berlin: De Gruyter.

Minkova, Donka (2018), 'English Word Clipping in a Diachronic Perspective', in P. Petré, H. Cuykens and F. D'hoedt (eds), *Sociocultural Dimensions of Lexis and Text in the History of English*, Amsterdam: John Benjamins, pp. 227–252.

Nübling, Damaris (2001), '*Auto – bil, Reha – rehab, Mikro – mick, Alki – alkis*: Kurzwörter im Deutschen und Schwedischen', *Skandinavistik*, 31: 2, 167–199.

Nübling, Damaris and J. Duke (2007), 'Kürze im Wortschatz skandinavischer Sprachen: Kurzwörter im Schwedischen, Dänischen, Norwegischen und Isländischen', in J. A. Bär, T. Roelcke and A. Stenhauer (eds), *Sprachliche Kürze. Konzeptuelle, strukturell und pragmatische Aspekte*, Berlin: De Gruyter, pp. 227–263.

Parkvall, Mikael (1998), 'O-words: Colloquial/Slangy Words Ending in <-o>', *Linguist List*, 9.360, https://linguistlist.org/issues/9/9-360.html (12 July 2018).

Schneider, Klaus P. (2013), 'The Truth about Diminutives, and How We Can Find It: Some Theoretical and Methodological Considerations', *SKASE Journal of Theoretical Linguistics*, 10: 1, 137–151.

Seuren, Pieter (2013), 'Frequency Linguistics – 2', https://pieterseuren.wordpress.com/2013/04/ (12 July 2018).

Sijs, Nicoline van der (2002), 'Verkortingen', *Onze Taal*, 71: 210–211.

Steinhauer, Anja (2000), *Sprachökonomie durch Kurzwörter: Bildung und Verwendung in der Fachkommunikation*, Tübingen: Narr.

Steinhauer, Anja (2015), 'Clipping', in P. O. Müller, I. Ohnheiser, S. Olsen and

F. Rainer (eds), *Word-Formation: An International Handbook of the Languages of Europe*, Berlin: De Gruyter, vol. 1, pp. 352–363.

Stockwell, Robert and D. Minkowa (2001), *English Words. History and Structure*, Cambridge: Cambridge University Press.

Urban Dictionary (1999–2019), *Urban Dictionary*, initiated by A. Peckham, www. urbandictionary.com (10 July 2019).

Vijver, Ruben van de (1997), 'The Duress of Stress: On Dutch Clippings', in J. Coerts and H. de Hoop (eds), *Linguistics in the Netherlands 1997*, Amsterdam: John Benjamins, pp. 219–230.

Wiese, Richard (2001), 'Regular Morphology vs. Prosodic Morphology? The Case of Truncation in German', *Journal of Germanic Linguistics*, 13: 131–177.

Würstle, Regine (1992), *Überangebot und Defizit in der Wortbildung: Eine kontrastive Studie zur Diminutivbildung im Deutschen, Französischen und Englischen*, Frankfurt am Main: Peter Lang.

Zabrocki, Ludwik (1962), 'Phon, Phonem und distinktives Morphem', *Biuletyn Fonograficzny*, 5: 59–87.

9

The Suffixes -*ismus* and -*ita* in Nouns in Czech

Magda Ševčíková

In this chapter, the interplay between borrowing and word formation (in particular, derivation) is documented on the example of the suffixes -*ismus* and -*ita*,[1] which are listed among the most common suffixes in loan nouns in Czech (e.g. Čechová et al. 1996: 93; Karlík et al. 2000: 140). These suffixes are of Greek origin, in Czech their Latinised version is used (Šimandl 2016). They have direct counterparts in English (-*ism* and -*ity*), German (-*ismus* and -*ität*), French (-*isme* and -*ité*) and other languages, as illustrated in (1).

(1)   a.   subjektivismus, subjektivita   CS
      b.   subjectivism, subjectivity   EN
      c.   Subjektivismus, Subjektivität   DE
      d.   subjectivisme, subjectivité   FR

Although most of the nouns in -*ismus* and -*ita* correspond both formally and semantically to nouns in one or even more foreign languages, and comply thus with the definition of internationalisms (Jiráček 1984; Ivir 1989), in the present chapter they are analysed as a part of the lexicon and, moreover, of the word formation system of Czech.

After a brief summary of how nouns with both suffixes have been approached in Czech linguistics so far (section 1), section 2 is devoted to the compilation and analysis of the language data set, the core of which is a list of nearly 1,100 nouns ending in -*ismus* and -*ita* extracted from a representative corpus of Czech (SYN2015, Křen et al. 2015). Attention then turns to derivatives which share their root with the nouns in -*ismus* and -*ita*.[2]

The observation that internationalisms are members of larger derivational families[3] or, in the word formation perspective, that they serve as bases for derivation of further words was discussed as one of the characteristics typical of internationalisms in West-Slavic languages by Waszakowa (2003); cf. also Buzássyová (2010) for Slovak. What is in focus here are the differences among the derivational families: particular nouns in -*ismus* and -*ita* share their roots with a different number of derivatives formed by different suffixes. By analysing the size and inner structure of derivational families, I point out that there are correlations between what a particular derivational family looks like and what meaning the derivatives involved have. The analysis then results in the description of several, most striking meanings of the suffixes -*ismus* and -*ita* in Czech in section 3. For each of the postulated meanings, a pattern is proposed that represents the inner structure of the respective derivational families.[4]

1. Nouns in -*ismus* and -*ita* in existing descriptions

Existing descriptions of the word formation system of Czech pay only marginal attention to nouns with loan affixes, including both suffixes analysed in this chapter. Loan affixes are listed only as alternatives to particular Czech formants in expressing particular meanings in all more or less recent descriptions (cf. Daneš et al. 1967 and the references in this section).[5]

In Dokulil et al.'s (1986) reference grammar of Czech, the suffix -*ismus* is mentioned only in connection with nouns with the suffix -*ista*, which denote 'followers of different movements referred to by a noun with the suffix -*ismus*' (cf. also Karlík et al. 2000: 118, otherwise references to relations between nouns with loan suffixes are exceptional). The suffix -*ita* is described as a suffix in foreign nouns of quality; these nouns 'refer to adjectives in -*ní*', but nouns without such a relation are listed, too.

Karlík et al. (2000: 140) list both suffixes -*ismus* and -*ita* at the end of the section on deadjectival nouns among 'final strings of loan nouns of quality of Greek-Latin origin', together with -*ita*, -*ika*, -*ie*, -*ance*/-*ence* and -*ura*. In Cvrček et al. (2013: 97ff.), both suffixes are found among formants in nouns that 'are not Czech formants [. . .] but foreign formants which are only adapted to Czech spelling'; the suffix -*ismus* is, however, given as an example of the small group of foreign formants which are combined with Czech words.

A more detailed description of both analysed suffixes is provided by the recent dictionary of affixes by Šimandl (2016). Nouns in -*ismus* are described as having mostly loan roots; if Czech roots are attested they tend to come from proper nouns. Šimandl divides nouns in -*ismus* into six groups according to their meaning (with six subgroups in the first one); examples are given with each meaning:

1. (a) political systems: *kapitalismus* 'capitalism', *marxismus* 'Marxism'
   (b) religious and philosophical systems: *buddhismus* 'Buddhism'
   (c) art movements: *kubismus* 'cubism'
   (d) scientific approaches/methods: *darwinismus* 'Darwinism', *strukturalismus* 'structuralism'
   (e) socially undesirable phenomena: *fanatismus* 'fanaticism', *kariérismus* 'careerism'
   (f) areas of interest: *alpinismus* 'alpinism'
2. personality traits and medical diagnoses: *pesimismus* 'pessimism', *autismus* 'autism'
3. functional systems: *organismus* 'organism', *mechanismus* 'mechanism'

4. linguistic and literature terms: *germanismus* 'Germanism', *paralelismus* 'parallelism'
5. terms from other scientific disciplines: *magnetismus* 'magnetism', *albinismus* 'albinism'
6. analogical coinages, rather for humorous effect: *saudkismus* 'Saudek-ism',[6] *jánabráchismus* 'me-to-my-brother-ism' (lit.), i.e. 'mutual backscratching'

While the question is raised by Šimandl (2016) whether nouns in *-ismus* can be considered to be formed in Czech if identical or very similar forms exist in other languages (especially in Latin and, subsequently, in German), nouns in *-ita* are described as being derived from loan adjectives, mostly ending in *-ní*, less often in *-cký*. If a related adjective is not available, nouns in *-ita* are considered to be loanwords. Šimandl (2016) describes the following groups of nouns in *-ita*:

1. nouns expressing a quality or a state of being: *stabilita* 'stability', *totalita* 'totality'
2. an isolated formation expressing an unspecified location: *lokalita* 'locality'
3. an isolated formation expressing an unspecified activity: *aktivita* 'activity'
4. two formations denoting a group of people: *admiralita* 'admiralty', *generalita* 'generals as a group'

Nouns in *-ita* commonly refer to objects, statements or behaviours characterised by a particular quality, too. As this meaning is considered a lexical shift, not another word formation meaning of these nouns, it is not included into word formation but is reflected in monolingual dictionaries. The noun *specialita* 'speciality' is described as a polysemous lexeme having three meanings in Filipec et al. (2005) and Kraus et al. (2005):

1. a special characteristic
2. an activity in which someone succeeds
3. a special product (in this meaning, the nouns are used in plural; see section 3.10)

The aim of this section was to illustrate that the picture provided by the available literature shows considerable lacunae and different criteria are fused in describing semantics of the suffixes *-ismus* and *-ita*.

2. Compilation and analysis of the language data

This section describes the data collection process and procedures used for analysing the data. In 2.1, the compilation of lists of nouns with *-ismus* and *-ita* from a large corpus is outlined. Then, 2.2 turns to the process of analysing the frequency lists in order to detect correlations between the use of different suffixes. Finally, in 2.3 I identify some significant generalisations about the patterns of use of these suffixes.

2.1 Compiling lists of nouns with the suffixes -ismus and -ita

For the purpose of the proposed study, I started with the compilation of lists of all nouns with the suffixes -ismus and -ita which are attested in the representative corpus of Czech SYN2015 (Křen et al. 2015).[7] The lists of words (types) in -ismus and -ita were post-processed in two steps. First, proper nouns, obvious errors, prefixed formations and compounds were excluded from the data set in order to simplify the data and focus on suffixation;[8] some examples of deleted formations are given in (2).

(2) a. abnormalita 'abnormality'
    b. nadrealismus 'surrealism'
    c. polyteismus 'polytheism'
    d. servomechanismus 'servomechanism'
    e. marxismus-leninismus 'Marxism-Leninism'

Second, normalisation was carried out because of the high degree of orthographic variation in loanwords in Czech, which increases the number of low-frequency words, especially of *hapax legomena*. Variants of the same noun that differed in the length of vowels, in a particular consonant or consonant groups (esp. *s:z*, *th:t*, *k:g*), in capitalisation and other issues obviously related to the adaptation of the words in Czech were replaced with a more (or the most) frequent variant and the frequency rates of all variants were summarised. For instance, the nouns *vampirismus/vampyrismus/vampýrismus* were normalised to *vampirismus* 'vampirism'. By these two steps, the original lists were reduced substantially as documented in Table 9.1.

Even after the reduction, the suffix -ismus has a much higher number of *hapax legomena* and appears thus to be more productive than -ita in Czech if borrowed and created formations are not distinguished (cf. Waszakowa's 2015 approach to foreign word formation in Polish) and an established measure correlating hapaxes to tokens (Baayen 1992) is used.

2.2 Identification of significant derivatives related to the analysed nouns

As already stated, most nouns in -ismus and -ita share their roots with other words in the Czech lexicon and can thus be seen as members of derivational families. The derivational families differ – among other aspects – in size, in suffixes included, and

Table 9.1 Final lists of nouns with the suffixes -ismus and -ita used for analysis (the original data before reduction are given in parentheses)

Nouns with the suffix	Absolute type frequency (reduced < orig.)	Absolute token frequency (reduced < orig.)	Absolute frequency hapax legomena (reduced < orig.)
-ismus	739 (< 1,219)	38,090 (< 41,740)	218 (< 500)
-ita	340 (< 555)	135,753 (< 151,234)	26 (< 87)

in mutual semantic relations among the formations. In order to identify formations which might be significant for the description of how the nouns in *-ismus* and *-ita* are used in Czech, a pilot study of 100 nouns in *-ismus* or *-ita* and related formations was carried out as the next step in preparing the data set.[9]

The differences which were put under scrutiny in the pilot study can be illustrated on the basis of derivational families in Table 9.2.

A noun with the suffix *-ismus* is involved in each of the families while the suffix *-ita* occurs in a single one (*subjektivita* 'subjectivity'). The suffix *-ista* occurs in *subjektivista* 'subjectivist', *kapitalista* 'capitalist' and *fotbalista* 'football player'. The noun *alkoholik* 'alcoholic' also denotes a person but uses the suffix *-ik*. The noun *kapitalista* 'capitalist' is five times less frequent than the noun *kapitalismus* 'capitalism'. *Fotbalista* 'football player' has 5,417 hits but *fotbalismus* 'footballism' is not attested in the SYN2015 corpus (it has eight hits in SYNv6).[10] *Alhokolik* 'alcoholic' is approximately 1.6 times as frequent as *alhokolismus* 'alcoholism'. Whereas the meaning of the noun *subjektivista* 'subjectivist' is defined simply as 'a follower of subjectivism' (Kraus et al. 2005), *alkoholik* 'alcoholic' is a person addicted to *alkohol* 'alcohol' or suffering from *alkoholismus* 'alcoholism', *fotbalista* 'football player' is a person who plays *fotbal* 'football' but is not suffering from *fotbalismus* 'footballism', which denotes rather an excessive pleasure in football.

As a result of the pilot study, the following formations were recognised to be significant for the analysis:[11]

- Adjectives with native suffixes (particularly, *-ní, -ký/-ský/-cký*) since they are considered to be base words for the nouns in *-ita* in available descriptions.
- Nouns with the native suffixes *-ost* and *-ství/-ctví*. The suffix *-ost* is the most frequent and productive suffix used for forming nouns of quality in Czech and thus competing with the nouns in *-ita*. The suffix *-ství/-ctví* occurs in nouns denoting religions, political approaches, etc., in Czech and may thus compete with *-ismus* with some roots.
- Nouns with the suffix *-ista* and personal nouns with other suffixes (including zero suffix).
- Adjectives ending in *-istický* (*-ist-ic-ký*) and *-itní* (*-it-ní*).

2.3 Splitting the data into subsets

In order to search for the above-listed formations in the corpus and to add them to the lists of nouns in *-ismus* and *-ita*, root morphemes were identified in both lists. There was an overlap between both lists in sixty-seven roots for which both a noun in *-ismus* and a noun in *-ita* were in the data. The remaining 672 roots which combined with *-ismus* but not with *-ita* were further split according to whether a noun in *-ista* was attested (188 roots) or not (484 roots). For 273 out of 340 nouns in *-ita*, a noun in *-ismus* was not available. These groups are referred to as:

- Subset A: sixty-seven roots both with a noun in *-ismus* and *-ita* attested.
- Subset B: 188 roots combined with *-ismus* but not with *-ita*, a noun in *-ista* is attested.

Table 9.2 Frequency lists of words that start with the strings *subjekt* 'subject', *kapit[aá]l* 'capital', *fotb[f[aá]l* 'football' and *alkohol* 'alcohol' in SYN2015

Frequency rank		Frequency		Frequency		Frequency		Frequency
1	subjekt	4,341	kapitál	2,172	fotbal	7,901	alkohol	8,324
2	subjektivní	1,578	kapitalismus	1,011	fotbalový	7,842	alkoholický	741
3	subjektivně	380	kapitálový	690	fotbalista	5,417	alkoholik	669
4	subjektivita	315	kapitalistický	538	fotbalistka	135	alkoholismus	420
5	subjektivismus	37	kapitalista	203	fotbálek	87	alkoholový	269
6	subjektivizovaný	14	kapitalizace	68	fotbalově	84	alkoholička	117
7	subjektivnost	14	kapitální	56	fotbalovost	21	alkoholicky	4
8	subjektivistický	13	kapitálově	40	fotbalistův	11	alkoholově	4
9	subjektový	10	kapitalizační	10	fotbalisticky	1	alkoholikův	3
10	subjektivizace	10	kapitalizmus	9	fotbalistický	1	alkohólát	2
11	subjektivizovat	6	kapitalizovat	9	fotbálkový	1	alkoholek	1
12	subjektivizující	5	kapitalizovaný	8	fotbál	1	alkoholizace	1
13	subjektivista	3	kapitálka	6	fotbalismus	0 (8)	alkoholní	1
14	subjektivum	2	kapitalistka	6				
15	subjektivace	2	kapitalisticky	5				
16	subjektovost	1	kapitalistův	2				
17	subjektivisticky	1						
18	subjektmí	1						

- Subset C: 484 roots with *-ismus* but neither *-ita* nor *-ista*.
- Subset D: 273 roots attested with *-ita* but not with *-ismus*.

The full list of roots (more precisely, strings from which the suffix *-ismus* or *-ita* was removed) for each of the subsets is given in Appendix 9.1.

For each subset, the formations listed in section 2.2 were extracted from the SYN2015 corpus (including absolute frequency rates)[12] and stored in a simple multiple-column format that could be sorted according to the form of any of the items involved or according to their frequency. Even though this subdivision was only preliminary, the subsets showed substantial differences in which suffixes they combine with. Statistics demonstrating how the subsets differed according to how many formations with the particular suffixes were found are summarised in Table 9.3.

The meaning of the formations analysed was determined using representative dictionaries, especially Kraus et al. (2005) and Filipec et al. (2005). The structural meaning based on the word formation rule was in focus here (Dokulil 1978; Štekauer 2005), lexical shifts that relate to individual lexemes were omitted.

OED (2018) was the main source of information on English equivalents. Even though etymologically English is only one of the sources of the nouns in *-ismus* and *-ita* in Czech, it is obvious already from these equivalents that most of the nouns are direct borrowings in Czech (cf. the account of recognising loanwords by Haspelmath 2009, or with a focus on neoclassical formations in Russian by Panocová 2015). Neither etymological nor comparative issues are, however, focused on in the present chapter. Information from dictionaries was supplemented with an analysis of corpus material (usually a random sample of ten sentences for each noun or adjective for at least a tenth of the derivational families in each Subset A to D was analysed).

In addition to dealing with the meaning of individual formations, the analysis focused on semantic relations between the formations and their word formation relations including exploration of the direction of motivation. In determining the direction of motivation between two related items, corpus frequency was applied as an important feature. A general assumption adopted here was that a base word is usually more frequent than its derivative (cf. Dokulil 1962; Sambor 1975; Panocová 2017).

Table 9.3 Absolute type frequency of words with the particular suffix (percentage related to a total of roots in each row/subset)

	N-ismus	N-ita	Adj with a native suffix	N-ost	N-ství/ -ctví	N-ista	Adj-istický	Adj-itní
Subset A	67	67	66	47	1	42	47	5
(67 roots)	100 %	100 %	99 %	70 %	1.5 %	62 %	69 %	7 %
Subset B	188	0	99	12	5	188	159	1
(188 roots)	100 %	0 %	53 %	6 %	3 %	100 %	85 %	0.5 %
Subset C	484	0	240	69	37	0	56	1
(484 roots)	100 %	0 %	49 %	14 %	8 %	0 %	12 %	2 %
Subset D	0	273	209	89	1	7	7	40
(273 roots)	0 %	100 %	77 %	33 %	0.4 %	2 %	2 %	15 %

The analysis, summarised for individual groups of formations in the following section, led to a proposal of a handful of more general patterns. As the study is based on a single corpus (though a large and representative one), formations that are not attested in the data but whose existence is anticipated by native-speaker intuition were searched for in a larger corpus (SYNv6). The study aims at an identification of the most relevant patterns but cannot aspire to cover the entire data.

3. A corpus-based analysis of the meaning of the suffixes -*ismus* and -*ita*

Nouns in -*ismus* demonstrate a variety of meanings. They are involved in nine patterns, described in sections 3.1 to 3.9. On the contrary, nouns in -*ita* turned out to be both semantically and derivationally simpler from the proposed perspective; three patterns were thus sufficient to describe these nouns (with nouns in -*ismus* in section 3.1 and without -*ismus* in sections 3.10 and 3.11).

The patterns are represented in Appendix 9.2. They do not correspond directly to the particular data subsets but, interestingly, usually have a core in one of the subsets. Thus, Pattern 1 covers the entire Subset A and is applicable to a part of Subset C. Patterns 2 to 6, 8 and 9 were identified in Subset B. Pattern 7 is realised in the data of Subset C. Finally, Subset D corresponds to Patterns 10 and 11.

The descriptions of the meanings are rather general, with the aim to find a general paraphrase of the word formation meaning of a whole group of derivatives rather than to capture the (lexical) meaning of individual formations. The data demonstrate a clear predominance of loan roots. When Czech roots occur, such an exception is explicitly commented upon in the discussion of the patterns.

3.1 Nouns in -*ismus* denoting an intellectual approach related to a phenomenon expressed by the noun in -*ita*

Roots that were attested both with the suffix -*ismus* and -*ita* turned out to form the richest derivational families in the data analysed. Nouns with the suffix -*ismus* express, at least in one of their meanings, an intellectual approach or movement, more specifically a political tendency, theological doctrine, philosophical approach, or art movement, e.g. (3a). Nouns in -*ita* express a quality, behaviour, statement, or a thing characterised by the quality, as in (3b), and were thus synonymous with the nouns in -*ost* (when available for the particular root, as in (3c)).

(3) a. konformismus 'conformism'   realismus 'realism'   naivismus 'naivism'
     b. konformita 'conformity'   realita 'reality'   naivita 'naïvety'
     c. konformnost 'conformity'   reálnost 'reality'   naivnost 'naïvety'

As adjectives with native suffixes are available for almost all nouns in -*ita* in Subset A (mostly in -*ní* in *objektivní* 'objective', seldom in -*ný* in *reálný* 'real')[13] and have mostly a higher frequency than the -*ita* nouns, these nouns are seen as direct derivatives of the adjectives in -*ní*. Nouns in -*ita* are thus considered to be synonymous with the nouns in -*ost*, both of them are derived from the same adjective in parallel. The higher frequency of *-ita* in most pairs of nouns in *-ita* and *-ost* is interpreted as evidence that foreign bases are preferably combined with a loan suffix.

The nouns in *-ista*, which were part of the derivational families too, denoted a person who holds a particular intellectual opinion or a follower of a particular movement and the noun is thus considered to be a derivative of the noun in *-ismus*, as in (4a).

(4) a. konformista 'conformist'   realista 'realist'   naivista 'naivist'
     b. konformistický 'conformist'   realistický 'realistic'   naivistický 'naivist'

The adjectives in *-istický* were used to express a relation to both the intellectual opinion/movement itself and to the person, as in (4b). Adjectives in *-itní* are related to the nouns in *-ita* but as they were attested only rarely they are not represented as constitutive items in these derivational families.

An open question remains whether the nouns in *-ismus* (and related derivatives in *-ista* and *-istický*) are related to the adjectives with native suffixes or, possibly, to the nouns in *-ita* and *-ost*. Even though this relation is not suggested in the available descriptions (Šimandl 2016), I propose to admit the existence of this relation since the intellectual opinion/movement denoted by the nouns in *-ismus* concerns, at least in general, the phenomenon expressed by the adjectives in *-ní* and the nouns in *-ita* and *-ost*. The relations among the derivatives in the derivational families analysed in this section (including the debatable links) are described by Pattern 1 (see Appendix 9.2).

For the sake of comparability of this and the other patterns across section 3, a unified pattern is used which consists of a total of nine boxes capturing the suffixes *-ismus* and *-ita* and all formations discussed in section 2.2 (plus some more if needed). Only those formations that are relevant for the particular meaning are 'active' (i.e. displayed in black) and derivational relations are marked using arrows leading from the assumed base to a derivative; the remaining boxes are 'deactivated' (displayed in grey). A special, dashed line is used to represent synonymy of two items (e.g. of nouns in *-ita* and *-ost* in Pattern 1). Only the more frequent of the synonymous items is connected with the base word (and with its derivatives if available); cf. the link between *-ita* and the adjective in *-ní* in Pattern 1. The relation of the less frequent item to the particular base word (and derivatives) is not explicitly marked so that the graph is not overloaded; cf. *-ost* and the adjective in *-ní* in Pattern 1.

Examples of derivational families associated with Pattern 1 are given in Table 9.4.

The frequency rates are based on SYN2015. The symbol [+] is used if the word was not attested in SYN2015 but was found in SYNv6. A cell is empty if the particular formation was found in neither of the two corpora.

3.2 Nouns in *-ismus* denoting a movement/approach related to a phenomenon expressed by a noun

The meaning of a movement or approach is conveyed also by nouns in *-ismus* with roots that are not attested with the suffix *-ita* in the data, as in (5).

Table 9.4 Derivational families related to Pattern 1 with absolute frequency in SYN2015

Adj-ní	N-ita	N-ost	N-ismus	N-ista	Adj-istický
konformní 'conform' 411	konformita 'conformity' 99	konformnost 'conformity' 5	konformismus 'conformism' 28	konformista 'conformist' 11	konformistický 'conformist' 4
naivní 'naive' 1,581	naivita 'naivety' 386	naivnost 'naivety' 7	naivismus 'naivism' 4	naivista 'naivist' 9	naivistický 'naivist' 19
	nudita 'nudity' 2		nudismus 'nudism' 14	nudista 'nudist' 19	nudistický 'nudist' 34
objektivní 'objective' 2,170	objektivita 'objectivity' 403	objektivnost 'objectivity' 42	objektivismus 'obejctivism' 16	objektivista 'objectivist' [+]	objektivistický 'objectivist' 41

(5)   a.   symbolismus 'symbolism' – symbol 'symbol'
      b.   avantgardismus 'avant-gardism' – avantgarda 'avant-garde'
      c.   extrémismus 'extremism'– extrém 'extreme'
      d.   kapitalismus 'capitalism' – kapitál 'capital'
      e.   anarchismus 'anarchism' – anarchie 'anarchy'

A noun in *-ista* and an adjective in *-istický* are combined with these roots and have a meaning similar to the one in the previous section. Unlike those in the previous section, these nouns in *-ismus* are semantically related to a simpler noun, given in (5), that refers to an object or action which is a central phenomenon of the movement.

In some of the families, an adjective with a native suffix is present, too, as in (6).

(6)   a.   symbolický 'symbolic'
      b.   avantgardní 'avant-garde'
      c.   kapitálový 'capital'

However, since the adjective is not available in all such families and semantically relates to the simpler noun, it is modelled as a derivative of this noun. See Table 9.5 and Pattern 2 (in Appendix 9.2).

The meaning of an approach or movement is further documented in nouns in *-ismus* for which neither a noun in *-ita* (as in section 3.1) nor a simpler noun (as here in this section) exists in the Czech lexicon. Here, the fact that these nouns are borrowings is more obvious than in the previous cases. Nevertheless, nouns in *-ista* and adjectives in *-istický* are attested for most of them. See the four lower rows in Table 9.5 for examples.

3.3 Nouns in *-ismus* denoting an approach proposed by a person

A specific pattern is realised in a number of derivational families which have a proper noun (usually, a surname) as their core element; cf. (7).

(7)   a.   bonapartismus 'Bonapartism'
      b.   darwinismus 'Darwinism'
      c.   leninismus 'Leninism'
      d.   viklefismus 'Wycliffism'

The noun refers to a person who proposed, practised, represented or inspired a specific approach to politics or to religious issues. The approach is denoted by the noun in *-ismus*, nouns in *-ista* refer to a follower of this approach (*-ista* is usually less frequent than *-ismus*). In most of the families, an adjective ending in *-istický* is available, with *leninismus* 'Leninism' and *viklefismus* 'Wycliffism' the adjectives *leninský* 'Leninist' and *viklefský* 'Wycliffist' are used instead. See Table 9.6 for more examples and Pattern 3 in Appendix 9.2.

This pattern is used frequently in Czech, as it is attested with stems based on proper nouns from the Czech-speaking environment, both older ones, as in (8a), and those

Table 9.5 Derivational families related to Pattern 2 with absolute frequency in SYN2015

Simpler N		N-ismus		N-ista		Adj-istický	
avantgarda 'avant-garde'	371	avantgardismus 'avant-gardism'	2	avantgardista 'avantgardist'	28	avantgardistický 'avantgardist'	5
extrém 'extreme'	858	extremismus 'extremism'	179	extremista 'extremist'	437	extremistický 'extremist'	193
imprese 'impression'	48	impresionismus 'impressionism'	68	impresionista 'impressionist'	72	impresionistický 'impressionist'	81
kapitál 'capital'	2,172	kapitalismus 'capitalism'	1,020	kapitalista 'capitalist'	203	kapitalistický 'capitalist'	538
		behaviorismus 'behaviorism'	86	behaviorista 'behaviorist'	40	behavioristický 'behaviorist'	21
		kubismus 'cubism'	144	kubista 'cubist'	17	kubistický 'cubist'	182
		populismus 'populism'	193	populista 'populist'	160	populistický 'populistic'	281
		sadismus 'sadism'	74	sadista 'sadist'	101	sadistický 'sadistic'	185

Table 9.6 Derivational families related to Pattern 3 with absolute frequency in
SYN2015

Proper noun		N-ismus		N-ista		Adj-istický	
Bonaparte	101	bonapartismus 'Bonapartism'	3	bonapartista 'Bonapartist'	2	bonapartistický 'Bonapartist'	1
Darwin	766	darwinismus 'Darwinism'	93	darwinista 'Darwinist'	15	darwinistický 'Darwinist'	17
Marx	558	marxismus 'Marxism'	226	marxista 'Marxist'	152	marxistický 'Marxist'	321
Thatcher(ová)	209	thatcherismus 'Thatcherism'	8	thatcherista 'Thatcherist'	4	thatcheristický 'Thatcherist'	1
Babiš	1,628	babišismus	1				
Masaryk	1,497	masarykismus	1				
Okamura	419	okamurismus	1				

that have emerged on the political scene only recently, as in (8b). In Table 9.6, the
three lower rows represent some examples.

(8) a. masarykismus – Masaryk, havlismus – Havel
     b. okamurismus – Okamura, babišismus – Babiš
     c. masarykovec, okamurovec

Even if the surnames are not of Czech origin (*Okamura*), they do not combine with the
suffix *-ista* but use the suffix *-ovec* to form personal names that, however, refer directly
to the surname, as in (8c), to indicate someone interested in the thoughts of the person.

3.4 Nouns in *-ismus* denoting a belief in someone

Nouns in (9) and several others denote, in general, a belief in a god, a spirit or a person
with special abilities.

(9) satanismus 'Satanism' šamanismus 'shamanism' šivaismus 'Shaivism'

From the word formation perspective, they are based on personal nouns or nouns
designating a function referring to these subjects. An adjective ending in *-istický* is
usually a part of the derivational families of this group; it refers to the belief itself.
Another adjective in *-ský*, if available, is related to the god/spirit. Examples are given
in Table 9.7 and Pattern 4 in Appendix 9.2.

This pattern was applied to the Czech pronoun *něco* 'something' in order to express
'a belief in something' (*něcismus* 'something-ism'), in (10).

Table 9.7 Derivational families related to Pattern 4 with absolute frequency in SYN2015

Noun (god/spirit)		N–ismus		N–ista		Adj–istický	
satan 'Satan'	443	satanismus 'Satanism'	33	satanista 'Satanist'	45	satanistický 'Satanistic'	24
šaman 'shaman'	547	šamanismus 'shamanism'	72	šamanista 'shamanist'	[+]	šamanistický 'shamanistic'	2
Višnu 'Vishnu'	17	višnuismus 'Vishnuism'	2	višnuista 'Vishnuite'	2	višnuistický 'Vaishnuite'	1

(10) Václav Havel tuším pojmenoval vyznání mnoha Čechů správně jako „něcismus",
   víra v něco nad námi, víra v existenci duchovních principů, sil a snad i nějaké té
   nepojmenované bytosti. (SYN2015)
   'Vaclav Havel, I guess, called the confession of many Czechs correctly
   "something-ism", belief in something above us, belief in the existence of spiritual
   principles, forces and perhaps some of the unnamed beings.'

3.5 Nouns in -ismus denoting a condition

Nouns referring to conditions (diseases, disabilities), though not very numerous in the data, are handled as a separate group due to their specific meaning. Derivational families of these nouns in -ismus are not rich. The nouns were related to a noun for a person suffering from the condition designated by the word ending in -ista, -ik or rarely having a zero suffix, as in (11), as well as to an adjective, mostly in -istický or -ický.

(11) a. autista 'autistic'
   b. astigmatik 'a person suffering from astigmatism'
   c. albín 'albino'

According to the dictionary (Kraus et al. 2005) as well as the corpus data, the adjective refers to the condition, not to the person, as shown in (12).

(12) Luciiny oči putovaly od revmatických prstů k vrásčité tváři a zalévaly se slzami.
   (SYN2015)
   'Lucy's eyes wandered from the rheumatic fingers to the wrinkled face and watered
   with tears.'

In (12), revmatický ('rheumatic'), does not have a corresponding noun in -ista. The missing relation between the adjective and the noun in -ista differentiates Pattern 5 from the other patterns in Appendix 9.2. Table 9.8 summarises the frequencies.
   OED's definition of albinism as 'the condition of being an albino' (OED 2018: albinism) might suggest that the noun in -ism is derived from the personal noun.[14] However, since in Czech the personal nouns are not available for all of the nouns in -ismus from this group and, if they exist, they have usually a lower frequency than

Table 9.8 Derivational families related to Pattern 5 with absolute frequency in SYN2015

N-ismus		N-ista/-ik		Adj-ický/-istický	
astigmatismus 'astigmatism'	76	astigmatik 'a person suffering from astigmatism'	[+]	astigmatický 'astigmatic'	4
autismus 'autism'	279	autista 'autistic'	177	autistický 'autistic'	170
mutismus 'mutism'	43			mutistický 'mutistic'	1
revmatismus 'rheumatism'	141	revmatik 'rheumatic'	9	revmatický 'rheumatic'	100

the noun in *-ismus* itself, I propose to describe the noun in *-ismus* to be prior to the personal noun in order to arrive at a coherent description of this semantic group.

3.6 Nouns in *-ismus* denoting an unhealthy or undesirable inclination

A group of nouns in *-ismus*, illustrated in (13a), expresses that a person (denoted by a noun in *-ista*, or rarely *-ik* in Czech, as in (13b)) has an inclination to a thing or activity to an extent that is unhealthy, socially undesirable or even dangerous.

(13) a. kokainismus 'cocainism'   kariérismus 'careerism'   alkoholismus 'alcoholism'
       b. kokainista 'cocainist'   kariérista 'careerist'   alkoholik 'alcoholic'
       c. kokain 'cocaine'   kariéra 'career'   alkohol 'alcohol'

The thing or activity itself is denoted by a noun, indicated in (13c), that does not have a negative feature in its meaning. An adjective ending in *-istický* is usually a part of these derivational families, too. In the derivational family of the noun *alkohol* 'alcohol', an adjective is missing, probably due to the suffix *-ik* in the personal noun instead of *-ista*.

Since the feature of unhealthiness or undesirability is involved both in the nouns in *-ismus* and in *-ista*, I assume that only one of them is derived from the semantically neutral noun by adding this feature, and the other one is derived from it (rather than both *-ismus* and *-ista* adding the negative feature to the noun in a parallel derivation). As for the direction of motivation, the higher frequency of the personal nouns in *-ista/-ik* (except for *klientelismus* 'clientelism') speaks in favour of this noun being the base and the noun in *-ismus* the derivative. Thus, for instance, *alkoholismus* 'alcoholism' or *morfinismus* 'morphinism' are seen as conditions of a person inclined to alcohol or morphium more than to a standard extent, *kariérismus* 'careerism' and *klientelismus* 'clientelism' as behaviour of a person who is focused on his/her career or clients too much. The nouns in (14) are also associated with this pattern (Pattern 6 in Appendix 9.2). See Table 9.9 for more examples.

Table 9.9 Derivational families related to Pattern 6 with absolute frequency in SYN2015

Simpler N		N-ista/-ik		N-ismus		Adj-istický	
alkohol 'alcohol'	8,324	alkoholik 'alcoholic'	669	alkoholismus 'alcoholism'	420		
kariéra 'career'	8,240	kariérista 'careerist'	97	kariérismus 'careerism'	12	kariéristický 'careeristic'	8
morfium 'morphium'	182	morfinista 'morphinist'	2	morfinismus 'morphinism'	1		
kecat 'to chat'	682	kecálista 'chatterbox'	5	kecálismus 'chatterbox-ism'	1		
potíž 'trouble'	8,503	potížista 'trouble-maker'	90	potížismus 'trouble-maker-ism'	[+]	potížistický	[+]

(14) a. onanismus 'onanism'
     b. recidivismus 'recidivism'
     c. klubismus 'clubbism'
     d. tradicionalismus 'traditionalism'

The word *fotbalismus* 'footballism' can be subsumed under the meaning of an unhealthy inclination, too, as illustrated in (15).

(15) Mířil na zbabělost, tupost, fotbalismus, brutalitu, zištnost, dobromyslnou prázdnotu [. . .] zasáhl právě ta ložiska duševní ubohosti, z nichž v podstatě pramení všechny druhy fašismů i stalinismů. (SYNv6)
'He focused on cowardice, dullness, footballism, brutality, acquisitiveness, good-natured emptiness [. . .] he struck those deposits of mental poverty which basically all kinds of fascisms and Stalinisms spring from.'

However, neither *fotbalista* 'football player' nor *fotbalistický* 'related to football players' from this family share the negative feature. They are both semantically neutral, *fotbalista* being formed according to an established pattern 'sport – sportsman', *fotbalistický* referring to the sportsman.
A handful of nouns with a Czech native stem belong to this group, as exemplified in (16).

(16) a. blábolismus 'nonsense-telling-ism'
     b. čutálismus 'kick-a-ball-about-ism'
     c. kecálismus 'chatterbox-ism'
     d. potížismus 'trouble-maker-ism'

Here, contrary to the nouns in -*ismus* with loan stems, the motivating words usually come from colloquial Czech (*čutat* 'to kick a ball about', but cf. the Standard Czech noun *potíž* 'trouble') and can have a negative feature in their semantics (*blábol* 'nonsense', *kecat* 'to chat'). Although these formations are not very recent (cf. Dokulil

1968; Ziková 2001), the contrast between the scientific register of the suffix and the colloquiality of the bases seems to be still effective in expressing criticism through irony. See the two lower rows in Table 9.9 for more detail.

3.7 The noun in -ismus with the meaning of being a person

Nouns with the suffix *-ismus* can also denote behaviour that is typical for a person. *Kanibalismus* 'kanibalism' is interpreted as a behaviour of a cannibal (*kanibal*), cf. analogous pairs in (17).

> (17) a. kanibalismus 'cannibalism'– kanibal 'cannibal'
> b. despotismus 'despotism' – despota 'despot'
> c. barbarismus 'barbarism' – barbar 'barbar'
> d. manažerismus 'managerialism' – manažer 'manager'

The behaviour is mostly negative, but not necessarily so. The analysis of the personal nouns as the motivating words for the nouns in *-ismus* is supported by a higher frequency of the personal nouns in most pairs. The personal nouns do not end in *-ista*, this suffix is not attested in the derivational families of this group.

In addition to the above-mentioned nouns, nouns based on either loan or Czech roots (as in (18a) and (18b), respectively) are interpreted according to this pattern. Table 9.10 gives an overview.

> (18) a. cynismus 'cynicism'
> flegmatismus 'phlegmatism'
> lesbismus 'lesbianism'
> patriotismus 'patriotism'
> pedantismus 'pedantism'
> voyeurismus 'voyeurism'
> workoholismus 'workaholism'
> b. pozorovatelismus 'observerism'

Adjectives in *-ský* are available in most families, referring to the person. An adjective in *-istický* is attested only with the nouns *kanibal* 'cannibal' and *voyeur* 'voyeur', still with a very low frequency (the suffix is therefore not activated in Pattern 7 in Appendix 9.2). In this pattern, the nouns in *-ismus* are synonymous with either a noun in *-ost*, or a noun in *-ství/-ctví*.

3.8 Nouns in -ismus denoting a word

A limited set of nouns in *-ismus* refers to a word or construction coming from a particular field (language, document, or area), as illustrated in (19). These nouns in *-ismus* are commonly used in the plural.

> (19) a. rusismus 'Russism' – ruština 'Russian language'
> b. germanismus 'Germanism' – němčina 'German language'
> c. japanismus 'Japanism' – japonština 'Japanese'

Table 9.10 Derivational families related to Pattern 7 with absolute frequency in SYN2015

Personal noun	Adj–ský/–ický	N–ismus	N–ost	N–ství/–ctví	Adj–istický
barbar 'barbarian' 1,288	barbarský 'barbarian' 395	barbarismus 'barbarism' 8	barbarskost 'barbarism' 2	barbarství 'barbarism' 145	
flegmatik 'phlegmatic' 47	flegmatický 'phlegmatic' 63	flegmatismus 'phlegmatism' 3	flegmatičnost 'phlegmatism' 3		
kanibal 'cannibal' 155	kanibalský 'cannibalistic' 49	kanibalismus 'cannibalism' 150		kanibalství 'cannibalism' 2	kanibalistický 'cannibalistic' 2
lesba 'lesbian' 229	lesbický 'lesbian' 212	lesbismus 'lesbianism' 2			
pedant 'pedant' 73	pedantský / pedantický 'pedant' 46 / 19	pedantismus 'pedantism' 2	pedantičnost 'pedantism' 2	pedanství 'pedantism' 12	
voyeur 'voyeur' 51	voyeurský 'voyeuristic' 11	voyeurismus 'voyeurism' 20		voyeurství 'voyeurism' 11	voyeuristický 'voyeuristic' 1
pozorovatel 'observer' 1,826	pozorovatelský 'observing' 56	pozorovatelismus 'observerism' 1			

    d. folklorismus 'folklorism' – folklor 'folklore'
    e. biblismus – Bible 'Bible'[15]

The nouns following *germanismus* or *japanismus* in (19b–c) indicate that these words are obvious borrowings in Czech since they are formally closer to the English counterparts (or to German, which might rather be the source language) than to any Czech word. Thus, the adjective *germánský* 'Germanic' exists in Czech but it differs from *germanismus* in meaning; the corresponding language is termed *němčina* 'German' in Czech. Similarly, *japonština* 'Japanese' differs formally from *japanismus*. The noun *moravismus* 'Moravianism' was derived in Czech according to this pattern.

    These nouns in *-ismus* are not in a direct relation to nouns in *-ista* or to adjectives in *-istický* (if attested). Both formations in *-ista* and *-istický* are related to a noun in *-istika* denoting a scientific discipline. The contrast is illustrated in (20). Additional examples are given in Table 9.11. Pattern 8 in Appendix 9.2 summarises the analysis.

    (20) a. germanismus 'Germanism'
           b. germanistika 'German studies' – germanista 'a researcher/student of German
              studies' – germanistický (in a relation to German studies or the researcher/student)

3.9 Nouns in *-ismus* synonymous with *-istika* denoting an activity or approach

A peripheral pattern covers a handful of nouns in *-ismus* that are synonymous with a noun ending in *-istika* and denote an activity, as illustrated in (21a–b).

    (21) a. žurnalismus 'journalism'
              dokumentarismus 'production of documentary'
              turismus 'tourism'
              kanoismus 'canoeing'
           b. žurnalistika 'journalism'
              dokumentaristika 'production of documentary'
              turistika 'tourism'
              kanoistika 'canoeing'

Table 9.11 Derivational families related to Pattern 8 with absolute frequency in SYN2015

N-ismus		N-istika		N-ista		Adj-istický	
rusismus 'Russism'	1 VS.	rustistika 'Russian studies'	19	rusista 'a researcher/ student of Russian studies'	11	rusistický 'related to Russian studies, the reaserchers/ students'	1
biblismus 'a word/phrase from Bible'	4 VS.	biblistika 'biblical studies'	21	biblista 'Biblist'	14	biblistický 'biblical'	8
folklorismus 'folklorism'	48 VS.	folkloristika 'folkloristics'	72	folklorista 'folklorist'	103	folkloristický 'folkloristic'	60

    c. žurnalista 'journalist'
       dokumentarista 'documentarist'
       turista 'tourist'
       kanoista 'canoeist'
    d. žurnál 'journal'
       dokument 'document'
       túra 'tour'
       kánoe 'canoe'

In this competition, nouns in -*ismus* have a lower frequency than those in -*istika*. For each base, these nouns are related to a noun that refers to a person, denoted by a noun in -*ista* as in (21c), who performs an activity or uses or produces a thing, given in (21d). An adjective in -*istický* relates to the person in -*ista* or to the -*istika*/-*ismus*. See Table 9.12 and Pattern 9 (in Appendix 9.2).

3.10 Nouns in -*ita* with roots that do not combine with -*ismus* denoting a quality

Nouns in -*ita* for which a noun in -*ismus* is not attested (Subset D) denote mostly a quality or a behaviour, statement or object defined by this quality, i.e. without a significant difference with respect to nouns in -*ita* in section 3.1 (Subset A). A synonymous formation with the suffix -*ost* is available for almost a third of the nouns; the loan suffix is preferred with most roots. Nouns in -*ita* (similarly to -*ost*) are commonly used in the plural. Plural forms are attested for 207 out of 340 nouns in -*ita* in the data set (Subsets A and D), referring mostly to more statements or things. An example is (22).

    (22) Nakonec jejich hovor vždycky sklouzl jen k banalitám. (SYN2015)
        'Eventually their conversation was always reduced only to banalities.'

The nouns in -*ita* and -*ost* can both be seen as derivatives of adjectives with a native suffix (mainly with the suffix -*ní*, rarely with -*ký*/-*cký*). The adjectives have a higher frequency than the nouns in -*ita*. The nouns in -*ost* were documented exclusively for roots for which an adjective in -*ní* (-*ký*/-*cký*) was present in the data. It thus seems to be justifiable to interpret these nouns in terms of derivation rather than borrowing in Czech (cf. section 1).

    Another correlation could be observed between the adjectives with native suffixes and adjectives in -*itní* (-*it-ní*). An adjective in -*itní* occurs only rarely in derivational families in which an adjective with a native suffix is available (cf. *imunní* – *imunitní* 'immune' in Table 9.13a; nevertheless, it is not involved in Pattern 10a). An adjective ending in -*itativní* (-*it-at-iv-ní*) is attested for four roots only; for none of them an adjective with a native suffix exists. Three patterns (Patterns 10a–c in Appendix 9.2; Tables 9.13a–c) are therefore proposed to capture the observation that the adjectives are attested mostly disjunctively.

Table 9.12 Derivational families related to Pattern 9 with absolute frequency in SYN2015

Simpler N		N-ista		N-istika		N-ismus		Adj-istický	
dokument 'document'	10,713	dokumentarista 'documentarist'	206	dokumentaristika 'production of dokumentary'	20	dokumentarismus 'production of dokumentary'	2	dokumentristický 'documentary'	28
kánoe 'canoe'	277	kanoista 'canoeist'	113	kanoistika 'canoeing'	77	kanoismus 'canoeing'	1	kanoistický 'canoeing'	16
túra 'hike'	447	turista 'tourist'	5,530	turistika 'tourism'	874	turismus 'tourism'	223	turistický 'touristic'	3,746

Table 9.13a Derivational families related to Pattern 10a

Adj-ní		N-ita		N-ost		Adj-itní	
imunní	255	imunita	942			imunitní	1,006
'immune'		'immunity'				'immune'	
obscénní	259	obscenita	59	obscénnost	50		
'obscene'		'obscenity'		'obscenity'			
rigidní	164	rigidita	43	rigidnost	2		
'rigid'		'rigidity'		'rigidity'			
senilní	94	senilita	50	senilnost	[+]		
'senile'		'senility'		'senility'			

Table 9.13b Derivational families related to Pattern 10b

N-ita		Adj-itní	
duplicita	84	duplicitní	68
'duplicity'		'duplicate'	
kalamita	324	kalamitní	48
'calamity'		'calamitous'	

Table 9.13c Derivational families related to Pattern 10c

N-ita		Adj-itativní	
autorita	2,847	autoritativní	471
'authority'		'authoritative'	
kvantita	343	kvantitativní	850
'quantity'		'quantitative'	

3.11 Nouns in -*ita* denoting a group of people

The nouns *admiralita* 'admiralty' and *generalita* 'generals' refer to admirals or gener-als, respectively, as a group (Kraus et al. 2005). The latter noun lacks the meaning of 'being general', which is listed as the main meaning of the English counterpart *general-ity* in OED (2018). They both correspond semantically to the German counterparts *Admiralität* and *Generalität* (DUDEN 2017). They can nevertheless be interpreted as derivatives of the army/navy ranks *admirál* 'admiral' and *generál* 'general' in Czech, forming a rarely applied Pattern 11 (in Appendix 9.2).

Derivations which constitute the individual Patterns 1 to 11 are summarised in Table 9.14.

4. Conclusion

As formations with loan affixes have been almost entirely ignored in available descrip-tions of the word formation system of Czech, the aim of the present study was to

Table 9.14 Overview of formations of Patterns 1 to 11

	N	N-ismus	N-ita	Adj with a native suffix	N-ost	N-tví	N-ista	N-istický	N-itmí
Pattern 1 "approach / movement"		+	+	+ (-ní)	+		+	+	
Pattern 2 "approach / movement"	+	+		+ (-ní / -ký)			+	+	
Pattern 3 "approach by someone"	+ (person)	+					+	+	
Pattern 4 "belief in someone"	+ (god / spirit)	+					+	+	
Pattern 5 "condition"		+					+ (or -ik)	+ (or -ický)	
Pattern 6 "inclination"	+	+					+ (or -ik)		
Pattern 7 "being someone"	+ (person)	+		+ (-ký)	+	+			
Pattern 8 "word"	+	+							
Pattern 9 "activity / approach"	+	+ (-istika)	+	+	+		+	+	
Pattern 10 "quality"	+		+						+
Pattern 11 "group of people"	+ (person)		+						

demonstrate that they can be approached as an integral part of the Czech lexicon and, importantly, to propose a bottom-up analysis of language data that aimed at a description of the semantics of the affixes.

Two loan affixes, -ismus and -ita, were analysed. They are both used to form abstract nouns but differ in many aspects. The suffix -ismus combines with bases that form larger derivational families than those of -ita but still most nouns in -ita share their root with several other derivatives, too. By analysing selected derivatives and their mutual relations across a large number of derivational families, I demonstrated that the size and inner structure of derivational families can provide significant knowledge about the meaning of the formations analysed. The meanings of the suffixes were described using patterns that involved the most relevant derivatives with explicitly marked derivational relations. Using the patterns, it is possible to explain semantic nuances that, to the best of my knowledge, have not been described with loanwords in Czech so far. For instance, the difference between nouns višnuismus 'Vishnuism' and marxismus 'Marxism', which are both based on proper nouns, is explained here by the pattern of 'belief in someone' vs. 'approach by someone' in an illustrative way.

The results of the study are necessarily limited by the data in validity; nevertheless, I believe that I was able to arrive at a systematic and detailed description of the nouns analysed and, more generally, to propose and verify methodological principles that can be used for description of not only the loan part of the Czech lexicon.

The effort to reveal word formation meanings of words by exploring the words derivationally related to them might recall Firth's (1957: 11) often quoted statement of knowing 'a word by the company it keeps', which was used by the author to support his pioneering corpus-based approach. In the present study, however, this criterion was shown to be applicable also to derivational (a sort of associative) relations in language.

Although comparative or contrastive issues are put forward when dealing with loanwords in a language, they are not addressed in the present study and require a separate investigation. An approach for how to compare whole derivational families in two or more languages has to be elaborated first.

Acknowledgements

This work was supported by the Grant No. GA19-14534S of the Czech Science Foundation. It has been using language resources developed, stored and distributed by the LINDAT/CLARIAH-CZ project (LM2015071, LM2018101).

Appendix 9.1 Subsets A to D (noun strings without the suffix -ismus/-ita; section 3.1)

Subset A (-ismus, -ita)

aktiv	final	komun	negativ	profesional	subjektiv
animal	formal	konform	neutral	progresiv	tonal
brutal	funkcional	kontextual	nud	provincial	univerzal
central	global	kontraktual	objektiv	racional	urban
destruktiv	human	linear	oportun	radikal	vital
dual	ideal	mental	paralel	real	vulgar
existencial	individual	modern	partikular	regional	vulkan
exkluziv	integr	monumental	personal	relativ	
expresion	intelektual	moral	perspektiv	sentimental	
fatal	intencional	nacional	plural	social	
femin	katolic	naiv	pozitiv	solidar	
feudal	kolektiv	nativ	primitiv	spiritual	

Subset B (-ismus, -ista)

abolicion	darwin	hindu	konjunktural	natural	rural
absolut	defét	iluzion	konkret	nihil	rus
advent	de	imag	konstitucional	nominal	sad
afor	determin	imperial	konstruktiv	okult	satan
alarm	dokumentar	impresion	kub	onan	secesion
alib	džihád	industrial	lenin	optim	separat
alpin	džin	institucional	lobb	organ	sex
altru	ego	instrumental	machiavel	oriental	sion
amerikan	ekolog	intuicion	maniche	pacif	slav
anarch	ekvilibr	iredent	manýr	parašut	solips
anim	encykloped	islam	mao	perfekcional	spirit
antagon	environmental	izolacion	marx	perfekcion	stalin
arab	evangel	jansen	masoch	pesim	struktural
ariv	exhibicion	japan	mašin	piet	suf
art	exorc	jehov	material	pluton	symbol
atom	extern	juda	maximal	poet	syndikal
aut	extrem	kalvin	mechan	popul	šinto
autonom	faš	kano	merkantil	pragmat	šiva
avantgard	fauv	kapital	mesian	progres	šovin
avantur	federal	kariér	metod	protekcion	tao
baha	fetiš	katastrof	militar	pur	te
bapt	folklor	kecál	minimal	ras	teror
behavior	frank	kemal	monarch	recidiv	thatcher
bibl	freud	klasic	mon	redukcion	tom
bohem	fundamental	klub	monote	reform	transcendental
bonapart	futur	kognitiv	morav	revanš	trock
buddh	gaull	kokain	morfin	revival	tur
centr	german	kolonial	motor	revizion	union
civil	gonochor	kolor	nac	roman	utilitar
dada	hédon	konceptual	narcis	royal	utop

Appendix 9.1 (*cont.*)

Subset B (*-ismus, -ista*) (*cont.*)

utrakv	vich	višnu	wahháb
ver	viklef	voluntar	žurnal

Subset C (*-ismus*)

abstinent	bat	dogmat	expanzion	hermet	kádár
adaptacion	behavioral	dokét	explozional	hero	kain
adult	bergson	dolor	expresiv	hetér	kaleidoskop
age	biblic	dramat	extraktiv	hirsut	kameral
agnostic	biolog	druid	ezoter	historic	kandaul
ahasver	bipert	dynam	fanat	histor	kanibal
akadem	blábol	džendr	federat	hitler	kaoda
akcion	blb	egalitar	fenomenal	hol	kartesian
akmé	bobošík	egot	fide	hoodoo	katabol
albin	bolšev	eidet	fikcional	horizontal	katech
alev	bön	eklektic	filantrop	houphouet	kemp
alkohol	botiš	eklekt	finit	humanright	klas
alp	botul	ekonom	fiskal	husit	klaus
amatér	bráhman	ekumen	flaut	hyen	klerikal
anabol	breatharian	eliminativ	flav	hyperic	klientel
anachron	britic	elit	flegmat	hypnot	kolaboracion
analfabet	brux	empiric	floral	chaot	kolokvial
angel	byrokrat	empir	ford	chasid	komenzal
anglic	car	endem	frazeolog	chauvin	komercional
anglikan	castr	energent	fruitarian	chem	komunitarian
ano	cav	energ	fyzikal	chilial	komunitar
apate	cylindr	engels	galic	chimer	konciliar
apokalypt	cyn	epikure	galvan	ideolog	konekcion
aprior	dalajlam	episkopal	gangster	idiot	konfesional
archa	dalton	ergot	gestalt	indiferent	konfucian
arian	dedukcion	erot	gestap	induktiv	konsekvencional
ariosof	deduktiv	erythr	gigant	infantil	konstitual
aristokrat	deflacion	esencial	gnostic	intecional	konstrukcion
aristotel	dekorativ	eskap	gradual	integral	konvencional
arminian	demokrat	estetic	graf	interakcional	konzervativ
artificial	démon	estet	hacktiv	interakcion	konzervat
asket	despot	etat	haider	interpretativ	konzumer
aster	dialekt	eudaimin	havl	intervencion	konzum
astigmat	didakt	eufem	hebra	introspekt	korporativ
atav	difuzion	europe	hegel	ismu	kreacion
atlet	dichro	evangelikal	hegemon	ital	kreten
autiritat	dichromat	evolucion	helén	jánabrách	kritic
automat	diletant	evrope	heliocentr	jedi	kryptorch
babiš	dimorf	existencional	henote	jin	kultural
bandit	dirig	exorc	herakleit	joc	kviet
barbar	divizion	exot	hermafrodit	josefin	kyn

Appendix 9.1 (*cont.*)

Subset C (*-ismus*) (*cont.*)

lacan	mening	ornamental	protestant	shopahol	totalitar
laic	mesmer	orporativ	provincional	schemat	totem
lama	metabol	ostrak	proza	sikh	tradicional
lamarck	meteor	pagan	prozelyt	situacional	traducion
l'art	metop	palud	psin	situacion	transformacion
lartpourlart	milenar	parazit	psych	skandinav	transform
latin	milenial	parcel	psycholog	skeptic	trial
lax	mimet	parcial	psychotic	slovak	tribad
lerroux	mithra	parkinson	ptyal	smetan	tribal
lesb	mithridat	parlamentar	punktuacion	snob	tritemat
lesefer	monast	parnas	punktual	sociolog	triumfal
lettr	mongol	parochial	puritan	somnambul	trop
leuc	monstrual	paternal	pussyriot	sovět	tru
liberal	mormon	patriarchal	putin	spec	túrán
libertin	mosaic	patriot	pyrrhon	spencer	uděláš
lichen	mozaic	paulin	pythagore	stoic	útrat
likvidacion	mut	pauper	quaker	strab	vagin
ludibrion	mutual	pedant	rekonstrukcion	supremat	vahháb
lumin	mystic	pelagian	republikan	sylog	vampir
luteran	nabrách	peripatet	retif	synerg	vandal
lyr	nan	person	revmat	synchron	védant
lysenk	naturan	piktorial	rezort	synkret	vegan
magmat	něc	pilát	rigor	syntet	vegetarián
magnet	neolog	platon	ritual	šaman	verbal
mach	nerv	pleochro	robot	ší	verifikacion
macho	nethol	pointil	romant	šíit	vítbárt
maloprop	neuděláš	polopat	salaf	šuk	vlezdoprdel
manažer	neurotic	polopatk	salám	švejk	vortic
man	neurot	populacion	saltacion	tabak	voyeur
marc	nikotin	porfyr	saph	tabu	wagnerian
masaryk	nimby	pozorovatel	savant	tantr	wagner
maskul	nom	pozz	scient	taš	warlord
mater	normativ	pragmatic	sedent	taurodont	wasteland
mazda	obskurant	praktic	sedlač	taylor	workohol
mccarth	okamur	preskriptiv	sekular	teoret	wyclif
mečiar	okazional	prezent	sensual	tetraedr	youth
mechanic	olympion	prezidencial	senzual	titan	záhir
melan	olymp	priap	serial	tito	zoroastr
melior	operacional	profamil	shaker	top	
mendel	orf	prognat	shawian	tory	

Subset D (*-ita*)

abraziv	adaptabil	adheziv	adva	agil	aktual
absurd	adaptibil	aditiv	afektiv	agresiv	alkal
acid	adaptiv	admiral	afin	akcesor	animoz

Appendix 9.1 (*cont.*)

Subset D (-*ita*) (*cont.*)

anomal	faktic	kolegial	multiplic	probabil	spontane
anonym	familiar	kolokabil	municipal	produktiv	stabil
antikv	fekund	komod	mutabil	profbil	stacionar
anxioz	fertil	kompatibil	mutagen	promisku	steril
asertiv	flexibil	komplementar	muzikal	proporcional	stupid
asociativ	fragil	komplex	narativ	prosper	submisiv
atonal	fratern	komplic	natal	pseudonym	subsidiar
atraktiv	frigid	konduktiv	nervoz	public	subtil
autentic	frivol	konektiv	nobil	reaktiv	sugestibil
autor	general	kontagioz	normal	receptiv	sugestiv
banal	generos	kontinental	nul	recesiv	superior
bestial	genial	kontinu	obez	reciproc	susceptibil
bilateral	gracil	kontraktibil	obscen	recut	suveren
binar	granular	konvertibil	obskur	reflexiv	synchronic
bipart	granul	konvex	oficial	regular	synonym
bon	gravid	kreativ	opac	rekviz	teatral
celebr	heterogen	kredibil	optimal	reliabil	teratogen
debil	homogen	kriminal	original	religioz	teritorial
deform	homonym	kurioz	osmolal	rentabil	termostabil
denz	hostil	kval	oxyhumol	responsibil	total
depresiv	humid	kvant	paranoid	reverzibil	toxic
difuziv	char	labil	part	rezistiv	tranzitiv
dimenzional	chiral	lasciv	pasiv	rigid	tripart
dispar	chronic	lateral	patern	rival	trivial
disperz	ident	legal	patogenic	rytmic	uniform
disponibil	imbecil	legitim	patogen	salin	univerz
diverz	impulziv	letal	periodic	sanh	util
duktil	imun	likvid	permeabil	seismic	valid
duplic	infantil	loajal	permisiv	selektiv	variabil
efektiv	infekcioz	lokal	permitiv	senil	verbal
elastic	inferior	luminoz	perverz	senior	vertikal
eliptic	intensional	major	piper	senzibil	virtual
emisiv	intenz	malign	plastic	senzitiv	virtuoz
emocional	intim	maskulin	plauzibil	senzual	viskoz
emotiv	invalid	matur	polar	servil	vizibil
etnic	invaziv	minor	popular	sexual	vizual
eventual	irbil	mobil	poroz	simplic	volatil
excentric	kalam	modal	portabil	simultane	vulnerabil
expanziv	kapac	modular	posesiv	singular	zonal
extenzional	kapilar	monstróz	potencial	sociabil	žovial
extenz	karcinogen	morbid	potencional	special	
exteritorial	kardinal	mortal	precioz	specific	
external	kauzal	motil	prior	specif	

Appendix 9.2 Patterns 1 to 11 described in sections 3.1 to 3.11

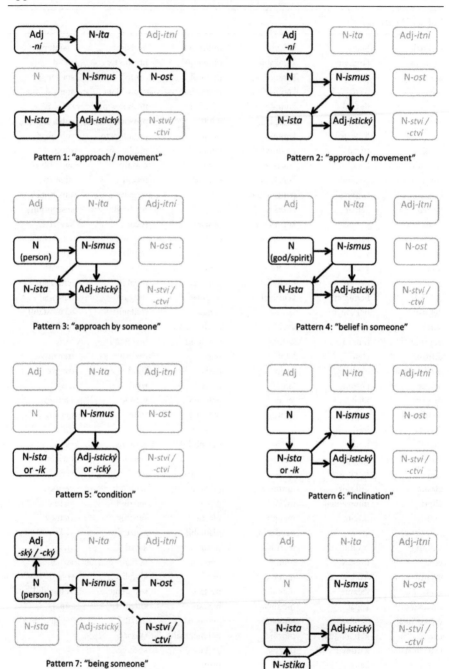

Pattern 1: "approach / movement"

Pattern 2: "approach / movement"

Pattern 3: "approach by someone"

Pattern 4: "belief in someone"

Pattern 5: "condition"

Pattern 6: "inclination"

Pattern 7: "being someone"

Pattern 8: "word"

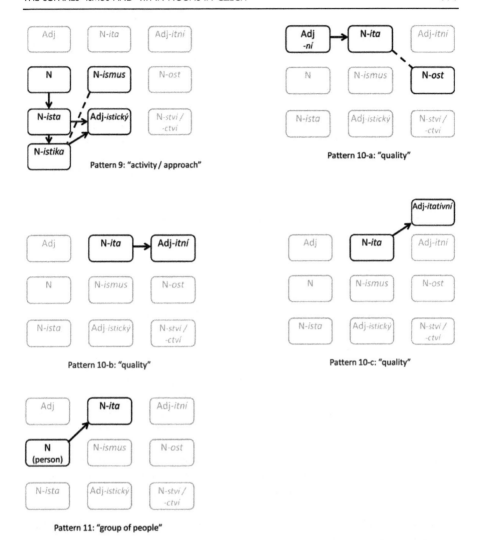

Pattern 9: "activity / approach"

Pattern 10-a: "quality"

Pattern 10-b: "quality"

Pattern 10-c: "quality"

Pattern 11: "group of people"

Notes

1. The suffix *-ismus* is used in Czech in several orthographic variants (*-ismus, -izmus,* rarely *-ismuz*). All these forms were taken into account during the compilation of the data used in the present study but, for simplicity, are referred to as *-ismus.* The variants *-esmus, -asmus* (in *marasmus* 'marasmus', *tenesmus* 'tenesmus'), which are rare and behave differently, are not included. For *-ita*, only feminine nouns are considered. Masculine animate nouns ending in *-ita* (e.g. *jesuita* 'jesuit', *husita* 'Hussite') are not covered.

2. In the chapter, both the terms *root* (root morpheme) and *stem* are used. The former refers to a morpheme that cannot be further analysed while the latter denotes,

less specifically, the part of a word without inflectional affixes (Aronoff 1994; Haspelmath and Sims 2010). Roots and stems are not together referred to as *bases* (cf. Bauer 1983: 20–21) since the term *base* is reserved for the opposition of a *base word* vs. a *derived word*.

3. The term *derivational family* is used here to refer to words that share a common root and are thus derivationally related (cf. Blevins 2016, and the 'morphological family of derivational related words' in Bonami and Strnadová 2018).

4. The patterns in section 3 are proposed as specific combinations of derivationally related words (form-and-meaning pairings) and come close to the notion of a derivational paradigm discussed by Štekauer (in Lieber and Štekauer 2014: 354–369) and elaborated recently by Bonami and Strnadová (2018).

5. In the Czech linguistic tradition, descriptions of the word formation system are organised according to a hierarchy of features: according to the part-of-speech category of the derivative as a first-level criterion, followed by the part-of-speech category of the base word (nouns from nouns, nouns from adjectives, etc.) and, finally, by the meaning of the derivatives (in accordance with Dokulil's 1962 concept of word formation types).

6. Jan Saudek is a Czech photographer (*1935).

7. SYN2015 contains more than 120 million tokens. Each of them is assigned a lemma (type) and a positional tag, in which the part-of-speech category and relevant inflectional categories are encoded. Using the search tool KonText (http://kontext.korpus.cz), the nouns in *-ismus* were searched for by the query [lemma=".*i[sz]mu[sz]"], which covers all orthographic variants of the suffix. The nouns in *-ita* were extracted by the query [tag="N.F.*" & lemma=".*ita"].

8. A prefixed formation was removed only if its non-prefixed variant was attested in the data. Similarly, compounds were deleted if their parts were present, otherwise they were kept in the data.

9. For this study, a randomised sample of 100 nouns was extracted from the lists of nouns in *-ismus* and *-ita*, i.e. nearly a tenth of 1,079 nouns in both lists (739 in *-ismus* and 340 in *-ita*, see Table 9.1), derivations that involve the same root were subsequently searched for in SYN2015.

10. SYNv6 is a non-representative corpus of Czech, which contains 4,834 million tokens (Křen et al. 2017).

11. Other formations which were still attested across the major part of the pilot sample were not included in the data since they were not expected to have a distinctive character, cf. the feminine nouns *individualistka* 'female individualist', *kapitalistka* 'female capitalist', *fotbalistka* 'female football player', *alkoholička* 'female alcoholic', or diminutives *fotbálek* 'football_DIM', *alkoholek* 'alcohol_DIM' in Table 9.2.

12. For the suffixes other than *-ismus* and *-ita*, not all derivatives attested in the corpus were included in the data but just those that share the root with some of the nouns in *-ismus* or *-ita*.

13. No adjective in *-ní/-ný* was attested only for *nudita* 'nudity' – *nudismus* 'nudism' since the adjective *nudný* 'boring' is related to *nuda* 'boredom' in Czech.

14. Such an explanation is not applied with nouns in *-ism* for other diagnoses in OED

(2018): *autism* 'a condition or state of mind characterized by patterns of thought [. . .]', *mutism* 'the state or condition of being mute or silent'.

15. The Czech noun *biblismus* denotes 'a word or expression from the Bible' (Kraus et al. 2005) and does not semantically correspond to *biblism* in English defined as 'adherence to the Bible as the sole rule of faith' in OED (2018).

References

Aronoff, Mark (1994), *Morphology by Itself: Stems and Inflectional Classes*, Cambridge, MA: MIT Press.

Baayen, Harald (1992), 'Quantitative Aspects of Morphological Productivity', in G. E. Booij and J. van Marle (eds), *Yearbook of Morphology 1991*, Dordrecht: Kluwer Academic Publishers, pp. 109–149.

Bauer, Laurie (1983), *English Word-formation*, Cambridge: Cambridge University Press.

Blevins, James P. (2016), *Word and Paradigm Morphology*, Oxford: Oxford University Press.

Bonami, Olivier and J. Strnadová (2018), 'Paradigm Structure and Predictability in Derivational Morphology', *Morphology*, 29: 2, 167–197.

Buzássyová, Klára (2010), 'Vzťah internacionálnych a domácich slov v premenách času' [The Relation between International and Original Words across Time], *Jazykovedný časopis*, 61: 2, 113–130.

Čechová, Marie, M. Dokulil, Z. Hlavsa, J. Hrbáček and Z. Hrušková (1996): *Čeština – řeč a jazyk* [Czech – Speech and Language], Praha: ISV nakladatelství.

Cvrček, Václav, V. Kodýtek, M. Kopřivová, D. Kováříková, P. Sgall, M. Šulc, J. Táborský, J. Volín and M. Waclawičová (2013), *Mluvnice současné češtiny 1* [Grammar of Contemporary Czech 1], Praha: Karolinum.

Daneš, František, M. Dokulil, and J. Kuchař (1967), *Tvoření slov v češtině 2: Odvozování podstatných jmen* [Word Formation in Czech 2: Derivation of Nouns], Praha: Nakladatelství ČSAV.

Dokulil, Miloš (1962), *Tvoření slov v češtině 1: Teorie odvozování slov* [Word Formation in Czech 1: The Theory of Deriving Words], Praha: Nakladatelství ČSAV.

Dokulil, Miloš (1968), 'Nepotřebujeme vyčkávače a zabukisty' [We Do Not Need (Words Like) *vyčkávač* and *zabukista*], *Naše řeč*, 51: 4, 255.

Dokulil, Miloš (1978), 'K otázce prediktability lexikálního významu slovotvorně motivovaného slova' [On the Question of Predictability of Lexical Meaning of Word-formationally Motivated Words], *Slovo a slovesnost* 39: 3–4, 244–251.

Dokulil, Miloš, K. Horálek, J. Hůrková, M. Knappová and J. Petr (1986), *Mluvnice češtiny 1. Fonetika, fonologie, morfonologie a morfematika, tvoření slov* [Grammar of Czech 1: Phonetics, Phonology, Morphophonology and Morphemics, Word Formation], Praha: Academia.

DUDEN (2017), *Die Deutsche Rechtschreibung*, Berlin: Bibliographisches Institut GmbH, 27th edn, www.duden.de (25 September 2018).

Filipec Josef, F. Daneš, J. Machač and V. Mejstřík (eds) (2005), *Slovník spisovné češtiny pro školu a veřejnost* 2, opravené a doplněné vydání [A Dictionary of Standard Czech for School and Public, 2nd updated edn], Praha: Academia.

Firth, John Rupert (1957), *Papers in Linguistics 1934–1951*, London: Oxford University Press.

Haspelmath, Martin (2009), 'Lexical Borrowing: Concepts and Issues', in. M. Haspelmath and U. Tadmor (eds), *Loanwords in the World's Languages: A Comparative Handbook*, Berlin: De Gruyter, pp. 35–54.

Haspelmath, Martin and A. D. Sims (2010), *Understanding Morphology*, London: Hodder Education.

Ivir, Vladimir (1989), 'Internationalisms: Marked or Unmarked', in O. Mišeska-Tomić (ed.), *Markedness in Synchrony and Diachrony*, Berlin and New York: De Gruyter, pp. 139–150.

Jiráček, Jiří (1984), *Adjektíva s internacionálními sufixálními morfy v současné ruštině (v porovnání s češtinou)* [Adjectives with International Suffix Morphs in Contemporary Russian (in Comparison to Czech)], Brno: Univerzita J. E. Purkyně.

Karlík, Petr, M. Nekula and Z. Rusínová (2000), *Příruční mluvnice češtiny* [Reference Grammar of Czech], Praha: NLN.

Kraus, Jiří, V. Červená, V. Holubová, M. Churavý, J. Klímová and V. Mejstřík (2005), *Nový akademický slovník cizích slov* [A New Academic Dictionary of Foreign Words], Praha: Academia.

Křen, Michal, V. Cvrček, T. Čapka, A. Čermáková, M. Hnátková, L. Chlumská, T. Jelínek, D. Kováříková, V. Petkevič, P. Procházka, H. Skoumalová, M. Škrabal, P. Truneček, P. Vondřička and A. J. Zasina (2015), *SYN2015: A Representative Corpus of Written Czech*, Prague: Institute of Czech National Corpus, Faculty of Arts, Charles University, http://www.korpus.cz (25 September 2018).

Křen, Michal, V. Cvrček, T. Čapka, A. Čermáková, M. Hnátková, L. Chlumská, T. Jelínek, D. Kováříková, V. Petkevič, P. Procházka, H. Skoumalová, M. Škrabal, P. Truneček, P. Vondřička and A. J. Zasina (2017), *Korpus SYNv6*, Prague: Institute of Czech National Corpus, Faculty of Arts, Charles University, http://www.korpus.cz (25 September 2018).

Lieber, Rochelle and P. Štekauer (eds) (2014), *The Oxford Handbook of Derivational Morphology*, Oxford: Oxford University Press.

OED (2000–2018), *Oxford English Dictionary*, edited by J. Simpson, Oxford: Oxford University Press, 3rd edn, www.oed.com (25 September 2018).

Panocová, Renáta (2015), *Categories of Word Formation and Borrowing: An Onomasiological Account of Neoclassical Formations*, Newcastle upon Tyne: Cambridge Scholars Publishing.

Panocová, Renáta (2017), 'Internationalisms with the Suffix -ácia and their Adaptation in Slovak', in E. Litta and M. Passarotti (eds), *Proceedings of the Workshop on Resources and Tools for Derivational Morphology*, Milan: EDUCatt, pp. 61–72.

Sambor, Jadwiga (1975), *O słownictwie statystycznie rzadkim* [About Statistically Rare Vocabulary], Warszawa: Państwowe Wydawnictwo Naukowe.

Šimandl, Josef (ed.) (2016), *Slovník afixů užívaných v češtině* [Dictionary of Affixes used in Czech], Praha: Karolinum.

Štekauer, Pavol (2005), *Meaning Predictability in Word Formation: Novel, Context-free Naming Units*, Amsterdam and Philadelphia: John Benjamins.

Waszakowa, Krystyna (2003), 'Internacionalizacija: Zapadnoslavianskije jazyki. Przejawy tendencji do internacjonalizaji w systemach słowotwótwórczych języków zachodnosłowiańskich' [Internationalization: West-Slavic Languages. Tendencies of Internationalization in the Word Formation Systems of West-Slavic Languages], in I. Ohnheiser (ed.), *Komparacja systemów i funkcjonowanie współczesnych języków słowiańskich. 1. Słowotwórstwo/Nominacja*, Opole: Universität Innsbruck and Uniwersytet Opolski, pp. 78–102.

Waszakowa, Krystyna (2015), 'Foreign Word-formation in Polish', in P. O. Müller, I. Ohnheiser, S. Olsen and F. Rainer (eds), *Word-Formation. An International Handbook of the Languages of Europe*, Berlin: De Gruyter, vol. 3, pp. 1679–1696.

Ziková, Markéta (2001), 'Substantivní neologismy a jejich parasystémový charakter' [Nominal Neologisms and their Parasystemic Character], *Naše řeč*, 84: 2, 81–89.

10

The Interaction between Borrowing and Word Formation: Evidence from Modern Greek Prefixes

Angeliki Efthymiou

In this chapter, I discuss two cases of Modern Greek prefixes whose extensive use in loan translations from foreign languages reveals a complex interplay between borrowing and word formation. The prefixes *υπερ-* and *αντι-* derive from Ancient Greek prepositions (*υπέρ* 'over, beyond' and *αντί* 'in front of, instead of', respectively), but, in the course of their grammaticalisation into prefixes, they have also developed some additional non-locational meanings: e.g. 'excess' (*υπερ-εργασία* [ipereryasía] 'overwork'), 'against, opposing' (*αντι-αμερικανικός* [andiamerikanikós] 'anti-american'). Given the extensive use of Greek prefixes in loan translations, I address the following questions:

- How does calquing influence word formation processes in contemporary Greek?
- Does borrowing affect the meaning of Modern Greek prefixes?

It is shown that borrowing constitutes a trigger for the expansion of the domain of use and the development of polysemy in Modern Greek prefixation (cf. also Rainer 2009). Furthermore, I investigate the factors that can account for the prevalence of all these loan translations, as opposed to direct borrowings. Moreover, I focus on how loan translations with *υπερ-* and *αντι-* are recorded in the *Practical Dictionary of Modern Greek* of the Academy of Athens (PDA 2014). The chapter is organised as follows. Section 1 gives some background information on lexical borrowing. Section 2 offers a brief overview of the relevant literature on the characteristics of the Modern Greek vocabulary, while section 3 discusses various issues concerning so-called *International Greek* and *international affixes*. Section 4 offers a brief presentation of the etymological and semantic properties of the prefixes under investigation. Section 5 explains how the data of this study were collected. Furthermore, it provides quantitative data which show that *υπερ-* and *αντι-* are extensively used in lexical borrowings in Modern Greek and that the vast majority of these borrowings are loan translations. Section 6 is dedicated to loan translations in Greek and their relation with linguistic purism.

It also discusses the treatment of loan translations in Greek dictionaries. Section 7 describes the main properties of loan translations with the prefixes αντι- and υπερ- and shows that the semantic domain of both prefixes was extended under a French or English influence so as to include more specialised meanings. Finally, section 8 summarises the findings of the present study.

1. Theoretical background

Linguistic borrowing involves the incorporation of features of one language (the donor or source language) into another (the borrowing or the recipient language). It has been studied by researchers working in a wide range of areas, from diachronic as well as synchronic perspectives. Linguistic material transferred from a source language into a recipient language may include anything from lexemes, affixes, morphological patterns and syntactic features, to phonemes, habits of pronunciation, intonation patterns and ways of framing discourse (Aikhenvald 2006: 15–18).

Lexical borrowing is by far the most common type of transference between languages and a well-studied issue in the literature (Winford 2003: 9). As stated by Weinreich (1953: 56), 'the vocabulary of a language, considerably more loosely structured than its phonemics or its grammar, is beyond question the domain of borrowing *par excellence*'. One of the best-known taxonomies of lexical borrowings, which I will also adopt in the present study, is that of Haugen (1950), who distinguishes three main types of borrowing:

- loanwords, which copy both the form and the meaning (e.g. EL κομπιούτερ [kombjúter] < EN *computer*)
- loanblends, consisting of at least one copied part and at least one native part (e.g. EL αγορέ [aγoré] 'boyish' from the word αγόρι [aγóri] 'boy' and the suffix -é borrowed from French)
- loanshifts, where only the meaning is copied (e.g. FR *grate-ciel* and DE *Wolkenkratzer* modelled after EN *skyscraper*)

Loanshifts can be further divided into semantic borrowings (when the meaning of a native word is extended on the model of its foreign equivalent; e.g. the new meaning 'computer device' that was added in the Greek word ποντίκι [podíki] from English *mouse*) and loan translations or calques (when two or more native morphemes are combined on the model of the combination of their foreign equivalents in a foreign model; e.g. German *Wochenende* from the English *weekend*). Loan translations and semantic borrowings belong to what is known in the literature as *indirect* or *partial borrowing* (Humbley 1974).

While lexical borrowing has attracted particular interest, the borrowing of morphology has generally attracted less attention in the literature. This can be explained in terms of the apparent relative infrequency of morphological borrowing (Gardani et al. 2015).

In recent years, several studies have highlighted the structural effects of borrowing based on large cross-linguistic data (e.g. Aikhenvald and Dixon 2006; Matras and

Sakel 2007). The latter also introduce a distinction between material borrowing and structural borrowing (also called *matter borrowing* and *pattern borrowing*). Material borrowing refers to borrowing of sound-meaning pairs (lexemes, stems, affixes, etc.), while structural borrowing refers to the copying of morphological or semantic patterns. Loan translations and loan meaning extensions are the most important types of structural borrowing, and loanwords are referred to as the most important type of material borrowing (see also Johanson 2002).

2. Greek diglossia and the characteristics of the vocabulary

Many lexical phenomena of Modern Greek can only be adequately described against the background of the long history of diglossia in Greece, which has had a profound influence on the structure of the vocabulary. Greek diglossia dates back to as early as the Hellenistic period (c. third–first century BC). In the Modern Greek state from the nineteenth century onwards, this involved the use of two varieties: *katharevousa*, a 'purist' written variety, which was a mixture of ancient and modern features and was reserved for formal and official purposes, and *demotic*, the 'popular' variety, used for spoken and informal occasions (Mackridge 1985; Horrocks 1997: 350). Katharevousa was supposed to 'protect' and 'purify' the language from foreign elements. Consequently, loans from Italian, Turkish and French were avoided through the coining of equivalents from Ancient Greek elements or by expanding the meaning of words that already existed in Ancient Greek (Petrounias 1995: 799; Stathi 2002: 303).

This diglossic situation was ended in 1976 when katharevousa was abolished officially. Nevertheless, the constitutional establishment of demotic as the official language of the Greek state could not extinguish completely the traces or the effects of the diglossic past of Greece. What is now known as Standard Modern Greek is based on demotic features supplemented with so-called learned elements from katharevousa (Mackridge 1985; Horrocks 1997: 362ff.), thus preserving features from both varieties at the phonological, morphological, syntactic and lexical levels. As a consequence, Modern Greek vocabulary is made up of lexical items of popular (or [–learned]) and learned origin (Petrounias 1985: 308–309, 378–381). The first may have two different sources:

- inherited from ancient and Hellenistic via Medieval Greek, i.e. words having always existed in the popular language. Examples of inherited words are γη 'earth', ήλιος 'sun', θάλασσα 'sea', or
- borrowed from other languages (chiefly Latin, Italian and Turkish). Many of these words are still in common use today, e.g. πόρτα (LA *porta*, 'door'), πιάτσα (IT *piazza*, 'market, taxi-rank'), τζάμι (TR *cam*, 'window-pane')

The second refers to words that have been coined in modern times under the learned (or purist) tradition. These words are in their vast majority of three sources (Petrounias 1995):

- Learned loans from classical or Hellenistic Greek, borrowed in an attempt to accommodate meanings of foreign words by expanding the meaning of ancient words that were thus reintroduced into the modern vocabulary (e.g. πολιτισμός, in GRC 'administration of public affairs' translates FR *civilisation*).
- Loan translations from Modern European languages (notably French and English) (e.g. μικροαστός < FR *petit-bourgeois*, ουρανοξύστης < EN skyscraper).
- Loans from internationalisms based wholly or partly on Ancient Greek and/ or Latin lexical elements (e.g. ψυχολογία < FR *psychologie*, κοινωνιολογία from κοινωνία 'society' + -λογία '-logia' < FR *sociologie*).

According to Petrounias (2010: 512), the case of loan translations in Modern Greek is more complex than what has been noticed for other languages due to the following reasons:

- First, the large amount of 'crossed borrowings' from Ancient Greek with a complete change of meaning to accommodate meanings of foreign words: the *signifiant* comes from classical or Hellenistic Greek, while the *signifié* comes from a modern language;
- Second, the existence of internationalisms, often overlapping with loan translations. In many cases, loan translations are based on internationalisms which in their turn originate in Ancient Greek, thus giving an Ancient Greek outward appearance, but in reality being a foreign word introduced to Modern Greek. Interestingly enough, these loans are occasionally termed as *emprunts de reconnaissance* ('recognition loanwords'), that is loanwords including two Greek elements, that native speakers recognise as Greek words, and easily transcribe with Greek characters (Anastassiadis-Symeonidis 1997).

As the same author maintains, it is not always easy to decide which composition elements are native (actual loans from Ancient Greek) and which come from international scientific vocabulary, because the same word or the same lexical element may have different sources:

- as inherited word (i.e. continually in the language for many centuries): e.g. αλλο-παρμένος ('with disturbed mind');
- as a learned loan from Ancient or Hellenistic Greek, e.g. αλλο-εθνής ('of foreign nationality');
- as a learned loan from international scientific vocabulary, e.g. αλλό-φωνο ('allophone').

Various issues concerning the so-called 'International Greek' and 'international affixes' are discussed in section 3.

3. International Greek and international affixes

According to Petrounias (1995), in the historical development of the Greek language two parallel strains can be noticed: one consists of *International Greek* the other is *Modern Greek*. The first refers to the vast number of philosophical, scientific and other terms present in the modern languages that have their lexical basis in Ancient Greek. The other is a full-scale language, but geographically and numerically restricted to Greece, Cyprus and the Greek communities abroad.

Words of Ancient Greek origin started entering European languages in large numbers during the renaissance in three ways (Petrounias 1995):

- they entered already in ancient times into Latin, and through Latin were transmitted to the modern languages: e.g. *ἐπιληψία* > *epilepsia*;
- they are direct modern loans from the old Greek language: e.g. *δημοκρατία* > *democracy*; *πολιτική* > *politics*;
- they are modern creations based on Greek or a combination of Greek and Latin lexical elements (prefixes, roots and suffixes): e.g. *psych-o-logy*, *syn-chrony*.

It is mainly the third case of modern creations that constitutes a boundless source for the creation of neologisms which tend to be internationalisms, passing from language to language, with slight differences in form or meaning, due to the characteristics of the particular languages (Adrados 2005: 285). The vast majority of them originated as scientific and technical terms, but a large number, e.g. *microbe*, gravitate into common use. In Western European languages, internationalisms are parts of a specific stratum of the lexicon, different from the native one. A considerable number of them are compounds, usually called *neoclassical compounds*, and sometimes they re-enter the Greek vocabulary as calques, in order to express the concepts that they were created for (Munske and Kirkness 1996; Lüdeling 2006).

As a consequence, the two strains (International Greek and Modern Greek) are converging today, since several hundred words or word formation material of International Greek are coming into Modern Greek through borrowing. The so-called *neoclassical* or *international* affixes and neoclassical compounds fit easily into Modern Greek and contribute to its overall conservative morphological outlook (Petrounias 1995; Manolessou and Ralli 2015). In English, for example, among the international prefixes we find *amphi-*, *aut(o)-*, *anti-*, *kata-*, *hyper-*, *hypo-*, *para-*, *syn-*, which are also found in other languages. There are also others.

In section 4, I will examine the etymological and semantic properties of two prefixes which have contributed to the creation of neological loan translations from foreign languages: *αντι-* and *υπερ-*, as used in *αντιπυρετικός* [andipiretikós] ('antipyretic'), *υπέρβαρος* [ipérvaros] ('overweight'), *υπερδύναμη* [iperδínami] ('superpower').

4. The Modern Greek prepositional prefixes *anti-* and *υπερ-* [iper-]

The prefix *υπερ-* derives from the Ancient Greek preposition *υπέρ* ('above, over, beyond'), cf. Bortone (2010: 291) and the *Dictionary of Standard Modern Greek* (DSMG 1998), but in the course of its grammaticalisation into a prefix it has also developed some additional non-locational meanings, such as excess, e.g. *υπερφορτώνω* [iperfortóno] ('to overload'). It seems that, according to Liddell and Scott's (1961) data and Bortone's (2010) descriptions, figurative meanings such as excess and high degree already appeared in a number of words in the classical period (e.g. *υπερθερμαίνω* 'to overheat') but became more productive in Hellenistic and Medieval Greek, as well as, later, in Modern Greek.

As regards the origin of the prefix *αντι-*, it derives from the Ancient Greek preposition *αντί*. *Αντι-* originally meant 'in front of, facing', but its spatial use was barely attested in Ancient Greek. In classical Greek the meaning of *αντι-* is almost always non-spatial: it mainly indicates non-spatial notions such as 'in exchange for', 'opposition' (Bortone 2010: 163). It might also be added that according to Liddell and Scott's (1961) description, Ancient Greek *αντι-* was mostly used with nouns and verbs.

As regards their semantic profile, in Modern Greek both prefixes exhibit extensive polysemy, expressing various meanings. In particular, according to the corpus-based semantic categorisation of Efthymiou et al. (2015), the meanings of *υπερ-* can be classified into two large semantic super-categories, namely 'spatial localisation' and 'non-spatial localisation'. The latter category is further distinguished into 'non-evaluative' and 'evaluative meanings'. 'Evaluative meanings' are distinguished into the subcategories of 'high degree', 'excess' and 'superiority'. The semantic classification proposed in Efthymiou et al. (2015) is illustrated in Figure 10.1.

As regards the productivity of *υπερ-* across the above-mentioned semantic categories, the findings in Efthymiou et al. (2015) suggest that there is a clear tendency of the

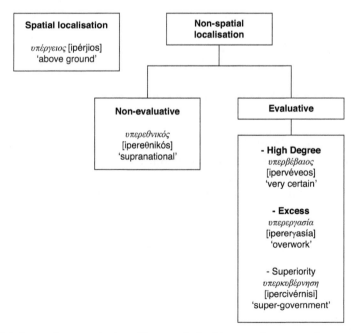

Figure 10.1 Semantic categorisation of lemmas derived by *υπερ-* into semantic categories (Efthymiou et al. 2015)

prefix towards evaluative meanings, like 'excess', 'high degree' and 'superiority', with a parallel decrease of spatial and non-evaluative meanings (for the semantic classification of evaluative meanings see Amiot 2004).

Moving now to the semantic contribution of αντι-, the principal meanings of the prefix are illustrated in (1).

(1) a. αντιαμερικανικός [andiamerikanikós] 'anti-American'
     b. αντιπυρετικός [andipiretikós] 'antipyretic'
     c. αντιήρωας [andiíroas] 'antihero'
     d. αντιπρόεδρος [andipróeðros] 'vice president'
     e. αντικλείδι [andiklíði] 'passkey'
     f. αντιπροσφορά [andiprosforá] 'counteroffer'
     g. αντιπρόταση [andiprótasi] 'counterproposal'

In (1a–c) we find different types of opposition. Whereas (1a) shows the meaning 'opposed to', (1b) illustrates 'attacking or counteracting' and (1c) 'not having the proper characteristics of x'. The sense of 'substitution' is illustrated in (1d–e) and that of 'requital or reaction' in (1f–g). These senses correspond to the descriptions of αντι- in PDA (2014) and DSMG (1998).

5. Data and preliminary remarks

The data of this study were collected from PDA (2014), a modern definitional, orthographic and etymological paper dictionary of Modern Greek with 75,000 entries. The number and the percentage of words prefixed with αντι- and υπερ- represented as borrowings (loan translations, semantic loans or loanwords) in the etymological part of the PDA are summarised in Table 10.1.

The figures and percentages in Table 10.1 trigger a number of observations. First, υπερ- and αντι- seem to be extensively used in lexical borrowings. Second, it appears that the vast majority of these borrowings are loan translations and that the number of semantic loans and loanwords (or direct loans) is much more limited. This finding confirms Petrounias's (2010: 511) observation that 'in Modern Greek the number of calques is inordinately high. In a medium to large dictionary they may well constitute over twenty per cent of the whole.' It also accords with the assumption that loan translations have led to a revival of many 'scholarly' elements from Ancient Greek such as

Table 10.1 Numbers of prefixed words extracted from the PDA

	αντι-	Share of all words	Share of borrowings	υπερ-	Share of all words	Share of borrowings
Entries	577	100		438	100	
Words represented as borrowings	359	62.2	100	210	47.9	100
Loan translations	291		81.1	191		91.0
Semantic loans	63		17.5	19		9.0
Loanwords	5		1.4	0		0

αντι- and *υπερ-* (see among others Petrounias 1995; Stathi 2002). Finally, the finding confirms Efthymiou's (2014) observation that a large number of Greek adjectives prefixed with *αντι-* are translated, mainly from French and English. Examples of borrowings with *αντι-* and *υπερ-* are given in (2), (3) and (4).

(2) a. αντιπραξικόπημα [andipraksikópima]
         (lit. αντι- + πραξικόπημα 'coup') < EN countercoup
     b. αντιαεροπορικός [andiaeroporikós]
         (lit. αντι- + αεροπορικός 'relating to aircraft') < EN anti-aircraft
     c. αντιαλκοολικός [andialkoolikós] < FR antialcoolique, EN antialcoholic
     d. αντιπαραγωγικός [andiparaγojikós]
         (lit. αντι- + παραγωγικός 'productive') < EN counterproductive
     e. αντιψυκτικός [andipsiktikós]
         (lit. αντι- + ψυκτικός 'refrigerant') < EN anti-freeze
     f. αντιβάιρους [andiváirus] < EN antivirus
     g. αντιφωνία [andifonía] 'antiphony'< GRC αντιφωνία 'disagreement, discord', IT antifonia, FR antiphonie, EN antiphony

(3) a. υπεραρκετός [iperarketós]
         (lit. υπερ- + αρκετός 'enough') 'superabundant'< FR surabondant
     b. υπεραιμία [iperemía] < FR hyperhémie, EN hyperaemia
     c. υπεραλίευση [iperalíefsi]
         (lit. υπερ- + αλίευση 'fishing') < EN overfishing
     d. υπεραπόδοση [iperapódosi]
         (lit. υπερ- + απόδοση 'performance') < EN outperformance
     f. υπεργενικεύω [iperjenikévo]
         (lit. υπερ- + γενικεύω 'generalise') < EN overgeneralise
     g. υπερατομικός [iperatomikós]
         (lit. υπερ- + ατομικός 'individual') < EN superindividual

(4) a. υπερβιβλίο [ipervivlío]
         (lit. υπερ- + βιβλίο 'book') < EN hyperbook
     b. υπέρβαρος [ipérvaros]
         (lit. υπερ- + βάρος 'weight') < EN overweight
     c. υπερήρωας [iperíroas]
         (lit. υπερ- + ήρωας 'hero') < EN superhero
     d. υπερκαταναλώνω [iperkatanalóno]
         (lit. υπερ- + καταναλώνω 'consume') < EN overconsume
     e. υπερθέαμα [iperθéama]
         (lit. υπερ- + θέαμα 'spectacle') < EN superspectacle

The etymological information in (2–4) is what PDA gives. As (2c), (2g) and (3b) show, in some cases PDA includes parallel types in two or more European languages. This means that it is not always possible to decide on the source language. Furthermore, (2), (3) and (4) show that *υπερ-* and *αντι-* represent not only the corresponding international prefixes *hyper-* and *anti-*, but also a number of foreign prefixes, such as English *over-* and *counter-* and French *sur-*. This phenomenon will be discussed in more detail in section 6.

6. Loan translations, linguistic purism and etymological information

In this section, I will address some questions relating to loan translations in Greek. First, section 6.1 considers their position with respect to linguistic purism. Then, section 6.2 discusses how this is reflected in the treatment of etymological information in dictionaries. Section 6.3 looks at the PDA in particular.

6.1 Loan translations and linguistic purism

Borrowing of meaning, instead of the use of direct loans, is attested in many languages, either in the form of loan translations with the creation of a new word (EL *μικροαστός* [mikroastós] from FR *petit bourgeois*) or in the form of semantic borrowing with expansion of meaning of an existing word to accommodate a foreign meaning (e.g. *ποντίκι* [podíki] from EN *mouse* in the sense of 'computer device'). In particular, loan translation (or calquing) is perceived as a process that translates 'morphologically complex foreign expressions by means of novel combinations of native elements that match the meanings and the structure of the foreign expressions and their component parts' (Hock and Joseph 1996: 264). As regards translational equivalence, calques can be arranged on a cline from morphological to semantic equivalence with the etymon (cf. Capuz 1997):

- loan translation: a precise rendering of individual constituents (e.g. DE *Wochenende* from the EN *weekend*, EL *βηματοδότης* [vimatoδótis] from the EN *pacemaker*),
- loan rendition: a rendering which deviates from the meaning or morphology, e.g. in DE *Wolkenkratzer* (lit. 'cloud scraper') is the equivalent for *skyscraper*, and
- loan creation: a free rendering which is formally independent of the etymon, e.g. in FR *planche à voile* (lit. 'board PREP sail') is prompted by the EN *windsurfing*.

In many cases the calquing process is not complete and only one part is translated, which results in the formation of semi-calques, e.g. *κοινωνιολογία* corresponding to FR *sociologie* (cf. section 2), with translation of the Latin element (see among others Petrounias 1995).

As Hock and Joseph (1996: 265) point out, 'calquing presupposes a certain familiarity with the donor language and its grammatical structure. Otherwise, it would not be possible to recognize that a given lexical item in the donor language is morphologically complex or to furnish a translation of the component parts.' As a consequence, loan translations are created by persons with a certain degree of understanding of the donor language morphology.

It might be added that calquing constitutes a tool for conscious creation of new words. According to Görlach (2003: 96–97), calques 'provide an excellent alternative to loanwords', especially in language-conscious communities whose members and/or authorities are against the excessive influx of foreign words, trying to keep their native language as intact as possible. Thus, purism 'appears to be a strong determining factor behind calquing'. In the same spirit, Petrounias (1995: 799) observes that using loan translations instead of direct loans seems less 'insulting' for the language, because the fact of borrowing is hidden.

As to loan translations in Modern Greek, we have seen in section 5 that their number is particularly high. Often it cannot be determined whether the source of the loan translation is English or French, since such words spread across many countries at the same time, and in several directions (cf. among others Petrounias 1995; Stathi 2002). According to Petrounias (2010: 511), the majority of these loan translations were created in the nineteenth century in order to hide the fact of borrowing, since for many educated people linguistic borrowing is a sign of what sometimes has been called *poverty* or *decadence*. In a similar vein, Stathi (2002) admits that many loan translations were created when katharevousa was the official state language, in order to designate achievements of science and technology. She also maintains that in contrast to the direct loans, loan translations are normally transparent and are not felt as foreign to the language (they obey the word formation rules of Modern Greek) (cf. Stathi 2002: 322). Along the same lines, Petrounias (1995: 799) notes that a superficial formalism, indifferent to the meaning of words can lead to the easy conclusion that the results of many indirect borrowings are really 'Ancient Greek'.

Petrounias also points out that loan translations, besides adding new words to Modern Greek, can also modify the morphological rules of the language due to a pattern taken over from the source language. According to him, this is what happened in the case of *πολυ-* in the meaning 'manifold':

> *πολυ-* combined with an unmodified substantive has probably originated with the word *πολυκλινική* from French *polyclinique*, itself often misinterpreted by speakers of that language [. . .] On the basis of this compound a new word was first created within Modern Greek: *πολυκατοικία* 'apartment-block'. Later, this pattern was expanded under English influence to use plural nouns as a basis as well. Examples are *multivitamins* and *multimedia* giving rise to *πολυβιταμίνες*, *πολυμέσα*, where *πολυ-* translates *multi-*. (Petrounias 1995: 796)

6.2 Loan translations and etymological information in Greek dictionaries

Etymological information is an expected type of information in historical dictionaries, but it is also common in many general-purpose dictionaries. Even if 'etymological knowledge is irrelevant to the functioning of the vocabulary' in a language, as Jackson and Zé Amvela (2007: 201) maintain, it can still betray the lexicographer's intention to prove and verify the rootedness and historicity of a particular language (Gallardo 1980; cf. also Tseronis 2002; Svensén 2009; ten Hacken 2018). According to Petrounias (1985), who was also responsible for the etymologies in DSMG (1998), this has been the case of past dictionaries of Greek, where the origins of Greek words were directly traced back to Ancient Greek and no foreign loanwords would easily be recognised as loanwords. Petrounias also argues that if the documented history of a language is extended to a long period of more than 3,500 years, it should be taken into account in the way etymologies appear in a dictionary, because they may reflect the ideas and the attitudes that the users have developed towards their language system (Petrounias 2001: 360–361). Interestingly enough, the same author admits that for over five years he had to conduct a protracted fight in order to include information on loan translations and semantic loans in DSMG, because the Supervising Committee of the Dictionary was obstinately opposed to the inclusion of such information in it. As a consequence of his efforts, with regard to loan translations, DSMG, unlike other previous dictionaries, accurately attributes the origin of words like *ουρανοξύστης* [uranoksístis] (< skyscraper) to loan translation (cf. Petrounias 1985; Tseronis 2002).

It is also interesting to note that in his review of the 'Specimen Edition' of DSMG, Burke (1989: 63) notes that the etymologies of DSMG highlight the fact that katharevousa also borrowed extensively from other languages, but many of these loanwords were concealed in their appearance. Similarly, Tseronis (2002: 26), in his review of DSMG, admits that the etymologies of the dictionary prove that the purist tradition of the past century was allegedly trying to purify Greek from foreignisms, but in reality ended up borrowing foreign words or their meaning extensively and concealing their true origin under an Ancient Greek form.

6.3 Loan translations and their treatment in the PDA

As regards etymological information, PDA, like DSMG, correctly attributes the origin of words like *ουρανοξύστης* ('skyscraper') to loan translation. In many lemmas, PDA records the time of the word's earliest attestation in the language, as illustrated in (5) and (6).

(5) a. αντιπραξικόπημα [andipraksikópima] < EN countercoup, 1963
     b. αντιπαράδειγμα [andiparádiγma] < EN counterexample, 1957
     c. αντιπυραυλικός [andipiravlikós] < EN antimissile, 1956
     d. αντιρατσιστής [andiratsistís] < FR antiracist, 1938
     e. αντιφασιστικός [andifasistikós] < FR antifasciste, 1924, EN antifascist, 1927
     f. αντιύλη [andiíli] < EN antimatter, 1950

(6) a. υπερβιβλίο [ipervivlío] < EN hyperbook, 1995
     b. υπερθέρμανση [iperθérmansi] < EN global warming, 1977
     c. υπερμαραθώνιος [ipermaraθónios] < EN ultramarathon, 1977
     d. υπερμοντέλο [ipermodélo] < EN supermodel, 1977
     e. υπερμέσα [ipemésa] < EN hypermedia, 1965, FR hypermédia, 1989
     f. υπερτροφή [ipertrofí] < EN superfood, 1915
     g. υπερκινησία [ipercinisía] < FR hyperkinésie, EN hyperkinesia

As (5) and (6) show, PDA considers English as the donor language of the vast majority of loan translations after 1950 and French as the donor language of loan translations before this. Interestingly enough, this decision on sources is in line with Petrounias (1995: 795), who maintains that 'it is safer, in case of doubt, to propose French for older loans as the default source'.

7. Grammatical and semantic categories of loan translations prefixed by αντι- and υπερ-

This section describes the main properties of the loan translations prefixed by αντι- and υπερ-. The analysis of loan translations extracted from the PDA shows that the vast majority of loan translations with υπερ- are nouns (142 out of 191). This finding is in line with previous research on borrowability scales. Haugen (1950) proposes (7), Muysken (1981) (8) and Matras (2009) (9).

(7)   Nouns > verbs > adjectives > adverbs, prepositions, interjections

(8)   Nouns > adjectives > verbs > prepositions > coordinating conjunctions > quantifiers > determiners > free pronouns > clitic pronouns > subordinating conjunctions

(9)   Nouns, conjunctions > verbs > discourse markers > adjectives > interjections > adverbs > other particles, adpositions > numerals > pronouns > derivational affixes > inflectional affixes

As regards the grammatical categories of loan translations with αντι-, the analysis of my corpus shows that the majority of loan translations found in the PDA are adjectives and nouns. This finding does not provide conclusive evidence for any of the hierarchies in (7–9) but concurs with Melissaropoulou et al.'s (forthcoming) claim that any borrowability scale is only representative of the specific donor-recipient language pair that was used for its formulation, referring to a specific language contact setting.

Table 10.2 presents the number and percentage of nouns and adjectives in loan translations with αντι-. Furthermore, if we contrast the high percentage of adjectives in neological loan translations with αντι- with the small number of adjectival derivatives in Ancient Greek (see section 4), it can be hypothesised that the morphological pattern of the prefix is influenced by borrowings from European languages. This hypothesis is in line with Petrounias's (1995) claim that loan translations can modify the morphological rules of the language due to a pattern taken over from the source language.

Table 10.2 Loan translations with αντι- in the PDA

	αντι-	share
Words represented as loan translations	291	100
Nouns	106	36.4
Adjectives	115	39.5
Other categories	70	24.1

Turning now to the semantic categories of loan translations prefixed with υπερ-, it can be observed that the vast majority of these borrowings display evaluative meanings such as 'excess', 'high degree' and 'superiority'. Interestingly enough, this observation concurs with the findings on the productivity of υπερ- meanings in Efthymiou et al. (2015). Examples of loan translations with υπερ- are given in (10) and (11).

(10) a. υπερφαγία [iperfajía] < EN hyperphagia
       (υπερ- + φαγ- 'eat' + -ia)

   b. υπερτροφία [ipertrofía] < FR hypertrophie, EN hypertrophy
       (< υπερ- + τροφή 'food, nourishment' + -ie/-ia)

   c. υπεργλυκαιμία [iperγlicemía] < FR hyperglycémie, EN hyperglycemia
       (υπερ- + γλυκύς 'sweet' + αἷμα 'blood'+ -ie/-ia)

   d. υπεραιμία [iperemía] < FR hyperémie, EN hyperaemia
       (< υπερ- + αἷμα 'blood' + -ie/-ia)

   e. υπερθερμία [iperθermía] < FR hyperthermie, EN hyperthermia
       (υπερ- + θερμός 'hot'+ -ie/-ia)

   f. υπερσυντηρητισμός [ipersindiritizmós] < EN ultraconservatism
       (lit. υπερ- + συντηρητισμός 'conservatism')

   g. υπερσύγχρονος [ipersínγronos] < FR ultramoderne
       (υπερ- + σύγχρονος 'modern')

   h. υπερπροστασία [iperprostasía] < EN overprotection
       (lit. υπερ- + προστασία 'protection')

(11) a. υπερπτήση [iperptísi] < EN overflight
       (lit. υπερ- + πτήση 'flight')

   b. υπερσιτισμός [ipersitizmós] < FR suralimentation
       (lit. υπερ- + σιτισμός 'feeding')

   c. υπερθέαμα [iperθéama] < EN superspectacle
       (lit. υπερ- + θέαμα 'spectacle')

   d. υπερανάπτυξη [iperanáptiksi] < EN overdevelopment
       (lit. υπερ- + ανάπτυξη 'development')

   e. υπεραπλούστευση [iperaplústefsi] < EN oversimplification
       (lit. υπερ- + απλούστευση 'simplification')

   f. υπερόπλο [iperóplo] < EN superweapon
       (lit. υπερ- + όπλο 'weapon')

   g. υπερσιβηρικός [ipersivirikós] < FR transsiberien
       (lit. υπερ- + σιβηρικός 'siberian')

   h. υπεραστικός [iperastikós] < FR interurbain
       (lit. υπερ- + αστικός 'urban')

As can be seen in (10a–e), a considerable number of loan translations belonging to the semantic category of 'excess' are medical terms carrying a negative, pathological sense (see also Efthymiou 2003; Efthymiou et al. 2015). The examples in (10a–e) also show that such loanwords are often constructed from Ancient Greek elements that native speakers recognise as Greek words.

Furthermore, (11a) and (11g) illustrate that there are also a small number of loan translations expressing the meanings of spatial localisation.

It is also interesting to note that one of the most productive meanings of *υπερ*-, the meaning of superiority, is not found in Liddell and Scott's (1961) description. This suggests, in my view, that this meaning was rarely attested or was not attested at all in classical Greek. Similar remarks can be made for the other two productive meanings of *υπερ*-, i.e. the meanings of excess and high degree. As already noted in section 4, Liddell and Scott's (1961) and Bortone's (2010) descriptions indicate that the Ancient Greek *υπερ*- was barely productive in these semantic domains (cf. also Efthymiou et al. 2015). Furthermore, the above examples, not only (10–11) but also (3-4) and (6), show that *υπερ*- represents not only the corresponding 'international' prefix *hyper*-, but also a number of other foreign prefixes, such as English *over*-, *ultra*- and *super*- and French *sur*-, *inter*- and *trans*- (cf. also Petrounias 1995 and Efthymiou et al. 2015 for similar remarks).

As regards the loan translations with *αντι*-, their principal meanings can be described as 'opposed to', 'attacking or counteracting', 'not having the proper characteristics of x', as illustrated in (12).

(12) a. αντιδιαβητικός [andiðiavitikós] < FR antidiabétique, EN antidiabetic
b. αντικαπιταλιστικός [andikapitalistikós] < FR anticapitaliste, EN anticapitalist
c. αντικυβερνητικός [andicivernitikós] < FR antigouvernemental, EN antigovermental
d. αντιαλλεργικός [andialerjikós] < FR antiallergique, EN antiallergic
e. αντιδημοκρατικός [andiðimokratikós] < FR antidémocratique, EN antidemocratic
f. αντιεπιστημονικός [andiepistikonikós]< FR antiscientifique, EN antiscientific

(13) a. αντιπραξικόπημα [andipraksikópima] < EN countercoup
b. αντεπανάσταση [andepanástasi] < FR contrerévolution

It is interesting to note that the meanings 'attacking or counteracting' and 'not having the proper characteristics of x' are not found in Liddell and Scott's (1961) dictionary. Furthermore, the examples in (13) illustrate that *αντι*- represents not only international *anti*-, but also the English prefix *counter*- and the French prefix *contre*-.

Given the high percentage of loan translations in the data of this study and given the fact that the relatively new meanings of 'superiority' for *υπερ*- and 'attacking or counteracting' and 'not having the proper characteristics of x' for *αντι*- have become very productive today, it can be argued that the semantic domains of *υπερ*- and *αντι*- are heavily influenced by borrowings from European languages, so as to include more specialised meanings. This conclusion is also in line with Petrounias's (1995) claim that loan translations can modify the morphological rules of the language. It also accords with Rainer's (2009) assertion that borrowing constitutes a trigger for the expansion of the domain of use and the development of polysemy in affixation.

8. Conclusion

In this chapter 566 lexical borrowings prefixed by *υπερ-* and *αντι-* were analysed. It was shown that *υπερ-* and *αντι-* are used extensively in lexical borrowings and that the vast majority of these borrowings are loan translations. Furthermore, the chapter provided data supporting the assumptions that in Modern Greek the number of calques is remarkably high and that loan translations have led to a revival of many learned elements from Ancient Greek (see among others Petrounias 1995; Stathi 2002). The study of the etymologies of loan translations with *υπερ-* and *αντι-* in the PDA also provided evidence supporting the claim that katharevousa borrowed extensively from other languages, but the true origin of the borrowings was concealed under a Greek form (Petrounias 1995; Tseronis 2002). Moreover, the analysis of the grammatical and semantic categories of the loan translations with *υπερ-* and *αντι-* has shown that calquing may trigger the expansion of the development of polysemy in Modern Greek prefixation.

References

Adrados, Francisco R. (2005), *A History of the Greek Language. From its Origins to the Present*, Leiden and Boston, MA: Brill.

Aikhenvald, Alexandra Y. (2006), 'Grammars in Contact: A Cross-linguistic Perspective', in A. Y. Aikhenvald and R. M. W. Dixon (eds), *Grammars in Contact: A Cross-Linguistic Typology*, Oxford: Oxford University Press, pp. 1–66.

Aikhenvald, Alexandra Y. and R. M. W. Dixon (eds) (2006), *Grammars in Contact: A Cross-linguistic Typology* (Explorations in Linguistic Typology 4), Oxford: Oxford University Press.

Amiot, Dany (2004), 'Haut degré et préfixation', in F. Lefeuvre and M. Noailly (eds), *Intensité, Comparaison, Degré. Travaux linguistiques du Cerlico* 17, Rennes: Presses Universitaires de Rennes, pp. 91–104.

Anastassiadis-Symeonidis, Anna (1997), 'Διαδικασίες κατά τη δημιουργία των όρων' [Term creation processes], *Proceedings of the 1st ELETO Conference 'Hellenic Language and Terminology'*, Athens: ELETO, pp. 77–87.

Bortone, Pietro (2010), *Greek Prepositions. From Antiquity to the Present*, Oxford: Oxford University Press.

Burke, John (1989), 'Review of the *ANE* (Specimen *ZHΘI*)', *International Journal of Lexicography*, 2: 156–165.

Capuz, Juan G. (1997), 'Towards a Typological Classification of Linguistic Borrowing', *Revista Alicantina de Estudios Ingleses*, 10: 81–94.

DSMG (1998), *Dictionary of Standard Modern Greek*, Institute for Modern Greek Studies of the Aristotle University of Thessaloniki.

Efthymiou, Angeliki (2003), 'Προθήματα ή πρώτα συνθετικά που δηλώνουν επίταση στη ΝΕ' [Prefixes or First Elements Denoting Intensification in Modern Greek], *Studies in Greek Linguistics*, 23: 519–528.

Efthymiou, Angeliki (2014), 'Λέξεις με αναντιστοιχία μεταξύ δομής και σημασίας: η περίπτωση των ελληνικών παρασυνθετικών επίθετων με αντι-' [Words without

Correspondence between Form and Meaning. The Case of Modern Greek Parasynthetic Adjectives with *anti*-], in Z. Gavriilidou and A. Revithiadou (eds), *Mélanges offerts à Anna Anastassiadis*, Kavala, Greece: Saita Publishers, pp. 34–49.

Efthymiou, Angeliki, G. Fragaki and A. Markos (2015), 'Exploring the Polysemy of the Modern Greek Prefix *iper*-', *Morphology*, 25: 4, 411–438.

Gallardo, Andrés (1980), 'Dictionaries and the Standardization Process', in L. Zgusta (ed.), *Theory and Method in Lexicography: Western and Non-western Perspectives*, Columbia, SC: Hornbeam, pp. 59–69.

Gardani, Francesco, P. Arkadiev and N. Amiridze (2015), 'Borrowed Morphology. An Overview', in F. Gardani, P. Arkadiev and N. Amiridze (eds), *Borrowed Morphology*, Berlin, Boston, MA and Munich: De Gruyter, pp. 1–23.

Görlach, Manfred (2003), *English Words Abroad*, Amsterdam: John Benjamins.

ten Hacken, Pius (2018), 'On the Interpretation of Etymologies in Dictionaries', in J. Čibej, V. Gorjanc, I. Kosem and S. Krek (eds), *Proceedings of the XVIII EURALEX International Congress, Lexicography in Global Contexts* (17–21 July 2018), Ljubljana: Ljubljana University Press, Faculty of Arts, pp. 763–773.

Haugen, Einar (1950), 'The Analysis of Linguistic Borrowing', *Language*, 26: 2, 210–231.

Hock, Hans H. and B. D. Joseph (1996), *Language History, Language Change, and Language Relationship: An Introduction to Historical and Comparative Linguistics*, Berlin: De Gruyter.

Horrocks, Geoffrey (1997), *Greek: A History of the Language and its People*, London: Longman.

Humbley, John (1974), 'Vers une typologie de l'emprunt lexical', *Cahiers de Lexicologie*, 25: 2, 46–70.

Jackson, Howard and E. Zé Amvela (2007), *Words, Meaning and Vocabulary: An Introduction to Modern English Lexicography*, London: Cassell, 2nd edn.

Johanson, Lars (2002), *Structural Factors in Turkic Language Contacts*, London: Curzon.

Liddell, Henry G. and R. Scott (1961), *A Greek-English Lexicon. A New Edition. Revised and Augmented Throughout by Sir Henry Stuart Jones*, Oxford: Clarendon.

Lüdeling, Anke (2006), 'Neoclassical Word-formation', in K. Brown (ed.), *Encyclopedia of Language and Linguistics*, Oxford: Elsevier, 2nd edn.

Mackridge, Peter (1985), *The Modern Greek Language: A Descriptive Analysis of Standard Modern Greek*, Oxford: Oxford University Press.

Manolessou, Ioanna and A. Ralli (2015), 'From Ancient Greek to Modern Greek', in P. Müller, I. Ohnheiser, S. Olsen and F. Rainer (eds), *Word-Formation. An International Handbook of the Languages of Europe*, Berlin and New York: De Gruyter, vol. 3, pp. 2041–2061.

Matras, Yaron (2009), *Language Contact*, Cambridge: Cambridge University Press.

Matras, Yaron and J. Sakel (eds) (2007), *Grammatical Borrowing in Cross-linguistic Perspective*, Berlin and New York: De Gruyter.

Melissaropoulou, Dimitra, A. Ralli and M. Marinis (forthcoming), 'Revisiting the Borrowability Scale(s) of Free Grammatical Elements: Evidence from Modern Greek Contact Induced Varieties', *Journal of Language Contact*.

Munske, Horst H. and A. Kirkness (eds) (1996), *Eurolatein: Das griechische und latein-ische Erbe in den europäischen Sprachen*, Tübingen: Niemeyer.

Muysken, Pieter (1981), 'Halfway between Quechua and Spanish: The Case for Relexification', in A. Highfield and A. Valdman (eds), *Historicity and Variation in Creole Studies*, Ann Arbor, MI: Karoma, pp. 52–78.

PDA (2014), *Χρηστικό Λεξικό της Νεοελληνικής Γλώσσας* [Practical Dictionary of Modern Greek], Athens: Academy of Athens.

Petrounias, Evangelos (1985), 'Τα λεξικά της νέας Ελληνικής, οι ετυμολογίες τους και οι Ετυμολογίες του λεξικού του Ιδρύματος Τριανταφυλλίδη' [The Dictionaries of Modern Greek, their Etymologies, and the Etymologies of the Dictionary of the Triantafyllides Institute], *Studies in Greek Linguistics*, 5: 307–416.

Petrounias, Evangelos (1995), 'Loan Translations and the Etymologies of Modern Greek', in G. Drachman, A. Malikouti-Drachman, S. Klidi and J. Fykias (eds), *Greek Linguistics '95, Proceedings of the Second International Conference on Greek Linguistics*, Graz: Neugebauer Verlag, vol. 2, pp. 791–801.

Petrounias, Evangelos (2001), 'The Special State of Modern Greek Etymology', in Y. Agouraki, A. Arvaniti, J. Davy, D. Goutsos, M. Karyolemou, A. Panayotou-Triantaphyllopoulou, A. Papapavlou, P. Pavlou and A.Roussou (eds), *Proceedings of the 4th International Conference on Greek Linguistics*, Thessaloniki: University Studio Press, pp. 360–366.

Petrounias, Evangelos (2010), 'Internationalisms Based on Ancient Greek Lexical Elements: A (Slippery) Bridge to Modern Greek', *Studies in Greek Language*, 30: 503–515.

Rainer, Franz (2009), 'Polysemy in Derivation', in R. Lieber and P. Štekauer (eds), *The Oxford Handbook of Compounding*, Oxford: Oxford University Press, pp. 338–353.

Stathi, Ekaterini (2002), 'Modern Greek', in M. Görlach (ed.), *English in Europe*, Oxford: Oxford University Press, pp. 301–329.

Svensén, Bo (2009), *Practical Lexicography: Principles and Methods of Dictionary-Making*, Oxford: Oxford University Press.

Tseronis, Assimakis (2002), 'Diglossic Past and Present Lexicographical Practices: The Case of Two Greek Dictionaries Language', *Problems & Language Planning*, 26: 3, 219–252.

Weinreich, Uriel [1953] (2011), *Languages in Contact: French, German and Romansch in Twentieth-Century Switzerland. With an Introduction and Notes by Ronald I. Kim and William Labov*, Amsterdam: John Benjamins.

Winford, Donald (2003), *An Introduction to Contact Linguistics*, Oxford: Wiley-Blackwell.

Part III Naming in Minority Languages

11

Loanword Formation in Minority Languages: Lexical Strata in Titsch and Töitschu

Livio Gaeta and Marco Angster

This chapter discusses the growing effect of borrowing on the word formation of Titsch and Töitschu, two Walser German varieties spoken in Northwestern Italy. Even if both communities of speakers are surrounded by a Romance-speaking area, the two varieties display strikingly different results due to distinct histories of contact.

The chapter considers the case of verb borrowing and the collapse of the stratal condition constraining certain word formation rules to apply only to non-native bases in Töitschu, the development in both varieties of a productive class of action nominals unknown to Modern Standard German and the emergence in Töitschu of phrasal verbs linked to the more general syntactic remodelling sustained by this variety. The chapter is organised as follows: after the introduction, section 2 briefly introduces the Walser communities, while section 3 discusses the issue of lexical strata in these varieties largely exposed to contact. In section 4 one case of borrowing is presented which shows how a derivational paradigm can be enlarged in a creative way; section 5 shows how far the contact can go when basic design features of a language are involved, while the final section 6 draws the conclusion.

1. A typology of borrowing phenomena

A common truism says that the presence of foreign elements within a language is due to language contact, which inevitably takes place in bi- or multilinguals. However, the latter normally form only a (small) subset of a linguistic community, from which the foreign elements subsequently spread across the whole community. In fact, language contact is highly sensitive to, among other factors, the intensity of the contact, the number of bilinguals in a community and the prestige of the contact language.

Another widespread truism is that language contact normally affects the lexicon to a stronger degree than the other components of the grammar. As for word formation and the lexicon, loan material is generally argued to be organised in different strata constraining the domain of application of certain word formation rules to bases belonging to a specific stratum and usually opposing native and non-native morphemes, which broadly reflect the origin of the word. For instance, German nouns ending with a full vowel are normally loans and take -*s* in the plural: *Kanu* ('canoe') / *Kanus*, *Kotau* ('kowtow') / *Kotaus*, etc. (cf. Gaeta 2008 for a survey). Similarly, Russian loan nouns ending with -*o* are normally neuter and invariable: *pal'to* ('coat'), *metro* ('underground'), etc. (cf. Timberlake 2004: 149). Finally, only English verbs belonging to the native stratum display the double-object alternation: *John gives* / *bequeaths* / **donates* / **delivers Mary a book* (cf. Dixon 2005: 120). However, the strata need not be thought of in terms of the etymology of a word, which is mostly unknown to the speakers, but rather in terms of specific (phonological, morphological, syntactic) properties, and in fact German native words ending in a full vowel can also follow the *s*-pattern in the plural (e.g. *Uhu* 'eagle owl' / *Uhus*, *Stau* 'jam' / *Staus*) while an English verb like *to pay*, which is etymologically a loanword, also admits the double-object construction, i.e. has entered the native stratum.

The issue of language contact and its impact on the stratification of the lexicon become dramatic when bi- or multilingualism is the norm across a linguistic community as extensive contact can lead to a growing impact of borrowing phenomena on a language. In particular, we will aim to distinguish four phenomena:

- borrowing of specific patterns replicating and/or expanding the model occurring in the donor language;
- borrowing of specific patterns elaborated in a radically 'creative' way directly inspired by the donor language;
- borrowing of specific patterns elaborated in a radically 'creative' way not directly inspired by the donor language;
- borrowing of more general design properties filtering from the donor language.

This typology will be exemplified with the help of data drawn from two small German-speaking linguistic islands found in Northern Italy which provide the optimal candidates for investigating cases of widespread language contact, as we will briefly discuss below.

2. Walser communities and data sources

Walser communities in Piedmont and Aosta Valley date back to the spread of settlers coming from the upper Rhône Valley (Wallis, CH) speaking a variety of Highest Alemannic in the late Middle Ages (cf. Russ 1990). Walser communities are spread out over a vast, discontinuous territory in the Alps and usually occupy the highest settlements in the relevant valleys. In addition to Wallis, where their place of origin is recognised, and several other Swiss cantons (especially Graubünden), dialectologists and historians have been able to identify Walser communities in France, Liechtenstein, Western Austria (Vorarlberg) and Northwestern Italy (Piedmont and Aosta Valley). The Walser communities of the latter area are the focus of our interest.

At present, only a handful of communities still exist in Northwestern Italy. They occupy the upper part of the valleys on the southern side of the Alps around the Monte

Rosa Massif and in Valle Antigorio. From North to South these communities are Formazza, Salecchio (and Bosco Gurin in nearby Canton Ticino, CH), Macugnaga, Rimella, Alagna in Piedmont and Gressoney and Issime in Aosta Valley. Even if they are geographically close to the border with Switzerland, some of the highest peaks in Europe separate most of these communities from Wallis and German speaking areas, thus making them linguistic islands in an Italian-speaking territory. Given their isolation from German-speaking areas, the small number of speakers (none of the relevant municipalities reaches 1,000 inhabitants) and the high altitude of these settlements (between 900 and 1,900 metres), these communities have witnessed a dramatic process of language shift in favour of Standard Italian and Gallo-Italic dialects in the last century. This has evidently had the effect of dramatically accelerating the process of language decay, ultimately leading to language death.

By contrast, during the same period the cultural prestige of Walser communities has increased, stimulating the birth of local cultural associations. The latter significantly enhanced the prestige of the Walser language and culture, promoting several publications of local amateurs, both in Italian and in the local language varieties, about traditional customs, historical, societal and environmental topics, as well as lexicographic works on which present orthographic conventions are based. This is a rich ethnographic and literary heritage that also constitutes a fundamental linguistic repertoire and a crucial source for researchers.

Two projects (DiWaC and ArchiWals, cf. Angster et al. 2017) have heavily drawn on this repertoire with the objective of collecting the textual and linguistic heritage and improving the documentation of the varieties considered by the projects (the varieties of Gressoney and Issime in Aosta Valley and those of Formazza, Rimella and Alagna in Piedmont, respectively). The data harvested are currently being uploaded to the variety-specific ArchiWals corpus (cf. www.archiwals.org) which will provide us with fine-grained searches enhancing corpus-based linguistic analyses on all varieties involved in the projects and which is the main source of the examples provided throughout this chapter.

3. Lexical strata and borrowed patterns in Walser communities

As mentioned in section 2 above, the Walser communities on the southern side of the Alps are surrounded by the Romance-speaking area and the speakers today are exposed to contact with more than one Romance variety. In this section, we will review the linguistic repertoire of Walser minorities in Italy and we will try to identify the most significant lexical strata recognisable in today's southern Walser lexicon. Finally, we will highlight the case of verbal borrowing in the varieties of Gressoney and Issime and the different outcomes of similar borrowing patterns.

3.1 Linguistic repertoires of the southern Walser communities

Situated on the Germanic-Romance boundary, the southern Walser communities are a clear case of language contact and of multilingual communities. The Walser varieties are not the only linguistic varieties spoken there and it is highly probable that the

neighbouring Romance dialects have slowly spread through these communities starting immediately after the time of first colonisation (cf. the survey in Eufe and Mader
2018). The sociolinguistic profile of each community is nonetheless different because,
despite the relative proximity of the settlements as the crow flies, they often lie in
separate valleys in which different Romance varieties are found (Francoprovençal in
Aosta Valley, several varieties of Piedmontese in Aosta Valley and Valsesia, Ticinese
Lombard varieties in Val d'Ossola).

The case of Gressoney and Issime in Aosta Valley is even more complex compared
to the other southern Walser communities, whose region, Piedmont, has only Italian
as the official language, because these communities are part of an autonomous region
in which French has had official status alongside Italian since at least 1948. However,
despite being in the same autonomous region and even in the same valley, the two
communities display a quite different sociolinguistic profile linked to a different
history of contacts between German- and Romance-speaking areas. Following Zürrer
(2009: 84ff.), we can summarise that, while Gressoney was a diglossic German-
speaking community until the beginning of the twentieth century, with German
serving as a written language and Piedmontese as an additional spoken variety beside
Walser German, Issime already had a completely different repertoire at the beginning
of the nineteenth century, with the complete absence of a written variety of German,
French being the only written language and Francoprovençal as an additional spoken
variety.

During the twentieth century this picture has further developed with the diffusion of Italian as a written language in both communities, the addition of French in
Gressoney and the growing importance of Italian as a spoken variety, something which
constitutes a general phenomenon in Italy, accompanied by a decrease of the use of
Romance dialects (Berruto 2018: 498–500). Today, Walser German is strongly endan-
gered and its transmission to young generations has almost been interrupted, while its
realm of use is increasingly connected to the activities of the local cultural associations
(Angster 2014: 115–119).

3.2 Lexical strata at the Germanic-Romance encounter

The dynamics of language contact and the historical development of language reper-
toires in the southern Walser varieties contributed in shaping the stratal composition
of their lexicon. Angster and Dal Negro (2017: 13–14) provide a tentative subdivision
of the lexicon of southern Walser varieties into four strata relating to three different
donor languages, in addition to the ancestral Middle High German (GMH) stratum,
which are used to classify the data included in the Atlas of Southern Walser German
varieties (cf. Antonietti et al. 2015).

In Figure 11.1 we charted Angster and Dal Negro's (2017) subdivision and adapted
it to our purposes with the addition of a stratum of German varieties that is meant
to include lexemes recognised as Germanic but not found in GMH.[1] This German
stratum forms a continuum stretching from arguably local lexical innovations to
lexemes coming from other German varieties (and especially Swiss German). In fact,
it is not easy to distinguish recent calques based on both Modern Standard German

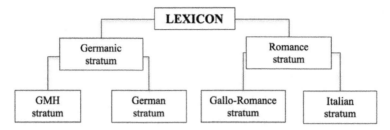

Figure 11.1 Historical language strata of southern Walser varieties

(DE) and Swiss German (GSW) such as, for instance, the form *rägeboge* ('rainbow'), found in Gressoney (see respectively DE *Regenbogen* and GSW *Rëge(n)boge(n)*), from arguably genuine local coinages like the Gressoney compound *rägetach* ('umbrella') (see DE *Regenschirm* and GSW *Rëge(n)schirm*, while a jocular form *Rëge(n)dach* is remarkably attested in GSW).

Furthermore, in Figure 11.1 a peculiar role is attributed to an Italian stratum as opposed to the rest of the Romance varieties as witnessed by words like *televisiòn* ('television') and *schkossò* ('electric shock') found in Gressoney. The rationale for this Italian stratum is the presence in these varieties of many recent borrowings drawn from (Standard or Regional) Italian, which contrast with arguably older borrowings which are clearly not part of the Italian lexicon. The borrowings of this second group, which constitute the Gallo-Romance stratum of Figure 11.1, form a heterogeneous set in which it is often hard to find out to which neighbouring Romance variety a word belongs.[2] An example of these difficulties is visible in the lexeme for 'chair' (cf. Angster 2012), which in most communities is a borrowing from Romance varieties coming from Latin *cathĕdra* – through an unattested stage [+]*catreca*[3] – and not from Standard Italian, where 'chair' is *sedia*. It is worth noting that these borrowings undergo several phonological and morphological processes of adaptation. On the one hand, a change of stress position takes place assimilating the Romance lexemes stressed on the penultimate syllable to Germanic initial stress (e.g. see Zürrer 2009: 131 for Issime). On the other hand, the lexemes are integrated into the native inflectional class of feminine nouns ending in *-u*: e.g. Issime *mattu* 'meadow', cognate of DE *Matte* 'mat, arch. meadow' (cf. Zürrer 2009: 133). Two different outcomes of Latin *cathĕdra* are attested.

(1) a. Mac. kadrjegu, Al. kariga, Rim. kedrigu
     b. Gr. karió, Is. karju[4]

Angster (2012: 188–189) shows that unreduced types like those attested in the Walser varieties spoken in Piedmont (1a), i.e. Macugnaga, Alagna and Rimella, are found in eastern Piedmontese and Lombard forms for 'chair'. On the other hand, reduced types of the kind found in the Walser varieties spoken in Aosta Valley (1b), i.e. Gressoney and Issime, are also attested in the Francoprovençal varieties of Aosta Valley as well as in the northwestern Piedmontese forms. Thus, it is impossible to draw any conclusion on which of the neighbouring varieties (either Francoprovençal or Piedmontese) might have served as source for the borrowing.

To conclude this short survey of the lexical strata in the Walser German varieties, it is worth noting that, despite the presence of borrowings from Romance varieties, which reaches its peak in the case of the varieties of Issime and Rimella, a substantial amount of the lexemes analysed in Angster and Dal Negro (2017), about half of all lexemes, belong to the ancestral GMH stratum of the lexicon.

3.3 Verbal borrowing in Gressoney and Issime

In this section we will take the case of verbal borrowings into account to show how a borrowed pattern can interact with native patterns in Titsch and Töitschu, the varieties of Gressoney and Issime, respectively.

DE displays a strategy to accommodate loan verbs, the stressed suffix *-ier(en)*, whose history, development and expansion in the Germanic branch of Indo-European languages is sketched in Wohlgemuth (2009: 230–232). The suffix emerged already in GMH and occurred with loan verbs from Old French and Latin in texts of the twelfth and thirteenth centuries (Wohlgemuth 2009: 230). Interestingly, *-ier(en)* derives from the Old French infinitive suffix *-ier* of one inflectional class going back to a subset of Latin verbs in *-āre* whose stem ended in a palatal, like Old French *jugier* ('to judge') or *traitier* ('to treat') respectively from Latin *iūdicāre* and *tractāre*, and testifies therefore to an inflectional affix which developed into a derivational loan verb marker.[5] Accordingly, when Old French verbs like *logier* ('to live') and *turnier* ('to tourney'), where *-ier* is an inflectional ending marking the infinitive form, were borrowed into GMH, the French inflectional ending *-ier* was retained phonologically, but re-analysed as a stressed verbal marker requiring the addition of the GMH inflectional endings and in particular the infinitive suffix *-en*: GMH *losch-ier-en*, *turn-ier-en*. The suffix *-ier(en)* has survived until the present and has in fact become extremely productive in DE (but also in German dialects, cf. Henzen 1965: 229) to form verbs, usually with non-native bases (*Alarm* 'alarm' > *alarmieren* 'to alarm', *Dose* 'can' > *dosieren* 'to dose', etc.), marginally with native bases (*Gast* 'guest' > *gastieren* 'to guest', *Haus* 'house' > *hausieren* 'to hawk').

Titsch behaves like DE and clearly displays a stressed loan verb marker (= LVM) *-iere* (the final *-e* being the marker of the infinitive) found in a wealth of lexemes (slightly fewer than 100 formations in the ArchiWals corpus) which in most cases parallel DE verbs and belong either to the Romance stratum, as in (2a), or to the Germanic one, as in (2b).

(2)   a. datiere ('to date'), abkopiere ('to copy') (DE datieren, abkopieren)
      b. halbiere ('to divide'), schattiere ('to shade') (DE halbieren, schattieren)

However, in some cases we also recognise formations based on Italian verbs which are unknown to DE (3a).

(3)   a. arif-ier-e   <   IT arrivare ('to arrive')
          arrive-LVM-INF
          ('to arrive')

     b. én-bòtòl-ier-e   <   IT imbottigliare ('to bottle')
          in-bottle-LVM-INF
          ('to bottle')

Note that the prefix *én-* in (3b), combined with *bòtellò* ('bottle'), is also found in other formations like *énkassiere* ('to cash in') (cf. DE *einkassieren*, IT *incassare*) or *énterniere* ('to inter') (cf. DE *internieren*, IT *internare*), and has to be analysed as the cognate of DE *ein-* found in *ein-flasch-en* ('to bottle') and cannot be taken as a borrowing from the corresponding Italian prefix *in-* of *imbottigliare*, because in the latter case we would expect place assimilation of the nasal.

We now turn our attention to Töitschu, where instead of *-ier(en)* an unstressed verb marker *-urun* is found, as illustrated in (4).

  (4) a. kassurun ('to break'), offensurun ('to offend'), pünnurun ('to punish'),
          remmursiurun ('to thank')
      b. casser ('to break'), offenser ('to offend'), punir ('to punish'), remercier ('to thank')

Zürrer (2009: 136–138) analyses the words in (4a) as hybrid formations consisting of a lexical part borrowed from the contact language – in this case French: cf. the words in (4b) – and of a morphological part, i.e. *-urun*, that he recognises as native. This ending is taken to be directly connected to the lexical root of the borrowed verbs, respectively *offens-*, *pun-*, *remerci-* and *cass-*, stripped of their original inflectional suffixes, i.e. *-er* and *-ir*. Zürrer (2009) traces the origin of the marker *-ur-* back to a set of native verbs belonging to the class of verbs ending in *-un* which display the phonological segment *-ur-* before the infinitive ending *-un*.[6] In dependence of the nature of this element, three different groups have to be distinguished:

1. deadjectival verbs, in which the base of the comparative is used: *ar-breit-ur-un* ('to widen') < *brait-ur*, comparative form of *brait* ('wide');
2. denominal verbs, in which the base noun displays the purely phonological ending *-er*: *hunghur-un* ('to go hungry, to starve') < *hungher* ('hunger');
3. denominal verbs, in which the base of the plural formed with the suffix *-er* is used: *chalb-ur-un* ('to calve') < *chalb-er*, plural form of *chalb* ('calve').

Each of the three groups has parallels in DE or in other German varieties: cf. DE *verbreitern* ('to widen'), *hungern* ('to go hungry, to starve'), and GSW *kalbern* ('to calve') (cf. DE *kalben*) respectively. It is important to stress that *-er-* becomes *-ur-* due to backward vowel harmony triggered by the ending *-un*.

Zürrer (2009: 137) argues that starting from these native formations the speakers interpreted the sequence of *-ur-* and *-un* as a single morpheme *-urun* (which also parallels GSW *-ere* and DE *-ern*) and started to apply it productively to verbs coming from the contact languages (French and to a lesser extent Italian) to adapt borrowings. The adaptation affects also the phonological make-up of these borrowed verbs, which results in the stress pattern of native words with stress on the first syllable (cf. also section 3.2 above). For instance, French *regretter* ('to regret'), stressed on the last syllable, is adapted as ['re]*grutturun*, while Italian *spostare* ('to move away'), stressed on the penultimate syllable, becomes [a'spos]*turun* stressed on the second syllable because the first syllable is re-analysed as a so-called 'non-separable' unstressed prefix.

We must add, to complete the picture reconstructed by Zürrer (2009), that apart from the loan verbs in (4a) and the three groups of verbs derived from native bases discussed above, *-urun* occurs also with native bases, as illustrated in (5).

(5) a. blétschurun ('to snow-spot') < blétschu ('snow-spot')
           gitzunurun ('to give birth to a goatling') < gitzu ('goatling')
     b. bisseturun ('to nibble') < bissetu ('snack') < biss ('bite')
           schowuturun ('to kick one's legs') < schowutu ('kick') < schu ('shoe')

With native nouns in which no etymological ending *-er* occurs, as in (5a), and with native nouns derived by means of the suffix *-etu/-utu*, as in (5b), we also find *-urun*.[7] Quite surprisingly, however, Zürrer (2009) does not mention the possibility that *-urun* might be the local outcome of GMH *-ieren* even though in Töitschu as well as in Titsch we find a long series of parallel formations as shown in Table 11.1.

In Table 11.1 the Töitschu verbs corresponding to DE forms as well as their corresponding French verbs are highlighted in dark grey. When no close similarity with DE forms is found, the Töitschu verbs either correspond to Italian verbs as shown by the forms highlighted in light grey in Table 11.1, *kurrudŝchurun*, *livelurun*, or they slightly deviate from any of the available models as shown by the forms *akupiurun* and *astüdiurun*.

While in the case of Gressoney the contacts with German-speaking areas documented until recent times offer themselves as an explanation of the presence of a post-GMH stratum of German – not necessarily Germanic – lexicon to which most *-ieren* formations belong, in the case of Issime the presence of such a stratum is harder

Table 11.1 Borrowed verbs in DE, Titsch and Töitschu compared with FR and IT

DE	Titsch	Töitschu	FR	IT	
abkopieren	abkòpiere	akupiurun	copier	copiare	('to copy')
diktieren	diktiere	dikturun	dicter	dettare	('to dictate')
funktionieren	fònziòniere	funktiunurun	fonctionner	funzionare	('to function')
garnieren	garniere	garnurun	garner	decorare, guarnire	('to decorate, to garnish')
korrigieren	kòrregiere	kurrudŝchurun	corriger	correggere	('to correct')
nivellieren	liwelliere	livelurun	niveler	livellare	('to level')
panieren	paniere	pannurun	paner	impanare	('to bread, to coat')
spionieren	spiòniere	aspéjunurun	épier	spiare	('to spy')
studieren	studiere	astüdiurun	étudier	studiare	('to study')

to explain. This is because of the interruption – at least as early as the nineteenth century – of substantial contacts with German-speaking areas discussed in section 3.1 above. This state of affairs lends apparent support to Zürrer's view, which opposes the development of *-iere* in Titsch from the GMH suffix *-ieren* to the peculiar development of *-urun* in Töitschu that is taken to be related only indirectly to the GMH loan suffix *-ieren*.

However, in our opinion the presence of a series of parallel formations displaying *-ieren/-iere/-urun* in DE, in Titsch and in Töitschu requires an explanation. In fact, if we look at the Töitschu data extracted from the ArchiWals corpus a clear asymmetry is observed, as illustrated in (6).

(6) a. aksepturun ('to accept'), markurun ('to mark') (cf. DE akzeptieren, markieren)
     b. arwéiturun ('to widen'), joamurun ('to lament') (cf. DE erweitern, jammern)

The verbs in *-urun* based on Romance bases (6a) outrank *-urun* verbs corresponding to DE *-ern* verbs (6b) by a factor of five to one (the former group includes about 250 formations, the latter approximately 50). Moreover, the possible common origin of *-iere* and *-urun* going back to GMH *-ieren* is not contradicted *stricto sensu* by the interruption of direct relations with the German-speaking areas by the Issime community in the nineteenth century.

On the other hand, *-iere* and *-urun* display remarkable differences which make the hypothesis of a direct relation of *-urun* with GMH *-ieren* difficult to accept and in need of support through further evidence. In this regard, we have already mentioned above that in Töitschu, backward vowel harmony has the effect of assimilating the unstressed vowels to the back vowel of the final syllable (cf. Zürrer 1999: 148–153 for a description of the phenomenon in inflected forms). Backward vowel harmony stands in a feeding relation with stress retraction to the first syllable in borrowings, because the latter has the effect of leaving the suffix *-ier-* unstressed and open to the influence of the back vowel of the following syllable *-un* (cf. section 3.2 above).

If this is enough to account for the form *-urun* instead of *-ierun*, we still have to explain why the borrowings are integrated into the class of *-un* verbs in spite of the occurrence in Töitschu of a verb class with *-en* which goes back to the GOH class *-ēn*, as shown by the verb *chaufen* ('to buy'). In this context, we should consider the examples in (7).

(7) a. spigal ('mirror') > spiglun ('to mirror'), stul ('stool, pile, stack') > stulun ('stack up'), vröin ('friend') > vröinun ('to befriend')
     b. gelw ('yellow') > gelwen ('to yellow'), gruass ('big') > gruassen ('to grow larger')

Besides the verbs going back to the GOH *-ōn* class, as for instance *machun* ('to make'), or displaying the verb marker *-urun* seen above, we also find dozens of denominal *-un* verbs derived from native stems displaying a causative or inchoative meaning (7a).[8] On the other hand, *-en* verbs are also derived to a limited extent from adjectival bases, modelling an inchoative meaning (7b).

In this light, we can formulate the hypothesis that the class of *-un* verbs was at some point the default class used to expand the stock of verbal lexemes in Töitschu. When the first *-ieren* verbs were borrowed, they underwent a process of adaptation consisting of three steps:

1. inclusion into the default class of *-un* verbs: *diktieren* > [+]*diktierun*;
2. stress retraction to the first syllable: [+]*dik*[ˈtiː]*run* > [+][ˈdik]*tierun*;
3. assimilation of the penultimate syllable to *-u-* due to backward vowel harmony: [+][ˈdikti]*run* > [ˈdiktʊ]*run*.

The effects of backward vowel harmony produced the merge of the group of loan verbs originally formed with the GMH suffix *-ieren* and the group of native verbs corresponding to DE *-ern* formations. In fact, since the default suffix *-un* was also used to form verbs like [+]*arbreiterun*, [+]*hungerun* and [+]*chalberun* (cf. GOH *hungirōn*), backward vowel harmony caused a full neutralisation between the two groups of verbs. This also led to the disruption of the stratal condition constraining the domain of application of certain word formation rules to bases belonging to a specific stratum. This condition is still valid in Titsch, where the suffix *-iere* is mostly restricted to non-native bases (8a) and the outcomes of the *-ern* verbs (8b) are kept neatly distinct.

(8) a. dosiere ('to dose'), fantasiere ('to fantasise'), kontròliere ('to control')
         (cf. DE dosieren, phantasieren, kontrollieren)
     b. verbreitrò ('to widen'), hòngrò ('to hunger'), chalbrò ('to calve')
         (cf. DE verbreitern, hungern, kalbern)

As a consequence, the suffix *-urun* in Töitschu appears nowadays as a productive means to integrate loan verbs in the lexicon, but also to form new verbs from local neologisms. At the same time, this shows that the peculiar development of Töitschu has led to a collapse of the synchronic relevance of the well-tailored strata depicted in Figure 11.1 above which appear to be still relevant for Titsch.

4. Creative elaboration of borrowed patterns

In this section we will turn our attention to action nouns in order to show how far the creative elaboration of a borrowed pattern can go in enriching a well-defined derivational paradigm (see Štekauer 2014 for the latter concept).

4.1 Action nouns in Greschòneytitsch

Like any well-behaved Germanic language, the derivational paradigm of action nouns both in Titsch and in Töitschu consists of the five different patterns displayed in Table 11.2.[9] As is shown by the figures in Table 11.2, the commonest ways to form action nouns in Titsch rely respectively on the suffix *-òng* (a), on the root-vowel alternations typical of Germanic languages (b) and on conversion (c). In addition, a number of other minor types occur (e), displaying further suffixes like *-é* and *-(t)scht*, possibly in combination with apophony. Quite surprisingly, however, a further type (d) is robustly

Table 11.2 The derivational paradigm of action nouns in Titsch and their DE equivalents

Derivational pattern	Greschòneytitsch	DE	Number of types
a. Suffix -*òng*	bessrò ('to heal') > bessròng ('to healing') fiere ('to lead') > fieròng ('direction') usstelle ('to exhibit') > usstellòng ('exhibition')	bessern > Besserung führen > Führung ausstellen > Ausstellung	112
b. Apophonic alternation	bisse ('to bite') > bés ('bite') goa ('to go') > gang ('(way of) walking') sprénge ('to jump') > spròng ('jump')	beißen > Biss gehen > Gang springen > Sprung	93
c. Conversion	antwòrtò ('to answer') > antwòrt ('answer') loufe ('to run') > louf ('run') redò ('to talk') > red ('talk')	antworten > Antwort laufen > Lauf –	72
d. Suffix -*etò*	chrétzò ('to scratch, scribble') > chrétzetò ('scribble') frässò ('to devour') > frässetò ('feast') flammò ('flame') > flammòtò ('blaze') fuscht ('fist') > fuschtetò ('punch')	??	56
e. Rest	dienò ('to serve') > dientscht ('service') toufe ('to baptise') > toufé ('baptism') verliere ('to lose') > verlòscht ('loss')	dienen > Dienst taufen > Taufe verlieren > Verlust	36

attested, which displays the feminine suffix -*etò* in combination with both verbal and nominal bases. In Töitschu, the suffix displays the form -*etu* or -*utu* in compliance with the vowel harmony discussed above: *chratzun* ('to scratch') > *chratzetu* ('scratch'), *messer* ('knife') > *messerutu* ('knifing'), etc.[10] Note that in contrast to the other types no clear equivalent of this suffix occurs in DE. On the other hand, this suffix is cognate with the feminine suffix -*ete* frequently found in High Alemannic and in Swabian referring to the abstract or concrete result of an activity, i.e. a certain quantity appearing at once, e.g. *Schüüsete* ('a shooting') and *Verschimpfete* ('a scolding') (cf. Russ 1990: 359, 379).[11] This suffix is taken to go back to a Latin or Romance ending, -*āta* or -*ēta*, which is attested in a few GOH borrowings like *miscellāta* ('mixture'), *scizzāta* ('dung'), *bliuwāta* ('hitting'), *screiāta* ('shouting'), *snuderāta* ('snot') (cf. Henzen 1965: 175). Note incidentally that the endings -*ò* and -*u* represent the normal way of adapting *a*-ending feminines coming from Romance languages in Titsch and Töitschu: e.g. Italian *gara* ('race') > Ti. *garò*, It. *benna* ('excavator grab') > Tö. *bennu*, etc. Moreover, these endings also represent the normal outcome of the old Germanic feminines reduced to Schwa in DE: Ti. *klockò* / Tö. *klocku* / DE *Glocke* ('bell'), Ti. *seifò* / Tö. *seifu* / DE *Seife* ('soap'), etc.

While their history and occurrence in Titsch and Töitschu are perfectly in line with the widespread diffusion of the suffix *-ete* in High Alemannic, the profile of the derivatives formed with the suffixes *-etò* and *-etu* is worth further investigation as it shows a consistent picture and displays striking similarity with a quite productive pattern found also in Italian and in other Romance varieties, but found only to a limited extent in French.

4.2 Derivatives formed with *-etò/-etu*

The derivatives formed with the suffix *-etò/-etu* come from two lexical bases, verbs and nouns. As for deverbal nouns, they typically select verbs denoting unbounded or atelic activities in Vendler's (1967) sense and produce action nouns provided with the meaning roughly sketched above.

(9) a. erschétte ('to shake')   > erschéttretò ('shake')
     b. fépple ('to tease')   > féppletò ('joke')
     c. frässò ('to devour')   > frässetò ('feast')
     d. läckò ('to lick')   > läcketò ('lick')
     e. lésmò ('to knit')   > lésmetò ('knitting')
     f. ròtschò ('to slip')   > ròtschetò ('slip')
     g. schnue ('to snow')   > schnuetò ('snowfall')
     h. schwétze ('to sweat')   > schwétzetò ('sweat')
     i. seikò ('to pee')   > seiketò ('pee')
     j. sifzkò ('to sigh')   > sifzkòtò ('sigh')
     k. stéffò ('to sting')   > stéffetò ('sting')

The activities can presuppose a human or more generally an animate agent as in (9b–e), or a non-volitional experiencer as in (9f) and (9j), or they can make reference to natural processes as in (9g–h), or they can profile either agentless natural processes or an agent lurking behind them as in (9a), (9i) and (9k). The crucial property, however, is that the activity is temporally unbounded while the derivative produces its corresponding bounded or semelfactive action noun referring to 'a single instantiation of the activity denoted by the base' which can easily be pluralised. A more varied picture emerges for denominal verbs.

(10) a. chorb ('basket')   > chorbetò ('basketful')
     b. flammò ('flame')   > flammòtò ('blaze')
     c. fuscht ('fist')   > fuschtetò ('punch')
     d. gabelò ('fork')   > gabletò ('pitchfork')
     e. hòre ('horn')   > hòrnetò ('butt')
     f. leffél ('spoon')   > leffietò ('spoonful')
     g. oug ('eye')   > ougetò ('glance')

These basically display three different meanings: (1) 'single quantity contained in N' if the base is a possible container, as in (10a) and (10f), or can be conceptualised as such as in (10d); (2) 'single blow of N' if the base is a possible instrument as in (10c) and (10e); (3) 'single instantiation of the activity involving N' if the base can be conceptualised as involving an activity as in (10b) and (10g). Note that the same derivatives can display different meanings: *gabletò* can also have the blow meaning, while *fuschtetò* can be conceptualised as referring to the typical activity involving a *fuscht*. On the other hand, *ougetò* can also be intended as a metaphorical blow of eye. Because of this intrinsic polysemy, it seems more plausible to assume a general, unspecified meaning 'single instantiation of a typical (abstract or concrete) property of the base'.

Finally, since verbs can easily be derived from nouns by means of conversion, in cases such as (11) both analyses are available, resulting in a double motivation.

(11) a. blétzk / blétzkò ('to flash')   > blétzketò ('flashing')
     b. fues ('foot') / fuessò ('to kick')   > fuessetò ('kick')
     c. hoamer ('hammer') / hoamrò ('to hammer')   > hoamretò ('hammer blow')
     d. näscht ('nest') / näschtò ('to brood')   > näschtetò ('brood')
     e. peitschò ('lash / to lash')   > peitschòtò ('lash blow')
     f. messer ('knife') / messrò ('to knife')   > messretò ('knife wound')
     g. stäcke ('stick') / stäckò ('to beat with a stick') > stäcketò ('blow with a stick')
     h. tésch ('table') / tésschò ('to set the table')   > tésschetò ('tableful')

This state of affairs supports the idea of a general, unspecified meaning which captures both deverbal and denominal derivatives stressing the unity of the derivational process involving -*etò*.

4.3 The Italian feminine past participle and -*etò*/-*etu*

In addition to the unspecified category of the base discussed in section 4.2, a second property of these suffixes is the striking similarity with the Italian (and, more in general, Romance, cf. Gaeta 2015) semelfactive action nouns that take the feminine form of the past participle: *mangiare* ('to eat') > *mangiata* (past part. *mangiato*), *cadere* ('to fall') > *caduta* (past part. *caduto*), etc. The semelfactive action noun can be characterised in all Romance languages (with the noteworthy exception of Romanian) as meaning 'a single instantiation of an activity typically connected with the base'.

They are provided with peculiar properties as they form bounded action nouns, typically from activity verbs, and flank other action nouns formed on the same bases, in particular those displaying the highly productive suffixes -*mento* and -*zione* as in (12a) and (12b) (cf. Gaeta 2002, 2017).

(12) a. insaponare ('to soap')   > insaponamento ('soaping') / insaponata
     b. accelerare ('to speed up') > accelerazione ('acceleration') / accelerata
     c. cadere ('to fall')   > caduta ('fall') / *cadimento / *cadizione
     d. entrare ('to enter')   > entrata ('entrance') / *entramento / *entrazione

Note, incidentally, that with unaccusative verbs this double series of derivatives from the same base is blocked as shown by (12c) and (12d). This is arguably due to the basic meaning of this procedure which can be formally expressed with the help of Booij's (2010) constructional framework.

(13) a. $[[\ldots]_{Vi}\text{-}mento/\text{-}zione]_{Nj} \leftrightarrow$ [the SitTyp involved by $\text{SEM}_i \ldots]_j$

    b. $[[\ldots <+dyn, -b>]_{Vi} \text{ FPP}]_{Nj} \leftrightarrow$ [the SitTyp $<+b>_j$ combined with $\text{SEM}_i \ldots]_j$

While the suffixes -*mento* and -*zione* do not display any particular selectional properties in that any verbal base can be taken to form an action noun denoting the situational type (SitTyp) identified by the basic meaning (SEM) of the verb (13a), the derivatives formed with the feminine past participle (FPP) are essentially more selective (13b). In fact, they only take dynamic <+dyn> and unbounded <–b> verbs and form nouns referring to a bounded <+b> SitTyp. With unaccusative verbs the application of the latter pattern applies at the output value insofar as their semelfactive meaning is immediately mirrored in the bounded nature of the SitTyp and blocks the possible selection of the other less restricted pattern. Such a mechanism in which a pattern is applied at the output value is well accommodated in Booij's constructional framework insofar as word formation patterns are expressed by means of lexical relations among partially specified constructions instead of rules presupposing an input-output relation.

Moreover, a suffix -*ata*, which actually corresponds to the specific form of the FPP of the default class -*are*, also combines with nominal bases displaying a number of meanings that basically correspond to those listed in (10) above for -*etò* also with respect to possible intrinsic polysemy as in (14a).[12]

(14) a. forchetta ('fork')   > forchettata ('fork full/pitchfork')

    b. gomito ('elbow')   > gomitata ('jab')

    c. occhio ('eye')   > occhiata ('glance')

Finally, in several cases a double motivation shows up, as illustrated in (15).

(15) a. martello ('hammer')/   > martellata ('hammer blow')

       martellare ('to hammer')

    b. ospite ('host')/   > ospitata ('appearance as host')

       ospitare ('to host')

Given the strict correspondence of the FPP and the -*etò* derivatives, it is straightforward to assume that a direct connection between the two patterns exists in the bilingual speaker's mind insofar as the Italian pattern supports and enhances the development of -*etò*, i.e. of the weak code. Some examples of corresponding pairs are given in (16).

(16) a. ròtschetò   scivolata   ('slip')

    b. schnuetò   nevicata   ('snowfall')

    c. schwétzetò sudata   ('sweat')

d. seiketò	pisciata	('pee')
e. gabletò	forchettata	('pitchfork')
f. hòrnetò	cornata	('butt')
g. ougeto	occhiata	('glance')
h. hoamretò	martellata	('hammer blow')

In fact, such a development has the effect of enlarging the derivational family of Titsch action nouns insofar as two types of action nouns can be formed from the same base, depending on the word formation pattern selected as shown by (17a–b) and (17c–d), respectively.

(17) a. $[[. . .]_{Vi} \text{-}òng]_{Nj} \leftrightarrow$ [the SitTyp involved by $\text{SEM}_i . . .]_j$

b. erschétte / scuotere $\rightarrow$ erschéttròng / scuotimento | action noun |

c. $[[. . . <\text{+dyn}, \text{–b}>]_{Vi} \text{-}etò]_{Nj} \leftrightarrow$ [the SitTyp $<\text{+b}>_j$ combined with $\text{SEM}_i . . .]_j$

d. *erschétte / scuotere $\rightarrow$ erschéttretò / scossa* | semelfactive action noun |

Note that unaccusative verbs normally select other procedures to form action nouns, namely the conversion pattern (see (c) in Table 11.2 above, e.g. *falle* 'to fall' > *fall*, *loufe* 'to run' > *louf*, cf. DE *fallen* > *Fall*, *laufen* > *Lauf*), or the apophonic pattern possibly in combination with the suffix *-t* (see (e) in Table 11.2 above, e.g. *achéeme* 'to arrive' > *ankònft*, cf. DE *ankommen* > *Ankunft*). However, in a few cases where an unaccusative verb selects *-etò/-utu*, other action nouns are normally blocked: *ròtschò* ('to slip') > *ròtschetò* / **ròtsch* / **ròtschòng* (cf. DE *rutschen* 'to slip' > *Rutsch* / *Rutschung*), mirroring the similar blocking effect observed for the Italian FPP in (12c–d) above.

Finally, the derivatives with *-etò/-utu* are particularly useful in periphrases selecting a support verb like *geen* ('to give'). In (18), from Töitschu, this expresses a particular emphasis on a single event extracted from a sequence of similar events.[13]

(18)	hets	gwettrut	un	hets	dondurut,				
	has.3SG.N	rain.PSTPTCP	and	has.3SG.N	thunder.PSTPTCP				
	hets	keen	an	dondurutu	das	het	gspoalten	a	larch
	has.3SG.N	given	a	thunder.UTU	that	has	broken	a	liarch

'It has rained and thundered, there has been a stroke of thunder [sic] which has broken a larch.'

This construction closely resembles the quite frequent Italian model exemplified in (19), which, similarly to English (cf. Dixon 2005: 459ff.), also has the effect of emphasising a single instantiation of the depicted event and selects the support verbs *fare* ('make') and *dare* ('give'), accompanied by an indefinite NP containing a FPP (cf. Gaeta 2002: 159ff.).

(19)	Ha	fatto	una	gran	tuonata	che	ha	spaccato	un	larice
	has	made	a	big	thunder.FPP	that	has	broken	a	larch

'There has been a big thunder which has broken a larch.'

Moreover, this construction is completely unknown in DE in which support verb constructions (DE *Funktionsverbgefüge* 'sequences with function verb') are quite widespread, but with an essentially different structure and value where the particular emphasis on a single instantiation of the event is absent (cf. Storrer 2006 for a survey).

4.4 The role of the Romance diminutive

A last observation on the development of the suffix *-età* / *-utu* relates to the possible influence of the feminine form of the Romance diminutive suffix *-etta* / *-ette* as it appears in a number of loanwords. Some examples are given in (20).

(20) a. FrProv.   brotsetta   >   Ti. brotschetò / Tö. brotschetu ('faucet')
     b. Fr.   serviette   >   Ti. schärvietò / Tö. sarvietu ('napkin')
     c. FrProv.   terretta   >   Ti. tärretò / Tö. terrutu ('tureen')

As we have already seen above, the feminine ending *-a* is normally adapted as *-ò* in Titsch and as *-u* in Töitschu which continue the old endings of the Germanic feminines reduced to schwa in DE. The influence of this pattern can be seen in the extension of the ending *-età* / *-utu* to native nouns like Ti. *gòrbetò* ('bill hook') (going back to GOH *churba* from Lat. *curvus* 'bowed'), or in cases where the etymological ending might be matched with *-età* such as Ti. *ruetò* ('rod' from GOH *ruota* cf. DE *Rute*) or Tö. *retzetu* from Fr. *recette* ('recipe' cf. DE *Rezept*), and crucially in nouns like Ti. *chorb* / Tö. *chuarb* ('basket'), Ti. *oug* / Tö *aug* ('eye'), etc. where a diminutive value was possible. The acquisition of the semelfactive action value, replicating the Italian model, might have been favoured by the frequent meaning extension 'diminutive' > 'singulative', as found for instance in It. *zuccherino* 'small sugar > piece of sugar' and in many other languages (cf. Grandi 2015 for a survey). In sum, the old loan suffix *-età* / *-utu*, ultimately coming from Romance *-ata*, has been partially enhanced by its formal identity with borrowings displaying a Romance diminutive suffix *-etta*, which – in spite of its etymological difference – has crossed its way with the old suffix via a common process of meaning extension.

5. Borrowing more general design properties

The borrowing of general design properties of a language is normally said to be possible only in the presence of dramatic changes caused by the generalised effects of language contact (cf. some discussion in Wohlgemuth 2009: 11–17). In this regard, we already observed how Töitschu, under a stronger influence of the surrounding Romance languages, gave up the stratal distinction between a Germanic and a Romance stratum discussed in Figure 11.1 above, which is perfectly preserved in Titsch. Let us now consider the examples in (21).

(21) a. DE Und, um   nicht zu   sterben, [hat$_{V+fin}$ er   [Gras und
          and   round   not   to   die   has   he   gras and
          Wurzeln]$_{NP}$ gegessen$_{V-fin}$]$_{VC}$
          roots   eaten

b. Ti. Ón   fer   nid   schtéerbe   [hatter$_{V+fin}$ [gras ón
       and   for   not   die   has.3SG.M   grass and
       wórtze]$_{NP}$ kässet$_{V-fin}$]$_{VC}$
       roots   eaten

c. Tö. Un   vür   nöit   schtearbe,   [hets$_{V+fin}$ kesse$_{V-fin}$]$_{VC}$
       and   for   not   die   has.3SG.M   eaten
       [weidi un wurtzi]$_{NP}$
       grass and roots

d. It. E   pe   non   morire [ha   mangiato]$_{VC}$ [erba   e radici]$_{NP}$
       and   for   not   die   has   eaten   grass   and roots
       'And he has eaten grass and roots to survive.'

In (21a), we find that in DE the so-called sentence bracket is determined by the two components of the complex verb (=VC). One bracket is the finite component (=V+fin) in second position, the other the non-finite components (=V−fin) in final position. The subject and the object are in between them, in the so-called middle field. In Titsch, this structure is maintained, as in (21b). However, in Töitschu the entire idea of a sentence bracket, including the middle field, is lost. Thus, the two components of the complex verb in (21c) are placed together, as they are in Italian (21d).

As is well known, in DE a similar sentence bracket is found with so-called particle verbs in which the particle element is separate from the lexical root and dislocated at the end of the sentence either alone (22a) or in combination with the non-finite component of the verbal complex (22b), in contrast to prefix verbs where separation is impossible (22c).

(22) a. Er ass Gras und Wurzeln auf / *aufass / *ass   auf Gras und Wurzeln
        he ate grass and roots   up / *up.ate / *ate   up   grass and roots
        'He ate grass and roots up.'
     b. Er hat Gras und Wurzeln aufgegessen / *gegessen auf Gras und Wurzeln.
        he has grass and roots   up.eaten   / *eaten   up   grass and roots
        'He has eaten grass and roots up.'
     c. Die Motten zerfrassen die Kleider   / *frassen die Kleider zer.
        'The moths ate away at the clothes.'

In concomitance with the loss of the general design property relating to the sentence structure, in Töitschu (23b) also particle verbs have disappeared in favour of phrasal verbs, while particle verbs are well preserved in Titsch (23a).

(23) a. Ti. heintsch demnoa Heilége mét   dem water
            have.3PL hence   saints   with the weather
            zéemegleit / *gleit zéeme
            together.put.PSTPTCP/put.PSTPTCP together
            'Hence they have combined the Saints with the weather.'

Table 11.3 Particle verbs in Titsch and their correspondents in Töitschu

	Particle verbs		Phrasal verbs		
Titsch	DE	Töitschu	Piedmontese	Northern Italian	
alecke	anlegen	lécken a			('to put to')
drélecke	hereinlegen	lécken i			('to put in')
élecke	einlegen	lécken dri	büté 'ndrinta	mettere dentro	('to put inside')
embrélecke	niederlegen		büté giü	mettere giù	('to put down')
uflecke	auflegen	lécken ouf	büté sü	mettere su	('to put up')
uslecke	auslegen	lécken ous	büté fora	metter fuori	('to put out')
vorlecke	vorlegen	lécken vür			('to put forward')
zuelecke	zulegen	lécken zu			('to put to')
zéemelecke	zusammenlegen	lécken zseeme	büté 'nsema	mettere insieme	('to put together')
			büté via	mettere via	('to put away')

b. Tö. z   bruat   hescht   gleit   i/*igleit sua
        the bread   have.2SG   put.PSTPART in   so
        'You have put the bread inside in this way.'

The re-analysis of particle verbs as phrasal verbs consisting of a verb immediately followed by a locative adverb is a generalised feature throughout the Töitschu lexicon, which stands in neat contrast with the conservative behaviour of Titsch resembling DE. This is illustrated in the contrasting examples in Table 11.3.

On the other hand, phrasal verbs are commonly found in Piedmontese and more in general in the Northern Italian varieties spoken there. Again, the disruption of the general design property relating to the sentence structure observed in Töitschu brings along the remodelling of a peculiar derivational pattern, the particle verbs, according to the syntactic model occurring in contact languages.

6. Conclusion

To sum up, intensive contact can lead to extensive borrowing of patterns of a growing complexity. In this regard, striking differences have been observed between the two Walser German varieties of Gressoney and Issime, which are both surrounded by Romance languages but display a significantly different contact situation.

As for the simple borrowing of morphological material, intensive contact can lead to the disruption of the stratal condition, as in the case of the suffix -urun in Töitschu with respect to its cognate -iere in Titsch and in DE. The case of the Titsch and Töitschu action nouns in -età / -utu shows that in the presence of intensive contact the derivational category of action nouns has acquired a new pattern which is very salient in the bilinguals' mind and has been partially elaborated in a creative way, combining morphological substance of a completely different etymological origin. Finally, borrowing more complex design features such as the pattern of phrasal verbs observed in Töitschu has to be related to its general syntactic remodelling compared to Titsch insofar as the former has completely given up the bracket sentence still preserved in the latter in favour of the Romance pattern.

Acknowledgements

Parts of this chapter were presented at the Workshop 'Interaction of Borrowing and Word-formation' held during the 50th International Annual Meeting of the Societas Linguistica Europaea (Zürich, September 2017). We are very grateful to those attending our talk and especially to Guido Seiler and Angela Ralli for their observations, as well as to Pius ten Hacken and Renáta Panocová. Needless to say, we are solely responsible for the views expressed and any remaining mistakes.

The general outline of the chapter, the analysis of the data and the drafting of the introduction and conclusion are due to a joint effort of both authors, however Marco Angster is responsible for sections 2–3 and Livio Gaeta for sections 4–5.

Notes

1. Note that in Figure 11.1 the ancestral GMH stratum also includes borrowings coming from Latin and Romance which are to be considered completely nativised, such as for instance *chaufen* ('to buy') and *schréiben* ('to write') found in Issime, and which are based respectively on Latin *caupō* ('innkeeper, retail dealer') / *caupōnārī* ('to chaffer') and on Latin *scrībere* ('to write'), already attested in the Old High German (GOH) borrowings *koufen* and *scrīban*.
2. Under Gallo-Romance we intend both Gallo-Romance varieties (e.g. Francoprovençal) and Gallo-Italic varieties (e.g. Piedmontese). The choice is made for simplicity's sake, but also because in the geographical area here considered the two dialectal domains border and, to some extent, overlap.
3. The $^+$ indicates a reconstructed form for which there is no evidence in written records.
4. In this chapter, all examples of Walser German or Romance varieties are written using the local writing system or as they are cited in the relevant sources. Note in particular the signs <é> and <ò> found in Gressoney which roughly correspond respectively to [ɪ] and [ʊ]. This implies that words can be written differently even if they sound alike (e.g. Gressoney *karió* and Issime *karju* are both [ˈkarjʊ]).
5. By the end of the thirteenth century, the inflectional class with *-ier* had already merged again with the class ending in *-er* in Old French (cf. Wohlgemuth 2009: 230).
6. The class of *-un* verbs in Issime developed historically from the second class of GOH weak verbs in *-ōn*. While already in the GMH period elsewhere in the German-speaking area this class merged with the GOH *-ēn* class, it is retained in the Swiss dialects of Wallis and in the Walser dialects (cf. Bohnenberger 1913: 15–16; Eufe and Mader 2018 for a recent survey).
7. We will come back to *-etu/-utu* derivatives in section 4.

8. In addition, a couple of deadjectival verbs are also found, e.g. *hialljun* ('to caress') < *hial* ('smooth'), *hielljun* ('to levigate') < *hiel* ('smooth') and *miarun/mierun* ('to increase, to raise') < *mia/mier* ('more').

9. Throughout this and the following sections the exemplification and the figures are based on Titsch data extracted from the ArchiWals corpus, but similar data are also found for Töitschu.

10. Unfortunately, vowel harmony is not consistently reported in the orthography and a certain variation is observed in the texts, as for instance *katzun* ('to kick') > *katzetu / katzutu* ('kicking'), *pannulurun* ('to paint') > *panneleretu* ('brush stroke'), etc. Moreover, it has to be added that vowel harmony also occurs in Titsch, although its effects are far less consistent than in Töitschu (cf. Zürrer 1999: 148ff.). Accordingly, alternative forms in *-òtò* such as *mésschlòtò* ('mixture') and *ofnòtò* ('batch') are found besides *mésschletò* and *ofnetò*.

11. Cf. Henzen (1965: 175–176): 'Auf *-ete* (südalem. noch *-eta*; aus rom. *-ēta* oder *-āta*?) gehen Feminina aus, die das Ergebnis einer Tätigkeit, namentlich aber eine gewisse Menge, die auf einmal erscheint, festhalten: *Kochete, Backete* was auf einmal gekocht, gebacken wird, *Läutete* Geläute, *Lachete* Gelache, *Rechete* das mit dem Rechen Zusammengeraffte, *Gablete* Gabel voll, *Zeilete* Zeile voll, *Rechnete* Abrechnung, Rechnung, *Strickete* Strickzeug, *Scheissete, Kotzete, Schnud(e)rete* Nasenschleim wie ahd. *scīzāta, snuderāta, screiāta*' [Feminine nouns which record the result of an activity, in particular however a certain quantity appearing at once, go back to *-ete* (southern Alemannic still *-eta*; from Romance *-ēta* or *-āta*?): *Kochete, Backete* what is cooked, baked at once, *Läutete* ringing, *Lachete* laughing, *Rechete* what is snatched with the rake, *Gablete* fork full, *Zeilete* row full, *Rechnete* reckoning, account, *Strickete* knitting, *Scheissete, Kotzete, Schnud(e)rete* nasal mucus like GOH *scīzāta, snuderāta, screiāta*].

12. The suffix *-ata* goes back clearly to the generalisation of the original FPP with nominal bases as also witnessed by the occurrence of the intermediate verb resulting from a conversion in older stages of Italian as for instance [+]*gomitare* ('to blow with an elbow') and [+]*occhiare* ('to eye').

13. We thank Michele Musso (Associazione Augusta, Issime) for pointing out to us this example extracted from an interview recorded in August 2018 (cf. Busso 2018).

References

Angster, Marco (2012), 'Isolamento e contatto. Stratigrafia del lessico dei walser meridionali dai dati del *PALWaM*', *Bollettino dell'Atlante Linguistico Italiano*, 36: 155–200.

Angster, Marco (2014), 'Lingue di minoranza e di maggioranza. 200 anni di lingue straniere a Gressoney (AO)', in V. Porcellana and F. Diémoz (eds), *Minoranze in mutamento. Etnicità, lingue e processi demografici nelle valli alpine italiane*, Alessandria: Edizioni dell'Orso, pp. 105–121.

Angster, Marco and S. Dal Negro (2017), 'Linguistische Distanz einschätzen: Der Fall von Walserdeutsch im Licht von lexikalischen Daten und soziolinguistischen

Parametern', in H. Christen, P. Gilles and C. Purschke (eds), *Räume, Grenzen, Übergänge. Akten des 5. Kongresses der Internationalen Gesellschaft für Dialektologie des Deutschen (IGDD)*, Stuttgart: Franz Steiner Verlag, pp. 9–25.

Angster, Marco, M. Bellante, R. Cioffi and L. Gaeta (2017), 'I progetti DiWaC e ArchiWals', in L. Gaeta (ed.), *Le isole linguistiche tedescofone in Italia: situazione attuale e prospettive future* (Workshop 24 February 2017), Special Issue of *Bollettino dell'Atlante Linguistico Italiano*, 41: 83–94.

Antonietti, Federica, M. Valenti and M. Angster (2015), *Piccolo Atlante dei Walser Meridionali*, Aosta: Tipografia Valdostana.

Berruto, Gaetano (2018), '18. The Languages and Dialects of Italy', in W. Ayres-Bennett and J. Carruthers (eds), *Manual of Romance Sociolinguistics*, Berlin and Boston: De Gruyter, pp. 494–525.

Bohnenberger, Karl (1913), *Die Mundart der deutschen Walliser im Heimattal und in den Aussenorten*, Frauenfeld: Huber.

Booij, Geert (2010), *Construction Morphology*, Oxford: Oxford University Press.

Busso, Vittoria (2018), 'Wi hewer mussu weerhun! Quanto lavoravamo!', *Augusta*, 50: 69–71.

Dixon, Robert M. W. (2005), *A Semantic Approach to English Grammar*, Oxford: Oxford University Press, 2nd edn.

Eufe, Rembert and A. Mader (2018), 'Das Walserdeutsche im deutschen und italienischen Sprachgebiet', in N. Eller-Wildfeuer, P. Rössler and A. Wildfeuer (eds), *Alpindeutsch. Einfluss und Verwendung des Deutschen im alpinen Raum*, Regensburg: edition vulpes, pp. 113–139.

Gaeta, Livio (2002), *Quando i verbi compaiono come nomi. Un saggio di Morfologia Naturale*, Milano: Angeli.

Gaeta, Livio (2008), 'Die deutsche Pluralbildung zwischen deskriptiver Angemessenheit und Sprachtheorie', *Zeitschrift für germanistische Linguistik*, 36: 1, 74–108.

Gaeta, Livio (2015), 'Action Nouns in Romance', in P. O. Müller, I. Ohnheiser, S. Olsen and F. Rainer (eds), *Word-Formation. An International Handbook of the Languages of Europe*, Berlin and New York: De Gruyter, vol. 2, pp. 1165–1185.

Gaeta, Livio (2017), 'Nomi deverbali in MIDIA', in P. D'Achille and M. Grossmann (eds), *Per la storia della formazione delle parole in italiano*, Roma: Cesati, pp. 221–241.

Grandi, Nicola (2015), 'Evaluative Morphology and Number/Gender', in N. Grandi and L. Körtvélyessy (eds), *Edinburgh Handbook of Evaluative Morphology*, Edinburgh: Edinburgh University Press, pp. 91–107.

Henzen, Walter (1965), *Deutsche Wortbildung*, Tübingen: Niemeyer, 3rd edn.

Russ, Charles V. J. (1990), 'Swabian. High Alemannic', in C. V. J. Russ (ed.), *The Dialects of Modern German*, London: Routledge, pp. 337–393.

Štekauer, Pavol (2014), 'Derivational Paradigms', in R. Lieber and P. Štekauer (eds), *The Oxford Handbook of Derivational Morphology*, Oxford: Oxford University Press, pp. 354–369.

Storrer, Angelika (2006), 'Zum Status der nominalen Komponenten in Nominalisierungsverbgefügen', in E. Breindl, L. Gunkel and B. Strecker (eds), *Grammatische Untersuchungen. Analysen und Reflexionen. Gisela Zifonun zum 60. Geburtstag*, Tübingen: Narr, pp. 275–295.

Timberlake, Alan (2004), *A Reference Grammar of Russian*, Cambridge: Cambridge University Press.

Vendler, Zeno (1967), *Linguistics in Philosophy*, Ithaca, NY: Cornell University Press.

Wohlgemuth, Jan (2009), *A Typology of Verbal Borrowings*, Berlin and New York: De Gruyter.

Zürrer, Peter (1999), *Sprachinseldialekte. Walserdeutsch im Aosta-Tal (Italien)*, Aarau, Frankfurt am Main and Salzburg: Sauerländer.

Zürrer, Peter (2009), *Sprachkontakt in Walser Dialekten. Gressoney und Issime im Aostatal (Italien)*, Stuttgart: Steiner.

12

Examining the Integration of Borrowed Nouns in Immigrant Speech: The Case of Canadian Greek

Angela Ralli and Vasiliki Makri

In virtually every country in the world linguistic minorities can be found as a result of immigration. In this context, linguistic interaction and contact-induced changes are apparent in the speech of immigrants and borrowing emerges as the outcome of language contact, leading to the transfer of various lexical elements, features and structures (see, among others, Haugen 1950; Poplack 1980; Poplack et al. 1988; Poplack et al. 1990; Sankoff et al. 1990; Myers-Scotton 2002; Clyne 2003).

This chapter is concerned with the speech of first-generation Greek immigrants who arrived in Canada in the period between 1945 and 1975, which has seen the bulk of Greek emigration. It scrutinises how the Greek language has evolved in a language contact situation,[1] where English is the donor and Greek the recipient.[2] In spite of the great interest this contact situation presents, it remains largely unexplored. In fact, this chapter constitutes one of the first attempts to investigate aspects of borrowing in the language of Greek immigrants in Canada and aspires to contribute to the study of immigrant speech in general. It aims to bring into focus the ways in which Greek immigrants resort to lexical transfer by mixing and blending Greek and English. It shows that there is a creative playing with resources spanning these two languages, in a way that underscores the linguistic resourcefulness of the speakers themselves as agents of innovations spread throughout the linguistic community. The end product of contact between Canadian English and Greek shows language-internal constraints of the recipient language that are uninterruptedly at work throughout the process of the integration of borrowed words (see also Hock and Joseph 2009 and Baran 2017 on this matter).

In order to show this, an answer is attempted to a series of general research questions, such as:

- What are the various types of linguistic practices with regard to borrowed words, as they are materialised in the process of their integration in the Canadian Greek transplanted communities?
- Is the typological distance between the analytic English and the fusional Greek an inhibitor in borrowing?

- Could specific types of integration be attributed to specific properties of the languages in contact?

More specifically, the chapter seeks to examine the performance of Canadian Greek speakers through the lens of noun transfer,[3] and explore:

- the concerted effect of linguistic factors, such as phonological, morphological and semantic, which determine the by-product of borrowing and its final formation;
- the principal role of morphological properties of Greek as an inflectionally rich language for the integration of loan nouns (see also Aikhenvald 2000, 2006; Ralli 2012a, 2012b, 2013; Ralli et al. 2015; Makri 2016a, 2016b, 2017 for similar contentions in Greek);
- the mandatory alignment to the fundamental Greek properties of inflection and gender assignment which forces loan nouns to be accommodated in the recipient language as masculine, feminine or neuter;
- an unequivocal preference for particular inflection classes, the most productively used ones, as well as for specific grammatical gender values.

In order to illustrate arguments and proposals, we investigate evidence from Greek spoken in four Canadian provinces, Québec, Ontario, Alberta and British Columbia, where the majority of Greek immigrants reside. The data are drawn from both written (e.g., among others, Maniakas 1991; Aravossitas 2016) and oral sources. As regards the oral sources, recorded interviews have been used for collecting spontaneous spoken Canadian Greek. These interviews are based on a structured questionnaire which was designed especially for the purposes of the research program 'Immigration and Language: Greeks and Greek-Canadians' (2016–2018), funded by the Stavros Niarchos Foundation. The questionnaire touches on three phases: origin/departure, arrival/settlement, and integration of immigrants. Consequently, the informants are invited to recount their personal immigration stories, which is a familiar topic to them.

The chapter is organised as follows: section 1 sketches the socio-historical background of Greek immigration in Canada and defines Canadian Greek as an immigrant language. Section 2 provides an overview of Greek morphology in comparison with English morphology. Previous accounts of noun borrowing in Greek and its dialectal variety are given in section 3, with an emphasis on grammatical gender assignment and inflection-class classification. The basic properties of Canadian Greek nouns and their integration into the native system are the topic of section 4, where the interaction of semantic, phonological and morphological factors ordaining gender and inflection class is examined. The chapter concludes with a review of the main arguments discussed in the article and the relevant bibliography.

1. Greek immigration in Canada and Canadian Greek as immigrant language

Greeks began immigrating to Canada at the end of the nineteenth century, when the contact situation came into being. For instance, in 1900 there were about 300 persons of Greek origin in the province of Québec,[4] in 1981, according to the Census of Canada, the number of Greeks in Québec was 49,420 (Maniakas 1991), while in 1983 there was an estimation of about 250,000 Greeks in the entire country (Constantinides 1983). As expected, these figures deviate from the real number of Greek immigrants in Canada because of illegal residence.

As already stated, our research focuses on Greeks who immigrated to Canada between the years 1945 and 1975. In the decades under examination, Canada welcomed people from various Greek towns and villages, who came in principle permanently, seeking better living conditions and employment. Nowadays, most of these people and their descendants form sizeable linguistic minorities dispersed throughout Canada, but mainly residing in the provinces of Québec, Ontario, British Columbia and Alberta.

Since the beginning, Canadian Greeks have tried to integrate into Canadian society, while preserving their native language and culture. In regions with a Greek population, there are Greek restaurants, shops, associations and schools, and Greek immigrants, at least those of the first generation, maintain communication with each other in their native tongue. Greek is used at home and within the community, with family and friends, as well as on formal occasions and in official institutions of the community (e.g. the Greek Orthodox Church and media). It is also alive in magazines, newspapers, TV and radio programmes, and is often enhanced with some features of local Greek varieties brought from the place of origin (see, for example, Ralli et al. 2018).

Apparently, Greek in Canada is a minority language in the country, with Canadian English, or Canadian French, depending on the province, being the major language in the Canadian community. It can also be defined as an immigrant language, since its speakers were exposed to Canadian English at some point in their adulthood, while many of them are sequential bilinguals, having become bilingual by first learning one language and then another (Myers-Scotton 2006). As is usually accepted, immigrant languages are those spoken by relatively recently arrived populations (as is the case for first-generation Greek immigrants in Canada), who do not have a well-established multi-generational community of language users (Clyne 2003). Several studies have shown that immigrants who come to a country later in their adulthood show little tendency to lose their ability to use their mother tongue and generally keep it as their primary language (Appel and Muysken 1987; Myers-Scotton 2002, 2006; Montrul 2008).

Migration, the movement of people, is equivalent to the movement of languages from their original geographic locations to new locations with new language ecologies. In this context, users of a particular language enter in contact with speakers of another language and are forced to linguistically interact with them, while language changes occurring as a result are studied within the framework of contact linguistics (see Thomason and Kaufman 1988; Thomason 2001; Winford 2003; Hickey 2010, among others). Pondering on the influx of Greek migrants in Canada, one can observe some significant modifications in their language repertoire. With the passing of the years and the improvement of their economic status, Greek speakers had a more active participation in the Canadian lifestyle and daily contact with English, the better knowledge and frequent use of which resulted in an increased level of borrowing. This borrowing is by and large seen at the vocabulary level, lexical transfer being the most frequent type of it, as acknowledged by several researchers (among others, Thomason 2001; Matras 2009). Hereupon, in this chapter, it would be enlightening to probe into the routes of lexical borrowing as manifested in the nominal system of Greek, its inflection and three-valued gender system, especially when the donor language is the poorly inflected and genderless English.

2. Greek and English nominal morphology: an overview

The Greek language is typologically fusional with rich morphology, showing a particularly productive system of compounding, derivation and inflection (Ralli 2005, 2013, 2016a). Nominal and verbal inflection are stem-based, where an inflectional suffix attaches to stems to specify a number of morphosyntactic features. For nouns and adjectives, these features are grammatical gender, case and number, while articles and some pronouns usually alter their forms entirely to encode this information. An illustration of Greek nominal inflection (namely the Standard Modern Greek one) is given in (1), where the forms of the definite article and the modifying adjective vary and morphosyntactically agree with those of the nouns.[5]

(1) a. ο   μεγάλος   δρόμος
         ο   meɣalos   ðromos
         the.MASC.NOM.SG   big.MASC.NOM.SG   road.MASC.NOM.SG
         'the big road'

     b. τη   μεγάλη   λωρίδα
         ti   meɣali   loriða
         the.FEM.ACC.SG   big.FEM.ACC.SG   lane.FEM.ACC.SG
         'the big lane'

     c. των   μεγάλων   βουνών
         ton   meɣalon   vunon
         the.NEU.GEN.PL   big.NEU.GEN.PL   mountain.NEU.GEN.PL
         'of the big mountains'

Nouns are distributed into eight inflectional paradigms, known as inflection classes (hereafter IC), on the basis of two criteria: stem allomorphy and the form of the ending (Ralli 2000, 2005). These classes are summarised in Table 12.1.

As Table 12.1 shows, many Greek nouns display an allomorphic variation (noted with the symbol '~'). This variation is morphological, in that it does not follow from the application of a productively used phonological rule; it originates from the diachronic development of the language. Table 12.2 gives an example of each class.

The four forms for each noun and number in Table 12.2 are the case values, that is, nominative, genitive, accusative and vocative. Assuming Ralli's (2000) division of Greek nouns into eight inflection classes, it is important to note that:

- IC1 nouns are masculine and feminine without stem allomorphy.
- IC2 nouns are masculine with stem allomorphy.

Table 12.1 Examples of stems for each inflection class illustrating the presence or absence of allomorphy (from Ralli 2000)

IC1	κηπ	cip	'garden'
IC2	μαθητη ~ μαθητ	maθiti ~ maθit	'pupil, student'
IC3	χαρα ~ χαρ	xara ~ xar	'joy'
IC4	πολη ~ πολε ~ πολ	poli ~ pole ~ pol	'town'
IC5	βουν	vun	'mountain'
IC6	χαρτι	xarti	'paper'
IC7	νεφ	nef	'smog, cloud'
IC8	χωμα ~ χωματ	xoma ~ xomat	'ground, soil'

Table 12.2 Greek noun inflection classes (from Ralli 2000)

IC1	IC2	IC3	IC4	IC5	IC6	IC7	IC8
				Singular			
κήπ-ος	μαθητή-ς	χαρά-ø	πόλη-ø	βουν-ό	χαρτί-ø	νέφ-ος	χώμα-ø
κήπ-ου	μαθητή-ø	χαρά-ς	πόλη-ς/ε-ως	βουν-ού	χαρτι-ού	νέφ-ους	χώματ-ος
κήπ-ο	μαθητή-ø/v	χαρά-ø	πόλη-ø	βουν-ό	χαρτί-ø	νέφ-ος	χώμα-ø
κήπ-ε	μαθητή-ø	χαρά-ø	πόλη-ø	βουν-ό	χαρτί-ø	νέφ-ος	χώμα-ø
cip-os	maθiti-s	xara-ø	poli-ø	vun-o	xarti-ø	nef-os	xoma-ø
cip-u	maθiti-ø	xara-s	poli-s/e-os	vun-u	xartj-u	nef-us	xomat-os
cip-o	maθiti-ø/n	xara-ø	poli-ø	vun-o	xarti-ø	nef-os	xoma-ø
cip-e	maθiti-ø	xara-ø	poli-ø	vun-o	xarti-ø	nef-os	xoma-ø
				Plural			
κήπ-οι	μαθητ-ές	χαρ-ές	πόλ-εις	βουν-ά	χαρτι-ά	νέφ-η	χώματ-α
κήπ-ων	μαθητ-ών	χαρ-ών	πόλε-ων	βουν-ών	χαρτι-ών	νεφ-ών	χωμάτ-ων
κήπ-ους	μαθητ-ές	χαρ-ές	πόλ-εις	βουν-ά	χαρτι-ά	νέφ-η	χώματ-α
κήπ-οι	μαθητ-ές	χαρ-ές	πόλ-εις	βουν-ά	χαρτι-ά	νέφ-η	χώματ-α
cip-i	maθit-es	xar-es	pol-is	vun-a	xartj-a	nef-i	xomat-a
cip-on	maθit-on	xar-on	pole-on	vun-on	xartj-on	nef-on	xomat-on
cip-us	maθit-es	xar-es	pol-is	vun-a	xartj-a	nef-i	xomat-a
cip-i	maθit-es	xar-es	pol-is	vun-a	xartj-a	nef-i	xomat-a

- IC3 and IC4 contain feminine nouns with stem allomorphy.
- The nouns of the other inflection classes are neuter, with only IC8 nouns having stem allomorphy.

As already mentioned, gender in Greek has a three-value system. According to Corbett (1991) grammatical gender is an inherent property of nouns. More specifically for Greek, Ralli (2002) has proposed that it is a feature of stems and derivational suffixes and that it is not overtly expressed by a specific marker, contrary to case and number which have their own fusional markers, realised as inflectional suffixes. Ralli has further proposed that in [+human] nouns, gender is related to the semantic feature of sex, in that male beings are grammatically masculine and female ones are feminine, while in [–human] nouns, the grammatical gender correlates with the morphological feature of inflection class. Moreover, from the three values, the neuter one is perceived as the unmarked gender option for all [–human] nouns, as suggested by Anastassiadis-Symeonidis (1994), Dressler (1997) and Christofidou (2003).

Compared to Greek, English is a typologically analytic language that conveys morphosyntactic features without usually resorting to overt morphemes. English has lost much of the inflectional morphology inherited from Indo-European over the centuries and has not gained any new inflectional morphemes in the meantime. With respect to its nominal system, Standard English has lost cases (except for the genitive case and the three modified case forms for pronouns) along with grammatical genders and has simplified its inflection. Thus, an important question that needs to be addressed is whether the typological remoteness between the two linguistic systems in contact affects loanword integration from one language to the other, since there is no direct mapping of morphemes from English to Greek.

3. Noun borrowing in Greek

For lexical borrowings, Haugen (1950: 214–215) distinguishes three basic groups on the basis of the notions of *importation* and *substitution*. Importation involves bringing a pattern, item or element into a language, while substitution refers to replacing something from another language with a native pattern, item or element (see also Appel and Muysken 1987: 164–165). For instance, Greek in its long history, has imported many words from Turkish and Italo-Romance and few patterns (Ralli 2016b, 2019). With respect to the latter, the Asia Minor Cappadocian dialect has adopted an agglutination pattern from Turkish nouns, while the material used remains Greek (see Dawkins 1916).

In Haugen's nomenclature, loanwords show morphemic importation without substitution, loanblends exhibit both morphemic substitution and importation, while loanshifts show morphemic substitution without importation. Our analysis makes avail of inflected and fully integrated material on the one hand, as well as non-integrated and thus uninflected material on the other, although sparingly found, which pertain to the category of loanblends and loanwords respectively in terms of Haugen's classification. However, for convenience purposes, we will use the term *loanword* invariably.

As commonly admitted in the relevant literature, lexical borrowings need to be adjusted to the morphological system of the recipient languages (Sankoff 2001; Winford 2003; Wichmann and Wohlgemuth 2008; Wohlgemuth 2009; Ralli 2012a, 2012b, 2016b). Expanding Wohlgemuth's (2009) postulation on loan-verb integration to loan-noun integration, in this chapter we will see that loan nouns can be integrated into Greek either by direct insertion or by indirect insertion. In direct insertion, the loan noun is plugged directly into the grammar of the target language with only the addition of an inflectional ending, since Greek contains compulsory and overtly realised inflection. Conversely, in indirect insertion, an integrating element is required to accommodate loan nouns. As is shown by Ralli (2016b) for the integration of loan verbs, the integrator can be taken from the range of native derivational affixes.[6]

One of the morphosyntactic features that plays an active role in borrowing in Greek is grammatical gender, and as pointed out by Anastassiadis-Symeonidis and Chila-Markopoulou (2003) it is compulsory for loan nouns to come to certain rearrangements in order to fit this category. Besides gender, nouns also need a native inflectional suffix denoting the features of case and number, in accordance with the Greek pattern of nominal inflection. Indicative examples of accommodated loan nouns in Standard Modern Greek are given in (2), where the original items are re-analysed as stems (2b is slightly modified), being supplied a gender value, while further combined with inflection denoting the features of case and number.[7]

(2) a. γιάπη-ς   EN   yuppy
         japi.MASC-s.NOM.SG

      b. κομπίνα   FR   combine
         kobina.FEM-ø.NOM.SG 'fraud'

      c. λεκέ-ς   TR   leke
         lece.MASC-s.NOM.SG 'stain'

      d. μόλο-ς   IT   molo.MASC
         molo.MASC-s.NOM.SG 'dock'

Loan nouns are, thus, transferred into Greek following a very predetermined pathway. However, a number of borrowed nouns in Standard Modern Greek remain uninflected and their phonological form is almost unaltered. In the absence of any overt inflectional marker, information about gender, case and number is only shown by the preceding article in (3a, c) or by another agreeing element, as for instance an adjective in (3b and 3d).

(3) a. το ασανσέρ   FR   ascenceur.MASC
         to.NEU.NOM.SG asanser
         'the elevator'

      b. νέο μακιγιάζ   FR   maquillage.MASC
         neo.NEU.NOM.SG macijaz
         'new make-up'

      c. το κέικ   EN   cake
         to.NEU.NOM.SG ceik
         'the cake'

      d. μεγάλο πάρτι   EN   party
         meγalo.NEU.NOM.SG parti
         'big party'

According to Aronoff (1994: 126), 'borrowings that do not fit the phonological pattern of any noun class are likely to be indeclinable' (see also Corbett 1991: 40–41 on this matter). Considering that in Standard Modern Greek consonants are not usually tolerated as noun-final ones (with the exception of [s] and [n] in certain slots of the inflectional paradigms, as shown in Table 12.2), one could suppose that loans ending in consonants are assigned the inflectional features with the mediator of another element, as in (3). However, this hypothesis does not apply to the English word *party*, which remains uninflected, in spite of the fact that its ending *-i* matches the endings of the most productive class of neuter nouns in Greek, that of IC6 (see the IC6 noun *χαρτί* 'paper').

In the existing literature (Ibrahim 1973; Poplack et al. 1982; Corbett 1991; Thornton 2001; Clyne 2003; Winford 2010), the chief factors influencing loanword integration are the following:

- The natural biological sex of the referent.
- The formal shape of the word in the donor language.
- Phonological analogy to the ending suffix of the recipient language.
- Semantic analogy to the semantically equivalent item of the recipient language.
- The gender of a homophonous noun with a different meaning in the recipient language.
- The default gender of the recipient language.
- A suffix being attached as an integrator.

Interestingly, these factors have already been observed in the borrowing of loan nouns in the Greek dialectal varieties, as shown in Melissaropoulou (2013, 2016), Ralli et al. (2015), Makri (2016a, 2016b, 2017), among others, where they are grouped into three general categories depending on their type and reference to the linguistic domain they belong to, namely semantic, phonological and morphological.

As Ralli (2002) proposed, in Greek, the semantic feature [+human] is the highest-ranked factor for the determination of gender in human nouns. This also applies to human nouns borrowed in Modern Greek dialects, as shown by the examples in Table 12.3, drawn from the dialects Pontic, Aivaliot, Heptanesian and Griko, the first two being affected by Turkish, while Heptanesian and Griko have been influenced by Italo-Romance.

Contrary to [+human] nouns, all the available gender values are attested in [−human] nouns, but the neuter noun, being a kind of default gender value, is assigned

Table 12.3 [+human] dialectal loanwords and their Turkish and Italian models

Greek dialect	Form	Transcription	Gloss	Model	Donor language
Pontic	τσοπάνος	tsopanos.MASC	'shepherd'	çoban	Turkish
Aivaliot	κιαγιάς	cajas.MASC	'caretaker'	kâhya	Turkish
Heptanesian	τζενεράλης	tzeneralis.MASC	'general'	generale.MASC	Italian
Griko		panefakulo(s).MASC	'baker'	panifaculo.MASC	Salentino
Pontic	ορόσπη	orospi.FEM	'prostitute'	orospu	Turkish
Aivaliot	καχπέ	kaxpe.FEM	'prostitute'	kahpe	Turkish
Heptanesian	ινφερμιέρα	infermjera.FEM	'nurse.woman'	infermiera.FEM	Italian
Griko		nina.FEM	'girl'	ninna.FEM	Salentino

Table 12.4 [–human] dialectal loanwords and their Turkish and Italian models

Greek dialect	Form	Transcription	Gloss	Model	Donor language
Pontic	καρταλίν	kartalin.NEU	'hawk'	kartal	Turkish
Aivaliot	ιλίκ(ι)	ilic(i).NEU	'marrow'	ilik	Turkish
Heptanesian	σοδισφάτσιο	soðisfatsio.NEU	'satisfaction'	sodisfazion.FEM	Venetian
Griko		fjoro.NEU	'flower'	fiore.MASC	Italian

Table 12.5 Heptanesian loanwords with their Italian models and the corresponding Standard Modern Greek words

Greek dialect	Form/Transcription/Gloss	Model: Italian/Venetian	Standard Modern Greek
Heptanesian	κάμπια kambia.FEM 'change'	cambio.MASC	αλλαγή alaji.FEM
Heptanesian	αγιούντα ajunta.FEM 'addition'	aggiunto.MASC	προσθήκη prosθici.FEM
Heptanesian	πιτόκα pitoka.FEM 'louse'	pidocchio.MASC	ψείρα psira.FEM

to loans, in case no other apparent tendency is present or predominant, as claimed by Dressler (1997), Anastassiadis-Symeonidis (1994), Anastassiadis-Symeonidis and Chila-Markopoulou (2003) and Ralli et al. (2015). For an illustration, see the examples in Table 12.4, from Ralli et al. (2015).

Concept association (Corbett 1991: 71; Clyne 2003: 147) may be a supplementary semantic criterion for gender assignment to [–human] loan nouns, according to which an existing synonymous noun in the recipient language may determine the gender value of a loan. Consider the words from Heptanesian in Table 12.5, where the gender of loans is regulated by that of native synonymous nouns.

Phonology has also proven to play a key role for the integration of [–human] loan nouns and their gender assignment. It refers to a certain matching of the final segments between the source nouns and those of the recipient language, which activates the form of inflection and gender of loans. In Table 12.6, the Italo-Romance endings -o and -a coincide with the typical endings of Greek native feminine and neuter nouns, respectively. Thus, the Italo-Romance *alegria* remains feminine in Greek, but the masculine noun *inverno* assumes the neuter value (see Ralli et al. 2015 and Makri 2016b for more examples).

Furthermore, the presence of a homophonous noun, but with a different meaning in Greek, may also determine the gender value allotted to a loanword, as illustrated in Table 12.7 with data from Heptanesian and Cretan.

Table 12.6 Loanwords with their Italian model and corresponding native nouns

Greek variant	Form/Transcription/Gloss	Model: Italian	Greek native noun
Standard	αλεγρία	alegria.FEM	χαρά
Modern	aleγria.FEM		xara.FEM
Greek (EL)	'glee, cheerfulness'		'joy'
Heptanesian	βέρνο	inverno.MASC	βουνό
	verno.NEU		vuno.NEU
	'winter'		'mountain'

Table 12.7 Dialectal loanwords with their Italian models and Standard Modern Greek equivalents

Greek dialect	Form/Transcription/Gloss	Model	EL
Heptanesian	φούντωμα	fondo.MASC	φούντωμα
	fudoma.NEU	'bottom' (Italian)	fudoma.NEU
	'roof bedrock'		'flare-up'
Cretan	φόρα	fora.FEM	φόρα
	fora.FEM	(Venetian)	fora.FEM
	'exterior'		'impetus'

Table 12.8 Integrators as used in some dialectal loanwords

Greek dialect	Form/Transcription/Gloss	Model	Integrator
Heptanesian	γάλικο	galo.MASC	-ικ(ο) ik(o).NEU
	γaliko.NEU	(Venetian)	
	'turkey'		
Griko	vardedd^{h}i.NEU	varda.FEM	-edd^{h}i.NEU
	'pack-saddle'	(Salentino)	
Aivaliot	παρτσάδ(ι)	parça	-αδι -aδi.NEU
	partsaδ(i).NEU	(Turkish)	
	'piece'		

Crucially, in the absence of any semantic or phonological motivation, morphology assumes the role for providing the means for the accommodation of loan nouns, in that sometimes the addition of an integrating element, that is, a derivational suffix, can facilitate the integration process and assign a gender value (Melissaropoulou 2013, 2016; Makri et al. 2013), as illustrated Table 12.8.

In the following section, the hypothesis that the same factors of semantics, phonology and morphology determine gender assignment is tested for Canadian Greek. Our claim is that if there is any comparable accommodation of loan nouns for this system as well, then it is confirmed that all Greek varieties follow the same path for integrating their loan nouns, irrespective of the donor language.

4. Canadian Greek

As is the case for other Greek varieties, and in accordance with the native morphological structures of nouns consisting of stems and inflectional suffixes (Ralli 2005, 2013, 2016a), an adopted English noun in Canadian Greek undergoes grammatical gender assignment, addition of an inflectional marker and classification to a specific inflection class, while for pronunciation purposes, a slight phonological modification may also occur. Consider the examples in (4–8), where loan nouns are classified into three categories according to their gender value and the [±human] feature. In these examples, the Canadian Greek form and its transcription are followed by the English source. If the Canadian Greek meaning is not the same as that of the English source, a gloss is given.

(4) a. μπόσης   bosis   boss
     b. σέφης   sefis   chef
     c. μπασέρης   baseris   bus driver
     d. πολισμάνος   polizmanos   policeman
     e. λοντράς   londras   laundryman
     f. λοντζάς   lontzas   lunch-room owner

(5) a. μπλόκος   blokos 'square'   block
     b. ρολός   rolos 'bun'   roll

(6) a. οπερέτα   opereta   woman operator
     b. μποσίνα   bosina   female boss

(7) a. μπάρα   bara   bar
     b. τζάρα   dzara   jar
     c. μαρκέτα   marceta   market
     d. μάπα   mapa   mop
     e. φρίτζα   fritza   fridge

(8) a. κάρο   karo   car
     b. μπόξι   boksi   box
     c. μπάσι   basi   bus
     d. μπίλι   bili   bill
     e. φλόρι   flori   floor
     f. στέσιο   stesio   station
     g. βακέσιο   vacesio   vacation
     h. τελεβίζιο   televizio   television

The examples in (4) and (6) are [+human], masculine and feminine respectively. The examples in (5) are [–human] and masculine, those in (7) [–human] and feminine, while (8) displays [–human] and neuter nouns.

The procedure to license the accommodation of English nouns by assigning gender, an inflectional marker and an inflection class corroborates the claim put forward by

Thomason and Kaufman (1988) and Repetti (2003, 2006) related to the manifest need for a morphological treatment of loanwords in languages with rich morphology, and extends properly to the morphologically abundant and stem-based Greek varieties, among which, Canadian Greek. That the native morphological properties prove to be particularly important in the integration of nouns is shown, among other things, by the fact that the speakers resort to the transfer of entire word forms but treat them as stems that necessitate gender assignment and the presence of an inflectional marker. When the original word ends in a consonant, a vowel is added to it, before the attachment of an inflectional marker. The quality of the vowel depends on two things: the grammatical gender and the inflection class assigned to the loan. If the word is assigned neuter gender, the vowel can be either [o] (IC5) or [i] (IC6). For instance, in (8), *car* assumes the [o], while *box*, *bus*, *bill* and *floor* take the [i]. Accordingly, [a] is the vowel added to feminine nouns (IC3) and [o] (IC1) or [i] (IC2) to masculine ones. Thus, in (7), *bar*, *jar*, *market*, *mop* and *fridge* take an [a], *block* and roll in (5a–b) are assigned an [o], while *boss* and *chef* in (4a–b) become μπόση,[8] and σέφη, respectively (-ς being the inflectional marker). Note that in Greek, the last position of nouns is morphologically salient, in that it flags membership to an inflection class. The most productive inflection classes of native Greek nouns are IC1, 2, 3, 5 and 6, cf. Table 12.2, and in fact these are also the inflection classes to which integrated loan nouns are assigned in Canadian Greek.

Interestingly, a Greek native derivational ending is sometimes added to the entire loan to add gender and a specific semantic value. For instance, the -ερη- [-eri] added to *bus* (μπασέρης [baseris] (4c)) yields the meaning of 'bus driver'.

More analytically, with respect to grammatical gender assignment, our data confirm the fact that semantics is the triggering factor, with the [± human] feature regulating a specific gender value in loans. As is the general rule in Greek (Ralli 2002, 2003), and already stated in section 3, [+human] nouns receive this value in alignment with biological sex.[9] This is illustrated in (9).

(9) a. πολισμάνος   polizmanos.MASC   policeman
     b. σέφης   sefis.MASC   chef
     c. μπόσης   bosis.MASC   boss
     d. οπερέτα   opereta.FEM   woman operator

In (9), [+human] masculine nouns are assigned to two different inflection classes, IC1 (9a) and IC2 (9b–c). As for feminine nouns receiving an -*a*, (9d), this preference can be ascribed to the very productive -*a* feminine nouns of IC3, as noted by Christofidou (2003: 105).[10]

It is worth noting that most Canadian Greek masculine nouns show a preference for inflecting according to IC2, which, in Greek, contains nouns ending in -*is* and -*as*.[11] Interestingly, the same tendency is also observed in Greek dialectal masculine loans (Makri 2016b), as in Table 12.9.

With respect to [+human] nouns denoting a profession, the application of an indirect integration strategy is often observed with the help of a native derivational suffix. This suffix is also responsible for providing the gender value to the noun, as illustrated in Table 12.10.

Table 12.9 Masculine loan nouns in some Greek dialects with their models

Greek dialect	Form/Transcription/Gloss	Model
Pontic	κολαγούζης kolaɣuzis.MASC 'driver'	kılavuz (Turkish)
Heptanesian	ινφερμιέρης infermjeris.MASC 'nurse.man'	infermiere.MASC (Italian)
Cretan	δατσέρης ðatseris.MASC 'customs officer'	dazièr.MASC (Venetian)

Table 12.10 Canadian Greek [+human] loan nouns and their integrators

Canadian Greek	Transcription	English	Integrator
μπαγκ-αδόρ-ος	bang-aðor-os *	banker	-αδορ -aðor.MASC
μπασ-έρη-ς	bas-eri-s	bus driver	-ερη -eri.MASC
λοντζ-ά-ς	lontz-a-s	lunch room owner	-α -a.MASC
λοντρ-ά-ς	londr-a-s	laundryman	-α -a.MASC
μποσ-ίνα-ø	bos-ina- ø	woman boss	-ινα -ina.FEM

Note: * -os, -s and -ø are the inflectional markers. See also Table 12.2.

For male humans, we assume that Canadian Greek speakers replace the English morphemes expressing the agent who performs the action (e.g. the words *man, owner* or the derivational suffix *-er*) by the common Greek derivational suffixes *-aðor-, -eri-* and *-a-* in Table 12.10, which are used for forming native professional nouns of masculine gender, as in (10).

(10) a. τραπεζι-έρη-ς trapezj-eri-s 'waiter' < τραπέζι trapezi.NEU 'table'

  b. γυψ-αδόρ-ος jips-aðor-os 'plasterboard technician' < γύψος jipsos.MASC 'plaster'

  c. λεφτ-ά-ς left-a-s 'rich man, filthy rich' < λεφτά lefta.NEU 'money'

As regards nouns denoting female humans, they opt for the derivational suffix *-ina* in the last line of Table 12.10, which productively produces feminine nouns in Greek out of masculine ones (Ralli 2005; Koutsoukos and Pavlakou 2009), as illustrated in (11).

(11) a. δικαστ-ίνα-ø ðikast-ina-ø 'woman judge' < δικαστή-ς ðikasti-s 'judge'
  b. γιατρ-ίνα-ø jatr-ina-ø 'woman doctor' < γιατρ-ός jatr-os 'doctor'

However, the presence of a derivational suffix is not compulsory, since there are also professional nouns that are accommodated with solely the addition of a simple ending, such as those in (9a) and (9d), repeated in (12).

(12) a. πολισμάνος polizmanos policeman
     b. οπερέτα   opereta   woman operator

Turning now to [–human] nouns, we observe a general distribution of loanwords to all three gender values, as is the case of native Greek [–human] nouns (Ralli 2002, 2003), with a slight preference to the neuter one, neuter being the unmarked gender value for [–human] entities, as already stated in section 2. For reasons of clarity, (13) repeats some examples from (5), (7) and (8).

(13) a. μπλόκος   blokos.MASC   block
     b. ρολός   rolos.MASC 'bun'   roll
     c. μάπα   mapa.FEM   mop
     d. μαρκέτα   marceta.FEM   market
     e. φρίτζα   fritza.FEM   fridge
     f. κάρο   karo.NEU   car
     g. φλόρι   flori.NEU   floor
     h. ρούμι   rumi.NEU   room

Contrary to [+human] masculine nouns, the selection of grammatical gender for the [–human] nouns seems to be *ad hoc*; moreover, their inflectional paradigm is predominantly that of the IC1, ending in *-os* in the citation form, contrary to that of [+human] masculine nouns which show a preference for the paradigm of IC2. The same strategy is also attested in the case of loans of some dialects, as demonstrated by Melissaropoulou (2013) and Makri (2016b), and as illustrated in Table 12.11.[12]

Masculine nouns among the [–human] loans are few though. The vast majority of them are assigned neuter gender, the default gender value, where no other clear motivation exists or prevails (Corbett 1991; Clyne 2003; Ralli et al. 2015), as in (14).

Table 12.11 Dialectal loanwords assigned to IC1 with their model

Greek dialect	Form/Transcription/Gloss	Model
Cretan	μπίκος bikos.MASC 'mining tool'	picca.FEM 'pole' (Venetian)
Heptanesian	σαγιαδόρος sajaðoros.MASC 'door bolt'	sagiador.MASC (Venetian)
Cappadocian	ασλάνος aslanos.MASC 'lion'	arslan (Turkish)

(14) a. κρέντιτο   kredito.NEU   credit
     b. μπίλι   bili.NEU   bill
     c. κοκονότσι   kokonotsi.NEU   coconut
     d. μεσίνι   mesini.NEU   machine

Like masculine nouns, neuter loan nouns belong to two different inflection classes; as already stated, they are attached a final -*o* and are assigned to IC5, but most of them receive a final -*i* and are assigned to IC6. Thus, Canadian Greek data corroborate Christofidou's (2003: 105) claim that consonant-ending inanimate loanwords are generally turned into neuter nouns in Greek with the addition of an [i] vowel.

As shown in (13c–e), a number of [–human] nouns can also be feminine. In contrast with the masculine ones, where there is no particular reason for the determination of the gender value, the feminine gender seems to be due to a semantic criterion which appeals to the existence of a synonymous feminine noun. For an illustration consider the examples in (15), where synonymous nouns in Standard Modern Greek influence the form and gender of English loans.

(15) a. μπάνκα   banka.FEM   EN bank   EL τράπεζα   trapeza.FEM
     b. μάπα   mapa.FEM   EN mop   EL σφουγγαρίστρα sfugaristra.FEM
     c. μαρκέτα   marceta.FEM   EN market EL αγορά   aγora.FEM
     d. σάινα   saina.FEM   EN sign   EL πινακίδα   pinaciδa.FEM

It is important to note that the same criterion is also at play in Australian Greek, as pointed out by Alvanoudi (2017: 8–10) who has identified some loanwords being assigned the same gender as the equivalent words in Standard Modern Greek, as illustrated in (16).

(16) a. φλάτι   flati.NEU   EN flat   EL διαμέρισμα   δiamerisma.NEU
     b. γρίλα   γrila.FEM   EN grill EL ψησταριά/σχάρα   psistarja/sxara.FEM

For the integration of [–human] feminine and neuter nouns, the role of phonology is also quite intriguing, since gender and inflection-class assignment can sometimes be motivated by the existence of a homophonous noun in the target language, most of the times with a different meaning, as in (17).[13]

(17) a. φρίτζα   fritza.FEM   EN fridge   EL φρίτζα   fritza.FEM 'banquette'
     b. μπάρα   bara.FEM   EN bar   EL μπάρα   bara.FEM 'barrier'
     c. οπερέτα   opereta.FEM   EN woman operator   EL οπερέτα   opereta.FEM
                                                                    'light opera'
     d. κάρο   karo.NEU   EN car   EL κάρο   karo.NEU 'carriage'
     e. στέκι   steci.NEU   EN steak   EL στέκι   steci.NEU 'hotspot,
                                                                    haunt'

It is worth pointing out the application of the phonological factor in the form of English loans in -*ion* as IC5 neuter nouns in -*o*, that is, as nouns which have undergone final -*n* deletion. This is illustrated in (18).

(18) a. βακέσιο   vacesio.NEU.IC5   vacation
     b. τελεβίζιο   televizio.NEU.IC5   television
     c. πολιστέσιο   polistesio.NEU.IC5   police station

A word-final -*n* deletion is not unknown in the history of Greek. It has occurred during the late medieval period (Browning 1969), while a trace of it exists in a very formal style of language, mainly in the accusative case (see Table 12.2). Therefore, we are tempted to assume that Canadian Greek speakers subconsciously match English [–human] nouns in -*ion* with native neuter nouns in -*o(n)*, before resorting to -*n* deletion and assigning them membership to IC5.

Finally, as mentioned in section 2, a number of loans in Standard Modern Greek remain uninflected and have entered the language as such. Crucially, most of them appear with the same unaltered form in Canadian Greek as well, as the examples in (19) show.

(19) a. κέτσοπ   cetsop   ketchup
     b. φούτμπολ   futbol   football
     c. πάρτι   parti   party

A possible explanation for the existence of these uninflected nouns could be the fact that they had already been inserted in Greek as such, that is, as types of international terms, prior to the speakers' immigration to Canada. It should be stressed though that, contrary to speakers in Greece, where other international items remain uninflected, there is a tendency among immigrants to assign them a neuter gender (as argued above [–human] nouns are predominantly neuter, unless other factors intervene) as well as inflection according to the most productively used IC6 paradigm. This is illustrated in (20).

(20) a. κέκι   ceci.NEU.IC6   EL κέικ ceik   EN cake
     b. γκαράζι   garazi.NEU.IC6   EL γκαράζ garaz EN garage

Therefore, Canadian Greeks may also diverge from speakers in Greece, sometimes showing a greater consistency to Greek morphological rules.

5. Conclusions

In this chapter we investigated noun borrowing in a language contact situation involving Greek as recipient and English as donor language in Canada. First, we have demonstrated that it is possible for the lexicon of a language (in this case, the fusional Greek) to be enriched by a linguistic system of distinct type (here the analytical English), provided that certain conditions are met. More specifically, the English noun loans are subject to complete integration into the Greek nominal system if they are re-analysed as stems, are assigned grammatical gender, and receive inflection according to the native inflection rules. Their adjustment brings to the forefront an unequivocal preference for the most productively used inflection classes in Greek, jointly with the choice of specific values of grammatical gender.

Second, we have shown that the Canadian Greek data confirm that there is a comparable accommodation of loan nouns for all Greek varieties, since they all follow the same paths for integrating their loan nouns, irrespective of the donor language. In accordance with previous work on loan integration in Modern Greek dialectal varieties, the principal grammatical factors dictating loan-noun integration are of semantic, phonological and morphological nature. Concerning the semantic factors at play, the [+human] feature is the key factor, with the obligatory alignment of masculine gender with nouns denoting male entities and feminine gender with nouns denoting female ones. Concept association may be a criterion for semantically-based gender assignment to [−human] nouns, while default neuter gender is attested when no other factors operate. Phonology operates in cases of homophonous words on the one hand, and of analogy to the recipient language ending segment on the other. More importantly, the morphology factor is in effect, since loanwords need an adjustment of their form, most often with the addition of a vowel in order to become a stem and be assigned a gender and inflection class.

Third, indirect insertion is also employed for loan accommodation in case that some loan nouns require an integrator, drawn from the range of Greek derivational suffixes, which is responsible for their gender and basic meaning.

In spite of contact with the analytic, thus morphologically simpler, English the data prove that Canadian Greek does not undergo a gender-value shrinkage or an inflectional simplification. In other words, the aspects of inflection and gender of Greek do not seem to become subject to English influence nor deteriorate in spite of the First Language Attrition phenomenon, which is the gradual decline in native language proficiency among migrants (Köpke and Schmid 2004), at least as far as first-generation Greek immigrants are concerned.

It is important to stress that the nominal system of Canadian Greek bears corroborating evidence to Ralli's (2012a, 2012b, 2016b) hypothesis that the accommodation of loan nouns in a language is not only the product of extra-linguistic factors (e.g. degree of bilingualism and/or heavy contact) but follows specific language-internal morphological, semantic and phonological constraints of Greek, which are at work throughout the process. However, investigation of second-generation immigrants may alter the picture.

Acknowledgements

This chapter is the product of a research conducted within the project 'ImmiGrec: Immigration and Language in Canada: Greeks and Greek-Canadians' (2016–2018). The authors would like to acknowledge the substantial financial contribution of the Stavros Niarchos Foundation, sponsor of the project, as well as the contribution of the three Canadian teams that have conducted the collection of oral material, led by Tassos Anastassiadis (McGill University), Sakis Gekas (York University) and Panayiotis Pappas (Simon Fraser University). A preliminary version of the article has been presented at the workshop 'The Interaction between Borrowing and Word Formation' (convenors: Pius ten Hacken and Renáta Panocová) of the 50th International Conference of Societas Linguistica Europaea, held in Zurich in September 2017. We wish to thank the organisers and the participants of the workshop for their most constructive comments.

Notes

1. In this article, *Greek* will be employed as a general term for all forms and historical stages of the language. *Modern Greek* is used for the language from the fifteenth century and *Standard Modern Greek* (EL) for the official language today (cf. Ralli 2013 for more details).
2. Until 1976, when French Québecois was established as the official language in Québec and one of the two official languages in Canada, the majority of Greek immigrants in Québec did not speak French and learned only English. As a result, the influence of French Québecois on the speech of first-generation Greek immigrants is very weak.
3. We examine solely loan nouns because of the scarce data of loan adjectives attested in both written sources and our corpus. We plan to investigate adjectives in future research.
4. In 1910 in Montreal, the first Greek Orthodox Church was built, and the first Greek language school was established (Maniakas 1983).
5. On first occurrence, Greek data will be given with a phonological transcription using characters of the International Phonetic Alphabet. Stress will not be noted on the transcribed data when it is irrelevant to the argumentation.
6. See Ralli (2016b) for the selection of derivational suffixes as possible integrators for verbal loans of Turkish and Romance origin.
7. When relevant to the argumentation, inflectional endings will be given separated from stems.
8. Although the English word *boss* ends in *-os*, like the native nouns of IC1, it is transformed into μπόσης [bosis] because, were the *-os* to be identified as the inflectional ending of IC1, only the consonant *b-* would have been left as the stem, something which contrasts with Greek stem patterns containing at least one syllable.
9. Alvanoudi (2017: 14) applies the same distinction in Australian Greek.
10. In Greek, there are also feminine nouns ending in *-i* (e.g. αυλή *avli* 'yard'), but the majority of feminine nouns of IC3 end in *-a*.
11. IC2 masculine nouns ending in *-as* (e.g. ταμίας *tamias* 'cashier') are fewer than those in *-is*. They are mainly used for masculine professional nouns, where *-a(s)* is a derivational suffix denoting profession (e.g. σκεπάς *scepas* 'roof man' < σκεπ(ή) *scep(i)* 'roof' + *as*).
12. Note, however, that the Modern Greek dialects do not behave the same as far as their inflection is concerned. For instance, while ασλάνος *aslanos* belongs to IC1 in Cappadocian, it is inflected according to IC2 (ασλάνης *aslanis*) in Aivaliot and Pontic.
13. See also Clyne (2003: 147) on the role of phonology.

References

Aikhenvald, Alexandra (2000), *Classifiers: A Typology of Noun Categorization Devices*, Oxford: Oxford University Press.

Aikhenvald, Alexandra (2006), 'Grammars in Contact: A Cross-linguistic Perspective', in A. Aikhenvald, and R. M. W. Dixon (eds), *Grammars in Contact: A Cross-linguistic Typology*, Oxford: Oxford University Press, pp. 1–66.

Alvanoudi, Angeliki (2017), 'Language Contact, Borrowing and Code Switching: A Case Study of Australian Greek', *Journal of Greek Linguistics*, 18 (1): 1–42.

Anastassiadis-Symeonidis, Anna (1994), Νεολογικός δανεισμός της Νεοελληνικής [Neological Borrowing in Modern Greek], Thessaloniki: Estia.

Anastassiadis-Symeonidis, Anna and D. Chila-Markopoulou (2003), 'Συγχρονικές και διαχρονικές τάσεις στο γένος της ελληνικής: μια θεωρητική πρόταση' [Synchronic and Diachronic Tendencies in Gender of Greek: A Theoretical Proposal], in A. Anastassiadis-Symeonidis, A. Ralli and D. Chila-Markopoulou (eds), Θέματα Νεοελληνικής Γραμματικής: Το Γένος [Modern Greek Grammar Issues: Gender], Athens: Patakis, pp. 13–56.

Appel, René and P. Muysken (1987), *Language Contact and Bilingualism*, London: Edward Arnold.

Aravossitas, Themis (2016), *The Hidden Schools: Mapping Greek Heritage Language Education in Canada*, PhD dissertation, University of Toronto.

Aronoff, Mark (1994), *Morphology by Itself*, Cambridge, MA: MIT Press.

Baran, Dominika (2017), *Language in Immigrant America*, Cambridge: Cambridge University Press.

Browning, Robert (1969), *Medieval and Modern Greek*, London: Hutchinson and Co. Ltd.

Christophidou, Anastasia (2003), 'Γένος και Κλίση στην Ελληνική. Μια Φυσική Προσέγγιση' [Gender and Inflection in Greek. A Natural Approach], in A. Anastassiadis-Symeonidis, A. Ralli and D. Chila-Markopoulou (eds), Θέματα Νεοελληνικής Γραμματικής: Το Γένος [Modern Greek Grammar Issues: Gender], Athens: Patakis, pp. 100–131.

Clyne, Michael (2003), *Dynamics of Language Contact*, Cambridge: Cambridge University Press.

Constantinides, Stephanos (1983), *Les Grecs du Québec*, Montréal: O Metoikos-Le Métèque.

Corbett, Greville (1991), *Gender*, Cambridge: Cambridge University Press.

Dawkins, Richard McGillivray (1916), *Modern Greek in Asia Minor. A Study of the Dialects of Sílli, Cappadocia and Phárasa with Grammar, Texts, Translations and Glossary*, Cambridge: Cambridge University Press.

Dressler, Wolfgang U. (1997), 'On Productivity and Potentiality in Inflectional Morphology', *Classnet Working Papers*, 7: 3–22.

Haugen, Einar (1950), 'The Analysis of Linguistic Borrowing', *Language*, 26: 210–331.

Hickey, Raymond (2010), *The Handbook of Language Contact*, Malden, Oxford and Chichester: Wiley-Blackwell.

Hock, Hans Henrich and B. D. Joseph (2009), 'Lexical Borrowing', in H. H. Hock and B. D. Joseph (eds), *Language History, Language Change, and Language Relationship: An Introduction to Historical and Comparative Linguistics*, Berlin: De Gruyter, 2nd edn, pp. 241–278.

Ibrahim, Muḥammad Ḥ. (1973), *Grammatical Gender: Its Origin and Development*, The Hague: De Gruyter.

Köpke, Barbara and M. S. Schmid (2004), 'First Language Attrition: The Next Phase', in M. S. Schmid, B. Köpke, M. Keijzer and L. Weilemar (eds), *First Language Attrition: Interdisciplinary Perspectives on Methodological Issues*, Amsterdam: John Benjamins, pp. 1–43.

Koutsoukos, Nikos and M. Pavlakou (2009), 'A Construction Morphology Account of Agent Nouns in Modern Greek', *Patras Working Papers in Linguistics*, 1: 106–126.

Makri, Vasiliki (2016a), 'Language Contact at the Service of Endogenous Forces: A Case Study of Neuterisation in Heptanesian', in A. Ralli (ed.), *Contact Morphology in Modern Greek Dialects*, Newcastle upon Tyne: Cambridge Scholars Publishing, pp. 109–144.

Makri, Vasiliki (2016b), 'Language Contact Substantiating the Realization of Gender in Heptanesian, Grecanico and Cretan', in A. Ralli, N. Koutsoukos and S. Bompolas (eds), *Proceedings of Modern Greek Dialects and Linguistic Theory 6*, Patras: University of Patras, pp. 113–124.

Makri, Vasiliki (2017), 'Gender Assignment to Romance Loans in Katoitaliótika: A Case Study of Contact Morphology', in *Proceedings of ICGL12, the 12th International Conference on Greek Linguistics*, Berlin: CEMOG, Freie Universität Berlin, vol. 2, pp. 659–674.

Makri, Vasiliki, N. Koutsoukos and M. Andreou (2013), 'Δανεισμός ονομάτων και απόδοση γένους στις Επτανησιακές Διαλέκτους' [Borrowing of Nouns and Gender Assignment in Heptanesian Varieties.], in A. Ralli (ed.), *Patras Working Papers in Linguistics: Morphology and Language Contact*, Patras: Laboratory of Modern Greek Dialects, vol. 3, pp. 58–72.

Maniakas, Theodoros (1983), *Sociolinguistic Features of Modern Greek Spoken in Montreal*, Master's thesis, McGill University.

Maniakas, Theodoros (1991), *The Ethnolinguistic Reality of Montreal Greeks*, PhD dissertation, University of Montreal.

Matras, Yaron (2009), *Language Contact: Cambridge Textbooks in Linguistics*, Cambridge: Cambridge University Press.

Melissaropoulou, Dimitra (2013), 'Lexical Borrowing Bearing Witness to the Notions of Gender and Inflection Class: A Case Study on Two Contact Induced Systems of Greek', *Open Journal of Modern Linguistics*, 3: 4, 367–377.

Melissaropoulou, Dimitra (2016), 'Loanwords Integration as Evidence for the Realization of Gender and Inflection Class: Greek in Asia Minor', in A. Ralli (ed.), *Contact Morphology in Modern Greek Dialects*, Newcastle upon Tyne: Cambridge Scholars Publishing, pp. 145–178.

Montrul, Silvina (2008), *Incomplete Acquisition in Bilingualism: Re-examining the Age Factor*, Amsterdam and Philadelphia: John Benjamins.

Myers-Scotton, Carol (2002), *Contact Linguistics: Bilingual Encounters and Grammatical Outcomes*, Oxford: Oxford University Press.

Myers-Scotton, Carol (2006), *Multiple Voices: An Introduction to Bilingualism*, Malden MA, Oxford and Victoria: Blackwell Publishing.

Poplack, Shana (1980), 'Sometimes I'll Start a Sentence in Spanish *y termini en espanol*: Toward a Typology of Code-switching', *Linguistics*, 18: 7, 581–618.
Poplack, Shana, A. Pousada and D. Sankoff (1982), 'Competing influences on gender assignment: variable process, stable outcome', *Lingua*, 57: 1, 1–28.
Poplack, Shana, D. Sankoff and C. Miller (1988), 'The Social Correlates and Lexical Processes of Lexical Borrowing and Assimilation', *Linguistics*, 26: 47–104.
Poplack, Shana, S. Wheeler and A. Westwood (1990), 'Distinguishing Language Contact Phenomena: Evidence from Finnish-English Bilingualism', in R. Jacobson (ed.), *Codeswitching as a Worldwide Phenomenon*, New York: Peter Lang, pp. 185–218.
Ralli, Angela (2000), 'A Feature-based Analysis of Greek Nominal Inflection', *Γλωσσολογία/Glossologia*, 11–12: 201–227.
Ralli, Angela (2002), 'The Role of Morphology in Gender Determination: Evidence from Modern Greek', *Linguistics*, 40: 3, 519–551.
Ralli, Angela (2003), 'Ο καθορισμός του γραμματικού γένους στα ουσιαστικά της νέας ελληνικής' [Gender Assignment in Modern Greek Nouns], in A. Anastassiadis-Symeonidis, A. Ralli and D. Chila-Markopoulou (eds), *Θέματα Νεοελληνικής Γραμματικής: Το Γένος* [Modern Greek Grammar Issues: Gender], Athens: Patakis, pp. 57–99.
Ralli, Angela (2005), *Μορφολογία* [Morphology], Athens: Patakis.
Ralli, Angela (2012a), 'Verbal Loanblends in Italiot and Heptanesian: A Case Study of Contact Morphology', *Italia Dialettale: Rivista di Dialettologia Italiana*, 73: 111–132.
Ralli, Angela (2012b), 'Morphology in Language Contact: Verbal Loanblend Formation in Asia Minor Greek (Aivaliot)', *Language Typology and Universals (STUF)*, 12: 185–201.
Ralli, Angela (2013), 'Greek', *Revue Belge de Philologie et d'Histoire*, 90: 939–966.
Ralli, Angela (2016a), 'Greek', in P. O. Müller, I. Ohnheiser, S. Olsen and F. Rainer (eds), *Word-Formation. An International Handbook of the Languages of Europe*, Berlin and New York: De Gruyter, vol. 5, pp. 3138–3156.
Ralli, Angela (2016b), 'Strategies and Patterns of Loan verb Integration in Modern Greek Varieties', in A. Ralli (ed.), *Contact Morphology in Modern Greek Dialects*, Newcastle upon Tyne: Cambridge Scholars Publishing, pp. 73–108.
Ralli, Angela (2019), 'Greek in Contact with Romance', in *Oxford Research Encyclopedia of Linguistics*, Oxford: Oxford University Press.
Ralli, Angela, M. Gkiouleka and V. Makri (2015), 'Gender and Inflection Class in Loan Noun Integration', *SKASE Journal of Theoretical Linguistics*, Special Issue: A Festschrift for Pavol Štekauer, 12: 3, 422–459.
Ralli, Angela, P. Pappas and S. Tsolakidis (2018), 'Όψεις του Παρατατικού στη Νέα Ελληνική των Ελλήνων μεταναστών του Καναδά' [Aspects of the Imperfect Tense in the Greek Language of Greek Immigrants in Canada], *International Meeting of Greek Linguistics* (April 2018), Thessaloniki: University of Thessaloniki.
Repetti, Lori (2003), 'Come i sostantivi inglesi diventano italiani: la morfologia e la fonologia dei prestiti', in S. Calimani (ed.), *Italiano e inglese a confronto*, Firenze: Franco Cesati, pp. 31–42.

Repetti, Lori (2006), 'The Emergence of Marked Structures in the Integration of Loans in Italian', in R. S. Ges and D. Arteaga (eds), *Historical Romance Linguistics: Retrospective and Perspectives*, Amsterdam and Philadelphia: John Benjamins, pp. 209–239.

Sankoff, Gillian (2001), 'Linguistic Outcomes of Language Contact', in P. Trudgill, J. K. Chambers and N. Schilling-Estes (eds), *Handbook of Sociolinguistics*, Oxford: Basil Blackwell, pp. 638–668.

Sankoff, David, S. Poplack and S. Vanniarajan (1990), 'The Case of the Nonce Loan in Tamil', *Language Variation and Change*, 2: 1, 71–101.

Thomason, Sarah (2001), *Language Contact: An Introduction*, Edinburgh: Edinburgh University Press.

Thomason, Sarah. G. and T. Kaufman (1988), *Language Contact, Creolization and Genetic Linguistics*, Berkeley: University of California Press.

Thornton, Anna-Maria (2001), 'Some Reflections on Gender and Inflectional Class Assignment in Italian', in C. Schaner-Wolles, J. Rennison and F. Neubarth (eds), *Naturally! Linguistic Studies in Honour of Wolfgang Ulrich Dressler Presented on the Occasion of his 60th Birthday*, Torino: Rosenberg and Sellier, pp. 479–487.

Wichmann, Søren and J. Wohlgemuth (2008), 'Loan Verbs in a Typological Perspective', in T. Stolz, D. Bakker and R. Salas Palomo (eds), *Aspects of Language Contact. New Theoretical, Methodological and Empirical Findings with Special Focus on Romancisation Processes*, Berlin: De Gruyter, pp. 89–121.

Winford, Donald (2003), *An Introduction to Contact Linguistics*, Oxford: Blackwell Publishing.

Winford, Donald (2010), 'Contact and Borrowing', in R. Hickey (ed.), *The Handbook of Language Contact*, Malden and Oxford: Wiley-Blackwell, pp. 170–187.

Wohlgemuth, Jan (2009), *A Typology of Verbal Borrowings*, Berlin and New York: De Gruyter.

13

Interaction among Borrowing, Inflection and Word Formation in Polish Medieval Latin

Michał Rzepiela

In contrast to the majority of chapters united in this volume that report on research conducted on modern languages, the present study analyses two historical languages by discussing classes of words attested in Polish Medieval Latin which might be interpreted both as borrowings (or loan translations) from Old Polish and as products of regular Latin word formation. Section 1 provides basic information on research data and indicates the specificity of Medieval Latin in terms of linguistic and extra-linguistic aspects. Section 2 provides a more detailed insight into the Latin used in medieval Poland. The degree of interplay between Latin and Old Polish is of particular interest, with emphasis on inflectional morphology as the method of transferring vernacular stems into Latin. Section 3 considers the role of inflection in Latin word formation from a more general perspective and discusses the competition between inflection and word formation as operations in Polish Latin. Section 4 distinguishes some lexico-semantic classes within which there may be interaction between borrowing and word formation. In addition, the section proposes a few more precise criteria for determining whether inflection or word formation operations have taken place in cases when lexemes with Latin stems appear and demonstrate 'unexpected' semantic and morphological parallels to Polish lexico-semantic classes. Further, the section evokes a series of agent names in Polish and Czech Latin in the light of the Štekauer's onomasiological theory, thereby referring to the loan translation *mercipotus* ('the sealing of a deal by making a celebratory toast') as a possible manifestation of the continuity between competition and collaboration. Section 5 summaries the conclusions.

1. The position of Latin in medieval Poland

The present study is based on data from the Polish Medieval Latin dictionary (*Lexicon mediae et infimae Latinitatis Polonorum*, LMILP), and draws from Weyssenhoff-Brożkowa (1991) which deals with the influence of Old Polish on Polish Medieval Latin, as well as from Rzepiela (2005) which treats word formation in Polish Medieval Latin. The data were also verified in related text sources and in the Electronic Corpus of Polish Medieval Latin (*eFontes*). Although the text sources taken into account in LMILP are from the period between the eleventh and sixteenth centuries, a majority of them originate from the fifteenth century, when the corpus of texts written in Latin began to grow rapidly in Poland and, simultaneously, those written in Polish also became more common.

A few generalities on the relationship between Old Polish and Medieval Latin are worth mentioning here. First, it must be mentioned that cross-linguistic transfers between Latin and Polish were not symmetric. As may be expected, in over 600 years (between the eleventh and sixteenth centuries), Latin had a much broader impact on Polish than did Polish on Latin. Similarly, in terms of linguistic prestige, Latin had always been the upper language with respect to Old Polish. The distinction between upper and lower language (Panocová 2015: 36, after Bloomfield 1933: 461) is relevant when the social position of the users of the two languages in contact is different. While Latin was mainly used by well-educated representatives of society, Old Polish (mostly as a spoken language) was used by the rest of the native population (generally, the less educated people). However, in contrast to Old Polish, Medieval Latin had never been an ethnic language, either in Poland or elsewhere. Consequently, all its users were bilingual (Rigg 1996: 73). In addition, even if Latin was exploited as a language of everyday communication, it could not be defined as being the common language of all ranks of medieval society.

The term *Medieval Latin* is used to refer to the language used in Europe during the Middle Ages. However, when accepting such a general definition, one often dismisses further reflection on the possible differentiation of this language with respect to its registers. Meanwhile, for sketching a map of the local variation of Latin, identifying the registers in which the influence of vernacular languages is most likely to be manifested is of primary importance. In Polish Latin, the interference with Old Polish can be almost exclusively observed in texts of lower register, for which the most spectacular examples of the phenomenon are provided by court records. When a court writer had to transform spoken speech into written form, he was occasionally forced to coin new terms because they were missing in Latin or unknown to him, or were known to him but only from his mother tongue. In such cases, the most spectacular translations from Polish to Latin occurred. Of course, the level of education of the writers, that is, their degree of knowledge of Latin, played a significant role. In addition, the linguistic norm in Medieval Latin, except perhaps for the well-established formulae (Rigg 1996: 75), was not fixed to the extent which could help writers to almost automatically reproduce all lexical, morphological and syntactic patterns that they actually needed.

The dynamics of the reciprocal interference between Latin and vernacular languages in the Middle Ages also reflected the geographical and ethnic conditionings of their coexistence. While Latin, during the entire period of the Middle Ages, was exposed to the impact of vernacular languages, this impact did not manifest itself with equal intensity everywhere (Plezia 1981: 132). The most striking difference in this regard can be observed when comparing Latin from the Romance-speaking countries (Rigg 1996: 73) with that used in Germanic and Slavic-speaking regions. In general, the more Latin was perceived as a completely foreign language, the lesser the changes observed with respect to the norm of classical Latin. Consequently, the distortions from the norm that arose under the influence of Old Polish were essentially marginal in Polish Latin and did not cause, in any case, any evolution that may affect the linguistic system of Latin. In principle, for example, morphological forms remained unchanged in Polish Latin (as well as in Latin of all other regions, except for those where Latin finally transformed into Romance languages) throughout the entire period in which it was in use.

2. Characteristics of Polish Medieval Latin

The extent to which Old Polish influenced Latin at the lexical level can best be illustrated with statistical data. Weyssenhoff-Brożkowa (1991: 16), who examined lemmas extracted from the portion of the LMILP comprising the letters A to O, counted 343 Polish-stem lexemes, while the total number of lemmas attested in this part of the dictionary amounted to 25,200 units, according to her examination. Then, Polish borrowings constituted only 1.36 per cent of the entire examined vocabulary. Even when taking into account only neologisms, that is, all words unknown from Ancient Latin, no matter whether coined in Polish Latin or in Latin of any other region (for example, lexemes such as *feudum* ('the estate or domain of a feudal lord') and its derivatives, *homagium* ('homage and fealty') and its derivatives, which are very specific to the Middle Ages and are attested both in Polish and in almost all other national dictionaries of Medieval Latin), Polish-stem lexemes still constituted only 5.35 per cent of the entire new coined vocabulary (1991: 16).

In turn, in what concerns the proportions of the entirely new vocabulary and the entirely inherited vocabulary from ancient Latin vocabulary, the examinations of Plezia (1958, 1970) and Rzepiela (2005) for Polish and of Prinz (1978) for German Latin show that these are in favour of inherited vocabulary (Rzepiela 2005: 35). It is worth noting that each of the investigations mentioned was conducted on different samples, although always based on data extracted from dictionaries, according to the state of advancement of related dictionaries, i.e. the part of the alphabet that is actually covered by them. While Plezia (1958) had access to data from only the first volume (A–B) of the LMILP and Prinz used data from the first and part of the second volume (A–Ch) of the German dictionary, Rzepiela had at his disposal those from six complete volumes of the LMILP (A–O). Nevertheless, despite these differences, the results from each of the calculations were, basically, similar, i.e. in favour of inherited vocabulary: Plezia (55 per cent vs. 45 per cent; in his second survey (1970) also including data from the volume on the letter C, 53 per cent vs. 47 per cent), Prinz (55 per cent vs. 45 per cent) and Rzepiela (57 per cent vs. 43 per cent).

Similar examinations were made by Bautier and Duchet-Suchaux (1983–1985) for data from the *Novum Glossarium Mediae Latinitatis* (NGML), a dictionary unifying lexical material from medieval France, the Iberian Peninsula and, to a lesser degree, from other parts of Europe. These authors checked the number of neologisms with regard to the selected letters of the alphabet, but each of them separately. In contrast with the results quoted above, in their survey, the number of neologisms prevailed. In addition, their observation with regard to hapax legomena is also of significance, viz. they definitely constitute the most numerous group among new coinages. For example, from among 890 new words related to the letter O, as many as 736 hapaxes were attested. The predominance of the hapax can also be observed in Polish Latin, although not on such a scale. According to Rzepiela (2005: 43) they constituted, among the letters A–O of the LMILP, 54 per cent of the noun neologisms coined by suffixation.

2.1 Characteristics of Polish borrowings in Medieval Latin

When discussing interference between Old Polish and Latin, certain fundamental structural similarities between those languages must be mentioned: they were both inflectional languages, for which the distinction of grammatical gender and number was relevant. This similarity doubtlessly encouraged mutual transfers between the languages. In turn, in order to determine the degree of assimilation of Polish-stem lexemes into Medieval Latin, it is important to pay attention to their frequency. According to Weyssenhoff-Brożkowa (1991: 25), a majority of them appeared once or twice or a maximum of five times, whereas only ten words remained in permanent use in Polish Medieval Latin. These were mostly used as bases for further derivational series (1).

(1)   a.   cmetho 'peasant'   >   cmethona 'peasant wife'   >   cmethonissa
           'peasant wife'
      b.   cmetho 'peasant'   >   cmethonicus, -i 'peasant son' >   cmethonicus
           'relating or belonging to peasant$_{ADJ}$' >   cmethonicalis 'relating or belonging
           to peasant'   >   cmethonaliter 'by peasant$_{ADV}$'

Such series prove that they were established as basic words and perceived by the users as a really stable part of Latin vocabulary. Since these words usually demonstrate correspondence with analogical series in Old Polish, one cannot exclude that competition between word formation and borrowing could have contributed to their popularity. The largest series are established by the nouns *cmetho* 'peasant' (1), *granicies* 'border' and *lotus* 'unit of weight called *lut*'. The lexemes derived from basic words usually motivate further derivatives of the series as in (1).

The most frequent Polish-stem words, unlike the rarest ones, are also attested in texts of higher linguistic register, such as ecclesiastical records, documents of royalty and the prince's chanceries. On the other hand, those that occur rarely and that are employed only occasionally, constituting the most numerous group of Polish-stem lexemes, must be interpreted as manifestations of code-switching and not of 'actual' borrowing. Weyssenhoff-Brożkowa (1991: 18) defines them, warily, as 'Polish words with Latin inflection'. The quotations presented in (2) illustrate typical communicative situations which favour code-switching from Latin to Polish:

(2)   a.   Andreas sibi dixit bis: 'non iuste me citasti et per tuum *chleboyeczczam*' – Item pro
           eo, quod violenter recia sua rapiebat.
           'Andrew said to him twice: "you didn't take me justly to the court, and to that,
           because of your dependant". That is as he took violently away his fish nets.'

    b. [. . .] quia cmethoni rethe violenter receipt
       [. . .] 'as he took violently away peasant's fish nets'.
    c. Laboratoribus circa currus 4 grossos, pro fustis et loppatis 33 grossos.
       'For those working at the cart 4 gross, for poles and shovels 33 gross.'
    d. eundo recte a torrente aut medio fluvio ad lyppam.
       'going straight from the stream or water, flowing in the middle, towards the
       linden'.

Examples (2a) and (2b) are fragments of two court records (StPPP VIII, 1886: 532) that report the same lawsuit (the controversy between a certain Andrew and a certain Clement), where (2a) originates from the record that presents the case, while (2b) originates from the record that informs about the sentence given in this case. One of the characteristics of Medieval Latin court records, when reporting statements of the trial participants, is alternation of direct and indirect speeches (Rzepiela 2013: 184–187). The scribe in (2a) is using direct speech to precisely summarise Andrew's position, who expresses his scorn towards Clement's servant by using the Polish-stem word *chlebojedźca* 'dependant', which outlines low social rank of the latter. Then, the literal quotation of Andrew's words reveals the connotative sense of his use of the vernacular word, which, however, could have barely been rendered in Latin by the scribe. That is probably why such code-switching was difficult to avoid here. The fact that this Polish-stem lexeme was, effectively, used by Andrew with a connotative meaning and was as such reported then by the scribe is additionally proved by (2b); in (2b), in contrast, the peasant-servant of Clement is defined using a word that is regularly used in Polish Medieval Latin to denote 'peasant', namely, *cmetho*. Example (2c) was taken from the accounts of the town Poznań (KsgPozn, 1892: 421). It is instructive in terms of how account books were created in the Middle Ages. The writers listed, as it seems, the expenses as they followed without discriminating them according to their types. Consequently, the expenses on workers, tools, materials or even food were included next to one another. It is also possible that the writers, when compiling these books, were forced to work quickly to provide a single final version. The author of the record quoted in (2c) must have apparently forgotten the Latin denomination of 'shelve', and all he could do was to immediately adapt the corresponding Polish lexeme *łopata* (here in its variant *loppata*) to the Latin inflectional paradigm. This explanation appears to be the more likely one, as in the LMILP the noun *pala*, commonly used in Latin to name 'shelve', is attested as a frequent word as well.

    Further, example (2d) is a passage taken from a document pertaining to the delimitation of the borders between the village of Dołęgi, near the city of Płock, and the neighbouring villages (DokList Pł I, 1975: 238). It draws borderlines by making reference to certain specific points in natural space, which was a typical procedure of delimiting borders in the Middle Ages. Two explanations of the code-switching occurring here can be provided: either the writer forgot or did not know the Latin noun *tilia* ('linden') and made a quick recourse to the corresponding Polish name *lipa* (here in its variant *lyppa*); or this word mentioned in the text was considered by the inhabitants as being somehow specific or having some specific connotation in order for them to treat it as a kind of proper name, for example due to its very characteristic shape. Then, it is possible that it is for this very reason that the writer recalling such an object preferred to make use of its Polish-stem denomination. Moreover, the electronic corpus *eFontes* shows that *tilia* was relatively frequently used in Polish Medieval Latin.

To briefly summarise the examples discussed above, it appears that the lack of knowledge of a lexical norm of Latin, that is, its vocabulary, among users was the most common reason for code-switching from Latin to Polish. It cannot be excluded, however, that in certain cases pragmatic and extra-linguistic factors could have also stimulated this phenomenon.

Going back to the statistics provided by Weyssenhoff-Brożkowa (1991: 18), nouns were established as the largest group, with 327 lexemes; the sets of verbs and adjectives were notably smaller, with each being represented by only eight lexemes. Among nouns, those adapted to the first Latin declension dominated, which was a total of 150 Polish-stem words. In second place were those adapted to the second declension, with a total of 125 words. In third place were those built according to the third declension, with a total of fifty-one words. Only one word, but of a high frequency, *granicies* 'border', was adapted to the fifth Latin declension, while none was adapted to the fourth. Since it is mainly lexemes belonging to the third declension that may be considered as those containing clearly separable derivational affixes, it is appropriate to conclude that inflection was a significantly more frequent method of absorbing Polish borrowings into Latin than word formation.

The method for adapting Polish-stem words to the third declension was basically to use the suffix -*(i)ō* (gen. -*(i)ōnis*), with the aid of which as many as forty-one lexemes were coined, mostly masculine nouns like *cmetho* in (1). This class will be discussed in greater detail in section 3.2. When discussing derivational morphemes in other declensions, it is worth mentioning the morpheme -*arius* in the second declension, illustrated in (3a–b).

(3) a. furarz PL   > furarius LA 'driver, carter'
     b. garbarz PL   > garbarius LA 'tanner'
     c. budnik PL   > budnicus LA 'stallholder'
     d. fortal PL   > fortale LA 'lump of salt' vs. natale LA 'birthday fest'

This morpheme was used to absorb Polish masculine nouns ending with the suffix -*rz* (*r'*), as being preceded by the thematic vowel *a*, it can also be interpreted as -*arz*. Consequently, by reason of its phonetic and functional similarity to the Latin -*arius* (with which it is diachronically related via German; *Słownik Prasłowiański* (Sławski 1976: 22)), the Polish-stem lexemes on -*arius* were developed as a specific class in Polish Medieval Latin (3a–b). My hesitation if the morpheme -*arius* should be treated as a derivational morpheme in this case comes from the fact that the entire Polish word, including the morpheme -*arz*, is adapted to a Latin inflectional paradigm. Consequently, insofar as this morpheme is regarded as corresponding to Latin -*ar*- in terms of phonetic similarity, the process of assimilation of Polish words, abstracting from their phonological adaptation, principally had an inflectional character that consisted of adding an inflectional ending -*(i)us*. Similarly, Weyssenhoff-Brożkowa (1991: 21) proposes the interpretation that Polish-stem nouns in -*arius* (namely, as masculine nouns) were regularly adapted to the second Latin declension by inflectional endings. What is indeed characteristic for second declension Polish-stem lexemes is that they receive an inflectional affix in variant -*ius* (3a–b) when they present a soft consonant ending stem (*r'*), and an inflectional affix -*us* (3c) when exhibiting a hard consonant ending stem.

In the same manner, the phonetic similarity of Polish and Latin morphemes and subsequent phonological adaptation of Polish morphemes to Latin phonological rules may explain the rise of the remaining nine neologisms of the third declension (Weyssenhoff-Brożkowa 1991: 22). For example, *fortal* 'lump of salt' PL (3d) takes inflectional forms according to the example of *natale* 'birthday fest' LA: *fortale* $_{NOM}$ – $_{ACC sg}$, *fortali* $_{ABL sg}$. etc.

2.2 Feminine nouns adapted to the first Latin declension

What is striking in the statistical summary discussed above is certainly the dominance of the feminine nouns adapted to the first Latin declension. Transfers from Polish into the first Latin declension were easier, as the stems of both Polish and Latin feminine nouns end with the thematic vowel *a*; thus, the Polish lexeme and its Latin equivalent represented the same shape in the nominative singular. For this reason, it came almost automatically to the users to transform Polish words into Latin ones. Pakerys (2016: 181) defines this type of adaptation as 'the replacement of inflectional markers in borrowing [. . .] based on the formal identity of nominative singular'. Although he provides an example of the transfer in the opposite direction, from Latin into a modern vernacular language, namely of the Latin anthroponym *Senec-a* into Russian, where it receives the form *Senek-a* (in the same manner the name of the Roman writer and philosopher was introduced into Polish), this example illustrates, in principle, the mechanism of lexical transfers of feminine nouns from Old Polish into Medieval Latin. The example provided by Pakerys concerns *a*-final masculine nouns, which within animate Latin borrowings constitute a small but characteristic group in Slavic languages (for example, in Czech, Kavitskaya (2005)). Now, however, let us turn to the Latin examples in (4).

(4)   a.   beczk-a 'barrel$_{NOM}$' PL/LA
        b.   beczk-ę 'barrel$_{ACC}$' PL
        c.   beczk-am 'barrel$_{ACC}$' LA

Generally, example (4a) illustrates an analogy to describe the above situation, which states that the phonological form of the borrowed word remains unaltered in the nominative. Thus, the ending of borrowed lexemes in Russian and Polish is identical to the Latin one in the nominative so that a borrowing can only be determined as adapted to the 'domestic' nominal morphology upon analysis of its inflected forms, which are different from the Latin ones, for example, PL and RU gen. *Seneki* vs. LA gen. *Senecae*. Similarly, Polish-stem feminine nouns, in Medieval Latin, can be recognised as assimilated units only if they exhibit inflection in Latin endings (4b) vs. (4c) throughout.[1]

3. The role of inflection in word formation: some general considerations

While the previous sections provided a few explanations with regard to why and when Latin words of Polish origin were introduced, users of Polish Medieval Latin chose inflectional affixes instead of derivational ones. Thus, from a theoretical viewpoint, it is interesting to question the status of inflectional affixes in the process of coining new words. As it has been often observed, operations which do not have recourse to derivational morphemes but only to inflectional ones, as well as those which do not change the form of words at all when transferring them from one grammatical class to another, are productive methods of word formation in certain languages. This indicates phenomena called *paradigmatic derivation*, *conversion* or *zero derivation* in the linguistic literature. These are illustrated in (5).

> (5)   a.   srebro$_{\text{NOM neut sg}}$ 'silver' > srebra$_{\text{NOM neut pl}}$ 'jewellery' PL
>   b.   writing$_{\text{PRESP/GERUND}}$ > writing$_{\text{N}}$ 'someone's style of writing' EN

Example (5a) is a manifestation of paradigmatic derivation, since the difference between newly coined and motivating words is marked by an inflectional morpheme of their plural forms, while the stem of derived and motivating words remain identical (cf. Štekauer 2014: 356). Of course, the change in inflectional morphemes is not limited here to a change in number but entails their semantic modification as well. In contrast, in the conversion in (5b), zero derivation is illustrated, as there is no change in the form of the new lexeme in comparison with that of the motivating word. However, this lexeme enters into the new grammatical and semantic categories. The question of a mutual relationship between inflection and word formation, which is of concern here, has been broadly discussed in the literature (Heinz 1961; Dokulil 1962; Waszakowa 1993; Booij 2000; ten Hacken 2014; Štekauer 2014), but mostly with emphasis on the internal organisation of each and on the degree of their regularity. The conclusions of such studies usually indicate that inflection and word formation are governed by more similar rules than one commonly believes. At the same time, one attempts not to blur certain lines between them (e.g. ten Hacken 2014). However, for me, the more interesting aspect of the phenomenon is that of possible interaction between inflection and word formation, and to question the extent to which the former may take over the role of the latter.

3.1 The status of inflectional affixes in word formation of Medieval Latin and Old Polish

The word formation operations which use inflectional morphemes in the way discussed occur with others that are characteristic of Slavic languages; it is worth questioning to what extent they are characteristic for Latin as well. Since the languages examined in this study are Latin and Old Polish, let us focus on examples from these languages (6).

> (6)   a.   bon-us$_{\text{masc}}$, bon-a$_{\text{fem}}$, bon-um$_{\text{neut}}$ 'good$_{\text{ADJ}}$' > bon-um 'good$_{\text{N}}$, goodness' LA
>   b.   dobr-y$_{\text{masc}}$, dobr-a$_{\text{fem}}$, dobr-e$_{\text{neut}}$ 'good$_{\text{ADJ}}$' > dobr-o 'good$_{\text{N}}$, goodness' PL

c. sapiens 'wise$_{PRESP/ADJ}$' > sapiens 'sage$_N$' LA
d. przychodzący 'coming$_{PRESP}$' > przychodzący 'comer$_N$, foreigner' PL
e. amic-us$_{masc}$ > amic-a$_{fem}$ 'friend' LA
f. kmotr-Ø$_{masc}$ 'godfather' > kmotr-a$_{fem}$ 'godmother' PL

Examples (6a–b) illustrate, both in Latin and Old Polish, a productive pattern of word class change that makes use of inflectional morphemes, and that is established by the nouns arising from adjectives. For Latin, this is a more characteristic conversion, while for Old Polish this is a paradigmatic derivation. In turn, this pattern exploited in the conversion of both languages was commonly used for coining the names of taxes, tributes or fees from neuter adjectives. These will be discussed further in section 4.1. Similarly, examples (6c–d) must be viewed as a clear manifestation of conversion, in this case going from the present participle (also occurring in the function of adjective) to nouns. In contrast, examples (6e–f) illustrate a change in inflectional class, with the shift from the second to the first declension in Latin and from the masculine personal declension with morphological zero in the nominative to feminine declension in Old Polish, which simultaneously entails a gender shift. Luraghi (2014: 200, 203, 211), whose example I use in (6e), discusses gender as a category at the border between derivation and inflection and insists on the phrases *inflectional class change* and *gender shift*. She uses them in contrast to derivation, thereby bringing about *gender motion* through the addition of a derivational affix which she interprets as 'not of a stem formation affix' (2014: 200). Such gender motion can be illustrated by the feminine nouns on *-trix*, which are derived from masculine ones on *-tor*.

This short overview of the methods involving inflectional affixes to coin new words in Latin and in Old Polish showed that these methods were productive in both languages. It is then reasonable to conclude that similarity of word formation patterns was, in this case, a factor that could encourage reciprocal transfers between both languages. The mechanism of inflectional adaptation, according to the rules observed in Ancient Latin, might have been considered as a completely 'legitimate' method of coining new lexical units by the users of its medieval continuation in Poland. In addition, the identical form of the nominative ending of Polish and Latin feminine nouns, apart from the fact that it was biased in favour of spontaneous coinages, might also be the cause that the distinction between Latin and Polish indigenous stems were not always perceived by the users as sharp. This was probably also the reason why so many hapaxes and other rare coinages appeared within Polish-stem lexemes. As argued in section 2.1, their low frequency suggests that they must have been a manifestation of code-switching.

3.2 Competition between inflectional and derivational affixes in Polish Medieval Latin

Evidence that inflectional endings might have been treated by the users of Polish Latin as a derivational device is provided not only by borrowed feminine nouns but also by the Polish-stem masculine nouns absorbed into the second Latin declension; in the second declension, the border between Polish-stem and Latin inflectional affixes was, in any case, more clearly marked in comparison with the structure of the lexemes of the first declension. This is also manifested in different variants taken by the suffix of the newly coined lexemes, depending on the structure of the Polish base word, cf. (3a–c). However, what is particularly striking is that the same Polish-stem lexemes appear in forms adapted to two different Latin declensions, second and third. In the latter case, they are adapted by means of the derivational affix *-(i)ō*, *(gen. -(i)ōnis)* as in (7a–b).

(7) a. creptuchus vs. creptucho   <   PL kreptuch 'bag for feed'
     b. konuchus vs. konucho   <   PL koniuch 'horse boy'
     c. balbus 'stammering$_{PRESP/ADJ}$'   >   Balbō 'stammerer$_N$'
     d. hortulus 'garden$_N$'   >   hortulō 'gardiner'

In Medieval Latin, the affix *-(i)ō* was widely used to absorb adaptations from vernacular languages, while in Ancient Latin it was used to coin names of a person's physical and mental characteristics, particularly their defects (Gaide 2002: 326). From here developed the class of Roman cognomens and nicknames, as illustrated in (7c). Another specific class was established by the names of functions and professions (7d) (Gaide 2002: 326); it is in this class that continuation primarily in Medieval Latin is found.

It is worth noting that there are differing opinions on whether the affix *-(i)ō* should be treated as a derivational or an inflectional morpheme. Leumann (1963: 239), Stotz (2000: 273) and Gaide (2002: 307) define it as a suffix and include it in chapters dealing with word formation, while Oniga (2014: 74) places it in inflectional morphology (as the consonant stem *-on* of the third declension).

In terms of the listed examples, one can, of course, account for the rise of such redundant pairs in Polish Latin by the ignorance of users that the words they intended to coin had already been in use. As we saw in section 1, what is possible as a linguistic norm was not always firmly fixed in Medieval Latin. Nevertheless, in a few cases, such pairs occur in the same source, written around the same time and by probably the same scribe. It even happens that they appear on the same page of the manuscript (Weyssenhoff-Brożkowa 1991: 30). Then, it is obvious that both affixes must have been treated by users as alternative but, at the same time, fully equivalent means of coining new words. It must be outlined that the difference between the pairs of the lexemes on *-us* and *-(i)ō*, as they occur in Ancient and Polish Medieval Latin, is that in the former they always establish a relationship of motivation (7c–d; cf. Väänänen 1963: 92; Gaide 2002: 311, 326–327), while in the latter they appear as independent coinages from one another (7a–b).

4. Competition between borrowing and word formation in Polish Medieval Latin

The manifestation of the interaction between borrowing and word formation in Polish Medieval Latin can most certainly be observed in the vocabulary pertaining to juridical practice, where one may expect the most reliable attestation of the phenomenon.

In particular, legal terms and words of common use coined by clerks when compiling court records are worth attention here. Since Latin, at least until the sixteenth century, was more commonly used in court than Polish but, at the same time, it was not possible to avoid Polish during the process, a particular kind of bilingualism emerged which resulted in the development of certain parallel lexico-semantic classes in both languages. However, in certain cases, the paradigm around which such classes are organised was previously unknown to Latin.

4.1 Parallel lexico-semantic classes

A very characteristic class in Polish Medieval Latin and, simultaneously, parallel to Old Polish is constituted by the names of inheritances making reference to a kind of consanguinity illustrated in Table 13.1 (Weyssenhoff-Brożkowa 1991: 49).

The Latin derivations in Table 13.1 seem to be a literal translation of the corresponding Polish derivations: the Latin suffix *-(i)tas* corresponds to the Polish suffix *-izna*; and the Latin names of consanguinity *ava*, *avus*, *patruus* to their Polish counterparts *baba*, *dziad*, *stryj*. Even if Latin lexemes do not stray from the derivational rules of Latin, i.e. they are coined correctly from a grammatical viewpoint, they establish new lexico-semantic patterns, not necessarily derivational ones. Further, denominal lexemes with the suffix *-tas* were attested already in late Latin, where they underwent a shift from abstract noun to concrete noun. They were used to designate human collectives, for example, *civitas* took the meaning of an 'ensemble of citizens', while *hereditas* took on the meaning of 'descendants'. They were also used to designate spaces and areas of land, *vicinitas* took on the meaning of 'neighbour's area' (Ernout 1954: 180; Löfstedt 1959: 155–156; Daude 2002: 252). In turn, in the Middle Ages, denominal derivatives with the suffix *-tas* were commonly employed in, among others, scholastic and scientific literature as designations of abstract qualities of various objects as well as of proper names, for example, *socratitas* < *Socrates* 'Socrates's nature' (Stotz 2000: 292–293). Nevertheless, denominal names of inheritances coined from the names of consanguinity occur, to the best of my knowledge, only in Polish Medieval Latin.

Another class of derivatives, common both for Old Polish and Polish Latin, is constituted by the names of tributes and impositions. The lexemes belonging to this group are neuters built with the suffix *-ale* as illustrated in Table 13.2.

Analogically, like in Table 13.1, Latin lexemes in Table 13.2 correspond structurally to Polish derivatives with the inflectional ending *-e*, in suffixal variants *-ne* and *-we*. Although the suffix *-ale* originating from the adjective suffix *-alis* was employed in Medieval Latin for coining neuters, which initiated a rather productive series, it is

Table 13.1 Latin and Polish patterns for inheritance names based on family relations

Family relation	LA base	LA derivation	PL base	PL derivation
Grandmother	ava	avalitas	baba	babizna
Grandfather	avus	avitas	dziad	dziadowizna
Paternal uncle	patruus	patruitas	stryj	stryjowizna

Table 13.2 Tributes and impositions in Polish Latin and Old Polish

Reason for payment	LA base	LA derivation	PL base	PL derivation
Tribute paid to feudal lord for the use of the forest	foresta silva	forestale silvale	las	leśne
Fee paid by the winning side in court	memoria	memoriale	pamięć	pamiętne
Fee imposed on everyone who crosses the bridge	pons	pontale	most	mostowe

only in Polish and Czech Latin that this suffix served to coin the names of tributes. Further, in Medieval Latin of other regions it was used to coin names of liturgical books, for example, *graduale* and *missale* as well as those of weight and length units, for example, *librale* and *pedale* (Stotz 2000: 337).

Weyssenhoff-Brożkowa (1991: 50) interprets the Old Polish class as established by nominalised adjectives in neuters which were afterwards rendered in Latin as neuter nouns, by analogy. It is the correct interpretation for synchronic motivation and, as such, it is presented in Table 13.2. It is presumed that it was borrowing which intervened here, so that Polish nouns were rendered as Latin nouns without any inter-mediate derivational operation, before being submitted to phonological adaptation. Consequently, one admits that even if the Latin class developed further, at some stage, autonomously (i.e. as word formation entailed by analogy), it would always be a noun that would motivate such a formation, as evident in the example *memoria > memori-ale*. Nevertheless, it is worth noting that such a sequence (from one noun to another) appears to be possible insofar as the related adjective on *-alis* is attested. Thus, the sequence *memoria > memoriale* can be barely imagined without the adjective *memorialis* being attested in the lexical thesaurus of Medieval Latin. Indeed, for all the lexemes in *-ale* quoted above we find corresponding adjectives attested in the dictionaries of Medieval Latin. For example, *forestalis* is missing in LMILP, but is attested in *Lexicon Bohemorum*. To conclude this digression, the existence of the related adjectives on *-alis* appears to be the only limitation for the open-ended and unrestricted formation of nouns in *-ale*, unless extra-linguistic factors such as the lack of imposition of certain conceivable taxes makes their use superfluous.

4.2 The concept of 'semantic niches'

The lexical couples listed in Tables 13.1 and 13.2 as representing the unity of suffix, word formation base and semantics can be, according to terminological preferences of different, mostly, structuralist schools, defined as *word formation type* (Dokulil 1962), *microstructure* (Dubois 2002), *microsystème lexicale* (Kircher-Durand 2002), *groupements associatifs ou série des mots* (Fruyt 1986) or even, as above (in section 4–4.1), *lexico-semantic class* (more about terminology pertaining to the specific classes of derivatives; Rzepiela 2019). However, for the purpose of this study, I would like to recall another term, namely *semantische Nische*, introduced by Baldinger (1950) and reinterpreted several times since then, recently by Hüning (2009). Hüning

(2009: 183) defines *semantic niches* as 'groups of words [. . .] kept together by formal and semantic criteria and extensible through analogy'. He views the value of this term in that it allows one to scale down the word formation description to units smaller than the category (2009: 183, 197) and hypothesises that *semantic niches* might represent the basic level of word formation. At this point, he meets with Dokulil, who calls them *word formation types* and expresses the opinion that they exhibit the most important word formation characteristics and constitute a nodal point in the nest of word formation relations (Dokulil 1962: 75; Dokulil et al. 1986: 220). Starting from a contrastive stance, Hüning outlines the usefulness of the term *niche* for examination of systematic differences between two languages. In his investigation, he focuses on morphological differences and contrasts between German and Dutch as two historically related languages.

However, when applying contrastive perspective to the data discussed in section 4, it is striking that no differences can be detected between corresponding Polish and Latin niches. They display a 100 per cent parallelism, not only in terms of structural and semantic characteristics but also in terms of completeness of the niche. They do not exhibit any gaps, since each Polish member of the niche corresponds to an equivalent in the Latin niche. Thus, this would mean that the Latin niche never functions autonomously with respect to the Polish one, which is also proved by the fact that Latin niches exploit lexico-semantic patterns that are not typical of Latin standards. Further, Hüning (2009: 187) argues that language comparison must deal not only with degrees of productivity but also with degrees of probability. Consequently, word formation must be focused not only on possible and impossible words and neologisms, which is the domain of productivity and rule-based processes, but also on likely and unlikely ones.

Accepting such a viewpoint may also make it easier to make a more unequivocal distinction between operations used for coinages that are considered to have arisen under influence of Old Polish. Let us consider only one example, the Latin lexemes with the morpheme *-arius*, as in (3a–b). I interpreted them on the basis of observed rules, namely, that they correspond to Polish nouns on *–arz* formally and semantically; moreover, due to the phonetic similarity of morphemes mentioned, they are easily adapted to Latin inflection borrowings from Old Polish. However, two other lexemes on *-arius* cause interpretive problems. They are illustrated in (8a and c).

(8) a. graniciarius LA vs. granicznik PL 'neighbour'
     b. granicies/granicia 'border' > granicialis 'boundary'
         granicies/granicia 'border' > graniciensis 'boundary
         granicies/granicia 'border' > graniciarius 'neighbour'
         granicies/granicia 'border' > granicitas 'boundary land'
     c. olborarius LA vs. olbornik PL 'tax coal extraction collector'
     d. olbora 'tax coal extraction' > olborius 'tax coal extraction collector'
     e. olbora 'tax coal extraction' > olborarius 'tax coal extraction collector' > olboraria
         'tax coal extraction'
     f. olborarius 'tax coal extraction collector' > olborariatus 'office of the tax coal
         extraction collector'

First, taking *The Dictionary of Old Polish* as a base, it is not possible to indicate corresponding lexemes on *-arz* either for *graniciarius* (8a) or for *olborarius* (8c), although they have stem-correspondent lexemes in Old Polish in the nouns on *-ik*. The irregularity they represent causes a gap within the semantic niche of the agent names on *-arius*, which are naturally coined from Polish stems. The lack of vernacular lexemes which correspond exactly to these two nouns suggests the need to consider another method than borrowing by which they could be coined. Word formation is more probable here, as both are not isolated words with a specific Polish stem but are part of the same derivational family developed around the basic word representing this stem (8b, d–f). This family can either establish the derivational paradigm in the narrow sense (8b), when individual words are directly derived from a single basic word (cf. Štekauer 2014: 363), or relate through motivation, when they do mutually motivate one another (8e, f). What must be added is that both basic words in (8), *granicies* and *olbora*, had a high frequency in Polish Medieval Latin, which is contrary to their derivatives. Thus, this factor could also work in favour of word formation, since because of their frequency these words could be identified easily by users as the starting point for new coinages.

4.3 A particular case of the continuum between competition and collaboration

In the Medieval Latin vocabulary, an important place is taken up by lexemes pertaining to commercial activity. A particularly interesting case in Polish and Czech Latin represents the family of derivatives that relate to the custom of sealing a deal by making a celebratory toast or occasionally even by giving a feast. This custom was widely adopted in medieval law. In Central Europe it appeared under German influence and, etymologically, it was the German compound *Litkouf* (combining the morphemes *lit* 'hot drink' and *kouf* 'purchase') that led to the rise of corresponding lexemes in Latin and in vernacular languages. Thus, we find the calque *mercipotus* (*merx* + *potus*) in the former and the borrowing *lithkup* in the latter, which indicates Old Czech and Old Polish.

Both in Czech and Polish Latin, the noun *mercipotus* led to the development of word formation series of agent names that designate either participants of the transaction or its witnesses (it is not always possible to establish precisely from text sources). *Lexicon Bohemorum* gives (9a) and LMILP (9b).

(9) a. mercipota, mercipotalis, mercipotarius, mercipotator, mercipotus, -i
         (< mercipotus, -us)
     b. mercipotalis (hl), mercipotaneus (hl), mercipotans, mercipotarius, mercipotator,
         mercipotor, mercipotus, -i (< mercipotus, -us)

However, what is surprising is that as many as seven lexemes are attested in the Polish Latin dictionary in the category of agent names (only two *hapax legomena*), of which five are coined with different suffixes (9b); the Czech Latin dictionary attests as many as five, of which four exhibit similar suffixal variation (9a). Then, the question that arises is how this abundance of synonyms can be explained. The series of synonymic coinages from the same base within the same category are in no way unusual in

Medieval Latin (Rzepiela 2005: 39–40). They could have occurred as a consequence of instability of the norm in Medieval Latin and, on the other hand, of insufficient linguistic competence of medieval scribes.

Nevertheless, it is obvious that in Polish and Czech Latin, the terms designating persons involved in the discussed sales contract were of great importance and played rather necessary roles. Interestingly, the Medieval Latin dictionaries of other regions do not contain any words designating such participants. The only words from the family concerned designating the transaction itself, namely *mercipotum, -i*, and *mercipotus, -us*, can be found in Dutch and German Latin dictionaries, respectively.[2] This fact can have great significance for explaining the abundance of the above-mentioned synonyms in Polish and Czech Latin. It appears that the names of persons assisting the transaction must have been newly coined each time by the users of Polish and Czech Latin, because of the lack of a Latin term that they could use spontaneously. The Old Polish and Old Czech agent name *litkupnik* 'witness or participant of the sealing deal', which in both languages was characterised by high frequency, must have served a pattern for them. In Polish Latin, and less often in Czech, it was also employed as a gloss being placed directly after Latin lexemes, occasionally even signalled by the adverb *alias*.

Another question arises with regard to why the scribes referring to a somehow specific local situation instead of vernacular borrowings **litkupo* or **litkupus*, for the coinage of which a paradigm productive in Latin could have been adopted easily, preferred to coin repeatedly missing agent names by referring to existing words in Latin, so by means of word formation. Vernacular borrowing, namely *litkupialis*, appears only in Czech Latin. It has a few attestations in the dictionary, but it was not used as a common term. A possible explanation for this is that the use of already existing words in Latin terminology pertaining to the discussed type of transaction was fixed to an extent that 'discouraged' any vernacular insertions when introducing new terms. It is also possible that the German etymology of vernacular *litkupnik* was, nevertheless, still clear for the users of Polish and Czech Latin (i.e. for the court writers) who, in contrast, correctly interpreted the Latin stem *mercipot-*, as the loan translation they effectively needed.

From a theoretical viewpoint, the situation described, whether it has arisen for this reason or another, can be interpreted as a particular case of the continuum between competition and collaboration, where the former is manifested in the interplay, but only at the onomasiological level (according to Štekauer's onomasiological theory), between vernacular *lithkupnik* and individual Latin agent names derived from words belonging to the family of *mercipotus*, and the latter merely in the multiplication of the derivatives in this family (whose founder *mercipotus* entered Latin as a calque). The line between competition and collaboration might have been blurred in the sense that the users of Polish and Czech Latin who aimed to fill the lexical gap did not introduce the missing word by borrowing from their own languages; however, they repeatedly had a vernacular word in their mind as a pattern, as a motivating word at the onomasiological level, when coining new words by means of word formation. Thus, they initiated a series of coinages from those existing in Latin stems, but previously absorbed to it as loan translation, which is a clear manifestation of collaboration.

5. Conclusion

Inflection established itself as the preferred method for absorbing Polish-stem lexemes to Medieval Latin. Apart from the general structural similarity between Polish and Latin (both inflectional languages), it was the phonetic similarity of Polish and Latin words, particularly in the case of feminine nouns ending with a thematic vowel *a* adapted to the first Latin declension, which eased almost all automatic lexical transfers from Polish into Latin. On the other hand, a majority of the Polish-stem lexemes in Latin was characterised by very low frequency and, thus, they must rather be considered as manifestations of code-switching. In turn, the competition between inflection and word formation was most clearly visible when the same Polish words were adapted both to the second and third Latin declensions, by means of inflectional and derivational affixes, respectively. These two types of morphemes were apparently perceived by the users of Polish Latin as equally 'legitimate' devices of coining new words.

In contrast, the interaction between borrowing and word formation was addressed in terms of parallel semantic niches occurring in Old Polish and Polish Medieval Latin. As long as no differences between them can be observed and Latin niches are organised according to a lexico-semantic pattern unknown in Latin, it is reasonable to accept that these arose as a result of loan translation. When analysing the phenomenon associated with this interaction from an onomasiological viewpoint, a certain continuum is noticeable between competition and collaboration. It was manifested in the vernacular lexeme *lithkupnik* 'witness or participant of deal sealing' basically never being absorbed as adapted to Medieval Latin, but nevertheless stimulating derivation of agent names in Polish and Czech Latin from the basic word *mercipotus* 'the sealing of deal by celebratory toast', which was previously itself adapted to Latin as a loan translation.

Acknowledgements

This study was conducted as a part of project nr. 31H 17 0444 84, Długosz 2.0. Elektroniczny Korpus i Narzędzia Analizy Języka Jana Długosza, supported by the Narodowy Program Rozwoju Humanistyki (NPRH) programme of the Polish Ministry of Science and Higher Education.

Notes

1. A good illustration of the phenomenon in modern inflectional languages is borrowings from Italian, for example, pizza, which remain unaltered in the nominative but undergo morphological and phonological adaptation in other cases (for more examples, also of borrowings from other languages than Italian, see Kavitskaya 2005; Comrie 2008; Kwiatkowska 2014).
2. It must be mentioned that Medieval Latin dictionaries for different regions of Europe take into account text sources from different time periods. While, for example, the French and partially pan-European Latin dictionary *Novum Glossarium Latinitatis* includes texts written between the eighth and twelfth centuries, the

German Latin dictionary *Mittellateinisches Wörterbuch* (MLW) includes texts written between 500 and 1280, the Dutch *Lexicon Latinitatis Nederlandicae Medii Aevi* between 700 and 1500, and the Polish (LMILP) and Czech Latin dictionaries *Latinitatis Medii Aevi Lexicon Bohemorum* between 1000 and 1500 (in addition, LMIPL takes into account the first part of sixteenth century). However, the latter two dictionaries include most abundantly texts from the fourteenth and fifteenth centuries. Therefore, abstracting even from ethnic and geographical contexts, they attest so many common phenomena for Polish and Czech Latin. I wish to thank Pavel Nývlt from the *Latinitatis Medii Aevi Lexicon Bohemorum*, Martin Fiedler and Helena Leithe-Jasper from the *Mittellateinisches Wörterbuch* and Katarzyna Jasińska from the Dictionary of Old Polish (*Słownik staropolski*) for providing me precious information and examples to support my statements.

References

Baldinger, Kurt (1950), *Kollektivsuffixe und Kollektivbegriff. Ein Beitrag zur Bedeutungslehre im Französischen mit Berücksichtigung der Mundarten*, Berlin: Akademie-Verlag [Veröffentlichungen des Instituts für Romanische Sprachwissenschaft].

Bautier, Anne-Marie and M. Duchet-Suchaux (1983–1985), 'Des néologismes en latin médiéval: approche statistique et répartition linguistique', *Archivum Latinitatis Medii Aevii*, 44–45: 43–63.

Bloomfield, Leonard (1933), *Language*, London: Allen & Unwin.

Booij, Geert (2000), 'Inflection and Derivation', in G. Booij, C. Lehman and J. Mugdan (eds), *Morphology. An International Handbook on Inflection and Word-Formation*, Berlin: De Gruyter, vol. 1, pp. 360–369.

Comrie, Bernard (2008), 'Inflectional Morphology and Language Contact, with Special Reference to Languages', in P. Siemund and N. Kintana (eds), *Language Contact and Contact Languages* (Hamburg Studies on Multilingualism 7), Amsterdam: John Benjamins, pp. 15–32.

Daude, Jean (2002), 'Les substantifs abstraits de qualité', in C. Kircher-Durand (ed.), *Grammaire fondamentale du latin Tome IX. Création lexicale: la formation des noms par dérivation suffixale*, Louvain, Paris and Dudley, MA: Éditions Peeters, pp. 225–305.

Dokulil, Miloš (1962), *Tvoření slov v češtině 1. Teorie odvozování slov* [Word Formation in Czech 1: The Theory of Deriving Words], Praha: Academia.

Dokulil, Miloš, K. Horálek, J. Hurková, M. Knappová and J. Petr (1986), *Mluvnice češtiny 1. Fonetika, Fonologie, Morfonologie a morfemika, Tvoření slov* [Grammar of Czech 1: Phonetics, Phonology, Morphophonology and Morphemics, Word Formation], Praha: Academia.

Dubois, Jean (2002), 'Dictionnaire de linguistique', Paris: Larousse Bordas VUEF.

eFontes (2019), *Electronic Corpus of Polish Medieval Latin (eFontes)*, scriptores.pl/efontes.

Ernout, Alfred (1954), *Aspects du vocabulaire latin* (Études et Commentaires, XVIII), Paris: Klincksieck.

Fruyt, Michèlle (1986), *Problèmes méthodologiques de dérivation à propos ds suffixes latin en –cus*, Paris: Klincksieck.

Gaide, Françoise (2002), 'Les substantifs masculines latin en *-(i)o, -(i)ōnis*', in C. Kircher-Durand (ed.), *Grammaire fondamentale du latin Tome IX. Création lexicale: la formation des noms par dérivation suffixale*, Louvain, Paris and Dudley, MA: Éditions Peeters, pp. 307–336.

ten Hacken, Pius (2014), 'Delineating Derivation and Inflection', in R. Lieber and P. Štekauer (eds), *The Oxford Handbook of Derivational Morphology*, Oxford: Oxford University Press, pp. 407–423.

Heinz, Adam (1961), 'Fleksja a derywacja' [Inflection and Derivation], *Język Polski*, XLI: 343–354.

Hüning, Matthias (2009), 'Semantic Niches and Analogy in Word Formation', *Languages in Contrast*, 9: 2, 183–201.

Kavitskaya, Darya (2005), 'Loan Words and Declension Classes in Czech', in G. Booij, E. Guevara, A. Ralli, S. Sgroi and S. Scalise (eds), *Morphology and Linguistic Typology. On-line Proceedings of the MMM4, Fourth Mediterranean Morphology Meeting* (21–23 September 2003), Bologna: Università degli Studi di Bologna, pp. 267–276.

Kircher-Durand, Chantale (ed.) (2002), *Grammaire fondamentale du latin Tome IX. Création lexicale: la formation des noms par dérivation suffixale*, Louvain, Paris and Dudley, MA: Éditions Peeters.

Kwiatkowska, Tatiana (2014), 'Gramatyczna kategoria rodzaju dla zapożyczeń w języku polskim i rosyjskim: paralele i różnice' [The Grammatical Category of Gender in Polish and Russian Cognates: Parallels and Differences], *Acta Polono-Ruthenica*, 19: 217–229.

Leumann, Manu (1963),'Lateinische Laut- und Formenlehre', in M. Leumann, J. B. Hofmann and A. Szantyr (eds), *Lateinische Grammatik*, München: C. H. Beck, vol. 1.

Lexicon Bohemorum (1977–), *Latinitatis medii aevi lexicon Bohemorum – Slovník středověké latiny v českých zemích*, edited by D. Martínková, Praha: Academia.

Lexicon Latinitatis Nederlandicae Medii Aevi – Woordenboek van het Middeleeuws Latijn van de Noordelijke Nederlanden (1977–2005), edited by J. W. Fuchs, O. Weijers and M. Gumbert-Hepp, Leiden: Brill.

LMILP (1953–), *Lexicon mediae et infimae Latinitatis Polonorum – Słownik łaciny średniowiecznej w Polsce*, edited by M. Plezia, K. Weyssenhoff-Brożkowa and M. Rzepiela, Wrocław-Kraków: Ossolineum, Instytut Języka Polskiego PAN.

Löfstedt, Einar (1959), *Late Latin*, Oslo: Aschehou.

Luraghi, Silvia (2014), 'Gender and Word Formation. The PIE Gender System in Cross-linguistic Perspective', in S. Neri and R. Schuhmann (eds), *Studies on the Collective and Feminine in Indo-European from a Diachronic and Typological Perspective* (Brill's Studies in Indo-European Languages & Linguistics), Leiden: Brill, vol. 11, pp. 199–231.

MLW (1967–), *Mittellateinisches Wörterbuch (Mittellateinisches Wörterbuch bis zum ausgehenden 13. Jahrhundert / MLW)*, edited by O. Prinz and A. Wellhausen, München: C. H. Beck.

NGML (1973–), *Novum Glossarium mediae latinitatis*, edited by J. Monfrin, F. Dolbeau, A. Guerreau-Jalabert and B. Bon, Bruxelles and Genève: Librairie Droz.

Oniga, Roberto (2014), *Latin: A Linguistic Introduction*, edited and translated by N. Schifano, Oxford: Oxford University Press.

Pakerys, Jurgis (2016), 'On the Derivational Adaptation of Borrowings', *SKASE Journal of Theoretical Linguistics* 13: 2, 177–188.

Panocová, Renáta (2015), *Categories of Word Formation and Borrowing. An Onomasiological Account of Neoclassical Formations*, Newcastle upon Tyne: Cambridge Scholars Publishing.

Plezia, Marian (1958), 'La structure du latin médiéval d'après les données fournies par le Ier volume du dictionnaire polonais', *Archivum Latinitatis Medii Aevii*, 28 (2): 271–284.

Plezia, Marian (1970), 'Remarques sur la formation du vocabulaire médiolatin en Pologne', *Archivum Latinitatis Medii Aevii*, 37: 193–198.

Plezia, Marian (1981), 'Le latin dans les pays slaves', *Colloques internationaux de Centre national de la recherche scientifique*, 589: 131–136.

Prinz, Otto (1978), 'Mittellateinische Wortneubildungen, ihre Entwicklungstendenzen und ihre Triebkräfte', *Philologus*, 122: 249–275.

Rigg, Arthur G. (1996), 'Medieval Latin Philology. Introduction', in F. A. C. Mantello and A. G. Rigg (eds), *Medieval Latin. An Introduction and Bibliographical Guide*, Washington, DC: The Catholic University of America Press.

Rzepiela, Michał (2005), 'Les néologismes créés par suffixation dans le latin polonais', *Archivum Latinitatis Medii Aevii*, 63: 35–44.

Rzepiela, Michał (2013), 'La langue des dépositions dans les comptes rendus judiciaires médiévaux. Étude d'après les sources polonaises', *Archivum Latinitatis Medii Aevii*, 71: 179–188.

Rzepiela, Michał (2019), 'Word-formation Type, its Reinterpretations, and Possible Equivalents', *SKASE Journal of Theoretical Linguistics* 16: 1, 130–145.

Sławski, Franciszek (ed.) (1976), *Słownik prasłowiański* [Dictionary of Old-Slavonic], Wrocław: Zakład Narodowy im. Ossolińskich, vol. 2.

Štekauer, Pavol (2014), 'Derivational Paradigms', in R, Lieber and P. Štekauer (eds), *The Oxford Handbook of Derivational Morphology*, Oxford: Oxford University Press, pp. 354–369.

Stotz, Peter (2000), *Handbuch zur lateinischen Sprache des Mittelalters*, München: C. H. Beck, vol. 2.

Väänänen, Veiko (1963), *Introduction au latin vulgaire*, Paris: Klincksieck.

Waszakowa, Krystyna (1993), *Słowotwórstwo współczesnego języka polskiego. Rzeczowniki z formantami paradygmatycznymi* [Word Formation in Contemporary Polish: Nouns with Paradigmatic Formatives], Warsaw: Wydawnictwo Uniwersytetu Warszawskiego.

Weyssenhoff-Brożkowa, Krystyna (1991), *Wpływ polszczyzny na łacinę średniowieczną w Polsce* [The Influence of Polish on Medieval Latin in Poland], Kraków: Instytut Języka Polskiego.

Primary sources (the abbreviations correspond to those being used in LMILP)

DokList Pł I, 1975 = Stella Maria Szacherska (ed.) *Zbiór Dokumentów i Listów miasta Płocka*, tom I 1065-1495, Warszawa: Państwowe Wydawnictwo Naukowe.

KsgPozn, 1892 = Adolf Warschauer (ed.) *Stadtbuch von Posen; die mittelalterliche Magistratsliste; die aeltesten Protokollbuecher und Rechnungen*; Bd1, Posen: Eigenthum der Gesellschaft,

StPPP VIII, 1886 = Bolesław Ulanowski (ed.) *Antiquissimi libri iudiciales terrae Cracouiensis*, Cacoviae: Sumptibus Academiae Litterarum.

Conclusion

14

Trends in the Interaction between Borrowing and Word Formation

Pius ten Hacken and Renáta Panocová

This volume originated from a concern that the disciplinary boundaries within the field of linguistics hamper the study of the interaction between borrowing and word formation. As explained in the introduction, borrowing is studied in fields such as lexicography and contact linguistics, whereas word formation is usually placed in morphology. The case studies in the volume look at particular phenomena in particular languages and linguistic environments. In this conclusion, we aim to summarise some findings by generalising about the case studies.

On the basis of the case studies, we identified three specific topics that are important in the interaction between borrowing and word formation and occur in several languages and linguistic environments. In the first three sections, we will therefore discuss neoclassical word formation, internationalisms and Anglicisms. The remaining two sections will be devoted to other observations in the domains of compounding and affixation. In the latter domain, we cover not only derivation but also word markers.

1. Neoclassical word formation

If there is a prototypical phenomenon linked to the interaction of borrowing and word formation, it must be neoclassical word formation. There is a sizeable literature about this topic, but most of it takes a single language as a focus. The way the main research questions are framed depends on one hand on the language in which neoclassical word formation is studied and on the other on the theoretical framework adopted for the study. From a morphological perspective, typical questions include whether neoclassical word formation is a separate phenomenon and what is the status of the neoclassical components in the language system. Thus, Bauer (1998) argues against a separate system of neoclassical word formation and Scalise (1984: 75–76) argues that neoclassical formatives are stems rather than affixes. From a lexicographic perspective, a central question is how individual formations can be traced back to their origin. In his overview of mechanisms in etymology, Durkin (2009: 108–110) discusses what he calls *neoclassical combining forms* in his chapter on compounding.

Much of the discussion of neoclassical word formation is based on English data. Joseph (Chapter 2, this volume) considers how borrowings from Greek and Latin into English affect the word formation system, in particular in technical vocabulary. One of his examples is (1).

(1)   a. otorhinolaryngologist
      b. oto – rhino – laryngo – log(o) – ist

The word in (1a) shows a structure that is not normally possible outside neoclassical compounding. It is a copulative compound with the first three components in (1b) combined in a coordination.

Whereas in English, compounding existed and only particular types of compound were added to the repertoire, Villalva (Chapter 4, this volume) argues that in Portuguese compounding itself was the innovation contributed by neoclassical word formation. Some of her examples are in (2).

(2)   a. odontologista   ('odontologist')
      b. toxicodependente   ('drug addict')

In (2a), we have a neoclassical compound. It consists of two components that are not Portuguese words but only occur in neoclassical formations. In fact, there is a near-synonym, *dentista* ('dentist'), with a vernacular base. In (2b), we have a compound that consists of two nouns. Both *toxico* ('poison', 'drug') and *dependente* ('dependent') are nouns that can also be adjectives. What Villalva shows is that the prevalence of compounds such as (2a) in neoclassical word formation paved the way for compounding with vernacular bases as in (2b).

In Panocová and ten Hacken (this volume), we take a different perspective. Instead of the influence on word formation, in our chapter it is the nature of neoclassical word formation as a system and its relation to borrowing and word formation that we focus on. We argue that some languages, e.g. English, have a system of neoclassical word formation, whereas others, e.g. Russian, have neoclassical formations but no such system. The system is the result of re-analysis. The difference between English and Russian is reflected in the analysis of a pair of words such as (3).

(3)   a. acrodynia
      b. акродиния ('acrodynia')

According to the model we propose, there are two types of borrowing involved, one from Ancient Greek and Latin, the other between modern languages. For English (3a) and Russian (3b), it is obvious that it is not possible that these words were borrowed from ancient languages, because the concept did not exist. The question is, then, whether they are the result of borrowing between modern languages or formation on the basis of the neoclassical formatives.

A crucial issue at this point is what it means for a word to be the result of word formation. The rules of word formation are vested in individual speakers' language competence. They are used first of all to understand new words and link them to other words in the mental lexicon. When we say that (3a) is rule-based in English and (3b) is a borrowing in Russian, what we mean is that there is a sufficiently significant community of speakers who have the rules for analysing (3a) in English, but this is not the case for (3b) in Russian. The idea that a community is *sufficiently* significant means that new neoclassical formations can originate from within this community. We do not imply that Russian speakers do not understand the structure of (3b). This is similar to English speakers' understanding of the structure of *kindergarten*. The evidence we adduce is therefore not evidence for the non-existence of a system of neoclassical word formation, but evidence that Russian speakers only know the structure passively, not as the result of a system they can use for the formation of new words.

Therefore, the case studies in this volume show on one hand how neoclassical word formation can influence the repertoire of word formation rules. In some cases, as in Portuguese, this even leads to a generalisation of the possibility beyond the neoclassical domain. On the other hand, there is the issue that the re-analysis of neoclassical borrowings gives rise to a system of neoclassical word formation. This will have to be determined for each language separately, which brings up the problem that the boundaries of a language as a system shared by a speech community are not empirical but depend on decisions that cannot be entirely linguistic in nature.

2. Internationalisms

The issue of internationalisms is not particularly prominent in the linguistic literature published in English. It is rather associated with the Slavic and German traditions of linguistics, cf. Braun et al. (1990), Waszakowa (2003), Buzássyová (2010). An internationalism is a word that appears in several languages, but not because these languages had it in their historical common core. Based on Buzássyová (2010), Panocová (2017: 61) gives the criterion of at least three genetically not immediately related languages, as in EN *communication*, IT *comunicazione* and SK *komunikácia*.

An issue that arises immediately is of course the delimitation of neoclassical word formation and internationalisms. In general, neoclassical formations fulfil the criteria for internationalisms. However, internationalisms are individual words, whereas neoclassical word formation is at least potentially a system. This difference can be illustrated by the two chapters in this volume that address internationalisms explicitly.

Ševčíková (Chapter 9, this volume) discusses the suffixes *-ismus* and *-ita* in Czech. In the Czech grammatical tradition, they are classified as *loan affixes*. Of course, it is not affixes that are borrowed, but words. The rule with the affixes to form new words can only originate from re-analysis of such borrowings.

As Marchand (1969: 307, 313) indicates for English *-ism* and *-ity*, the origin of the suffixes ultimately can be traced back to Latin and Ancient Greek. As such, they have a similarity with neoclassical word formation. However, Ševčíková shows how in Czech a rather different system of related derivations can be traced. In a large collection of data from a Czech corpus, she recognises eleven patterns of derivationally connected words in which at least one of the words is a noun with *-ismus* or *-ita*. The most elaborate pattern is the one illustrated in (4).

(4) a. reálný   ('real')
     b. realita   ('reality')
     c. reálnost   ('reality')
     d. realismus   ('realism')
     e. realista   ('realist')
     f. realistický ('realistic')

In (4b) and (4d), we find the two suffixes Ševčíková focuses on. The other suffixes illustrated in (4) may also have a native origin, as (4a) and (4c). Patterns such as this emerge through a bottom-up analysis of corpus data. They are instantiations of what Štekauer (2014) calls *derivational paradigms*.

A somewhat different situation is described by Efthymiou (Chapter 10, this volume) for Greek. In Greek, the historical link with the neoclassical elements is more complex than in other languages, cf. Mackridge (2009). On one hand, most neoclassical formatives are of Ancient Greek origin; on the other, the position of Modern Greek with respect to Ancient Greek has been a controversial political issue for more than two centuries. Efthymiou discusses prefixed words such as (5).

(5) a. αντιαλκοολικός ('antialcoholic')
     b. υπεραλίευση   ('overfishing')

Obviously, the prefixes *αντι-* and *υπερ-* are originally Greek. They also exist in Greek as prepositions, but with a different meaning. The basic meanings of the prepositions *αντί* and *υπέρ* are 'instead of' and 'for; more than', respectively. In (5) we see that the prefixes now have an additional meaning that is related to, but not included in, this prepositional meaning. In (5a), *αντι-* means 'against', a meaning that appeared in neoclassical contexts in various languages. In (5b), *υπερ-* means 'in excess', applied here to *αλίευση* ('fishing'). Whereas (3a) can also be analysed as a borrowing from English (or another language that has a cognate form), (3b) must be based on a re-analysis of neoclassical words with *hyper-*, borrowed in Modern Greek, so that *υπερ-* was assigned this additional meaning.

The Czech data in (4) and the Greek data in (5) illustrate two ways in which the re-analysis of internationalisms can affect the word formation system. In (5), the re-analysis concerns affixes the speakers recognised as part of their language. They were assigned additional meanings, but there was no need to change the organisation of the word formation system in order to accommodate them. In (4), the suffixes were more exotic, so that they were taken as a basis for a more elaborate system. This system is what Ševčíková characterises in terms of eleven derivational paradigms. Neoclassical word formation constitutes a higher degree of complexity. It is rather a system for combining formatives than a pattern of connected suffixation rules. This leaves *internationalism* as a descriptive term with little theoretical impact.

3. Anglicisms

Even though COED (2011) defines *Anglicism* as 'a word or phrase that is peculiar to British English', in linguistics it is rather used in the sense of a borrowing from English in another language. When we consider borrowing in the last half century, there is no doubt that most borrowings are Anglicisms in the latter sense. Görlach (2001) gives a systematic overview of Anglicisms in sixteen European languages. On this basis, Anglicisms are an important, if not the predominant, subset of internationalisms. Indeed, Buzássyová (2010) treats *Anglicism* as a hyponym of *internationalism*. It is important to see, however, that the criteria for identifying Anglicisms and internationalisms are partly independent. Anglicisms do not have to have any cognates in other languages.

A property shared by Anglicisms and internationalisms is that they are in principle individual borrowings. While they have long raised strong opposition and fears of undermining the structure of the borrowing language, e.g. Étiemble (1964), the influence on the structure of the language should first be demonstrated. For Italian, Cacchiani (Chapter 6, this volume) aims to find out how Anglicisms affect the rules for compounding on the basis of a large number of examples. A selection of the various types is given in (6).

(6) a. wellness centre
     b. parco divertimenti   ('amusement park')
     c. night   ('nightclub')
     d. wedding planner
     e. zanzara killer   ('killer mosquito')

In (6a), we find a typical example of a borrowed compound. It is an N+N compound adopted in Italian in the same form and with the same meaning as its English counterpart. The problem with this type of compound in Italian is that, as far as Italian has N+N compounds, they are left-headed, as illustrated in (6b). To the extent that this construction occurs more frequently in recent Italian word formation, we can see this as a phenomenon similar to surge in the Portuguese compounding noted in section 1. As far as (6b) is influenced by English *amusement park* it is a calque. A phenomenon Cacchiani observes in Italian is the reduction of the form to the first component, illustrated in (6c). We also find this in French, e.g. *skate* ('skateboard'). Here the compound that is right-headed in English is reduced as if it were left-headed, as regular Italian and French compounds. Particularly confusing are pairs such as (6d–e). On the surface, the only structural difference seems to be that the left-hand element is taken from English in (6d) and from Italian in (6e). However, as the gloss shows, (6d) is right-headed and (6e) is left-headed. Cacchiani explores a number of English formatives in Italian which trigger right-headed structures. It is not easy, however, to come up with proper generalisations.

On the basis of Patton (1999), Joseph (Chapter 2, this volume) gives examples such as (7) illustrating a similar phenomenon in Russian.

(7)   a. директор офиса   ('office director')
      b. офис-директор   ('office director')

In (7a), we have a classical Slavic construction corresponding to Germanic compounds. It is a left-headed construction with a genitive noun as the right-hand element. In the case of the parallel construction in Polish, although it is traditionally considered a syntactic construction (cf. Szymanek 2010: 218), ten Hacken (2013) argues that it should be seen as belonging to compounding. The compound in (7b) has the same constituents and the same meaning but it is a right-headed construction with an uninflected non-head.

A different approach to identifying the influence of English borrowings on word formation is taken by Bloch-Trojnar (Chapter 7, this volume). She addresses the influence of English on the frequency and type of use of one specific word formation rule in Polish, analysing the formation of deverbal adjectives with the suffix -alny, illustrated in (8).

(8)   a. obserwowalny   ('observable')
      b. modifikowalny   ('modifiable')
      c. mierzalny   ('measurable')

As (8) indicates, the meaning of -alny is comparable to English -able. The Polish suffix is often said to attach preferably to [–native] verbs, as in (8a–b). This may be in part due to a few specific verbal endings such as the one illustrated in (8b). As (8c) shows, it is also possible to attach the suffix to a [+native] verb, in this case mierzyć ('measure$_v$'). Bloch-Trojnar shows that the productivity of the -alny rule, in the sense of what Corbin (1987) calls rentabilité, i.e. producing a large number of new items, has increased significantly since Grzegorczykowa and Puzynina (1973). On the basis of an analysis of frequency over time, she attributes this to an increased contact with English. Because in English any transitive verb has (at least potentially) a corresponding adjective in -able, Polish speakers started assuming that this should also be the case in Polish.

Together, these three case studies illustrate how Anglicisms can affect the word formation system in different and perhaps unexpected ways. The Italian case presents itself in a rather chaotic but very visible way. Russian data replicate the picture of competing left-headed and right-headed structures, but at least the case marking disambiguates them. The Polish case is much more subtle. It presents itself as rule-based, but the actual effects can only be discovered by a detailed frequency analysis of corpus data.

4. Other cases of compounding

When we consider the interaction of borrowing and word formation, compounding seems to take a privileged position. We have already encountered examples of compounding in the sections on neoclassical word formation and on Anglicisms, but there are a number of case studies in this volume that feature compounding and do not fall into these classes. Given that the source of the borrowing cannot be English, this section deals mainly with historical cases.

A well-known example from the history of English, discussed by Joseph (Chapter 2, this volume), is the V+N compounds of the type illustrated in (9).

(9)   a. pickpocket
      b. hidebottle

The status of the rule underlying the examples in (9) is somewhat controversial. It is obvious that a number of examples such as (9a) were borrowed from French. Whether they count as compounds depends on the definition of compounding that is adopted. Ten Hacken (2010) argues that they are rather phrasal derivations (or conversions). More important for our purposes here is the question whether they are rule-based. As Joseph points out, Marchand (1960) lists seventy-four cases, but many of them are no longer recognisable to modern speakers of English. As an argument that there is nevertheless a rule underlying them, Joseph mentions Baldwin's (1970) study of compounds in the work of an American humorist, from which (9b) is taken. The question to be asked here is, then, whether (9b) and similar cases are the result of a word formation rule or of analogy. Given the specific context of humour, analogy is quite a likely source. As Mattiello (2017) suggests, analogy often works with results of word formation, in particular if the rule is no longer available. Of course, the availability of a rule is a matter of individual speakers, so that there is no point in trying to settle this issue at the level of a language.

Another historically oriented case study is Stundžia (Chapter 5, this volume). He aims to identify the influence of German on Lithuanian compounding on the basis of an eighteenth-century bilingual dictionary produced in a Lithuanian-speaking area of East Prussia. In the historical context of language contact, it is to be expected that German would influence Lithuanian. That German has a strong tendency to compounding is well known. Given that the dictionary is German-Lithuanian, the extent of the influence in this domain can be measured not only by positive evidence, based on the occurrence of compounds in Lithuanian, but also on the basis of negative evidence, when German compounds are rendered by other constructions, avoiding a direct translation of the German structure.

Compounding in Lithuanian is not recursive. This is a feature shared with Slavic languages such as Polish, cf. ten Hacken and Kwiatek (2013). Stundžia found that this non-recursion constraint was never violated in the dictionary. He further identifies two types of calque in Lithuanian, illustrated in (10).

(10) a. budelbernis   ('butcher's assistant')
      b. kalnaltorius   ('mountain altar')
      c. rotponis   ('council member')
      d. rotponas   ('council member')

Lithuanian nominal compounds have an inflectional paradigm that is indicated by, for instance, the ending -is in (10a). When we find an ending -as or -ius, as in (10b), this means that the inflection class is determined by the final member, not by the compounding rule. Therefore, we can say that (10a) is a more integrated compound than (10b). The existence of doublets such as (10c–d) is analysed by Stundžia as a sign that the integration was still in progress. Contrary to the situation in Italian and Russian discussed in section 3, however, the influence of German on the Lithuanian compounding system is quite limited.

The interaction of compounding with inflection also plays a role in the last case study to be summarised in this section, the Modern Greek construction discussed by Joseph (Chapter 2, this volume) and exemplified in (11).

(11) a. λέξη-κλειδί   mot-clé   ('keyword')
     b. παιδί-θαύμα enfant-prodige ('child prodigy')

In (11), we let the Greek examples be followed by the French counterpart and an English translation. Compounds such as these are sometimes classified as copulative, in the sense of Bloomfield (1933: 235), because, for instance, a keyword is both a key and a word. However, the semantic contribution is not symmetric, because it is a kind of word, but not a kind of key. In (11a), we can therefore say that the Greek and French words are left-headed and the English translation is right-headed, which suggests that French rather than English is the donor language. In (11b), Joseph indicates German *Wunderkind* as the origin. In that case, the word order was adapted in French and the French form was the basis for further borrowing, with English keeping the French order, although it is left-headed.

An interesting phenomenon in Greek occurs in the oblique cases of compounds such as (11). Whereas typical compounds in Greek are right-headed and have the inflection only on the second component, the compounds in (11) are either inflected on the first component, leaving the second in the nominative singular, or on both components. This is reminiscent of the rules for the plural formation of compounds in French, cf. Grevisse (1980: 304–306).

The three case studies summarised in this section indicate that it is possible at least in some cases that a compounding construction emerges under the influence of borrowing, which has properties that do not coincide with those of previously existing compounding constructions. If we analyse (9) as compounds, they are exocentric, which is atypical in English. The Lithuanian compounds in (10) have at least in part an inflection class that does not follow from the general rule of compounding. The Greek compounds in (11) follow the French model in their semantic and morphological headedness rather than the general rule for Greek determinative compounds.

5. Affixation: derivation and word markers

The idea that the lexicon is divided into different strata is often encoded in terms of a feature [±native]. Bloomfield discusses 'foreign-learned forms' (1933: 154). In such a division, it is obvious that neoclassical formations belong to the [–native] stratum. Gaeta and Angster (Chapter 11, this volume) discuss how two related and neighbouring dialects spoken by Walser communities in Aosta Valley behave differently with respect to the preservation of this stratal division. The complex history of the dialects has led to an interplay of Germanic and Romance strata, each further divided into a standard language variety and local dialects. In one dialect, Titsch, we find the examples in (12), in the other, Töitschu, the examples in (13).

(12) a. halbiere   halbieren DE   ('divide')
     b. arifiere   arrivare IT   ('arrive')
     c. verbreitrò   verbreitern DE   ('broaden')

(13) a. aksepturun   akzeptieren DE   ('accept')
     b. arwéiturun   erweitern DE   ('widen')

In (12) and (13) the examples in the dialects are followed by the German or Italian cognates and a translation. The suffix -*ier* marks a [–native] verb stem in German. In Titsch (12), this suffix is preserved with the same function. (12b) shows that Italian loanwords are assigned to the [–native] stratum. However, the [+native] verb in (12c) has a different suffix. In Töitschu (13), the vowel of the affix changes to -*u*-, but as (13b) demonstrates it loses its distinctive [–native] meaning and also applies in cases corresponding to (12c). Gaeta and Angster note that this loss of the stratal distinction coincides with a loss of the typical verb second structure in German main clauses, where the inflected verb appears in second position and other verb forms at the end.

Apart from stratal markers of the type illustrated in (12), many languages have a system of gender classes and inflection classes for nouns. As nouns are the most frequent word class in terms of types and they are generally borrowed more easily than other word classes, the problem of assigning borrowed nouns to an appropriate noun class is a prominent one in such languages.

Rzepiela (Chapter 13, this volume) discusses how this problem of noun class assignment is solved in Polish Medieval Latin. The use of Latin as the language of the law required borrowing of many nouns from Polish for which no Latin correlates were available. Latin has genders and inflection classes that are partly correlated with gender. Some examples of how this assignment problem was solved for loanwords from Polish are given in (14).

(14) a. garbarius LA   garbarz PL   ('tanner')
     b. beczka LA   beczka PL   ('barrel')

In (14a), a Polish ending -*arz* was reinterpreted as correlate of the Latin suffix -*arius*, assigning the noun to the second declension and masculine gender. In (14b), the ending -*a* occurs both in Polish as a marker of feminine gender and in Latin as a marker of the first declension and feminine gender. This coincidence is limited to the nominative singular, but it facilitated borrowings of words of this class. Rzepiela outlines how class assignment rules of this general type were supplemented by various partial generalisations, based on a mixture of phonological and semantic criteria.

Ralli and Makri (Chapter 12, this volume) describe another situation in which this problem of gender and inflection class assignment has to be solved. They study

Canadian Greek, the heritage language spoken by Greek immigrants to Canada and their descendants. In terms of the properties of the languages involved and the socio-linguistic context, the situation is very different from Rzepiela's study, but there is a striking similarity in the repertoire of solutions. Some examples are given in (15).

(15) a. μπόσης   ('boss')
     b. μαρκέτα   ('market')
     c. στέκι   ('steak')

In (15a), the masculine ending -ης is added, because the referent is perceived as masculine. In (15b), the feminine ending -α is added, because the Greek word for 'market' is feminine, αγορά. In (15c), there is a homophonous Greek word. Although it has a completely unrelated meaning, 'haunt', it provides a motivation for the choice of a final vowel and the assignment to the corresponding gender class. Thus, we find direct semantic motivation, semantic motivation mediated by the translation and phonological motivation.

There are different perspectives on word markers. Whereas the study by Rzepiela and that by Ralli and Makri focused on word markers for the integration of borrowings, Hamans (Chapter 8, this volume) considers a case where it is arguably the word marker that is borrowed. He traces the use of the suffix -o in cases such as Dutch (16).

(16) a. aso   asociaal   ('antisocial')
     b. depro   depressief ('depressed')
     c. duffo   duf   ('dull')

In the Dutch cases in (16), the short form with -o is a noun derived from the adjective given after it. The meaning is 'a person that is [A]'. In (16a), the -o is part of the adjective and the adjective is clipped after the -o. In (16b), the adjective is clipped after the first syllable and the -o is added. In (16c), the adjective is monosyllabic and the -o is suffixed. The process changes the adjective to a [+human] noun. It tends to select adjectives with a negative connotation or add such a connotation. Hamans identifies similar cases in English and suggests an analysis in which the -o is originally an Italian word marker, taken over in American English. In German and Swedish, the distribution of the -o diverges somewhat. Hamans explains the differences on the basis of the existence of competing suffixes in those languages.

In the case studies summarised in this section, the word formation processes have a rather restricted semantic contribution. They have in common that they focus on word markers. In three of the case studies the borrowing language is rather weak. Gaeta and Angster discuss dialects with a few elderly speakers, Ralli and Makri a heritage language, and Rzepiela a legal language without native speakers. Nevertheless, any borrowed word must be able to fit in with the phonological, inflectional and syntactic properties of the language. It is remarkable that the two case studies of nominal borrowing show a very similar repertoire of class assignment strategies, despite significant differences in other parameters. In the final case study, it is the word marker that spreads among languages of the same family. This word marker is not semantically empty, although its denotative meaning is not very strongly articulated.

6. Concluding remarks

In the presentation of the case studies in the introduction, they were divided into three parts. Part I is on compounding, Part II on affixation and Part III on naming in minority languages. In Parts I and II, the contribution of borrowings to the word formation system is in focus, whereas in Part III the competition between word formation and borrowing as competing naming mechanisms is more important. In this concluding chapter, we highlighted a number of common themes. Neoclassical word formation occurred in several case studies as a mechanism by which borrowing and word formation collaborate. Internationalisms and Anglicisms appear first of all as borrowings. The extent to which they connect with the existing word formation system in the receiving language as well as the relative importance of the number of borrowings determine how the conflict between tendencies to adapt the borrowings to the system or the system to the borrowings will develop. In the case of compounding, there is a genuine possibility that a number of similar borrowings will be re-analysed as a new type of word formation rule, even if this is not in line with the existing system. In the case of minority languages, strategies for the integration of borrowings in the language system play an important role.

References

Baldwin, Alice (1970), 'James Thurber's Compounds', *Language and Style, An International Journal*, III: 3, 185–197.

Bauer, Laurie (1998), 'Is There a Class of Neoclassical Compounds and If So is it Productive?', *Linguistics*, 36: 403–422.

Bloomfield, Leonard (1933), *Language*, London: Allen and Unwin.

Braun, Peter, B. Schaeder and J. Volmert (eds) (1990), *Internationalismen. Studien zur interlingualen Lexikologie und Lexikographie*, Tübingen: Niemeyer.

Buzássyová, Klára (2010), 'Vzťah internacionálnych a domácich slov v premenách času' [The Relation between International and Original Words across Time], *Jazykovedný časopis*, 61: 2, 113–130.

COED (2011), *Concise Oxford English Dictionary*, edited by A. Stevenson and M. Waite, Oxford: Oxford University Press, 12th edn.

Corbin, Danielle (1987), *Morphologie dérivationnelle et structuration du lexique*, Tübingen: Niemeyer.

Durkin, Philip (2009), *The Oxford Guide to Etymology*, Oxford: Oxford University Press.

Étiemble, René (1964), *Parlez-vous franglais ?*, Paris: Gallimard.

Görlach, Manfred (2001), *A Dictionary of European Anglicisms*, Cambridge: Cambridge University Press.

Grevisse, Maurice (1980), *Le bon usage: Grammaire française avec des Remarques sur la langue française d'aujourd'hui, onzième édition revue*, Paris and Gembloux: Duculot.

Grzegorczykowa, Renata and J. Puzynina (eds) (1973), *Indeks a tergo do Słownika języka polskiego pod redakcją Witolda Doroszewskiego* [Reverse Index to the Dictionary of the Polish Language Edited by Witold Doroszewski], Warszawa: Wydawnictwo Naukowe PWN.

ten Hacken, Pius (2010), 'Synthetic and Exocentric Compounds in a Parallel Architecture', *Linguistische Berichte Sonderheft*, 17: 233–251.

ten Hacken, Pius (2013), 'Compounds in English, in French, in Polish, and in General', *SKASE Journal of Theoretical Linguistics*, 10: 97–113.

ten Hacken, Pius and E. Kwiatek (2013), 'Nominal Compounds as Naming Devices: A Comparison of English and Polish Land Surveying Terminology', in P. ten Hacken and C. Thomas (eds), *The Semantics of Word Formation and Lexicalization*, Edinburgh: Edinburgh University Press, pp. 83–101.

Mackridge, Peter (2009), *Language and National Identity in Greece, 1766–1976*, Oxford: Oxford University Press.

Marchand, Hans (1960), *The Categories and Types of Present-Day English Word Formation. A Synchronic-Diachronic Approach*, Wiesbaden: Otto Harrassowitz.

Marchand, Hans (1969), *The Categories and Types of Present-Day English Word-Formation*, Munich: C. H. Beck, 2nd edn.

Mattiello, Elisa (2017), *Analogy in Word-formation: A Study of English Neologisms and Occasionalisms*, Berlin and Boston: De Gruyter.

Panocová, Renáta (2017), 'Internationalisms with the Suffix -*ácia* and their Adaptation in Slovak', in E. Litta and M. Passarotti (eds), *Proceedings of the Workshop on Resources and Tools for Derivational Morphology*, Milan: EDUCatt, pp. 61–72.

Patton, David (1999), *Analytism in Modern Russian: A Study of the Spread of Non-Agreement in Noun Phrases*, PhD dissertation, The Ohio State University.

Scalise, Sergio (1984), *Generative Morphology*, Dordrecht: Foris.

Štekauer, Pavol (2014), 'Derivational Paradigms', in R. Lieber and P. Štekauer (eds), *The Oxford Handbook of Derivational Morphology*, Oxford: Oxford University Press, pp. 354–369.

Szymanek, Bogdan (2010), *A Panorama of Polish Word Formation*, Lublin: Wydawnictwo KUL.

Waszakowa, Krystyna (2003), 'Internacionalizacija: Zapadnoslavianskije jazyki. Przejawy tendencji do internacjonalizaji w systemach słowotwótwórczych języków zachodnosłowiańskich' [Internationalization: West-Slavic Languages. Tendencies of Internationalization in the Word Formation Systems of West-Slavic Languages], in I. Ohnheiser (ed.), *Komparacja systemów i funkcjonowanie współczesnych języków słowiańskich. 1. Słowotwórstwo/Nominacja*, Opole: Universität Innsbruck and Uniwersytet Opolski, pp. 78–102.

Author Index

Subject Index